Governing after War

Governing after War

Rebel Victories and Post-war Statebuilding

Shelley X. Liu

OXFORD
UNIVERSITY PRESS

Oxford University Press is a department of the University of Oxford.
It furthers the University's objective of excellence in research, scholarship,
and education by publishing worldwide. Oxford is a registered trade mark of
Oxford University Press in the UK and in certain other countries.

Published in the United States of America by Oxford University Press
198 Madison Avenue, New York, NY 10016, United States of America.

© Oxford University Press 2024

All rights reserved. No part of this publication may be reproduced, stored in a retrieval system,
or transmitted, in any form or by any means, without the prior permission in writing of Oxford
University Press, or as expressly permitted by law, by license or under terms agreed with the
appropriate reprographics rights organization. Inquiries concerning reproduction outside the scope
of the above should be sent to the Rights Department, Oxford University Press, at the address above.

You must not circulate this work in any other form and you must impose this same condition on any acquirer

Library of Congress Cataloging-in-Publication Data

Names: Liu, Shelley, author.
Title: Governing after war : rebel victories and post-war statebuilding / Shelley Liu,
Goldman School of Public Policy, University of California, Berkeley.
Description: New York : Oxford University Press, [2024] |
Includes bibliographical references and index.
Identifiers: LCCN 2023052082 (print) | LCCN 2023052083 (ebook) |
ISBN 9780197696712 (paperback) | ISBN 9780197696705 (hardback) |
ISBN 9780197696729 (epub)
Subjects: LCSH: Insurgency. | Nation-building. | Political stability. |
Conflict management. | Postwar reconstruction. | Resource allocation. |
Economic assistance. | Natural resources—Management. | Civil-military relations.
Classification: LCC JC328.5 .L58 2024 (print) | LCC JC328.5 (ebook) |
DDC 355.02/8—dc23/eng/20240110
LC record available at https://lccn.loc.gov/2023052082
LC ebook record available at https://lccn.loc.gov/2023052083

An Overview of the Book

This book explores how wartime processes affect post-war state-building efforts by examining the governing strategies of rebel groups that win control of the state. Post-war governance is a continuation of war: though violence has ceased, the victor must consolidate its control over the state through a process of internal conquest. This means carefully making choices about resource allocation toward development and security. *Where does the victor choose to spend, and why? And what are the implications for ultimately consolidating power and preventing conflict recurrence?*

Resource allocation is a political decision and, in the post-war arena, politics is shaped by wartime processes. The book theorizes armed actors' wartime ties with civilians as an important predictor of post-war governing strategies. During war, armed actors sought to establish control over local life by building a base of support and forming ties with civilians through politicization and rebel governance. After war, the victor continues to rely on its wartime ties to bolster support, gather intelligence, and stamp out dissidence. Control can therefore be sustained at relatively low cost, meaning that these wartime strongholds are not priorities for post-war resource allocation.

Instead, for political survival, the victor abandons its base and directs resources toward conquering the rest of the state from the top down. Where possible, it engages in co-optation through development, preferring to enhance state capacity for establishing control. Where civilians reject such co-optation however—in areas where rivals sustain ties with civilians—the victor turns toward coercion, increasing military spending to mete out violence against civilians. The balance between development and security spending is paramount because, if this strategy is successfully implemented, the victor consolidates power. However, failure to allocate sufficient resources to these regions increases the likelihood of renewed instability. This is where wartime ties with civilians are particularly valuable: budget constraints decrease as the depth and breadth of the victor's wartime ties with civilians increase. This allows the victor to more efficiently target resources, reducing the likelihood of conflict recurrence.

The book brings together qualitative and quantitative evidence from two disparate cases in sub-Saharan Africa: the Zimbabwe Liberation War and the First Liberia Civil War. The empirical chapters combine interviews, focus groups, administrative datasets, and archival data collected during fieldwork with fine-grained census, survey, and conflict data to provide an in-depth examination of sub-national variation in wartime rebel behavior and post-war governing strategies. For cross-national variation on conflict recurrence, I analyze these two cases alongside four additional civil wars in Burundi, Rwanda, Côte d'Ivoire, and Angola to demonstrate the importance of wartime civilian ties for post-war control. The book's central insights point to war and peace as part of a long state-building process, and cautions against treating the post-war landscape as a blank slate under a new government. Findings offer implications for recent rebel victories—from South Sudan to Afghanistan—and, more broadly, for understanding the termination, trajectories, and political legacies of such conflicts around the world.

Contents

List of Figures	ix
List of Tables	xi
Acknowledgments	xiii
Acronyms	xvii

Part I. GOVERNING AFTER WAR

1. **Introduction**	3
2. **State-building through Rebel–Civilian Ties**	26

Part II. RESOURCE ALLOCATION

3. **Introducing the Cases**	75
4. **The Zimbabwe Liberation War (1972–1979)**	88
5. **The Liberia Civil War (1989–1996)**	133

Part III. CONSOLIDATING POWER

6. **Divergent Trajectories across Rebel Victories**	185
7. **External Comparisons**	204

Part IV. IMPLICATIONS

8. **Implications and Future Research**	251

Appendix A Security Challenges after War	267
Appendix B Zimbabwe Liberation War	269
Appendix C First Liberia Civil War	281

Bibliography	291
Index	309

List of Figures

2.1 The process of consolidation	38
2.2 Post-war politics under threat of counter-rebellion	65
2.3 Consolidating power after civil war	68
2.4 Failure to consolidate power after civil war	71
3.1 Liberia's ethnic populations	81
4.1 Zimbabwe conflict timeline	89
4.2 Social control coding	106
4.3 Mount Darwin district	107
4.4 Gukurahundi operations in the Matabeleland provinces	119
4.5 Voter registration plot	124
4.6 Education parallel-trends plots	128
5.1 Liberia conflict timeline	135
5.2 NPFL presence	137
5.3 Territory maps	159
5.4 Chief replacement and appointment under Taylor	164
6.1 LURD and MODEL coverage	192
App.1 Voter registration plot with additional birth cohorts	276
App.2 Parallel Trends for Gains in Educational Attainment	285
App.3 Parallel trends for gains in educational attainment (excluding Monrovia)	286

List of Tables

1.1 Rebel victories that eliminated wartime rivals	16
2.1 Wartime social control and organizational capacity in war-affected areas	55
4.1 Votes for main parties	110
4.2 Voter registration	123
4.3 Educational attainment	130
5.1 Chief replacement	165
5.2 Chief replacement	166
5.3 Education and literacy	179
6.1 Recruitment areas	195
6.2 War-appointed chiefs and second war conflict years	196
6.3 Rebel social control and post-war state stability	199
7.1 Comparisons: Primary and secondary cases	206
A1 Rebel victories and post-war security challenges	267
B1 Post-war coercive capacity (Afrobarometer Rural Sample 1950–1986)	275
B2 Public goods provision (Census Rural Sample 1950–1971)	275
B3 Voter registration (80% Shona)	276
B4 Voter registration placebo checks	277
B5 Education attainment robustness checks	277
B6 Education attainment robustness checks	278
B7 Education attainment robustness checks (different samples)	279
B8 Placebo outcomes for educational attainment DiD	279
B9 Education placebo checks	280
C1 Wartime chief appointments (rural sample)	281
C2 Education attainment (Census sample 1970–1992)	282
C3 Education attainment placebo outcomes (Census sample 1970–1992)	282
C4 Post-war security	283
C5 Chief replacement (clan level)	284
C6 Education and literacy robustness checks	287
C7 Balance across placebo outcomes for educational attainment DiD	288
C8 Education and literacy	289

Acknowledgments

As I reflect on this project's journey, I am filled with a deep sense of gratitude to the many individuals and institutions that have supported me along the way. This book represents the culmination of years of research, writing, and reflection, and it would not have been possible without the unwavering support of so many. To everyone who has played a role in supporting my research, providing feedback, or simply offering words of encouragement, I owe a heartfelt thank you.

This book would not have been possible without the many individuals in Liberia and Zimbabwe who have shared their stories and experiences with me. I thank them for being so welcoming and for their willingness to participate in my research: their generosity in recounting their personal experiences of violence and conflict has enriched my understanding of the complex nature of these phenomena. Their voices and perspectives are critical to understanding the realities of war and peace, and their small acts of kindness have left an indelible mark on my scholarship. I am truly humbled and privileged to have had the opportunity to work with them, and their contributions to this book are immeasurable.

I thank my advisors at Harvard, who have seen this project through every step of the way. Jeff Frieden, my chair, has an unparalleled ability to break down and identify gaps in logic. The book is far stronger with his advice and constructive criticism, and I thank him for pushing me to think harder, to simplify, and to consider the implications and relevance of my ideas beyond the cases I study. Gwyneth McClendon's methodical and detailed advice has been invaluable throughout this project, and I have learned a tremendous amount from her insights on fieldwork and research. Finally, I owe so much thanks to Horacio Larreguy, who has been a dedicated teacher and advisor since I arrived at Harvard. He has supported and pushed my research efforts beyond my comfort zone. His guidance and insights are undoubtedly visible throughout this entire book.

At Berkeley, I have been lucky to receive so much support from my colleagues. In addition to their mentorship and guidance, Leonardo Arriola, Susan Hyde, Aila Matanock, Scott Straus, and Daniel Sargent provided such helpful guidance and constructive comments during my book workshop. Much heartfelt thanks also to Ana Arjona and Zachariah Mampilly, who

xiv Acknowledgments

traveled all the way to California to attend the workshop. All of their insights and constructive criticism have been invaluable in helping me refine and improve the book. I am grateful for the time and energy that they have invested in helping me bring this project to fruition. I must thank the Institute of International Studies for generously hosting this workshop, and in particular Claudia Gey for pulling it all together. More broadly, I also sincerely thank Henry Brady, Ryan Brutger, Jennifer Bussell, Solomon Hsiang, Dorothy Kronick, Edward Miguel, and Martha Wilfahrt for their support and advice. I feel so fortunate to have been part of such a supportive and intellectually stimulating community.

Further afield, this book could not have been completed without so many people who have challenged me and provided me with valuable feedback along the way. This began far before I embarked upon this project: I owe a great debt of gratitude to my earliest mentors, whose guidance has been instrumental in shaping the scholar I am today. I would like to extend my sincere appreciation to Bob Bates, whose book initially sparked my interest in studying development and violence in sub-Saharan Africa. Throughout the course of researching and writing this book, Bob has provided invaluable feedback and insights that have helped to shape and refine my argument. His wealth of knowledge and willingness to share his extensive library of resources have been critical in the development of this work. Before graduate school, I am grateful in particular for Chris Blattman, Tanisha Fazal, and Nicholas Sambanis, who have provided me with strong foundational knowledge on conflict and development and set me on the research path leading to this book. Above all, they have instilled in me a passion for seeking out new methodologies, thinking independently, and embracing the unknown in research. I am truly grateful for the lasting impact they have had on my research. As the project developed, I must thank so many others for their comments and discussions at various workshops, for reading drafts of the project during various stages, for fieldwork advice, for their friendship, and countless other acts of kindness: Antonella Bandiera, Jeremy Bowles, Kaitlyn Chriswell, Dara Kay Cohen, Colleen Driscoll, Guy Grossman, Meg Guliford, Connor Huff, Adrienne LeBas, David Jud, Philip Martin, Ben Morse, Munya Munochiveyi, Pablo Querubin, Pia Raffler, Cyrus Samii, Jake Shapiro, Megan Stewart, Kai Thaler, Monica Toft, Alice Xu, and Lauren Young. My sincerest gratitude also to David McBride, anonymous reviewers, the editorial team at Oxford University Press, and Kelley Friel for all their help in turning this research into the final book.

Undertaking this research would not have been possible without the invaluable support, guidance, and generosity of the many people I have met and collaborated with during my fieldwork. In particular, I am deeply grateful to Murphy Bella and Alex Kendima in Liberia, as well as Chikwava Sigauke, Kuda Netsayi, and Gerald Mandisodza in Zimbabwe, for their assistance in facilitating access to critical data and resources, providing me with essential contacts, and offering their time and expertise to guide me through the intricacies of the research process. It is difficult to overstate the critical role that they played in ensuring the success of my fieldwork, and I am forever indebted to them for their invaluable contributions. Moreover, I would like to express my gratitude to many other individuals who have immeasurably helped me along the way. Kou Gbaintor-Johnson, Jonako Bindah, Yusuff Sarnoh, Alfred Chikomba, Nicholas Nyachega, Shylock Muyengwa, and countless others have generously offered their support and advice, shared their insights and experiences, and facilitated my access to information and data sources that were essential to completing this project. Their willingness to go out of their way to help me and their commitment to this research are deeply appreciated.

I am deeply grateful for the invaluable support and encouragement that I have received from a wide range of institutions and individuals in the pursuit of my research. The Weatherhead Center for International Affairs, the Institute for Quantitative Studies, the Harvard Africa Center, and the United States Institute of Peace have provided generous funding that made my fieldwork and research possible. Being a Peace Scholar has been an incredible experience, and I feel privileged to have had the opportunity to interact with so many brilliant scholars who are pushing the boundaries of our understanding of conflict and its consequences. The project has benefitted significantly from various workshops and seminars at Harvard University, UC Berkeley, UC San Diego, UC Irvine, WZB Berlin, and Duke University, and also conferences including the American Political Science Association, International Studies Association, Midwest Political Science Association, Boston Area Working Group in African Political Economy, the Harvard-MIT-Tufts-Yale Political Violence Conference, and the Northeast Workshop in Empirical Political Science. I truly thank all participants and discussants: the insights and feedback that I received from these various venues have been instrumental in shaping and refining my arguments, and their thoughtful criticisms and suggestions have enriched my manuscript tremendously.

Finally, I would like to express my heartfelt appreciation to my family and friends, whose love and encouragement have sustained me throughout the

xvi Acknowledgments

ups and downs of this journey. My family has been an unwavering source of support throughout the years. Although my parents and sister may not share my interest in the subject, they have always listened to me talk about my research and offered their encouragement. I am, above all, immensely grateful to my husband and best friend, Tony, for his patience and willingness to brainstorm with me. His support and enthusiasm for my work have been an endless source of motivation and comfort.

Acronyms

Zimbabwe

ZANU/ZANU-PF Zimbabwe African National Union/ -Patriotic Front
ZANLA Zimbabwe African National Liberation Army
ZAPU Zimbabwe African People's Union
ZIPRA Zimbabwe People's Revolutionary Army

Liberia

ECOMOG Economic Community of West African States Monitoring Group
INPFL Independent National Patriotic Front of Liberia, Prince Johnson faction
LPC Liberia Peace Council
LURD Liberians United for Reconciliation and Democracy
MODEL Movement for Democracy in Liberia
NPFL National Patriotic Front of Liberia
NPP National Patriotic Party
NPRAG National Patriotic Reconstruction Assembly Government
ULIMO-J United Liberation Movement of Liberia for Democracy, Roosevelt Johnson faction
ULIMO-K United Liberation Movement of Liberia for Democracy, Alhaji Kromah faction

Burundi

CNDD-FDD Conseil National Pour la Défense de la Démocratie–Forces pour la Défense de la Démocratie
Palipehutu-FNL Parti pour la libération du peuple Hutu - Forces Nationales de Libération
Frolina Front de Libération Nationale

Rwanda

RPF Rwanda Patriotic Front
FAR Forces Armées Rwandaises
ALiR Armée pour la Libération du Rwanda

xviii Acronyms

Cote d'Ivoire

FN Forces Nouvelles
FANCI Forces Armées nationales de Côte d'Ivoire

Angola

MPLA Movimento Popular de Libertação de Angola
FNLA Frente Nacional de Libertação de Angola
UNITA União Nacional Para a Independência Total de Angola

Power and violence are opposites; where the one rules absolutely, the other is absent. Violence appears where power is in jeopardy, but left to its own course it ends in power's disappearance.

Arendt, 1970

PART I
GOVERNING AFTER WAR

1
Introduction

How do rebel victors govern after winning war? Although ex-rebel governments often espouse political goals at the national level, there is also significant sub-national variation in how they govern once in power. What explains this sub-national variation, and how does it affect rebel victor-governed states' post-war security and political trajectories?

Take Zimbabwe's post-war experiences, for example. Zimbabwe gained independence from Great Britain in 1980 after two decades of political and military struggle. At the handover ceremony, Robert Mugabe—leader of the Zimbabwe African National Union-Patriotic Front (ZANU-PF)—promised national reconciliation after years of guerrilla warfare: "The wrongs of the past must now stand forgiven and forgotten... If yesterday I fought you as an enemy, today you have become a friend and ally with the same national interest, loyalty, rights, and duties as myself" (Ross, 1980). Mugabe emphasized that he would prioritize the reconstruction of rural Zimbabwe, focusing on land, education, and health. The international community was optimistic about his seemingly pragmatic approach to governance despite his Marxist tendencies. Lord Soames, the last governor of colonial Rhodesia, who was charged with transitioning the colony into an independent nation, praised Mugabe's politics: "What he wants to do coincides in many ways with what we would like to see him do" (AFP, 1980). American newspapers highlighted Mugabe's good relations with the West and proclaimed that Zimbabwe "will be a functioning, majority-rule, pluralistic democracy—one in which the rights and interests of minorities will be safeguarded, including the white minority" (Kilian, 1980). In 1981 Zimbabwe joined the African, Caribbean, and Pacific Group of States, which gave it access to preferential trade, aid, and investment from the European Economic Community. Aid dollars soon began to flow.

The ruling ZANU-PF party made good on its promises in many ways. It rolled out a series of bold and large-scale projects across the state that promised to revolutionize health care, education, and bureaucracy. With the help of regional allies and the international community, the

---

Governing after War: Rebel Victories and Post-war Statebuilding. Shelley X. Liu, Oxford University Press.
© Oxford University Press 2024. DOI: 10.1093/oso/9780197696705.003.0001

4 Governing after War

new government embarked upon vaccination programs and established a community health program. It also implemented an ambitious education policy that entailed expanding primary schooling and also opening up secondary schooling (previously reserved for the children of the colonizers) to Black Zimbabweans. This required widespread school construction across the country and training a new cohort of teachers to meet the sudden increase in the demand for education. The government quickly implemented a hierarchical community-based development system that it announced would democratize its decision-making processes and help it meet each community's specific needs. During the war, ZANU soldiers and political figures had promised land reform to ensure that landless farmers who lived in communal areas under the colonial government would be granted their own farmland. After the war, the new ZANU-PF government sought to fulfil this promise by buying back land from White farmers to redistribute land rights. Despite growing pains and some complaints about the efficacy of the reforms' implementation processes, the new government did earnestly engage in post-war development.

Yet, whispers of violence surfaced after less than two years. Despite the exuberance associated with the country's recent independence and the seemingly widespread support for the new government—ZANU-PF had won the 1980 elections in a landslide—some civilians viewed its win as illegitimate. Thus the party feared for its political survival. Though the government began nominally as a coalition between the ruling party and its opposition (the Zimbabwe African People's Union (ZAPU), ZANU-PF's wartime rivals), members of the opposition were soon accused of secretly plotting a new civil war and were subsequently ousted in 1982. ZANU-PF covertly trained a private militia, called the Fifth Brigade, tasked with eliminating the opposition. From 1983 to 1986, the Fifth Brigade committed unspeakable mass atrocities in the provinces of Matabeleland North and Matabeleland South in western Zimbabwe, where ZAPU enjoyed strong support—particularly among the minority Ndebele ethnic group (Catholic Commission for Justice and Peace, 1997) that comprised less than 20% of the country's population. The ethnic cleansing was carried out in an attempt to establish a one-party state—a far cry from the democracy that the international community and nongovernmental organizations (NGOs) working in Zimbabwe had hoped for.

Zimbabwe's disappointing trajectory toward political exclusion and coercion, despite the ruling party's apparent widespread civilian support and promising development projects, is not unique. Several other new governments that came to power after civil war have pursued similar governing strategies. For example, in 2001, ten years after Eritrea gained independence, the former chair of the country's Constitutional Commission lamented: "There was a very good beginning, a very promising beginning. We all hailed Isaias and his colleagues in creating an enabling environment to lead to democracy and we were waiting for that when he and his group—in my view—hijacked the constitution" (Cobb, 2001). Though the new Eritrean government enjoyed a broad mandate and was immensely popular among civilians, it brutally crushed dissidents and eliminated any viable opposition to its rule. Nor is such behavior unique to sub-Saharan Africa: the Sandinistas in Nicaragua were well known for their developmental policies as well as their violent actions toward those who opposed their rule. The Khmer Rouge exhibited similar behavior after winning the Cambodian Civil War in 1975. These new governments—rebel victors—were willing to engage in state-building through development *and* to use violence. Rebel victories have repeatedly dashed the international community's hopes of positive peace-building and reconstruction through development and democracy. As it turns out, development need not accompany democracy, and post-war processes that start out democratic often (and rapidly) revert to authoritarianism.

That state-building projects, particularly those led by ex-rebel governments, involve violence should perhaps not come as a surprise. Successful state-building projects all over the world have featured relatively coercive measures that allowed rulers to consolidate power over the entire state. Scott (2009) explains that in Southeast Asia, "Much, if not most, of the population of early states was unfree; they were subjects under duress . . . Living with the state meant, virtually by definition, taxes, conscription, corvee labor, and for most, a condition of servitude." We generally accept the thesis that "war made the state and the state made war" (Tilly, 1992)—that state legibility was unwelcome for peasants seeking to escape state control in Southeast Asia, Africa, and Europe (Scott, 2009; Herbst, 2000; Bates and Lien, 1985), and that successful state-building meant "stationary bandits" who methodically extracted from citizens and punished them for noncompliance (Olson, 1993). The broader question is why these post-war governments engaged in state-building in the first place. The current norm against conquest (Fazal, 2011; Atzili, 2011) makes it less necessary for rulers to consolidate control over the entire state to stay in power (Herbst, 2000). Why, then, do these post-war rulers bother to build the state beyond their strongholds if they can win reelection by simply relying on votes from their supporters?

The patterns of distributive politics—the allocation of public goods and favors—appear to be different in post-war contexts when rebels win control. Numerous studies on distributive politics in a variety of developing contexts have highlighted the benefits of engaging in patrimonial politics and

6 Governing after War

clientelism by favoring one's own group to sustain power (Bates, 1974; Golden and Min, 2013). Political parties in democracies and competitive authoritarian regimes all over the world deliver goods and services to partisans who vote to keep them in power, leading to an uneven distribution of resources.[1] Even nondemocratic rulers must appease their winning coalition within a limited selectorate (De Mesquita et al., 2005), which entails sending more resources "home" to sustain support.

New governments that come to power after winning a war, however, seem to act differently. In post-apartheid South Africa, the African National Congress (ANC) was expected to honor a major wartime promise to its base to redistribute land from White farmers to landless Black peasants who had their land taken away under colonialism. Yet despite having the necessary domestic support, it has still not done so. Nearly three decades later, land reform continues to be a major issue in the country; new leftist political parties have recently emerged promising to do what the ANC has so far refused to entertain. On the flip side, unlike previous Rwandan rulers, the post-war Tutsi-led Rwandan Patriotic Front (RPF) government has bolstered rural state-building efforts that benefit the majority-Hutu population. As I discuss in Chapter 7, President Paul Kagame's policy of national unity likely explains this development, but it is also notable that the RPF government has, in parallel, silently marginalized Hutu politicians and bureaucrats in favor of Tutsi supporters. South Africa and Rwanda are two extreme examples of a resource allocation puzzle: as I show in Part II of the book, in post-independence Zimbabwe and Charles Taylor's Liberia—two very different types of rebellions and rebel victories—the new post-war governments avoided rewarding supportive regions after the conflict and instead provided public goods beyond their base. What were the political reasons for doing this?

1.1 The Book's Subject and Argument

This book is about rebel victors and their post-war resource allocation toward *violence* and *development* to establish control, and ultimately why some

---

[1] In Latin America, a ruler's ideology has been shown to predict supporters, which in turn predicts how resources are allocated (Calvo and Murillo, 2004; Stokes et al., 2013; Holland and Palmer-Rubin, 2015). Ethnicity has traditionally served as the main heuristic for identifying supporters and targeting resources in sub-Saharan Africa (De La O, 2013; Baldwin, 2013; Koter, 2013), although ties to the state are now increasingly recognized as particularly important for accessing state resources (Bowles, Larreguy, and Liu, 2020; Brierley, 2020; Brierley and Nathan, 2019). In Asia, ethnicity and religion both matter, but ultimately a candidate's ability to target strongholds with public goods and resources is the best predictor of future support (Chandra, 2007; Thachil, 2014; Auerbach and Thachil, 2018).

victors successfully consolidate power while others return to civil war. I argue that post-war governments do not act like peacetime governments because post-war politics impose different conditions on rulers' behavior. Victors face an existential threat because civil wars reoccur relatively frequently. Thus ex-rebels cannot stay in power simply by putting together a winning coalition among the selectorate; they must build up the state to consolidate their rule.

While this constraint affects all post-war governments, rebel victors also have a different set of strengths. Depending on how the war was fought, they come to power equipped with a variety of knowledge and tools that are useful for sustaining control over civilians at the local level. This book explores wartime rebel governance and state-building activities as a precursor to post-war politics. It highlights the importance of wartime social control through rebel–civilian ties for understanding: (1) governing decisions when a rebel group wins power and (2) how likely it is that rebels' control will be consolidated smoothly depending on wartime endowments.

To understand political decisions about how resources are allocated after war, we must examine the constraints imposed by war. Prior studies have explored how politics affects *who gets what* in various contexts and regime types around the world.[2] Post-war landscapes are characterized by heightened insecurity and a fragile peace. Thus when a new government comes to power after civil war, it makes governing choices with security threats and political survival in mind. What strategies do new governments use to minimize the security threats from rivals and maximize political survival? How do citizen preferences and agency condition the new government's decisions? And what explains whether these decisions help the new government to consolidate control and prevent conflict recurrence?

This book takes into account the preferences of the new government, its rivals, and ordinary citizens to develop a theory that uses armed actors' wartime ties with civilians to predict post-war governing strategies. During war, armed actors—rebel groups and government forces—contest militarily for power and control over territory. To achieve these goals, rebel groups seek to establish social control over local life by building a base of support and forming ties with civilians through politicization and perhaps even rebel governance. Such politicization may be based on ideology, ethnicity, nationalism, or economic appeals; the utility of these unifying frameworks varies across conflicts and even sub-nationally within conflicts. For instance, in Chapter 7 I discuss how the União Nacional Para a Independência Total de Angola

---

[2] See Hicken (2011) for a thorough review of clientelism; and Golden and Min (2013) for an overview of the distributive politics literature.

8   Governing after War

(UNITA) pursued different wartime socialization strategies in Ovimbundu and non-Ovimbundu areas in Angola. Civilians may reject rebel groups' attempts to politicize, or find them unpersuasive; where rebels lack a military presence on the ground, they may struggle to form durable relationships with civilians. However, where rebel attempts to *influence* the population are successful and their military *presence* is strong enough, rebels can cultivate ties with a subset of civilians to whom they can entrust supporting tasks such as providing wartime intelligence and organizing the community to provide the food and materials necessary to wage war. Rebels can exploit these ties to insert themselves into—or even change—the local political structure to exert substantial control over civilian life at the sub-national level during (and after) the war (see Part II).

Just as war is "the continuation of politics by other means" (Clausewitz, 1982), post-war politics is a continuation of war: when one group wins and takes control of the state, political contestation continues sub-nationally. The winning side now governs, but many citizens will be either indifferent or hostile to its rule. Thus it must consolidate its control over the state through a process of *internal conquest*. The victors ought to continue to rely on the civilians they established strong ties with during the war to bolster their support in the post-conflict period, gather intelligence, and stamp out dissidence. Since post-war control can be sustained at a relatively low cost, these wartime strongholds are not priorities for post-war resource allocation.

Instead, to maximize the likelihood of political survival, the victor abandons its base and directs resources to conquering the rest of the state from the top down. Its strategies are meant to win supporters and eliminate internal challengers while incurring the lowest fiscal and reputational costs. Where possible, the victor engages in co-optation, attempting to bolster the state's reach by deploying loyal bureaucrats and increasing development to win civilian support, spread state legitimacy, and increase the state's capacity for control. The types of development policies that are likely to be strategically implemented during this period ought to fulfill three criteria. First, they should be popular with ordinary citizens if they are to successfully function as co-optation. Second, they ought to be visible, so the general population can credit the victor with reform success. These two criteria are important for establishing *legitimacy*: spending on public goods that are popular and visible (such as health, education, security, and rebuilding local infrastructure) signals government efficacy, which bolsters support for the victor (Azam, 2001). The third criterion is the development initiatives' contribution to state *legibility*: during the fragile post-war period, the victor will prefer policies that are not only popular but can help establish state control. Put another way, development should contribute to the state-building process by anchoring state presence within key communities while winning legitimacy. Throughout the book, I draw evidence primarily from education and school expansion policies, a type of major reform that legitimates the state and increases its legibility (Paglayan, 2020).

While this strategy of increasing resource allocation toward such development reforms can work in parts of the state, it will not be successful everywhere. Sometimes civilians reject state reforms because they consider them an imposition. Indeed, state-building should be less effective in areas where the victor's rivals established ties with civilians during the war, since these rivals may still be embedded in those communities. In these areas, civilians will likely reject the victor's attempts at co-optation and may join a counter-rebellion, thus heightening the security threat. If the victor fails to establish legibility in an area that may challenge its power, it will more likely turn to coercion: it ought to allocate resources to engage in violence against civilians, seeking to sever their ties with the rivals and open up space to penetrate unfriendly terrain.

Does this strategy—controlling the base while engaging in co-optation and coercion elsewhere—prevent a new civil war? In Part III of the book I argue that civilian ties help the victor allocate resources to development versus violence. If the victor strikes the right balance, they can eliminate security threats and consolidate control over the state, thus completing the process of internal conquest. However, the failure to allocate sufficient resources to areas outside of its political base increases the likelihood of renewed instability, since rivals will find it easier to recruit and indifferent civilians will be angered by the slow rate of post-war reconstruction. Meanwhile, overspending on violence has negative reputational effects both domestically and internationally, and may close valuable channels for political and economic support.

Wartime ties with civilians are also important for preventing this return to violence. Since the victor relies on these ties to control its wartime strongholds at low cost, the budget constraints decrease as the depth and breadth of the victor's wartime ties with civilians increase. The more civilians the victor can rely on to exert control, and the more spread out they are across the state, the fewer resources are needed to consolidate control. Wartime ties therefore allow the victor to more efficiently target resources to smaller areas; thus more resources can be dedicated to both development and violence. In sum, *the victor's wartime ties with civilians play a direct role in reducing the likelihood of conflict recurrence.*

My argument builds on a core insight from bellicist theories of state-building: that state stability requires both political and military power, which

10 Governing after War

are generated by deploying a combination of development and coercion. When a war ends, the victor must ensure that it controls not just the capital, which is generally satisfied with its successful ascent to power; crucially, it must also retain control over its constituency to stay in power. This control is not won just because the civil war has ended. Rather, war fragments and increases political polarization during a critical time, making it harder to establish control and centralize power. If the war broke out due to the previous regime's inability to project state power, then the new regime must be able to do so to survive. Civil war-making by armed actors introduces ground-up strategies to consolidate the victor's control. Methods of establishing control during rebellion, chiefly forming ties with civilians and reshaping local political institutions, help ex-rebels complete their internal conquest after winning war.

1.2 Scope Conditions

1.2.1 Civil Wars Ending in Rebel Victories

My theory applies to countries where civil wars have recently ended in a rebel victory. In the longer run, once power has been consolidated, the patterns of resource allocation likely differ. Though many states that have not experienced significant levels of violence are weak and fragile, without a shock to the system such as that caused by a civil war, governments would not be motivated to change the state's institutions. These states engage in corrupt or clientelistic behavior that involves rewarding their core in an effort to increase either (1) the loyalty of their winning coalition (in authoritarian countries) or (2) voter turnout from their strongholds (in developing democracies). The argument I make in this book does not travel well to these non-conflict contexts since weak but relatively peaceful states do not face the threat of conflict recurrence. The post-war context is important because if the state is uneasy and armed groups are ready to fight, the government expends fewer resources on creative methods of winning elections and more on ensuring that citizens do not join their armed rivals and resume war.

The book draws its evidence from rebel victories over time in sub-Saharan Africa, leaning most heavily on evidence from two disparate cases—the Zimbabwean Liberation War and the First Liberian Civil War. The logic of my argument should apply beyond this region to all rebel victories after civil war that meet two conditions. First, the victor should fear internal threats after winning the war. This condition is fairly unrestrictive: across the conflicts in sub-Saharan Africa, for example, all but two—the South West Africa People's Organisation (SWAPO) in Namibia and the African Party for the Independence of Guinea and Cape Verde (PAIGC) in Guinea Bissau—faced overtly violent threats from an armed opposition group after the war.[3] The second condition is that the post-war settlement must not involve a power-sharing arrangement, for two reasons. First, shared power means the opposing sides require support from their bases, either at the polls or in the event of a return to war. They must therefore turn their attention inward to consolidate their control over their key supporters. The second reason is that political parties that share power do not unilaterally enact policy across the state: in classic consociational governments, for example, ex-rebel parties are responsible for implementing policies within their own constituencies (Lijphart, 1969).

In establishing scope conditions, it is important to highlight that I do not differentiate between anti-colonial wars, secessionist conflicts, and rebellions. While the first two may be considered different from rebellions because they seek to drive an arguably external power out of the state, across cases such as Angola, Eritrea, Mozambique, and South Sudan, Zimbabwe, the post-war landscapes in all three types of conflicts are the same: though external forces are unlikely to constitute internal threats after war, the victor contends with internal rivals that often arise out of opposing independence movements.

1.2.2 How Is Victory Achieved?

Definitions of rebel victory in the scholarly literature tend to focus on military victory, and are thus restricted to groups that win decisively and take control with no peace agreement (Toft, 2010). However, in another common scenario, peace accords are nominally signed but certain clear winners take control of the government through their size, strength, and support during post-war elections. These cases of *political* victory are important to include in studies of rebel incumbents because their victory—though not necessarily secured by force—is codified and legitimized by law.[4]

---

[3] Namibia and Guinea Bissau also arguably faced internal rivals, but their wartime strength allowed them to eliminate these rivals prior to the conflict's end.

[4] Because the lines between military and political victories are blurred, prior studies disagree on the full universe of cases. However, clear military victories include cases such as the Ethiopian Civil War or the Chinese Revolution, while political victories include cases like the First Liberian Civil War, the Zimbabwean Liberation War, and the terminal Burundian Civil War.

12 Governing after War

I do not distinguish between military and political victories because they both lead to the same outcome: a rebel group becomes the ruling party after a civil war. In developing an argument about the value of wartime civilian ties and the resource allocation strategies used to consolidate power, military and political victories are only distinguishable as a scope condition if (1) military victories only relied on military power to exert control during and after the war, and thus exploit no rebel–civilian ties; or (2) military victories eliminate rivals prior to the war's termination, and thus the ruling party does not need to consolidate power as outlined in my theory.

However, neither condition is borne out empirically. Regarding the first condition, even military victories do not necessarily overlook rebel governance and rely only on military power. Military victories such as in Côte d'Ivoire, Eritrea, and Uganda all engaged heavily in rebel governance and subsequently exploited wartime rebel–civilian ties to establish post-war dominance. With respect to the second condition, military victories focus on capturing the center, which can occur without eliminating rivals—as happened in Angola, Mozambique, and Rwanda. These rebel governments spent their initial post-war years attempting to spread their institutions and supporters; they faced violence in rival strongholds and attempted to use top-down development to exert control. Some were more successful than others, depending on the degree to which their rivals sustained their wartime strongholds. As I show in Chapter 7, the Movimento Popular de Libertação de Angola (MPLA) was forced to abandon its development strategy as its rival UNITA's influence spread quickly into unsecured terrain. Even under military dominance, no rebel group can dominate completely: in cases such as the National Patriotic Liberation Front (NPFL) in Liberia (Chapter 5), wartime territorial control and military strength did little to sustain post-war power.

1.3 Contributions

1.3.1 State-building after War

This book seeks to explain how victors stay in power after war and how their governing choices can be situated within a broader state-building process. The bellicist state-building literature contends that the ruler—a political party or individual that controls the state—extracts from civilians in their domain in exchange for protection from violence. According to these state-building theories, states impose control by promising security—following the logic of organized protection rackets (Tilly, 1985) or stationary bandits

(Olson, 2000)—and enjoy sufficient legitimacy to enact violence against their rivals in retaliation. As rulers attempt to expand their territory, they seek to increase taxation in order to wage war. This is because winning and controlling larger swathes of territory requires rulers to engage with local allies, build a larger army, and extend the arm of the state through bureaucracy and the police force (Tilly, 1992, 175).

Core bellicist theories focus on interstate disputes; yet state-building occurs not just to prepare for territorial expansion, but also to guard against internal violence and other threats to the regime. While the notion that "war made the state" primarily refers to extracting taxes to gird the state's borders, the state's internal strength must similarly be considered for consolidating power. This book advances our understanding of state-building by expanding upon the bellicist argument to theorize about state-building after civil war, where the victor pursues a logic of internal conquest. Such a conquest entails expanding state power from the victor's sub-national stronghold into uncontrolled terrain—where loyalty is weak or fractured and rivals may easily arise. To consolidate control over the state, the victor must maintain stability within (and throughout) the country to provide for citizens while preventing violent rivals, which involves not only eliminating armed groups, but also establishing the bureaucratic and development capacity to reduce the population's appetite for rebellion in the first place.

A rich literature has examined how such state-building strategies might look. Scott's (1999) seminal study, for example, examines state legibility projects as a method of accounting for citizens who seek to remain undetected. In the same way, states attempt to "see"—or at least project the ability to do so—to discourage citizen dissent (Lewis, 2020; Tapscott, 2021). The need for information extends to the development space, motivating rural reforms (Albertus and Kaplan, 2012; Albertus, 2020) that dampen dissent and reduce the likelihood of conflict while simultaneously increasing the state's counterinsurgency capacity. In other words, *legitimation* projects—which cement the victor as the legitimate ruler of the entire country—are also an important aspect of state-building.

In the book, I link both legibility and legitimation concerns to a framework for understanding post-war state-building through internal conquest. I conceptualize victors as meting out coercive violence and implementing popular development initiatives at the same time: they bolster their fighting forces and eliminate rivals, while attempting to win over the population and ensure cooperation or loyalty by investing in public goods and services. This increases both state legitimacy and legibility, and enables the consolidation of control.

14 Governing after War

Highlighting the importance of legitimation after civil war enhances our understanding of distributive politics. While ruling parties often direct resources toward supporters to maximize votes and stay in power during peacetime (Nichter, 2008; Koter, 2013), post-war governments must prevent conflict from recurring in hostile terrain. This book advances this conversation by arguing that the threat of instability significantly changes the usual distributive politics calculus: the victor cannot be satisfied with winning power through plurality or majority; she must actively deter support for rivals and minimize any potential dissent to prevent ballooning insecurity. Resources must therefore be allocated accordingly; supporters—who would normally enjoy favoritism—must now take a back seat. The victor allocates resources to development as a tool of co-optation, and to violence as a tool of coercion.

The political logic of post-war state-building and distributive politics—co-optation through popular development, or coercion where co-optation is not possible—leads to two questions. First, where is co-optation possible, and why? Second, how can the victor spend resources to co-opt and win new supporters without generating dissent from its stronghold? The book links the rebel governance literature to the state-building literature to argue that the answer to these two questions lies, at least in part, in the ties that armed groups form with civilians. Scholarship on rebel governance has already elucidated the myriad ways in which rebel groups attempt to govern and exert control over civilian populations during war. These rebel–civilian ties provide the organizational capacity to rebel during war. After war, they can give the victor the capacity to exert control on the ground after war in a variety of ways.

To that end, the book's theory emphasizes that it is *social* control during war that matters for understanding post-war state-building, control, and stability: the geographic coverage of the rebel's *territorial* control during war matters less than the actual ties that rebels form with civilians for consolidating post-war power. It is certainly the case that social and territorial control may often overlap largely because rebels are more likely to form ties with civilians when they control the territory in which they live; however, the degree of overlap between territorial and social control depends on the timing, military strategy, and other such factors. It is important to remember that not all rebel groups form ties when controlling territory. Additionally, not all ties require the absolute control of territory either: As I show in Chapter 4, the victorious rebels in Zimbabwe did not truly establish territorial control but were successful in exerting social control over the civilian population. On the other hand, as I show in Chapter 5, the conflict in Liberia ended with greater territorial control but no rebel–civilian ties, and the victor failed to consolidate its power after the war. In the end, social control and rebel-civilian ties were more useful than territorial control through relative military force.

1.3.2 Conflict and Political Development in Sub-Saharan Africa

This book advances the study of conflict and political development in sub-Saharan Africa. Rebel victories comprise a significant percentage of civil war termination around the world (one-fifth to one-third, depending on the source), but they play a particularly important role in sub-Saharan Africa: of the twenty-eight states that have experienced civil wars in this region over the last fifty years, rebels have won more than half (eighteen). These rebel victors have proven to be remarkably resilient: only three were ousted in subsequent civil wars.[5] Rebel victors in fifteen of the eighteen states successfully consolidated power after winning the war and subsequently established strong political parties amid weak opposition. Today, all but two of these states—Guinea Bissau and Democratic Republic of Congo—are governed by ex-rebels with little or no party turnover (Table 1.1).[6] These ex-rebel parties have sustained their hold over politics and have—by institutionalizing their war machines and often violently eliminating potential challengers after a civil war—established single-party dominance.

The states listed in Table 1.1 highlight three patterns. First, since the end of decolonization in sub-Saharan Africa, every decade has experienced the victory of a rebel that has consolidated its power. They cover various "types" of groups, include anti-colonial rebellions (Guinea Bissau, Angola, Mozambique, Zimbabwe, Namibia), secessionist rebellions (Eritrea), and rebellions against an authoritarian regime (the remainder). Second, international politics influence whether these conflicts begin—and how they terminate. Decolonization in the 1970s and the end of the Cold War in the early 1990s both triggered a surge in civil wars.[7] The ebb and flow of conflicts based on

---

[5] In Chad, the victor was replaced by a new rebel group (the Mouvement Patriotique du Salut, MPS), which then proceeded to consolidate power.

[6] In Guinea Bissau, the ruling Partido Africano para a Independência da Guiné e Cabo Verde (PAIGC) was overthrown in a civil war in 1998. The PAIGC has returned as a major political party in the country the end of civil war in 1999. In the Democratic Republic of Congo, Joseph Kabila of the Parti du Peuple pour la Reconstruction et la Démocratie (PPRD) handed power over to Felix Tshisekedi in the December 2018 election. However, Tshisekedi was accused of colluding with Kabila to defeat Kabila's true opponent, Martin Fayulu. Tshisekedi formed an alliance with Kabila's party after coming to power in 2019, and eventually took full control in 2021.

[7] When the USA and the Soviet Union provided abundant support during the Cold War, regimes tended to be corrupt with poor bureaucratic and economic development, no monopoly over violence, and little governmental social control reaching the state's borders (Bates, 2015). This environment was ripe for

16 Governing after War

Table 1.1 Rebel victories that eliminated wartime rivals

Country (party)	First year	Years in power	Experienced turnover	In Power in 2023
Guinea Bissau (PAIGC)	1974	24	✓	
Angola (MPLA)	1975	48		✓
Mozambique (FRELIMO)	1975	48		✓
Zimbabwe (ZANU-PF)	1980	43		✓
Uganda (NRA)	1986	37		✓
Chad (MPS)	1990	33		✓
Namibia (SWAPO)	1990	23		✓
Ethiopia (EPRDF)	1991	32		✓
Eritrea (PFDJ)	1993	30		✓
Rwanda (RPA)	1994	29		✓
South Africa (ANC)	1994	29		✓
Congo Brazzaville (CLP)	1997	26		✓
Dem. Rep. Congo (AFDL/PPRD)	1997	23	✓	
Burundi (CNDD-FDD)	2005	18		✓
Côte d'Ivoire (RDR)	2010	13		✓

international politics highlights the future's uncertainty as the United States and China ramp up their contestation for global power, and as the rise of transnational Islamist movements threatens regional instability.

The third and most important pattern is that these rebel victories have produced remarkably resilient political parties, some of which have now been in power for more than forty years. In many cases, individual party leaders have changed over time but the party remains dominant. Although we often associate these rebel groups and their post-war regimes with their leaders—such as Samora Machel in Mozambique, Mugabe in Zimbabwe, or Pierre Nkurunziza in Burundi—the parties have continued to dominate without them through the domestic structures for control that spread across the state under their rule.[8] These institutions, rather than the individual leader, tend to help the party maintain its grip on the nation.

The longevity of these ex-rebel parties therefore requires further investigation and highlights the importance of understanding how civil wars have shaped post-war politics. Prior research on rebel regime survival often focuses on revolutionary actors and has primarily examined the role of civil–military relations and elite politics in preventing elite defection, coups, and counterrevolutions; such studies primarily examine security *after* the post-war

---

guerrilla warfare, allowing discontented citizens living in hard-to-reach rural areas to organize militarily and rebel against the state.

[8] As I show in Liu (2023), rebel victories today tend to be less personalistic, with less powerful chief executives who are more beholden to the party than the other way around. They also tend to engage in violent clientelism, choosing intimidation rather than vote buying.

political situation has stabilized (Clarke, 2022; Lachapelle et al., 2020; Levitsky and Way, 2022; Martin, 2020; Meng and Paine, 2022). Yet, I show in Appendix Table A1, wartime rival threats are common during post-war instability, and often precede intra-party threats; elite defections from the ruling party are more likely to come *when* the party has stabilized and consolidated control. This book therefore differs from the revolutions literature in two respects. First, because civil war (and civil war resumption) often relies on civilian recruitment, the book explores citizen–state relationships rather than elite politics: how victorious rebel regimes relate to, and exert control over, the people and territories they govern in order to prevent civil war recurrence. Second, it seeks to understand why some rebel victors are able to stay in power during the initial period of post-war instability in the first place.

The book's theoretical focus thus allows us to investigate how rebel victories' successes and failures in wartime and post-war governance affect the long-term state-building process. Do rebels remake the state in their quest to prevent conflict recurrence, and if so, how? Rebel victors' potential for a fresh new start explains the international community's enthusiasm and willingness to fund post-war reconstruction after many rebel victories: after all, a completely new government represents an opportunity to change a state's political and economic path. However, as I point out throughout the book, particularly in Chapter 8, the victor's state-building efforts are unevenly applied based on wartime processes, and follow distinct political logics.

My argument helps explain how these dominant rebels-turned-parties exploited their wartime experiences to consolidate power after the war, and illuminates the political implications of their long-term dominance.[9] Under guerrilla warfare (Mao, 1961), rebel groups attempt to exert control over the civilian population by forming ties with key civilians, engaging in politicization, and establishing rudimentary institutions for intelligence and control.[10] Thus, victorious rebels can use lessons learned during the war as a blueprint for how best to reshape the state's institutions to better exert control, sometimes strengthening the state in the process. Rebel victories therefore represent a critical juncture during which a new set of political actors can redefine political cleavages, spread its own institutions of control, and attempt to project authority across the entire territory (Migdal, 1988; Liu, 2022).

---

[9] In Liu (2023) I examine the path dependence on how and where violence is used to establish control.

[10] A flourishing literature within conflict studies focuses on even more sophisticated forms of rebel governance, including how rebels remake the state sub-nationally and engage in a variety of governing functions to win civilian support, extract taxes, and demonstrate their competence (Arjona, Kasfir, and Mampilly, 2015; Mampilly, 2011; Suykens, 2015; Magouirk, 2008).

To be clear, I am not arguing that rebels are necessarily revolutionary actors who will implement positive and socially transformative change based on what we observe from them during war. The question of whether we can expect wartime rebel governance—including health, justice, education, and other such contributions to state-building—to carry over into peacetime when rebels attain power and access to state wealth is outside the scope of this book.[11] I instead examine the *organizational endowments* of victorious rebels as tools for post-war state-building under security fears: when rebels face crises, what organizational capacity can they leverage to quickly address threats? When victors engage in internal conquest, they use many tools derived from their wartime experiences. The crux of my argument is that victors use their civilian ties to "hold down the fort" while attempting to recruit more supporters and replicate the institutional structures that successfully gathered intelligence and maintained control during the war across the rest of the state. In some ways, rebels do learn how to govern from war.

This argument has significant implications for our understanding of how these parties and states are structured today. It implies that ties with civilians during civil war not only increase post-war stability, but also play a major role in stifling political plurality as the victor invests in expanding its capacity to control civilians across the state. Since wartime rebel–civilian ties grow *not* out of democratic exchange, but during war under the constant shadow of coercion and physical insecurity, there is path dependence in how social control—through coercion and the threat of violence—is exerted during and after war. Ex-rebel parties are durable and authoritarian across sub-Saharan Africa and the world more broadly, and their post-war state-building activities may suggest why this is the case. I show in Chapter 4 that in post-war Zimbabwe, the victor's civilian ties on the ground were instrumental in leading reconstruction, from aid distribution to mobilizing the community to improve education. However, the victor also used its wartime ties to the youth population to build militias and employ electoral intimidation due to fears that its rival was arming itself to resume conflict. Other rebel regimes, such as in Burundi, Eritrea, and Uganda, also engaged in both positive and negative peace-building. When the goal is to consolidate power and prevent rivals from successfully mounting a military challenge, state-building seeks to build authoritarian control, and preexisting ties with civilians help achieve that outcome.

---

[11] See Thaler (2018); Huang (2016).

1.4 Research Design

1.4.1 Evidence from Zimbabwe and Liberia

The book's theory generates sub-national and cross-national hypotheses; the research design therefore reflects these two levels of analysis. At the sub-national level, I use a most-different research design. I examine two disparate cases, the Zimbabwean Liberation War (1972–1979) and the First Liberian Civil War (1989–1996), and use qualitative and quantitative evidence to show how political survival shapes post-war resource allocation strategies. Despite significant differences in the wars' *raison d'etre*, demographics, and context—and the divergent outcomes we would expect from these conflicts—both rebel groups strategically used cooperation and coercion to achieve their aims. For example, both groups formed ties with civilians to exert wartime control. Their post-war governing strategies also followed surprisingly similar patterns that emphasized surviving an internal challenge to their rule. The Zimbabwe and Liberia cases underscore the importance of understanding how wartime dynamics condition rebel behavior and cooperation with civilians independently of rebel aims, and how such cooperation empowers new classes of local supporters to help the victor consolidate control.

The Zimbabwean Liberation War was a Marxist–Leninist and nationalist war for independence, fought during a decades-long political struggle that formed part of a broader set of independence movements across southern Africa. Rebels in Zimbabwe enjoyed significant support from regional allies in Angola, Zambia, and Mozambique as well as international allies such as Tanzania, China, and the Soviet Union. The war's victor, ZANU, enjoyed the support of the country's overwhelming ethnic majority. By appealing to ethnic kinship, the sheer demographic majority ought to have bypassed the need to engage in internal conquest. Yet, as I show in Chapter 4, ZANU found its position precarious: control was not easy to exert outside its wartime areas of operation, where it had formed civilian ties. Co-optation was necessary even among co-ethnics, and even as the victor used the technocratic rhetoric of Marxist–Leninist bureaucratic state-building after the war, it targeted development resources to some areas and unleashed mass violence in others.

Liberia has a long tradition of neo-patrimonialism; its civil war is considered one of the most chaotic and brutal in history. It was rooted in both Muammar Gaddafi's pan-Africa movement that employed revolutionary rhetoric as well as rivalry between two minority ethnic coalitions that was fueled by government politicization. The Liberian Civil War quickly became embroiled in the region's race for natural resources; the country's diamonds, iron, rubber, and timber funded the conflict. The eventually victorious NPFL won support from several ethnic groups but failed to establish a majority coalition. Despite Liberia's neo-patrimonial institutions and the conflict's roots in ethnic rivalry, I show in Chapter 5 that the victor did not necessarily default to paying off wartime supporters after the war. To be sure, bribes and informal payments were made: neo-patrimonialism persisted from before the war, and shaped how the rebels established control during the conflict, as well as their subsequent post-war governing strategies. However, they were directed outside the victor's wartime strongholds toward areas the NPFL hoped to co-opt, highlighting the logic of internal conquest. Security-related resources played a significant role in post-war politics, targeted at areas that rejected the victor's attempts at co-optation.

1.4.2 Comparing Zimbabwe and Liberia to Four Secondary Cases

Although both cases strategically allocated resources to maximize the chances of political survival, these efforts to control, co-opt, and coerce failed in Liberia. This highlights the cross-national dimension of the argument: the breadth and depth of wartime ties with civilians affect the victor's budget constraints, which in turn reduces the likelihood of consolidating power because sufficient resources must be allocated to successfully stave off rebellion. Within a decade after the war's end, Zimbabwe's victor cemented control and the country has evolved into a one-party state; Liberia's victor succumbed to a second civil war and was ousted from power. I argue that military contestation during Liberia's civil war drastically decreased the breadth and depth of its ties with civilians on the ground and simultaneously decreased the likelihood of co-optation elsewhere. After the war, the victor in Liberia sought to co-opt, but spread its resources too thinly across the state and was confronted with a security–development trade-off. As more resources were channeled to security, fewer were available for development—which pushed civilians to join the rebellion, to the detriment of consolidating power. Liberia's post-war experience highlights how rebel strength during war, as proxied by military dominance or territorial control, does not necessarily translate easily to the post-war consolidation of power.

Because the Zimbabwean and Liberian conflicts are so different across multiple dimensions, it is difficult to make a strong case based only on a controlled comparison of them. I therefore situate their experiences within a broader set of secondary case studies: Angola's War for Independence (1961–1974), the Burundian Civil War (1991–2005), the Rwandan Civil War (1990–1994), and the Côte d'Ivoire Civil War (2002–2011). These additional cases allow me to account for alternative explanations arising out of ethnicity, ideology, prewar institutional strength, and international context.

I first investigate the Angolan War for Independence and the Côte d'Ivoire Civil War. The Angolan War for Independence was similar to Zimbabwe's civil war at the beginning but grew more similar to the Liberia case after independence. Though the victor was ideological in character and the war was fought over independence—some of the Zimbabwean rebels had been trained in Angolan camps—the lack of ties with civilians forced the victor to defend its position against three successive counter-rebellions launched by a socially embedded opposition. Though the new Angolan government started as a revolutionary movement dedicated to its ideological foundations, it devolved into a neo-patrimonial state that relied heavily on oil wealth to fight increasingly expensive civil wars. Its post-war experience mirrored the opportunism that characterized Liberia's civil war and post-war politics. Côte d'Ivoire presents the opposite scenario. The country is adjacent to Liberia, and shared the same regional political context and pre-war neo-patrimonial institutions as those that plagued Liberia. The conflict was similarly rooted in ethnic tensions rather than ideology, and the armed groups even recruited Liberian mercenaries from the Liberian Civil War. Unlike in Liberia, however, the 2011 rebel victory in Côte d'Ivoire has consolidated power and established post-war peace over the last decade.

I then compare Burundi's Civil War, which featured strong and widespread rebel–civilian ties, with that of Rwanda, which had almost no civilian ties, to illustrate how wartime ties (or the lack thereof) led to very different outcomes in these two adjacent countries. These two cases allow us to "control" for the role of confounding factors in divergent post-war outcomes for three reasons. First, neither of these conflicts was ideological or revolutionary; thus the use of such political appeals to facilitate organizational capacity played far less of a role in both wartime and post-war control. Second, while the victorious rebel group in Burundi was affiliated with the ethnic majority (Hutu), so was its rival, which eliminates the ethnic advantage in this case altogether. Third, the pre-war governments in both Rwanda and Burundi were institutionally strong (Chemouni, 2016), and sociopolitical factors were comparable across the two countries. In sum, the differences in post-war development decisions in Burundi and Rwanda are more likely attributable to whether the victorious rebel groups in both countries were able to control civilians and form local ties during the civil war.

1.4.3 Fieldwork and Evidence

In the two main cases, Zimbabwe and Liberia, I utilize data collected from fieldwork to provide in-depth qualitative and quantitative evidence. My theory of wartime control and post-war stability cannot be tested experimentally: the wars I examine have long ended, and most of the immediate post-war history has already played out. For quantitative testing, I therefore rely on a series of quasi-experimental designs and leverage historical data collected by various governments, administrations, and organizations to test my hypotheses. In the four secondary cases, I use secondary sources for qualitative testing.

Decades after the conflicts have ended, the ease of conducting in-person research in Zimbabwe and Liberia reflects the legacies of both civil wars and the long-run political restrictions that have developed over time. My fieldwork first brought me to Liberia, which offers an open research environment: civilians and ex-combatants were not afraid to speak of their wartime experiences, their opinions about the previous and current governments, or their expectations about Liberian politics moving forward. Government agencies were willing to help procure data, but there were no archival materials available from the pre- or immediate post-war period. Zimbabwe's research environment was far different. The government had placed increasingly severe restrictions on political freedoms. Numerous conversations with scholars, NGO leaders, and government employees made it clear that it would have been unwise to broadly solicit interviews from civilians and ex-combatants about the ZANU-PF government or the Liberation War due to well-founded fears of government reprisal. The government also heavily restricts outside researchers from accessing data in-country.

The types of data I collected and use to test my hypotheses in both countries reflect the differences between the two contexts. In Zimbabwe, I focused on archival research and collected data from the National Archives of Zimbabwe, the Jesuit Archives, and the Mafela Trust with the help of two Zimbabwean research assistants. This data includes reports from missionaries and Rhodesian government officials during the civil war, newspapers, and rebel records collected after the war such as wartime diaries and oral interviews with ex-combatants and civilian collaborators. I also use death records for both rebel groups that fought in the Liberation War and digitized Rhodesian military maps to determine the locations of various counterinsurgency campaigns. Finally, I supplemented this archival data by interviewing a small number of elites who did not fear the government. I used this qualitative data to code a novel measure of wartime rebel control and military contestation under the two rebel groups, ZANU and ZAPU, in Zimbabwe. I then used this measure to conduct quantitative analyses along with secondary survey responses collected by Afrobarometer and the 2012 Zimbabwe Population Census.

In Liberia, I draw primarily from ex-combatant and elite interviews, as well as focus group discussions with civilians who lived in the country during the civil war. My ex-combatant interview subjects ranged from rank-and-file ex-combatants to elite commanders of multiple rebel groups. This provides an insightful picture of rebel–civilian relations both as a survival strategy and a military expansion strategy. My elite interview subjects played a role in local or national government during the First Civil War. The focus groups consisted of civilians who were of the same ethnic group, and who therefore experienced the war in different areas of the country. This strategy allowed me to target civilians who had very different experiences, which more accurately depicts civilians' motivations for engaging in rebel–civilian relationships under different levels of social control. Building on this qualitative data, my quantitative data from Liberia draws on administrative data that I gained access to during my fieldwork, including post-war information from the 2008 Housing and Population Census and local government hiring records, and also existing conflict data from the Uppsala Conflict Data Program Georeferenced Event Dataset (UCDP GED).

My use of different types of data across my two main cases naturally raises questions about biases: the information from interviews and focus groups that I conducted as a foreigner may be different from the information gathered from interviews conducted by researchers and archivists from Zimbabwe. In addition, my qualitative coding of rebel–civilian ties during the wars may differ from an approach that uses existing conflict data; the quality of administrative data may also differ across the two contexts given constraints in state capacity. While I am unable to standardize all the data I use, I strive where possible to triangulate across multiple sources and draw on information from various viewpoints to increase confidence in the comparisons at the sub-national level. I describe the data and these efforts in more detail in Part II.

1.5 Overview of the Book

The book is organized as follows. Chapter 2 introduces my theory of rebel–civilian relations and situates civil war within a broader state-building framework. It first explains why rebel–civilian ties during civil war facilitate rebel governance and can help rebels establish social control over civilians in a particular area. I next introduce a typology that describes the degree of social control that rebels should exert in different territories based on the strategic interactions among rebels, civilians, and other armed groups. I then lay out hypotheses regarding post-war state-building following rebel victory. The chapter ends by discussing how civil war and rebel victory can be viewed as the first step in a broader state-building process, in which the victorious party consolidates power through one or more rounds of contestation with potential challengers before establishing a monopoly over violence.

Part II explores the sub-national variation in resource allocation. I evaluate the theory and mechanisms using the two primary case studies. This part begins by introducing the cases in Chapter 3, explaining the historical contexts of the two rebellions and situating them within the broader regional and international politics of their time. Chapters 4 and 5 then examine the ZANU rebels in the Zimbabwean Liberation War and the NPFL rebels in the Liberian Civil War, respectively. In both cases, I show that the rebels formed ties with civilians, which they leveraged to help them fight the civil wars. Most such ties were destroyed in Liberia and the remaining ties were fragmented, while in Zimbabwe, rebels' ties to civilians strengthened as the war progressed. In both cases I then explore how the victor made post-war resource allocation decisions based on its expectations of whether it could control civilians, co-opt them through development, or coerce through violence.

In Part III, I examine cross-national variation in post-war state stability. Does the resource allocation strategy succeed in staving off counter-rebellion? In Chapter 6, I begin with a discussion of why the victor in Zimbabwe consolidated power while in Liberia it did not. I once again evaluate rebel–civilian ties, explaining how the breadth and depth of these ties help us understand why Liberia eventually faced a security–development tradeoff that led to Taylor's overthrow. Broadening this analysis, I categorize the eighteen rebel governments in sub-Saharan Africa based on the breadth and depth of their ties to civilians and the resulting degree of social control they truly exerted in the state. I demonstrate that this categorization correlates with post-war conflict recurrence and state stability. In Chapter 7, I illustrate the mechanism of wartime rebel–civilian ties using four secondary cases— Angola, Côte d'Ivoire, Burundi, and Rwanda—which help account for alternative explanations and provide external validity to the argument.

Part IV concludes by discussing the policy implications of my findings. While rebel politicization and the formation of civilian ties during war increase post-war stability and help consolidate power, it may be difficult to exert social control during peacetime using institutions established at gunpoint. I argue that victors tend to create a single-party state as the ruling party militarily eliminates challengers and co-opts potential allies under the banner of peace and stability. The final chapter discusses these long-term implications and how the international community can best direct its aid provision and civil society support on the ground.

2
State-building through Rebel–Civilian Ties

This chapter develops a theory of how rebel–civilian ties affect post-war governance, and adopts a state-building framework to examine two questions about how wartime processes affect post-war governance. First, when rebels win control of the state, what governing strategies do they use—and why? Second, under what conditions do these governing strategies help the victor consolidate power?

I argue that rebel victors share one common goal: they seek to prevent conflict recurrence and consolidate power after winning control of the state. To achieve this goal, they should strategically allocate resources toward popular *development* and *security* across the state depending on where they developed wartime ties with civilians. Such ties decrease the cost of governance and help mitigate economic constraints during a period of high political tensions characterized by the threat of a return to war. Rebel–civilian ties in wartime strongholds help the victor control civilians living in these areas at low cost, which allows the government to allocate a greater proportion of its resources to areas outside of such strongholds to build bureaucratic capacity, win new supporters, and eliminate rivals. Whether this approach prevents a return to conflict depends on the breadth and depth of rebel–civilian ties across the state: if the victor enjoys widespread and deeply embedded organized ties with civilians, it is more likely to successfully consolidate power.

This chapter is divided into five sections. The first section provides an overview of the literature and lays out potential pathways from war to post-war stability after a rebel victory. Second, it proposes a state-building framework that links war and post-war governance, defines key concepts, and identifies the relevant actors. The third section examines how (and why) rebel–civilian ties are formed during war. The fourth and fifth sections then explain how these ties are used after war to assert control. The chapter concludes by returning to the state-building framework and summarizes the complete timeline: how civil war, rebel victory, and post-war governing decisions fit within the broader process of consolidating power.

Governing after War: Rebel Victories and Post-war Statebuilding. Shelley X. Liu, Oxford University Press.
© Oxford University Press 2024. DOI: 10.1093/oso/9780197696705.003.0002

2.1 Insights and Puzzles from Conflict Scholarship

While rebel victories are sometimes credited with being better able to eliminate multiple sovereignties and sustain post-war peace,[1] rebel regimes' resilience varies substantially. Within sub-Saharan Africa, for instance, rebel victors in, Burundi, Côte d'Ivoire, Eritrea, and Zimbabwe consolidated control after eliminating domestic security threats. Rebel victors such as those in Uganda, Mozambique, and Ethiopia faced renewed civil war but eventually staved off imminent challengers and retained power for long periods of time. The remainder—Angola, Chad, Liberia, and South Sudan—were quickly challenged by wartime rivals and plunged into civil war again. In these cases, the victor's power was significantly threatened, and some were overthrown altogether.

In short, some rebel governments are able to consolidate power, while others capture control but quickly face one or numerous existential security crises. Prior research highlights four potential mechanisms that explain why some rebel victors are able to consolidate power while others are not: (1) political support, (2) greater will (and capability) for governance, (3) military strength, and (4) elite politics. This section examines each potential mechanism in turn.

2.1.1 Political Support

Conflict scholarship has theorized extensively on how (and why) rebels win political support from civilians, focusing on ethnicity and ideological appeals. The relevance of these two arguments depends on the time period and location of the conflict (Kalyvas, 2001). Ethnicity is a common political grievance in Africa: Across the continent, conflicts take root and acquire popular support when rebel leaders or elites exploit inequalities and cross-community grievances. Particularly where the state is weak and resources are scarce, sub-national cleavages and competition over state goods can lead to in-group favoritism or resentment—instigating conflict between sub-national ethno-religious groups (Bates, 1974; Fearon and Laitin, 2011). Neo-patrimonialism and inter-group competition then manifest as grievances against the state, which increases the likelihood of violent demands for access to the state's wealth (Østby, 2008; Cederman, Weidmann, and Gleditsch, 2011).

---

[1] See, for example, discussions of rebel military victories in Toft (2010) and Mason et al. (2011).

28   Governing after War

However, identity-based explanations are not relevant everywhere. Beyond sub-Saharan Africa—particularly in Latin America, but also around the world during the Cold War period—ideology has been theorized as a unifying framework through which rebels can politicize, organize, and use to sustain legitimacy (Wood, 2003). Ideological rebellions adhere to a set of ideas that are not primarily resource driven or opportunistic, and may be more likely to feature less violence and greater support from citizens (Green, 2018; Thaler, 2012). International and domestic political forces have shaped which ideologies capture popular attention; Marxist–Leninist conflicts and (nationalist) independence movements are the most common type of ideological rebellions. Past studies in this strand of the literature have argued that rebel groups adhere to ideology for both instrumental and normative reasons (Sanín and Wood, 2014), and that conflicts with such goals—including nationalist, secessionist, or independence aspirations—lead to sub-national state-building (Thaler, 2018; Stewart, 2018).

Rebel victors that are popular because they successfully politicized co-ethnic or partisan ties may be expected to create a more stable post-war environment. If they successfully politicized along ethnic identity-based cleavages, they will enjoy post-war support based on these cleavages even if they did not form ties during the war to exert social control. This would suggest that state stability may be derived from ethnic dominance. If so, civil war will either harden preexisting cleavages or create new ones, but post-war stability depends on which groups support the state. A government that is affiliated with a majority ethnic group may receive intrinsic support from the local population after the war and may then, accordingly, ensure state stability through ethnic dominance. Zimbabwe, one might argue, is an example of this; however, as I show in Chapter 4, ethnic support was not the primary reason for why the victor consolidated control.

The broader literature on conflict incidence, however, does not support this mechanical relationship between ethnic support and state stability. An argument purely about citizens' ethnic support would suggest that conflict and stability are based on each ethnic group's share of the population. Yet theories about the distribution of power, ethnic fractionalization, and polarization suggest there are complicated relationships between ethnicity and violence (Østby, 2008; Esteban, Mayoral, and Ray, 2012; Posner, 2004a; Cederman, Weidmann, and Gleditsch, 2011; Cederman, Wimmer, and Min, 2010). The existence of an ethnic majority, for example, does not rule out the possibility that an ethnic minority will successfully wage a counter-rebellion against a new rebel government; indeed, ethnic dominance may *increase* the likelihood of civil war (Collier and Hoeffler, 2004). There are several historical cases of ethnic minorities successfully launching a civil war—such as the Rwandan Patriotic Front and the National Patriotic Front of Liberia. Nor are ethnic categories stagnant: they are often aggregated or manipulated to increase their political relevance (Posner, 2004b; Green, 2022). Where rulers rely on co-ethnicity to sustain stability, pure political support from civilians is unconvincing as an alternative explanation.

It is also possible that citizens may be more heavily influenced by partisan ties, and their support (or lack thereof) of the state's actions. For example, the rebel victors of the civil wars in Eritrea, South Africa, and Zimbabwe enjoyed fervent partisan support. However, as I show in subsequent chapters, partisanship fails for the same reason as co-ethnicity: unless citizens homogeneously support the victor, partisans of rival groups may be equally fervent—and willing to resume civil war. Political polarization and factionalization along any cleavages are detrimental to sustaining peace, particularly when the political system is unstable (Walter, 2022; Goldstone et al., 2005). The civil wars following the Angolan War for Independence demonstrate how civilian support matters when multiple groups offer the same policy options. Though all major rebel groups fought for the country's independence, citizens in various parts of the country supported different rebels and believed that their preferred group would be better at governing the new nation. This, ultimately, led to conflict resumption.

2.1.2 Pre-war Institutions and Governing Capacity

Alternatively, if pure political support does not increase the likelihood of post-war stability, perhaps rebel victors will consolidate power more quickly if their governing capacity is higher. A country may be easier to govern either because its pre-war institutions are stronger, or because the rebel victors are better at governing.

With respect to pre-war institutions, variation in institutional setup is undoubtedly important for understanding post-war trajectories since there is path dependence in institutional strength (David, 1994; Mahoney, 2000; Pierson, 2000). However, pre-war institutions cannot explain the entire story: If this were the case, the type of conflict termination should play little or no role in post-war trajectories. Rather, we can better understand civil war, termination, and post-war trajectories under the critical junctures framework proposed in Collier and Collier (1991). Antecedent conditions, including pre-war institutions, culminate in the second step—the shock that is civil war. The civil war termination type goes on to explain which post-war path the country takes, as conflict may end in rebels taking control, the government remaining in control, or various forms of power sharing. Finally, these divergent paths would subsequently affect the civil war's aftermath and long-run legacies. Framed in this way, it is not that pre-war institutions don't matter; however, wartime processes still have a considerable influence on post-war outcomes.

Treating the conflict termination type as a critical juncture variant that shapes post-war trajectories means that *who* comes to power may matter a great deal: The eventual victor's governing ability may help explain post-war state stability. Governing ability may in turn have grown out of rebel governance experience at the sub-national level during the civil war. This logic is well explained in Toft (2010), who argues that rebel military victories produce longer periods of post-war peace because they are both more institutionally capable and are perceived by the public as being more legitimate. This explanation touches on the literature on rebel governance: Scholars have increasingly explored how rebels govern during war—by imposing the rule of law and engaging in sub-national state-building by taxing citizens and providing public goods—in order to establish control and gain legitimacy (Huang, 2016; Sanchez de la Sierra, 2017). Some studies of rebel governance, for example, look at the bureaucratic foundations of sub-national penetration, from building village-level networks to creating a communist party structure (Kalyvas, 2015) to the importance of pre-war institutions for sub-national state-building (Mampilly, 2011).

Rebel groups provide law, order, public goods, and protection not only due to state weakness and lawlessness (Wikham Crowley, 2015), but also to demonstrate their political goals (Suykens, 2015; Magouirk, 2008). Prior research in this area focuses on rebel groups that grow out of, and thrive under, state collapse and lack of governance by more formal authorities. Where the state lacks the capacity to provide order and public goods, rebel groups represent a better alternative for governance (Revkin, 2021). At the very least, rebel militaries have a *de facto* monopoly over violence in the areas they occupy, which deters banditry and enforces local laws even if they were set by the rebels rather than the state (Wikham Crowley, 2015). Rebel groups—particularly those that are more ideological—also build local systems of taxation and judicial courts, provide public goods, and maintain other sub-national bureaucratic structures to demonstrate and promote governance (Huang, 2016; Podder, 2014; Stewart, 2018).

A governing capacity argument would suggest that rebels' post-war governing activities are linked to their wartime governing activities. In Huang's (2016) account of rebel governance, citizens learn to make demands by engaging with rebel rulers, and therefore are more likely to make demands after the war—resulting in good governance and democratization overall. We may reasonably expect that this would, in turn, decrease appetites for conflict recurrence. Returning to rebel motivations and comparing ideological versus opportunistic wars, one might further argue that rebels with strong ideological goals and development ideals may be more willing to engage in post-war governance (Thaler, 2018). If this is the case, these ideological victors should not only be better at programmatic governance in theory; they may also win broad citizen support for their development-minded governance. By contrast, opportunistic rebels may *decrease* the likelihood of post-war state stability. Natural resources increase the benefits of predation and coercive behaviors (Weinstein, 2006), attracting the wrong type of rebels—those that predate and engage in violence. After winning control of the state, such victors will continue to be incapable; predatory rulers who choose to enrich themselves and their cronies and will fail to transform the state (Ross, 1999). Compared to ideological rebellions, resource-driven rebel victors may rapidly lose citizen support. They may also encourage renewed violence as others, noting that wealth is concentrated at the top, choose to rebel out of both greed and grievance (Dube and Vargas, 2013).

While rebel governing capacity undoubtedly plays a factor in the victor's post-war success, the relationship is not so simple. The theory I propose draws heavily upon the rebel governing capacity literature and takes its logic as a building block for understanding post-war governance. However, depending on the actions of their rivals, rebels-turned-victors are both constrained in—or are pushed to expand—their wartime and post-war governing activities regardless of programmatic intent. In short, it is not enough to take into account the victor's governing capacity post-war, but also their rival(s)' capacity to resist such governance.

2.1.3 Military Strength and Territorial Control

An alternative to rebel governing capacity is military strength—the ability to exert territorial control and maintain social order through coercive force. Kalyvas's (2006) seminal work on the logic of territorial control, certainty over information, and civilian victimization during the Greek Civil War provides a parsimonious explanation of how rebels use violence depending on their military strength. His predictions of indiscriminate versus discriminate violence hinge on whether rebels are able to discern the accuracy of civilian intelligence—which is in turn based on their degree of territorial control. This argument is a military one: rebel motivations, politicization, and efforts to increase legitimacy play a far lesser role in determining whether civilians and rebels cooperate to further the war effort. Such arguments about rebel group strength suggest that groups that are strong during the war ought to not only be more likely to win the war, but also continue to be strong after it. This possible conclusion is borne out by research on rebel parties, which argues that the strong militarism and internal cohesion of successful rebel groups lead to strong mass-based rebel parties (Lyons, 2016; Sindre, 2016).

Existing research finds that strong rebels are more likely to win war because patterns of wartime violence under different armed groups crucially affect citizens' political decisions as war transitions into peace. Citizens seek peace and security, and thus may choose to support or reject political actors based on the perceived returns to their support. Kreiman and Masullo (2020) find, for example, that citizens who were victimized by the Revolutionary Armed Forces of Colombia were more likely to support its peace deal with the government in Colombia, while those who were victimized by paramilitaries were more likely to reject the agreement. Rebels with greater military prowess and territorial control also tend to enjoy larger vote shares in elections (Ishiyama and Widmeier, 2013). Daly (2019) argues that citizens vote militarily strong rebels into government *despite* wartime violence because stronger rebels can credibly commit to providing security and maintaining peace. The flip side to this logic is that stronger rebels can commit to *spoiling* the peace—a strategy that multiple groups (including the rebel victors in Zimbabwe and Liberia) have used in their campaign threats. Territorial control and rebel–civilian cooperation during war may therefore simply be a credible sign of rebel military strength, which both increases citizen support and decreases the likelihood of instability given power disparities.

However, even though strong rebels are more likely to win control of the state, linking wartime power to post-war strength leads to a puzzle. Even militarily strong rebels rarely control the entire country during war, and this is particularly true for rebels that win political victories. How, then, can wartime territorial control in one part of the country affect post-war stability in uncontrolled areas? To consolidate power, post-war governance must extend throughout the country—including to areas that continue to support the victor's rivals. Thus rebel strength in one region is not sufficient to project power over rival territories after the war. While Toft (2010) argues that a rebel military victory more likely "effectively eliminates one side or, more commonly, damages it to the point where it must abandon its political objectives," this is not necessarily the case. Rivals do not disappear entirely even if they have been convincingly defeated in a military sense; in rival terrain, rivals may have a greater military capacity to fight back and more likely have strong support from civilians. They may therefore not be easily overwhelmed by the victor's popularity elsewhere in the state, or its military strength. For example, I show in this book that the victor in Liberia enjoyed overwhelming territorial control but failed to consolidate its power. I demonstrate that *social* control through organized civilian support ends up being more important over the long term.

This puzzle—how wartime strength affects post-war stability in areas outside the rebel group's military control or political base—is pertinent to all three mechanisms discussed earlier (political support, governing capacity, and military strength). While all three certainly matter for thinking about post-war political support, the criticism famously made in Centeno (1997)—that intra-state wars exacerbate internal fractionalization—and ultimately weakens the state—still applies. A new rebel government cannot simply rely on preexisting support from the majority to impose control over an unwilling minority, especially given the heightened polarization and uneasy peace that characterizes most post-war periods. Unless the victorious rebel group is militarily strong enough to have successfully overtaken and established control throughout the state by the end of the war, it will struggle to extend power beyond its wartime strongholds. In short, whether it is through pure political support, a greater capacity for governance, or military strength in rebel strongholds during the war, we must still question how these translate to territories that do not support the rebel victors.

2.1.4 Elite Politics and Civil–Military Relations

A final possibility is that rebel victors may avoid the problem of internal fractionalization and civilian discontent altogether if they have a firmer grasp on elite politics and stronger civil–military relations, which would allow them to quash any dissent that may arise. In this case, sub-national variation in state capacity, civilian support, and local embeddedness would not matter.

If questions of counter-rebellion and conflict recurrence can be settled at the elite level, the victor may not need to worry about discontented territories at all. Meng and Paine (2022), for example, argue that rebel victors are durable because they have more stable power-sharing arrangements between the political and military elites. Empirically, rebel victors are therefore more likely to appoint military elites as minister of defense; this reduces the threat of coups, meaning that rebel victories are more likely to become durable and stable authoritarian regimes compared to authoritarian regimes that are not ruled by rebel victors. The revolutionary regimes literature helps us

34 Governing after War

understand why violently imposing social change can lead to such durable authoritarian regimes. These studies suggest that rebel victors may be able to take this important step because these ruling parties—particularly revolutionary ones—develop more cohesive cores and loyal armies during their violent struggle (Levitsky and Way, 2022; Lachapelle et al., 2020). This, in turn, generates greater trust between the political and military wings.

Arguments about elite politics and power sharing between political and military leaders, however, only explain the reduced risk of coup threats arising from military leaders—*not* the threat of civil war recurrence in the post-war period. Decoupling coup threats from civil war recurrence is theoretically and empirically important because they originate from different actors: while coups emerge from members of the political elite or the military, civil war recurrence can (and often does) include armed actors that were kept out of the ruling coalition during the post-war transition. Even among negotiated power-sharing governments, coalitions of rivals are often formed due to wartime strategy and break down quickly once war is won (Christia, 2012)—which may devolve into civil war between wartime rivals once again. In Appendix Table A1, I record each African rebel victory's first wartime rival challenge and first intra-party challenge in the post-war period, along with a brief description of the security contexts after the rebel victors had won. Fifteen of the twenty rebel victories experienced internal unrest from wartime rivals within the first two years of being in power. In short, civil war recurrence is frequent, and therefore a constant fear in a post-war context (Walter, 2004; Call, 2012); counter-rebellion and counterrevolution after major social upheaval similarly involve numerous forms of resistance from both the top down and the bottom up (Clarke, 2022). Thus, rebel victors' ability to secure politics at the top does not mitigate fears of opposition from discontented territories.

Related arguments about revolutionary regimes and counterrevolutionary threats expand beyond coup threats to highlight that strong civil–military relations help rulers impose control through the threat of repression. Violent revolutions are reasoned to yield durable regimes and are less likely to be overthrown because they tend to produce loyal armies (Clarke, 2022), which are especially important for staving off counterrevolution or conflict recurrence. This body of scholarship also points to the importance of being able to wield repressive violence when necessary (Hazelton, 2017; Arreguin-Toft, 2001), which is undoubtedly an important part of consolidating power and preventing counter-revolts. Interacting this argument with the military capacity argument mentioned earlier, the implication is that rebel victors' militaries are not only stronger; rank-and-file fighters are more willing to stick with their leader and go to the lengths needed to establish violent control.

This implication suggests three complications. First, even if the military is loyal and cohesive, outright violent repression is not always a winning strategy: violence is more likely to be effective when it is targeted at specific areas (Downes, 2007) because this helps the repressor more thoroughly exert complete control through military strength. Second, and relatedly, moderate levels of repression are not useful: violence mutes the opposition only if it is so severe that it prevents civilians from engaging in political action (Zhukov, 2023). Together, these two complications suggest that to understand *how* loyal militaries are able to sustain control so effectively, we must also try to understand how rebel victors can minimize the territories over which they need to exercise violence: sub-national variation still matters. To avoid military constraints and reputation concerns on the international stage, the rebel victor should seek to balance the degree—and territorial spread—of violence they can, and are willing to, use.

The third complication applies to both elite power-sharing arguments and repression arguments: there is substantial cross-national variation in the degree of cohesion between the political and military wings of rebel-turned-incumbent parties (Martin, 2020). Not all rebel victors are revolutionary in nature—thus they may not exhibit the cohesion that (Levitsky and Way, 2022) describe—but even loyal armies defect when the regime seems likely to fall (Bellin, 2004). In other words, complete reliance on a loyal and cohesive military is unlikely to be a preferred strategy during times of political instability. Beyond the temporal variation in military loyalty, there are also spatial differences in civil–military cohesion across the state: some rebel commanders ally more closely with the victor, while other commanders may have stronger ties to the territories they controlled during the war. (Martin, Piccolino, and Speight, 2021). Such sub-national variation points to the importance of understanding when (and where) the military is more or less likely to choose to stand with the rebel victor when facing counter-rebellion threats.

2.1.5 Building on Prior Research

The literature just summarized serves as stepping stones to help recognize how rebel victors build wartime advantages—and leverage them to achieve post-war governance. These theories lead to three important unanswered questions. How does wartime political support translate into tangible benefits during post-war governance? How do rebel victors leverage (sub-national) wartime governing capacity and military strength to project power across the state after war? And how do cohesive civil–military relations help rebel victors

36 Governing after War

consolidate power and avoid conflict recurrence when political support and governing capacity come up short?

In the rest of the chapter, I propose a theory that explores these questions to help bridge the gap between these arguments. I situate civil war within a state-building process to explain how victors exploit their wartime experiences to engage in internal conquest after war. This, in turn, helps explain how likely they are to be able to consolidate control over both their rivals and their supporters.

2.2 State-building as a Theoretical Framework

This book conceptualizes rebel victory, post-war governance, and potential subsequent civil war(s) as part of a long process of consolidating control over the state. In this framework, civil war represents not a singular period of conflict within a weak state, but rather the first step toward state-building through the territorial and political expansion of control (Soifer, 2008) from the sub-national to the national arena. While civil war represents a break-down of the state and enmity between various segments of the population (Centeno, 1997), it can also be viewed as a process in which one distinct sub-national territory must conquer the other(s) through bellicist state-building strategies—mixing the use of violence and development to obtain a monopoly over violence throughout the nation.

The logic of my argument begins with wartime politicization. During a civil war, rebel groups attempt to politicize civilians. In some cases, they manage to establish social order—in essence to consolidate social control over a portion of the state; these groups become "stationary bandits" that command cooperation (Olson, 1993). The political geography of wartime control under various armed groups and the state thus sets the stage for post-war political cleavages: when one armed group wins, this wartime political geography defines the sub-national quasi-states engaged in the post-war struggle for complete political and military control.

When war subsides, the victor ought to attempt to use its military and insti-tutions to expand into territories that it was unable to control during the civil war. To do so, it seeks to establish social contracts with citizens while deploy-ing both violence and development for coercion and co-optation. According to this argument, although the victor does not necessarily face pressures to engage in state-building from true external challengers (Herbst, 2000), it should eliminate internal challengers. By linking wartime politicization and rebel–civilian ties to post-war governance under a broader state-building framework, the state's physical borders can be viewed as the limits of the new rebel government's attempts to expand its power. This expansion of control is undertaken during the tense but nominally peaceful time following the end of the civil war. During this period, the victor's supporters are euphoric while rival supporters are angered by their exclusion from the government. Just as groups of people have historically sought to escape unwanted state control (Scott, 2009), rival supporters will resist the advances of the new government.

The victor's task is therefore to impose its form of governance and control on a new population that seeks to be free from its rule entirely. The victor undertakes both *legibility* projects, rendering its citizens and their actions visible to the state; and *legitimation* projects, policies that establish the victor as the only legitimate ruler of the country's territory. This framework comports with prior studies on state-building that—as Berwick and Christia (2018) note—take both a *long durée* approach and a shorter-term institution-building approach to enhancing state capacity. Within this frame of thinking, my argument draws on previous work that highlights the role of co-optation through deployed bureaucrats and public goods provision (Soifer, 2015; Ansell and Lindvall, 2020), legibility exercises (Lee and Zhang, 2017), ideological indoctrination (Paglayan, 2020; Scott, 2008), performative governance (Ding, 2022), and violent coercion (Hazelton, 2017)—all for the purpose of imposing political and social control (Mann, 1984; Migdal, 1988).

There are, of course, significant differences between a rebel victor attempting to expand its influence after war and a conquering ruler. A conquering ruler, for example, would by law be unable to install its own military structures across the areas it is seeking to conquer, and it would certainly not be inheriting a territory with a bureaucracy and other state structures that can be galvanized to extend its power. However, while the new rebel government is now the *de jure* head of the entire country, these state institutions are often weak or almost nonexistent in parts of the state—especially where rivals were able to sustain control during the war. Rivals may find it easy to resume conflict in these areas, both because areas with poor state capacity are vulnerable to guerrilla warfare methods (during both the first civil war and the post-war period, e.g. Fearon and Laitin, 2003; Hendrix, 2011) and because rivals may have a greater capacity to rebel in areas where they sustained control and support. Further, if state institutions are staffed with individuals who are associated with the previous regime, they may resist the new ruling party despite working for the state. Thus, as I argue in what follows, the new ruling party may be best served by rebuilding or modifying state institutions in the image of its own wartime institutions, and overhauling bureaucratic appointments to install supporters. This act of rebuilding the state to establish a monopoly over violence and social control bears a striking resemblance to the actions a ruler must take during territorial conquest.

The advantage of conceptualizing the resumption of war as a continuing conflict within the state-building process, rather than as a distinct second civil war, is the recognition that subsequent periods of peace and war are often a continuation of the initial conflict. They involve the same actors, even if they take on new names or join new rebel organizations; they are fought over the same political issues, and feature the same local cleavages. Most importantly, conflict resumption often relies on the same sets of military and social networks within the same territories.[2] A major finding from the peace settlement literature is that civil war recurrence is likely because it is easy for ex-rebel commanders to remobilize their ex-fighters for various violent activities (Daly, 2016). Thus, just as war is a "continuation of politics by other means" (Clausewitz, 1982), post-war politics is an extension of wartime struggles for power. The new rebel government's ability to eliminate these multiple sovereignties within a territory (Mason et al., 2011) and monopolize the use of force (Weber, 1946) *after the war has ended* must be considered part of the conflict process.

Figure 2.1 depicts civil war and the post-war consolidation of power in their simplest form. It illustrates that the consolidation process begins during the civil war, when the rebel groups attempt sub-national state-building in their areas of operation. In some areas the rebels are successful, while in others they are unable to establish control. After winning the war, the victorious rebel group becomes the new government and enjoys a short period of interim peace. During this time, its opponents regather their strength to foment counter-rebellion. To address this threat, the new rebel government seeks to conquer the rest of the ostensibly foreign territory within state boundaries.

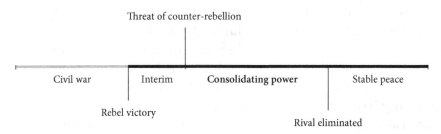

Figure 2.1 The process of consolidation

---

[2] The revival of conflict should be considered categorically different from relatively more uncommon cases in which the new post-war state faces a new and different rival that was not involved in the civil war, such as the Cabinda civil war in Angola.

These post-war acts of conquering enemies and winning supporters are crucial to the process of consolidating power: only when the new government's violent rivals are eliminated is there stable peace.

This model can be complicated and extended in numerous ways. In many cases, the period of consolidating power leads to a second (or subsequent) civil war before the rival is eliminated. Thus, the consolidation period may extend far longer than depicted in Figure 2.1, oscillating between interim peace and consolidation conflicts until the violent rivals are eliminated. In a final set of cases, the new rebel government fails to consolidate power and is overthrown. In those cases, the newly victorious rival armed group must begin the process from scratch. I discuss these scenarios in greater detail at the end of the chapter, after fully explaining the logic of the rebel government's post-war governing decisions.

2.2.1 Establishing Relevant Actors in Post-war Politics

This book investigates how the victor's efforts to obtain citizens' support and impose social order and control during war affects its post-war governing strategies to consolidate power. I have thus far proposed a theoretical framework that conceptualizes civil war and post-war governance as a continuous process of rebel victors establishing and consolidating power over the state. The relevant actors in this framework are those who play a role in state politics during the immediate (peaceful) post-war period and in later episodes of potential conflict when the victor faces its rivals to consolidate its control.

According to the scope conditions laid out in Chapter 1, a rebel group can win control over the state through either military or political means.[3] Throughout the book, I use the terms *rebel government* and *victor* interchangeably to refer to the rebel group that won the civil war, and is now engaging in post-war governance. The victor's potential *rivals* in the immediate post-war period that are relevant to my theory are often armed groups that lost the first conflict and seek to contest the new rebel government for power in a counter-rebellion. These rivals may include other rebel groups that fought in the civil war; any new or splinter groups that formed during or after the first war due to discontent with the victor's rule; and/or the ex-ruling party that lost civil war and thus lost control of the state.

---

[3] This means that even if the rebel group comes to power through a political process or nominally shares power with other political parties or armed groups as part of a peace agreement, the ruling party can be the *de facto* winner if it substantially dictates governing policy.

40 Governing after War

Finally, I reference three additional groups of actors—civilians, bureaucrats, and the army—that play important roles in the post-war consolidation of power through state-building.

First, *civilians* consist of myriad subgroups—such as religious and ethnic leaders, elders, youths, men and women—that have different incentives during and after war.[4] Civilians generally refer to individuals who, in the *wartime context*, were not formal members of a rebel group's civil or military apparatus. However, many civilians would have been involved in the war effort in some capacity, for example as porters, cooks, spies, or local organizers. In the *post-war context*, different groups of civilians have varying incentives to accept or reject the new rebel government. While in the bellicist state-building framework a ruler is able to extract resources and support from civilians in exchange for public and private goods such as jobs, bribes and gifts, or local community-level development, in the post-civil war landscape this is complicated by civilian loyalties that are divided between all the armed actors involved in the war. In short, the rebel government faces a subpopulation of civilians who are loyal to its rivals. If a war was fought over identity politics, it is often especially difficult to extend governance: sticky ethnic loyalties and grievances do not die down easily and may be hardened by war, making it difficult for the rebel government to penetrate unfriendly territory and reach out to civilians while the state remains weak (Rohner, Thoenig, and Zilibotti, 2013; Grossman, Manekin, and Miodownik, 2015).

The second group of actors, post-war *bureaucrats*, are individuals who assumed a (generally nonmilitary) role within the rebel group during the civil war. Post-war bureaucrats are sometimes drawn from wartime political commissars, mid-ranking members of the political wing, or even well-educated ex-combatants who seek to transition from the military to the civil side of government. These bureaucrats may be partisans of the new rebel government, who can be deployed to sub-national political positions such as county administrators, mayors, or councilors. They may also be paid supporters, who seek to bolster the rebel government's rule to sustain patronage from above. Unlike the regular civilians just described, bureaucrats operate at a higher administrative unit than the local level. They are entrusted to carry out the new rebel government's development and governance decisions from the top down.

Third, the *army* consists of two broad categories of armed actors associated with the victor's new government: (1) the formal army, which is the newly composed state military and (2) an informal army, which may include victo-

---

[4] The relevant civilian subgroups vary from war to war; the Zimbabwe and Liberia case studies provide a more detailed description of the types of civilian groups that are salient in those contexts.

rious ex-guerrillas who were not integrated into the army. After a civil war, the national army will largely comprise the rebel government's military wing, those who fought for the victorious rebel group. My theory assumes that the victor will integrate a substantial portion of its own rebel fighters into the state army or gendarmerie to establish an internal monopoly over violence. Ex-government forces, which once constituted the army, either acquiesce to be integrated into the new state army or defect to become rivals in any subsequent war. Other rival rebel groups' ex-combatants may similarly be partly integrated if military integration forms part of a negotiated peace agreement.[5] Regardless of the extent of integration, however, rival soldiers who are integrated in this way—whether they are ex-government forces or rival rebel groups' ex-combatants—tend to be treated as "outsiders" who are less trustworthy than those who fought in the victorious rebel army (Glassmyer and Sambanis, 2008; Krebs and Licklider, 2016); they tend to be persecuted and are more likely to desert if a counter-rebellion erupts.

The second type of armed actor—the victor's unofficial new army—is more likely to consist of ex-combatants who are not integrated into the national army, but are loyal to the victor and can be armed. Rebellions involve numerous combatants from multiple armed groups, many of which are not integrated into the army. These soldiers return home as ex-combatants among the civilian population, but the new rebel government can still call on them when necessary. Unintegrated ex-combatants were generally lower-ranking soldiers during the civil war who received less military training and have less discipline than their integrated counterparts. They may choose to return to their original communities, or they may resettle in the state capital or other large cities to avoid local stigma and persecution. Ex-combatants may have been demobilized during a formal disarmament, demobilization, rehabilitation, and reintegration process, but can be easily remobilized to fight using the original rebel networks, such as through connections with their commanders or other rank-and-file guerrilla soldiers.

2.2.2 The Victor's Constraints and Strategies

After winning a civil war, the victor's ultimate goal ought to be to sustain and consolidate power.[6] Yet, at least three constraints hinder this goal. First,

---

[5] Peace agreements negotiated to end civil wars fought between multiple rebel groups may formally integrate rivals into the new state army, as was the case in both Zimbabwe and Liberia.

[6] While many rebel governments have other goals, ranging from predation to programmatic development, it stands to reason that all rebel groups primarily wish to stay in power after having fought a lengthy war to secure their current position.

existing state institutions under the ex-government are likely to be weak: had they been strong, the initial civil war and subsequent rebel victory would have been unlikely in the first place. These institutions, and the individuals who work in them, may also be loyal to the ex-government. The rebel government should therefore strive to remake bureaucratic institutions to ascertain loyalty and increase institutional strength to prevent conflict recurrence (Mann, 1984). Second, the post–civil war landscape is complicated by polarized civilian loyalties, as the rebel government faces a subpopulation of civilians who are loyal to potential rivals (Centeno, 1997). Rival supporters tend to be territorially concentrated, making these areas a dangerous breeding ground that future rivals could recruit from. The third constraint is that conflict destroys infrastructure and capital, and the costs of reconstruction are high. Despite the availability of international aid, resource constraints heighten post-conflict political tensions and tie the rebel government's hands.

The victor is more likely to be able to consolidate power and ensure state stability if it performs core state-building functions—rebuilds weak state institutions and subdues rival supporters—*despite the budget constraints*. At its simplest, this means successfully allocating resources between two governing strategies: (1) bureaucratic development and public goods provision and (2) military spending.

The rebel government will likely need to pursue more than one of these strategies to successfully consolidate power. Although public goods can be used to help win over a population (Berman, Shapiro, and Felter, 2011; Beath, Christia, and Enikolopov, 2012), such endeavors are difficult and expensive, and hardened divisions mean that rival strongholds cannot be won over quickly enough (if at all). Indeed, it will be difficult to build bureaucratic and developmental capacity in areas that reject state institutions altogether. Pure military repression is useful, but should be deployed judiciously; it should not be a rebel government's only strategy for exerting control (Downes, 2007). Violence is unlikely to win over undecided civilians, and may backfire by increasing support for rivals among civilians who would otherwise have been open to supporting the new regime (Arreguin-Toft, 2001). Thus, the rebel government should use both strategies, which involves making crucial decisions about where public goods and security should be targeted to minimize both state spending and the likelihood of civil war resumption.

To reduce the costs of providing goods and security, the victor can rely on a third governing strategy: the rebel group can leverage its wartime ties with key civilian supporters, who can in turn organize their communities to exert social control and even provide their own goods and security in the immediate post-war period. During wartime, guerrilla fighters bargain with civilians for material support and may attempt to partner with, or co-opt, local civilian institutions or militias as a governance tactic (Arjona, Kasfir, and Mampilly, 2015). As part of this process, rebels form ties with civilians in various communities—such as traditional or religious leaders, youth or women's groups, and rebel party committees—who help sustain order and impose rebel control during war.

Rebel–civilian ties vary extensively depending on how the conflict progressed in a particular area (Kalyvas, 2006), rebel governing arrangements (Arjona, 2016; Mampilly and Stewart, 2021), and the origins of the rebel group's military and political knowledge (Stewart, 2021). These ties are never truly voluntary—relationships formed under threat of violence cannot be— but they vary in terms of their coercive nature and strength. At one end of the spectrum, rebel–civilian relations may be transactional and coercive, meaning that rebels may engage with civilians through one-shot interactions. These engagements tend to begin with rebels demanding information and food with the threat of physical harm, and end with one or both sides leaving the area after the interaction is finished. These are not meaningfully considered rebel–civilian ties.

At the other end of the spectrum, rebel–civilian ties may be characterized by various degrees of organized cooperation. Such ties feature heavily in multiple conflicts around the world, and play a major role in rebel groups' organization and survival. In Burundi, for example, the Imbonerakure were civilian youths organized within various communities who became associated with the victorious rebel group during the country's civil war. These youths were tasked with tax collection and reconnaissance in territories occupied by rebel soldiers. In Uganda, rebels convened civilian committees in several villages, which comprised "villagers selected as trustworthy contacts to supply NRA detachments with food, recruits and intelligence" (Kasfir, 2005). In Aceh, Indonesia, key organized supporters included women who formed a support organization Inong Balee; civilian village government officials who served as intermediaries in interactions with the rebels; and Islamic leaders who provided spiritual guidance, conferred legitimacy, and collected alms (Barter, 2015b, 348–349). In El Salvador, campesinos engaged in various forms of high-risk collective action to provide support for rebels (Wood, 2003). As I describe later in the chapter, these types of rebel–civilian ties were also prominent in both Zimbabwe and Liberia to varying degrees.

Such rebel–civilian ties allow rebels to reach and organize individuals who may not personally maintain ties with rebels, which helps the new rebel government consolidate post-war control. After the war, these ties can be leveraged to exert local social control, and perhaps even be delegated local governing functions on the rebel government's behalf. Wartime institutions can be remobilized after the war to increase the efficiency of local extraction or goods provision, maintain security, and ensure continued support. For example, civil wars often overturn social hierarchies; youths and women often become active members of local security and spy networks (Utas, 2003; Kumar, 2001; O'Gorman, 2011). These new positions can be mobilized in the post-war period for on-the-ground security against potential rivals, and to provide information about potential dissident activity. On the more supportive end, popular sentiment may help reduce the cost of positive state-building and reconstruction efforts. For example, wartime political brokers may be traditional, ethnic, or religious leaders who aided rebels in the provision of law, security, and public goods during the war (Barter, 2015a). After the war, they can more easily galvanize the community and help organize civilian-led post-war reconstruction and local goods provision.

2.2.3 The Importance of Organized Ties for Post-war Control

My theory focuses on how wartime politicization and socialization strategies can explain differences in the post-war consolidation of power. I contend that nascent governments emerging out of rebel victory often fiscally and politically overextend themselves after war because they are suddenly faced with governing far more people and a much larger territory. Thus, minimizing such overextension is key to their survival. Successful rebel governments are those that used a wide array of mobilization strategies to form ties with civilians and successfully exerted social control (Migdal, 1988) over the civilian population through guerrilla warfare. These factors help rebels increase support and establish wartime social control, which in turn helps the victor consolidate power after the conflict ends.

A central aspect of wartime rebel–civilian ties is the importance of *organizational capacity*, meaning that only *organized* civilian support for the rebel government can provide assured assistance through local formal and informal social control. As I show qualitatively in subsequent chapters, these civilian ties provide organized support to impose control on the ground during the war, and remain organized after the war for the same purpose. They therefore differ from peacetime ethnic or partisan supporters. While co-ethnicity may increase cooperation (Habyarimana et al., 2007), local organizational capacity from wartime institutions can more quickly boost such productivity immediately after the war and reduce the costs of sustaining control. Without such capacity, the rebel government must seek and identify additional sympathetic co-ethnic local leaders who have a proven organizational capacity and are willing to be state agents—a costly and time-consuming process (Gottlieb and Larreguy, 2020). The state may also fear that sympathetic co-ethnic local leaders may be more loyal to their communities than to the state (Hassan, 2020; Baldwin, 2013).

Similarly, ideological partisans should be more valuable to the rebel government if deeply embedded local party structures can mobilize civilians for party activities. Even if post-war sentiment is generally positive toward the new government, citizens have (perhaps unrealistically) high expectations for their new government. As I show in Zimbabwe (Chapter 4), major roles that party structures and local conduits play include (1) reducing citizen demands, (2) imposing structure and rules on local communities, (3) preventing dissent, and (4) monitoring and conveying information to the state. As Lewis (2020, 177) describes in Uganda, local institutions developed during the war as part of rebel governance increased the victor's informational penetration, which "enabled the state to identify incipient insurrections and to 'nip them in the bud.'" These functions require organization: local ideological support without collective action or access to state decision-makers cannot help exert control. During the tense and polarized post-war period, such organization also needs to be readily available.

In sum, my argument does not focus on citizens' political support for the ruling party. Rather, I argue that wartime social control—which may derive from either political support or fear, or more likely a combination of both—creates a blueprint that allows the new rebel government to more easily continue exerting control from the capital. Focusing on the rebel group's *ability to control* citizens allows us to examine conflicts in a different light. Although some forms of wartime organization and social order can be attributed to Marxist teachings, ethnic patronage, or revolutionary zeal, they are not exclusive to specific types of wars; nor are they necessarily observed in all wars that are purportedly of a certain type. Instead, rebel groups—even those based on opportunism—engage in sub-national social control and form long-term relationships with local civilians under their control when it is strategically advantageous (and possible) for them to do so during wartime (Lidow, 2016; Sanchez de la Sierra, 2017). Such behaviors are undertaken to advance the rebel group's local organizational capacity, in effect amounting to sub-national state-building to achieve a monopoly over violence and social control at the sub-national level.

My argument, which analyzes the civil war to post-war governance process using a state-building framework, focuses on two aspects of state-building: (1)

establishing coordination capacity: "the capabilities of state agents to organize collective action"; and (2) creating compliance capacity: "the ability of state leaders to secure compliance with their goals" (Berwick and Christia, 2018). My approach departs from much of the bellicist state-building literature, which examines extractive capacity as the primary indicator of state capacity (Besley and Persson, 2009; Tilly, 1992; Sanchez de la Sierra, 2017; Garfias, 2018). My theory speaks primarily to coordination and compliance capacity because these aspects of state-building are particularly important for consolidating political power, maintaining state stability, and eliminating potential violent rivals when the state is constrained by time and political polarization during post-war reconstruction.[7] Preventing conflict recurrence requires quick action, and victors that successfully consolidate power during the brief window of peace must wield both "despotic" and "infrastructural" power (Mann, 1984): the ability to impose their decisions as well as the "institutional capacity . . . to penetrate its territories and logistically implement decisions." This means having the both the capability and territorial reach to exert social control (Soifer, 2008).

2.3 When and Where Organized Rebel–Civilian Ties Are Formed

The crux of my argument is that a new rebel government can reduce the costs of *post-war* governance by relying on the wartime ties it formed with local civilians and institutions in the rural periphery to exert social control. Rebel-civilian ties are relationships that rebels form with civilians while fighting civil war. Rebels and civilians may cooperate through one-shot transactional interactions on one end of the spectrum, to repeated cooperation on the other end of the spectrum. When rebels and civilians cooperate or collaborate repeatedly to help push forward rebel goals, they form what I refer to as rebel-civilian ties: relationships that allow rebels to embed themselves within local communities and establish social control through civilian conduits.

Why (and how) do rebel groups form these rebel-civilian ties? I draw on a rich body of scholarship on rebel governance to argue that rebels need not be motivated by forward-looking reasons (although they are not precluded from being so motivated) when they form ties with local civilians: these ties do

---

[7] The fiscal capacity to independently fund state policies requires economic development and some level of citizen wealth. Post-war contexts are characterized by severe resource constraints given the cost of large-scale reconstruction, and external aid is key.

State-building through Rebel–Civilian Ties 47

not necessarily arise only because rebels are planning to govern after the war. Rather, rebel groups might form ties with civilians in various communities simply for war-making reasons—to increase their organizational capacity for extraction and information gathering. Further, rebels are better able to form the types of wartime civilian ties that are useful for post-war governance in areas where they maintain a high military *presence* and exert *influence* over the civilian population.

2.3.1 Why Rebels Seek to Form Ties with Civilians

During war, rebels attempt to change the social order in the community by selectively empowering groups of civilians, thereby forming rebel–civilian ties. This is often out of war-making necessity: while fighting asymmetrically in the rural periphery, rebels must enlist the support of local communities to extract materials, gain support, and recruit new fighters in order to sustain guerrilla warfare (Mao, 1961). To win community support, rebels seek opportunities to gain local legitimacy and build their extractive capacity. They may appropriate the legitimacy of preexisting cultural institutions (Hoffmann, 2015; Förster, 2015): for example, rebels commonly collaborate with local elders or ethno-religious leaders, whose blessing indirectly generates civilian support for the rebels (Mampilly, 2011; Barter, 2016). Concurrently, they may gather and empower supporters, and co-opt or build new local militias (Wikham Crowley, 2015). If the rebel group succeeds in these activities, it can build new systems for extraction, such as quasi-bureaucratic structures, and informal security apparatuses for the purposes of reconnaissance and maintaining order. The power that rebels and their civilian supporters exercise in a territory is mutually reinforcing: as rebel power increases, the power of their supporters increases as well; as rebels win the support of well-respected local leaders, their own legitimacy increases accordingly.

In addition to extraction and the provision of social order, wartime rebel–civilian ties can also encourage locals to support rebel group goals and compel regular civilians in rural communities to cooperate with the rebels. Rebel politicization can boost community-level social capital in certain cases, as rebels increase the amount of resources employed to promote a sense of belonging and decrease efforts to produce violence. Rebel rhetoric played a strong role in enlisting the support of the rural population in both Zimbabwe (nationalism) and Liberia (ethnicity), and in most rebellions around the world. For example, Mampilly (2015) shows that the use of nationalistic symbology in rebel-held territory in South Sudan, Sri Lanka, and the Democratic

Republic of the Congo (DRC) allowed rebels to influence civilian thinking and increase civilian identification with the rebel government. This in turn decreased the need for violence in inducing civilian support, and increased the efficiency of the war machine in providing materials and support for the rebels.

Overall, the rebel–civilian ties built through these efforts help rebels exert *social control*—compliance, participation, and legitimation (Migdal, 1988, 32)—over the community, which compels (or coerces) civilians to aid the war effort. By relying on its civilian ties for extraction and security provision, rebel groups deputize, and thus empower, key local individuals to work on their behalf. While rebel governing apparatuses and politicization efforts often seem all encompassing, many civilians seek to avoid associating themselves with armed groups or in playing any part in civil wars (Kalyvas, 2006). The rebels' civilian supporters draw and organize support from the local population; many would not go out of their way to participate in the war effort otherwise. Thus, the community follows rebel rules with minimal violence precisely *because* of rebel–civilian ties.

The benefits of social control over a community explain why the formation of rebel–civilian ties and the establishment of rebel governance do not depend on the type of rebel group: this preference for control over civilian life should hold true for all rebel groups, regardless of their overarching goals. Though rebels vary in their desire to take political control, secede, or simply enrich themselves, increasing their ability to extract and control by creating sub-national governing structures advances all such goals. Bureaucracy grows out of extractive necessity (Tilly, 1992); this governing system remains the most efficient way to win wars (Spruyt, 1996). Much in the same way, sub-national governance through informal civilian institutions allows rebels to gather resources and accurate information most efficiently, which increases their chances of winning.[8] As rebel groups build new systems for extraction, they can deputize local individuals to collect taxes and food from the community. They can also further delegate local security, entrusting reconnaissance matters to local civilians. These acts of governance all increase efficiency and the likelihood of victory.

Rebels are unable to form ties with civilians everywhere. In some areas, politicization and legitimacy-building exercises are effective; in other areas, rebels resort to greater violence to induce cooperation. A significant portion of prior work on rebel–civilian relationships focuses on understanding and predicting the conditions under which rebels perpetrate violence against

---

[8] While rebel governance does not necessarily increase the likelihood of victory—which depends more on military strength—rebels nonetheless consider organized civilian participation a crucial aspect of war-making (see, for example, Lidow [2016] in an opportunistic conflict or Mao [1961] in an ideological war).

civilians. Weinstein (2006), Green (2018), and Lidow (2016), for example, point to the importance of rebel troop cohesion for civilian victimization. In these accounts, troop cohesion—achieved through slow recruitment and depending on civilians for support, the use of ideological education, or steady payments through rebel commanders—increases good behavior and decreases civilian victimization. When attempting to quickly build cohesion, rebel groups may resort to civilian victimization to generate comradery between strangers (Cohen, 2016).

These arguments go some distance toward explaining the treatment of civilians, but even within each intra-state war, the types of violence perpetrated against civilians tend to vary in different parts of the country based on local dynamics and demographics (Hägerdal, 2019). In Bates' (2015) explanation of predation under authoritarian regimes, financial insecurity erodes the social contract between citizens and the state—a logic that can be extended to wartime victimization or the lack thereof (Sanchez de la Sierra, 2017). Kalyvas's (2006) logic of territorial control through military means provides a parsimonious explanation of how rebels choose between discriminate and indiscriminate violence. Discriminate punishment is needed to induce civilian cooperation (Rueda, 2017), but is complicated by local political struggles between rivals (Balcells, 2017).

In sum, theories of rebel violence and relations with civilians provide clear predictions about the incentives for civilian compliance (regardless of compromise or coercion), and how the political and military terrain might predict rebel incentives to harm or govern. I next summarize these predictions and use them as building blocks to explore how wartime strategic violence, recruitment, and induced compliance can be used to incorporate civilians into the rebel machine. The supporting roles that civilians play during war, in turn, can endure long after the war has ended.

2.3.2 Time Horizons in Rebel–Civilian Relations

Theories of repeated interaction highlight the importance of time horizons for increasing cooperation between different actors (Axelrod, 1980). Accordingly, cooperation between rebels and civilians should increase under long-time horizons, as cooperation is more likely to be beneficial for both parties under these conditions (Olson, 2000).

For rebels, cooperation becomes more efficient when they remain in an area for longer periods of time, encouraging wartime sub-national governance and spurring the development of on-the-ground information institutions. They become stationary bandits (Olson, 2000; Sanchez de la Sierra, 2017) who prefer to decrease the use of coercive violence, choosing instead to establish civilian institutions they can use to collect resources more efficiently. These wartime sub-national governing structures increase rebel operating efficiency but require high levels of civilian participation, which decreases rebels' incentives to use excessive violence as punishment. This is the case in Kalyvas (2006) and Balcells (2017), in which civilian-provided information is clearer and more trustworthy in areas over which rebels have full military control, leading to lower levels of indiscriminate rebel violence against civilians. In both studies, violence is perpetrated against those who are considered sellouts or defectors, in an attempt to ensure full social control. Similarly, in Arjona (2015), rebels prefer to cede some control to local institutions as long as they continue to benefit through taxation, rather than perpetrate indiscriminate violence against unyielding civilians and risk losing them as a source of income altogether.

From the civilian point of view, cooperating with rebel groups and complying with wartime institutions can be similarly beneficial over the longer term, especially in areas that are untouched or sparsely governed by the state. At a minimum, cooperation increases truthful information and recruitment while reducing the likelihood of being turned over to the government (Kalyvas, 2006). Rebels provide security for the local population, primarily against other rebel groups or the government, but also against roving bandits who commit acts of petty violence and robbery (Wikham Crowley, 2015). Wartime governance can further lead to public goods provision beyond security and the administration of justice in rebel-occupied areas (Huang, 2016). If rebels stay in an area long enough to establish local economies and generate income, they are more likely to provide for civilian welfare by building or repairing public structures (Martin, 2020), or providing food or agricultural aid (Nindorera, 2012). Educated individuals in the rebel army may facilitate schooling for local communities (Chung, 2006). Numerous historical rebellions around the world feature such state-building activities (Huang, 2016), including both of my main case studies (Zimbabwe and Liberia) and the four secondary cases.

Long time horizons, however, are difficult to establish and maintain during war in areas where there is active conflict. Rebel groups seeking control over the center also often seek to capture territory;[9] the government forces act to defend territory through counterinsurgency operations. These different actors thus encroach upon each other's terrains, with the aim of capturing enemy territory. Where rebel groups and government forces are able to take

---

[9] Secessionist rebel groups, by contrast, care only about a certain part of state territory.

(or regain) territory but are unable to hold onto it for long, heightened military contestation for territorial control means a greater focus on fighting between the rival armed groups—to the detriment of building civilian ties (Lidow, 2016).

Under such military contestation, time horizons are shorter and rebels act as roving bandits (Olson, 2000). Military contestation means potentially greater mobility for rebels, as they may be frequently forced out of various areas. Greater mobility then increases the benefits of predation for the rebels, as they are no longer tied to a certain location and have no expectations of repeated interactions. When rebels do not expect to remain in control of an area for a long period of time, they are discouraged from collaborating with local elders, preexisting institutions, and civilian groups. They are less likely to focus on politicizing civilians—and more inclined to fail in such efforts— due to the increased presence of other armed groups; thus the likelihood of cooperation between rebels and civilians decreases. Under military contestation we should therefore anticipate lower levels of rebel *influence*, as well as mutually beneficial cooperation and rebel governance.

In addition, rebel governance is secondary to rebel military survival: rebel groups focus on building institutions and bureaucracy for extraction and public goods provision *only after* they have established stability and security within a territory. Thus, as military contestation increases, rebels focus their resources on defense and expend primarily on conflict and violence. The need for additional resources may also lead to coercion: since they are not building sub-national institutions and are primarily focused on fighting against other armed groups, reliance on the local population takes the form of looting and violent extraction rather than taxation in exchange for governance.

From the civilian perspective, the short time horizon also substantially increases the risk of cooperation under military contestation. Where rebels are the primary armed group in the community, cooperation with the rebel group is mutually beneficial and provides civilians with additional benefits such as protection and, sometimes, public goods. However, high levels of contestation between armed groups introduces confusion and social mistrust because civilians are never sure which group will be dominant in the near future (Kalyvas, 2006). Civilians know that collaborators with one armed group will undoubtedly be singled out if the area is taken over by a different group. The cost of collaboration is high, even if the civilian is ideologically aligned with one group over others. Thus, individuals cooperate by providing food or information as a last resort—under threat of violence or death—rather than coordinate with other civilians in the community.

Finally, military contestation shortens time horizons not only by increasing predation, but by displacement. As violence increases, civilians—particularly collaborators—are more likely to flee to relatively peaceful areas, away from potential persecution. Displacement is often a major reason why areas that were once under stable rebel control suffer from a lack of governance once they are taken over militarily by another armed group: when a previous in-control armed group leaves, civilians who participated in its wartime institutions are often the first to leave. This may be because of security reasons, as they will be identified by others in the community as having worked for the previous armed group, and will be punished by the new rebels in charge. In addition, however, retreating rebel groups sometimes take civilians with them into the bush as porters, cooks, and work staff; thus rebel supporters are torn away from their community when military contestation occurs. In short, even if rebels are initially able to exert social control over an area, military contestation erases these previous gains.

2.3.3 How Rebel Group Presence and Influence Affect Civilian Interactions

A rebel group's ability to lengthen time horizons in an area, establish social control, and form organized rebel–civilian ties depends on two crucial criteria—rebel *presence* and *influence* over that area.

The *presence* of a rebel group describes the density of members of various warring factions in an area, which in turn correlates with their absolute military capability, their capabilities relative to other groups, and their judgment regarding the need to occupy a particular territory. That is, a warring group may be absent from an area either because the locality has (1) already been captured by a stronger group or (2) the area is not strategically useful for war. There may also be an overlapping presence of multiple groups involved in the conflict over the years. Finally, there is temporal variation: a community may experience high or low levels of rebel presence at different points of the conflict.

Existing theories from the rebel governance literature suggest the importance of a strong rebel presence: the rebels' ability to successfully govern depends heavily on the type and frequency of their interactions with the community. Studies of rebel–civilian institution-building during civil war implicitly assume that a full rebel presence in an area is important (Kasfir, 2015). Arjona (2015), for example, explores Colombia's rebel–civilian relations in territories with a high rebel military presence, and argues that rebels can change institutions and impose rigid new rules of governance and justice when prior civilian institutions are too weak ("rebelocracy"); if existing institutions are strong, rebels are forced to work with these original civilian structures to build a cordial relationship for the purposes of taxation and governance ("aliocracy"). Frequent and cordial interactions between rebels and existing ethnic, religious, or cultural groups also take place in a variety of conflicts, including identity-based (Côte d'Ivoire: Förster [2015]; Martin [2020]), separatist (Indonesia: Barter [2015*a*]), resource-based (Kivus regions of the DRC: Hoffmann [2015]), and ideological wars (Greece: Kalyvas [2015]).

However, simply maintaining a presence in a community is not enough. Rebels may be present in a territory but either fail to—or not wish to— connect or come into repeated contact with civilians living in the territory. As mentioned earlier, in contested territories with a strong presence from multiple groups, each group would find it difficult to exert social control over the civilian population due to competing political ideas, greater levels of violence, and civilian displacement.

Thus, a second criterion, *influence*, also helps explain where rebels are likely to exert social control and form ties with civilians. By influence, I mean the degree to which civilians profess loyalty to the rebel group(s) and act in accordance with their goals. Rebel–civilian ties are more likely to form if rebels increase civilian trust and support in the group's goals through various unifying frameworks such as ethnicity, religion, or ideology. This influence can help increase the efficiency of the rebels' bureaucracy and decrease the costs of governance, allowing the rebel group to establish more civilian ties and increase its social control without diverting funds from war-making (Barter, 2015*a*).

There are three pathways through which rebels may gain influence over the civilian population. First, rebel influence over community behavior may be tied to full territorial control (Kalyvas, 2006): if a group has a complete and constant monopolistic presence within a territory such that no other armed group can enter the area, it likely exercises a strong influence and full social control over the civilian population due to wartime socialization. However, territorial control is *not* a necessary condition for rebel influence over a population. In a second channel, a strong rebel presence may increase the group's influence over civilians due to successful rebel politicization, particularly if no other armed group is present and politicizing the area (Mao, 1961; Wood, 2003). This is particularly likely if the rebel group has the time and space to conduct political education in the case of ideological conflicts (Huang, 2016; Weinstein, 2006; Sanín and Wood, 2014) or to rouse

54 Governing after War

identity-based sentiments in the case of ethnic conflicts (Jok and Hutchinson, 1999; Cederman, Wimmer, and Min, 2010). Finally, rebels can gain influence through a third channel: a group's influence over a population can be based on pre-war factors that predispose support, particularly if the group has professed identity-based origins (ethnicity, religion, language, region). This means that civilians can support a rebel group *even if it does not actively attempt to politicize or increase its presence in an area.*

If a community is affected by the conflict, then rebel influence over its territory tends to be affected by other groups' relative influence. Influence between rival armed groups (both rebels and government forces) may be zero sum, such that an increase in one group's influence over a territory decreases the influence of other groups. Alternatively, no group may have significant influence as the number of rebel groups involved in that area increases. This may happen if multiple armed groups attempt to establish their own politicization and thus, overall, all fail to meaningfully influence the community. Finally, if multiple armed groups operate in an area, each group may focus on defending territory rather than seeking to politicize—thereby resulting in little or no influence over civilians.

These insights from the rebellion literature can be summarized into two observable implications about how rebel groups' presence and influence affect the likelihood of forming cooperative rebel–civilian ties.

Implication 1 *Rebels are more likely to form cooperative rebel–civilian ties to exert social control where they have a high presence and strong influence.*

Implication 2 *Military contestation between armed groups decreases the likelihood that rebels and civilians will form cooperative ties.*

2.4 Post-War Social Control and Organizational Capacity

In this section I use these two observable implications as building blocks to theorize about sub-national variation in post-conflict organizational capacity where a rebel group wins the war. This subsequently informs post-war governing strategies and the consolidation of power.

Table 2.1 summarizes the degree of social control and organizational capacity that arises based on the various types of rebel engagement with different types of territories. It is important to note that levels of rebel presence and influence can differ from year to year, as rebels are not necessarily stationary;

Table 2.1 Wartime social control and organizational capacity in war-affected areas

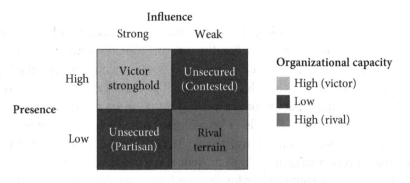

their influence may change based on levels of violence and rebel presence. The categorization depicted in the table describes wartime social control in aggregate *by the end of the war*, taking into account the length of time that rebels were present in certain areas as well as the level of competition for influence between different armed groups. For example, where the eventual victor had strong civilian ties at the beginning of the war but lost them to rivals during the same conflict, the area would be considered a rival stronghold despite initial social control. The flip side is also true: if the eventual victor successfully expanded into a rival stronghold by forming rebel–civilian ties in these areas, while the rivals' ties to civilians were destroyed, that would be considered the victor's stronghold at the end of the conflict.

Victor strongholds are identified by a high wartime presence and a strong influence over civilians—leading to high post-war organizational capacity for the civil war victor. In this ideal type, rebel–civilian relations should be highly durable, and rebels should engage in rebel governance by creating parallel administrative structures for extraction and security apparatuses to guard against state incursion. The high presence of one group in such areas means that both rebels and civilians have an incentive to cooperate, while the strong level of influence suggests either that (1) other warring groups have a relatively low presence or (2) other groups have a presence, but civilians' loyalties lie with one group over others. Cases of near-monopolistic territorial control—such as the impenetrable rural north during the Côte d'Ivoire Civil War—fall under stronghold areas; in other stronghold areas, the rebel group does not maintain a monopoly over violence but continues to exercise a high degree of social control. For example, in some cases the government continues to have access to the area through coercive military force, including the use of aerial weapons. Other groups may continue to have an ineffectual presence. Indeed, since social control under rebels is defined by a monopoly over civilian *ties*, strongholds do not preclude government access—only a lack of government social control.

Outside of its strongholds, the victor must also contend with *unsecured* terrain—territories in which it has low organizational capacity. Unsecured terrain may be *contested*, meaning the rebel government maintained a high presence but weak influence during the war. Such areas are characterized by low organizational capacity for both the eventual winner and rivals because multiple armed groups—rebels or government forces—have attempted (but failed) to exert social control over the territory for long. Because more than one armed group maintains a high presence in the area, but influence is low, civilians are either split in their loyalties or have none. There is often greater military action between armed groups in contested terrain, leading to temporary and transactional rebel–civilian relations as a result of increased violence, coercion, and high levels of displacement. In these cases, civilians are coerced into sporadically providing information or materials to various groups.

In unsecured *partisan* terrain, the victor maintains a low wartime presence but continues to exert a strong influence due to pre-war factors that predispose support. In these areas, civilians support the group politically, but have little wartime organization directly tied to the victor during war. Rebels may choose to maintain a low presence in certain areas, despite predisposed support, for several reasons. These territories, for example, may be militarily unimportant, or have few food sources or natural resources with which to finance it. Stronger rebel groups that can forge ahead might therefore choose to simply recruit quickly before leaving supportive areas in favor of more strategic locations from which to base their operations. Alternatively, militarily strong rebel groups might quickly make their way toward the capital rather than engage in longer-term guerrilla warfare, preventing them from turning partisan areas into strongholds featuring sub-national governance.

Finally, areas with both low presence and weak influence provide the victor with not only no support during the war, but also heightened security issues afterwards. These are *rival terrain*: they are either (1) rival strongholds in which other rebel groups may have maintained a strong presence and influence, and thus engage in substantial sub-national governance and organizational capacity on behalf of future rivals or (2) rival partisan areas. From the victor's perspective, rival strongholds and rival partisan areas both threaten the victor's eventual consolidation of power. This is not only due to intrinsic political support for their rivals, but also, crucially, because the victor has equally poor information about on-the-ground activity in these regions due to its low presence and influence. Thus, while rivals may distinguish between their own strongholds (high organizational capacity) and purely partisan terrain (low organizational capacity), the victor may find it very difficult to distinguish between the two and find them both to be serious security threats.

By rival terrain, I mean not only rival rebels but also ex-government-supporting regions: this includes ex-government strongholds, where the deposed ex-government has strong and organized ties to local formal or informal governing institutions and actors. Unlike rival rebels however, the strength of the ex-government's ties on the ground is more likely to be defined by pre-war relationships and institutions rather than wartime relationship-building. This is because governments are unlikely to expand their ties during war: while rebel groups seek territory and spread across the country, government troops presume territorial control and seeks to defend its territory. Thus, in areas where government forces and rebels clash, absent robust hearts-and-minds operations that emphasize working with local communities, government troops are more likely to be focused on counterinsurgency than building organized ties with civilians. On the other hand, regions that already support the ex-government are less likely to be affected by the war and, if violence does not reach these areas, a government military presence is not needed. These areas should therefore continue to follow the status quo and—particularly in the case of prototypical weak governments that are likely to experience civil war in the first place since they lack a strong and organized government—civilian institutions on the ground can hasten a counter-rebellion after a rebel victory.[10]

2.5 How Rebel–Civilian Ties Affect Post-war Governance

After winning the civil war, the victor employs targeted strategies to penetrate different types of territories based on their degree of resistance to state control; sub-national variation in rebel–civilian ties shapes the new government's strategies for consolidating power. The victor makes decisions regarding its (a) *strongholds*, where it has a high capacity to sustain control due to its preexisting links with civilians; (b) *rival terrain*, where it suspects

---

[10] While a robust local party structure may sometimes be considered a government stronghold, these tend to be Marxist parties that engage in high levels of grassroots action growing out of a prior civil war. In other cases, governments may have preexisting ties with traditional leaders. However, these are not *strengthened* during war, only *defended* if rebels attempt to destabilize the area.

58 Governing after War

its rivals have a strong organizational capacity; and (c) *unsecured terrain*, which may be either contested or partisan, and where neither group maintains organizational capacity.

2.5.1 Resource Allocation

Wartime structures and rebel–civilian ties do not disintegrate after the war: where rebels enjoyed strong ties with civilians during the war, they will continue to enjoy these ties afterwards. While the new rebel government may be under pressure to reward those who supported it during the civil war, it will likely continue to rely on these ties and wartime institutions to sustain post-war social control. It can therefore avoid allocating significant resources to stronghold areas, allowing it to spend in other parts of the state to win supporters and consolidate control.

In short, war increases the post-war local organizational capabilities of stronghold areas, since wartime institutions can easily be remobilized for post-war governance. The ties are galvanized after the war to sustain local governance and impose control by buoying political support through politicization on the victor's behalf, gathering information about potential discontent, and—most importantly—using intimidation to eliminate political challenges. As I show in Zimbabwe, this control can be built upon both mass support and coercion: it prevents dissent even if dissent is in the minority.

Individuals who were affiliated with these informal institutions during the civil war have an incentive to continue this link afterwards for three reasons. First, much like the elders whose power in the local community is elevated by serving the winning side during the war, individuals—security teams, reconnaissance teams, and the like—can experience a boost in social standing in a community that supported the victorious rebels.[11] Youth and women who led wartime civilian efforts, for example, may participate in youth and women affairs in the community during the post-war period. This change in social power alters the dynamics within communities, as social standing becomes intricately linked to association with the new rebel government. The second reason that individuals continue to participate in informal institutions after the war is that the existence of wartime social networks and collaborative teams increases the efficacy of recreating such informal institutions for community-based reconstruction and aid. Pro-government chiefs or leaders

---

[11] As I discuss in Chapter 4, the village committees and collaborators in the Zimbabwean Liberation War are a good example of this.

may even exploit such links to organize local governance on behalf of the rebel government and/or to continue to extract from the local population. Finally, supporters in stronghold areas may share an ideological affinity with the new rebel government as well as friendship with ex-rebels who hold government posts, and thus derive an intrinsic benefit from taking part in efforts that aid the state in local governance.

Further, wartime capacity-building solidifies rebel–civilian ties, and post-war legitimacy cements the power of those who were put in charge of local institutions during the war. Ethnic or religious leaders and traditional chiefs appointed during the war are elevated in the post-war period for the purposes of governance. While the new rebel government may or may not directly reward them with patronage payments, their wartime status may be formalized after the war with a local bureaucratic post. Marxist rebel victors— for example, in Greece, China, and Uganda—transitioned wartime party cells to state bureaucracy when they take over the government. These rebel supporters act as local state agents after war, ensuring continued compliance with (and support for) the new rebel government.

Sub-national Hypothesis 1 *The rebel government leverages high organizational capacity in its wartime strongholds and ties with civilians to facilitate local political control after the war.*

Outside of its wartime strongholds (i.e., in unsecured or rival terrain), the rebel government has fewer (or no) supporting structures with which to maintain political control. To exert social control over these areas—where it anticipates greater resistance to state control because it lacks local agents—the rebel government ought to allocate more resources and reconstruction efforts to consolidate its power.

The rebel government may choose to allocate resources in various ways in an effort to increase state capacity and exert social control. I argue that new rebel governments attempt to exert control using public goods spending primarily in unsecured terrain, whether that is contested or purely partisan areas: these territories are more likely to have either mixed support for the rebel government and other rivals, or potential support with no grassroots organizational capacity for state control. Since these areas have low organizational capacity overall, the rebel government deploys loyal supporters to bolster its capacity: these supporters become bureaucrats who can make decisions about development and public goods spending. In addition, these bureaucrats can attempt to expand the victor's successful wartime institutions to remake the rest of the state in its own image.

60 Governing after War

Deployed bureaucrats' strategic decisions about where, and how, to confer state-funded goods should increase both support for the party (Berman, Shapiro, and Felter, 2011) and state capacity (Soifer, 2015): previous research on the relationship between welfare spending and civil unrest has found that increased social spending on welfare programs such as health and education mitigates small-scale conflict and thus diffuses the desire to rebel (Bodea, Higashijima, and Singh, 2016; Taydas and Peksen, 2012). In such cases, the state can avoid some grievance-based decisions to rebel by providing public goods. After the war, individuals look to the new rebel government to deliver the promises made during the war and subsequent election, and expect speedy reconstruction and development during the new period of peace.

It is important to note that while wartime politicization better resembles grassroots campaigns for civilians on the ground, post-war politicization in unsecured (partisan or contested) terrain is more likely to be interpreted as the new rebel-controlled central government attempting to impose control. Since the victor was unable to fully penetrate these territories during the war, it cannot rely on local elites to build political control and establish social control after the war without top-down supervision. It would therefore need to penetrate and embed itself into local politics for three reasons. First, even in co-ethnic areas, local leaders have no ties to the rebel government without wartime relations. They are more likely to respond to (or be swayed by) within-community pressures or other cleavages, making them less reliable than wartime political brokers (Baldwin, 2013). Second, it may be more difficult to correctly identify sympathetic and effective local leaders, which can lead to costly mistakes during a period of fragile peace (Gottlieb and Larreguy, 2020). Third, there may simply be fewer local leaders in unsecured areas. Wartime rebel–civilian relations in high-capacity strongholds produce multiple political brokers—local leaders, youth, women, and others—in one community. Yet the rebel government may only identify one local leader, such as the chief, where wartime organizational capacity is low.

Supporters as deployed bureaucrats play two roles: they (1) expand governing capacity by trying to replicate the new rebel government's familiar institutions and (2) mobilize support on the ground. These newly appointed local government officials, who may enjoy little local legitimacy, retain their authority by being the conduit through which the community accesses developmental funding from the central state. As Soifer (2015, 65) theorizes, local officials with no private capacity have a greater incentive to perform well and focus on state-building, which increases development in the short run and helps "shape identities and communities in ways that make them easier to control" in the long run. The state, in turn, disburses public goods to attract supporters and increase state capacity in these crucial territories, allowing the rebel government to consolidate power.

Sub-national Hypothesis 2 *In unsecured—contested and partisan—areas, the rebel government builds capacity and increases its influence over civilians by deploying bureaucrats to expand its wartime institutions and providing public goods to win supporters.*

We should expect the new rebel government to wish to use the same co-optation strategy in rival terrain—to bolster its reach by deploying bureaucrats and investing in development. Such a strategy, if successful, would engender more goodwill from the international community— an important ally for funding post-war reconstruction. The state may also attempt to buy out local leaders with patronage payments and local government posts. Folding rival terrain into the new state apparatus would allow the rebel government to extend its authority into impenetrable areas and impose social control.

However, this strategy of simply expanding institutions through deployed bureaucrats is likely to be too dangerous and uncertain for the victor to attempt during the fragile post-war peace. Attempts to co-opt an unwilling population through capacity-building development exercises can easily fail if civilians formed strong and durable ties with rival groups during the war. While the rebel government may seek to expand its wartime institutions into these territories, rivals' continued ties with citizens makes it easier for local residents to reject the new government's institutions either out of genuine support for rival groups or because of rival coercion. Civilians in rival strongholds are more likely than those in areas with no ties to rivals to refuse state control (Centeno, 1997; Mehler, 2009), thereby resisting any attempts at state co-optation through bureaucratic development and public goods provision. In short, the state's reach in rival strongholds is limited, and is unlikely to increase even with new attempts to establish social control due to the rebel government's low influence and presence, combined with its rivals' high presence and influence.

Faced with a resentful population that can be readily recruited for a new civil war, the rebel government should be more likely to allocate resources to security in rival terrain. These areas pose the greatest security threat since ex-rebels or ex-government forces can regroup to foment counter-rebellion against the new government. To guard against such challenges, the rebel government should devote a larger portion of its military spending to these areas to quash any potential counter-rebellions. Specifically, military action

62 Governing after War

is dedicated to breaking down ties to rivals by targeting civilians—with the goal of reducing both recruitment into rival ranks and civilian aid to counter-rebellion efforts (Valentino, Huth, and Balch-Lindsay, 2004).

Sub-national Hypothesis 3 *In rival terrain, the rebel government increases its security spending to break down rivals' relationship with civilians, weaken rivals' organizational capacity, and increase the likelihood of consolidating control.*

Why doesn't the rebel government simply pay off its own supporters and avoid engaging with the rest of the state? Authoritarian leaders of weak states often pursue such a strategy, as they prefer to neglect large parts of the country in favor of nurturing their own elite networks.

This strategy can be comfortably deployed if the authoritarian leader does not fear violent insurrection from areas with low state capacity—more likely during more stable political periods where the rival-supporting regions are poorly organized and unlikely to pose a real challenge. In the immediate post-war context, however, the political landscape has not yet reached a stable equilibrium: a peace process does not simply eliminate wartime security problems. If there are multiple competing sovereignties, an organized and potentially violent rival would make it particularly dangerous for the new rebel government to reward only its supporters. Put another way, even if the rebel government can count on electoral victories to stay in power, *it still faces security concerns*: it must still eliminate the possibility of civil war recurrence in rival terrain. While rival strongholds are initially the most threatening due to their links with civilians, rivals can quickly spread to unsecured terrain. To consolidate power, the rebel government must therefore first establish control over unsecured terrain to block the spread of rival recruitment efforts beyond rival strongholds.

An alternative strategy—to simply begin with violence and bypass attempts to co-opt and win support altogether—is less preferred for several reasons. While state-building and the consolidation of power is undoubtedly a coercive affair, outright violent coercion can damage the rebel government's reputation. Post-war reconstruction requires international goodwill and aid, and human rights shaming may push donors away (Lebovic and Voeten, 2009; Woo and Murdie, 2017; Peksen, Peterson, and Drury, 2014).[12] In addition, while violence can be effective (Hazelton, 2017), barbarism as a

---

[12] It is important to note, however, that implementing economic sanctions for bad human rights behavior is also a political decision, and numerous factors complicate the relationship between the two variables. See, for example, Nielsen (2013) and Dietrich and Murdie (2017).

counterinsurgency strategy is not a perfect solution. Downes (2007), for example, finds that violence as a counterinsurgency strategy increases in effectiveness as civilian support for rivals and the size of the area decrease. Arreguin-Toft (2001) reasons that barbarism works in the short term, but is politically costly in the long run. In short, victors should prefer *not* to deploy violence unless it is necessary—in rival strongholds where civilian ties to the victor's rivals prove too difficult to sever.

2.5.2 Consolidating Power

I have thus far argued that to consolidate power—in an effort to ensure post-war stability and political dominance—the rebel government must be able to keep the peace by eliminating potential rivals and preventing civilians from joining counter-rebellions. In unsecured terrain with low capacity during war (i.e., contested and partisan areas), the victor spends primarily on public goods to hasten recovery. Spending in rival strongholds tends to focus on security, since counter-rebellions are most likely to begin in such areas. The hypothesized resource allocation decisions should apply at least until the rebel government is satisfied that there is no longer a threat of the conflict resuming—that it has successfully completed the internal conquest and retained control during the period of post-war fragility.

When rivals attempt to mount a new challenge to the victor, civilians and rivals observe the victor's decision-making process and respond accordingly. Civilians can either join rivals in a new rebellion or accept the victor as the new government. However, not all civilians have the same opportunity—or face the same costs associated with—making such decisions. Those who live in the victor's strongholds are least likely to join rivals and rebel against the victor because the victor's wartime rebel–civilian ties continue to allow the new rebel government to exert social control through its local conduits. Similarly, local governance infrastructures, as well as the rebel government's high degree of influence in the area during the first war, make citizens in strongholds less likely to join a counter-rebellion.

Knowing this, and leveraging their own ties with civilians, rivals should therefore recruit for counter-rebellion first in their own strongholds and then in contested terrain. Citizens living in rival strongholds are more likely to have an affinity with rivals that governed these areas during wartime, and are already organized based on those wartime networks. Contested terrain often acts as a "border" between rival and government strongholds; thus, as conflict spreads beyond rival strongholds, it moves toward contested terrain.

64 Governing after War

Then, once contested areas are won over, a counter-rebellion will move militarily into areas where the rebel government enjoys greater influence but fewer wartime ties (partisan areas) before finally expanding to the rebel government's wartime strongholds.

However, conflict need not easily spread into contested terrain, since citizens often have mixed incentives to join a counter-rebellion. Compared to those living in rival strongholds, citizens in contested terrain are more likely to have experienced greater violence and conflicting politicization attempts from numerous armed groups during the first civil war. They may have experienced coercive behaviors from multiple sides as well as higher levels of displacement. These civilians are unlikely to rebel outright, since they have no (or split) allegiances and no system of organization on behalf of the rebel government or any of its rivals. Whether civilians in contested areas will join a second rebellion against the new rebel government thus largely depends on (1) the intensity of their *grievances* against the government versus rivals— both of which used violent coercive methods in their (unsuccessful) attempts to establish dominant social control and (2) the government's ability to spread its *influence* and build organizational capacity.

Both factors, relative grievance and government influence, are mitigated by the degree and speed of post-war reconstruction. These factors not only increase support for the government by winning "hearts and minds;" they also allow the government to increase its reach and institutional strength in unsecured areas. By providing public goods and reconstruction, the government engages in local politicization: it deploys pro-government bureaucrats, restaffs local institutions, determines the educational curriculum, and supplies targeted development funding. Thus, as spending to improve the quality of life increases, citizens in unsecured terrain are more likely to side with the victor than the rival. However, if the victor is unable to co-opt unsecured terrain quickly enough, rivals have a greater chance of recruiting there. Figure 2.2 summarizes the strategies that victors and civilians pursue during the post-war period.

Sub-national Hypothesis 4 *Conflict recurrence is more likely to spread from rival to contested terrain if the government fails to establish top-down control— by building a bureaucracy and funding adequate development—to win over civilians.*

When can victors avoid losing unsecured terrain? The state's ability to expand its influence increases with the degree to which it established wartime rebel–civilian ties and exerted social control—both with regard to

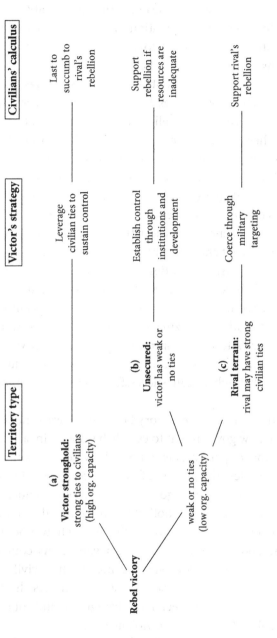

Figure 2.2 Post-war politics under threat of counter-rebellion

the geographical spread (*breadth*) and the strength of these ties (*depth*)—that can be deployed from the top down to formalize post-war state control.

The *breadth* of rebel–civilian ties increases with the rebel victor's successful territorial expansion during war, meaning that it was able to influence a wider subset of the country's population. Thus, rebellions that last longer and affect the entire country tend to have greater breadth than limited regional rebellions. Breadth matters because, as I argue in this chapter, a rebel government that exercises control over the state has fewer resource constraints. Since rebel–civilian ties help sustain control at low cost after the war, the rebel government can allocate more resources for coercion and co-optation elsewhere in the state to consolidate its power. All else equal, as the size of wartime strongholds increases, this resource allocation is targeted at geographically limited rival strongholds and unsecured terrain. This increases the likelihood that the rebel government will be able to maintain security by deploying adequate levels of development and violence—thereby preventing post-war violence from escalating into a second civil war.

Breadth, however, is not enough: rebel groups can have deep and embedded ties or shallow and transactional ties as a result of their civilian interactions. The depth of these ties is important because the deeper and more embedded they are within society—meaning the victor was more successful at formalizing and institutionalizing these ties during the war—the more it can trust these links to exert control after the war. Activities associated with rebel governance tend to feature, and perhaps even require, deep ties with localities so that rebels can successfully negotiate compliance from civilians.

Depth plays a major role in my theory because the wartime ties I describe not only allow the new government to establish stability in strongholds; they also provide a cohort of partisans who know how best to expand into unsecured terrain to complete the process of internal conquest. If ties to civilians are sparse and shallow, the rebel government's resource allocation strategy will fall short. Once rivals gain a foothold into contested terrain, it is much more difficult to consolidate power without reverting to war because a failure to provide public goods increases citizen grievances. As counter-rebellion spreads into areas that were contested during the first civil war, security decreases for civilians living in these areas and intensifies their grievances. State forces are spread thinly between rival strongholds and contested terrain, decreasing their ability to contain the violence.

The rebel government faces a *security–development trade-off*: it must divert spending from co-optation to coercion. This becomes a dilemma because the rebel government's influence over civilians decreases as it spends more on fighting the war. During this time, rebels attempt to recruit from these new territories, and are more successful if civilians believe the government is providing neither goods nor security. In this scenario, rivals that are able to maintain a military presence can more easily recruit fighters. The result is that previously contested zones slowly come under rival control, decreasing the rebel government's reach.

Cross-national Hypothesis *As the breadth and depth of the victor's rebel–civilian ties increase, it is more likely to consolidate power.*

It is also possible that rebel victors fought limited regional rebellions and established deep ties with civilians by implementing comprehensive rebel governance structures in areas where they had social control, but failed to achieve geographical breadth. My theory implies that such ties are still valuable. In Chapter 6, I show that geographically limited rebel victors with more in-depth ties still tend to return to civil war. Yet they are more likely to win the second war, meaning they are less likely to lose their bid to consolidate power than rebel groups that have relatively shallow and limited ties. The reason is that victors with strong ties benefit from wartime learning and have a stronger organizational capacity to engage in co-optation across larger swathes of unsecured terrain—even if their influence is not *ex ante* broad enough to immediately eliminate threats of violence.

Uganda is a good example. Although its rebellion was geographically contained, the victors had engaged in deep rebel governance and rebel party-building during the civil war. Thus the victors maintained strong social control over a small segment of the population, but were able to establish a strong foundation. Due to its limited breadth, it faced rebellions after the war's end; however, the depth of its rebel–civilian ties added to the group's organizational capacity, and the victor was able to learn from and draw on its experiences during the war to replicate its wartime institutions across the state. As Mamdani (1988, 1168) describes:

> The fact was that in its exceptionally short stay of five years in the bush the NRA's military presence extended to no more than half the country, and its political hold to even less. As a result, even though it had sympathy in larger sections of the country, the NRA lacked an organised base in over half the country. This fact not only dictated the necessity for a united front government, it also called for an extremely creative application of united front tactics if these were not to turn into an unprincipled reconciliation with organised forces of the old order which would hold back any attempt to usher in fundamental social change.

In short, Uganda eventually experienced conflict recurrence, but the victor was ultimately able to consolidate power by proliferating its wartime party structures to increase watchfulness and gather information about potential dissent (Lewis, 2020).

2.6 Summarizing the Sequence of Events

This chapter outlines the book's overall argument—that post-war governance decisions can be predicted by the geographic distribution of wartime social control, and that the new rebel government can harness rebel–civilian relations forged during war to extend state control. I examine two dimensions, rebel presence and rebel influence in a territory, to determine the degree of social control that rebels exercise within that territory during the civil war. When presence and influence are high, rebels are more likely to build wartime ties with civilian and local governance institutions. This allows the group to induce cooperation and extract resources from the local population during the war. Conversely, areas that experience high levels of military contestation between different armed groups generate more coercive rebel–civilian ties with no governing institutions.

Returning to the state-building framework introduced at the start of the chapter, Figure 2.3 illustrates the process of state-building through rebel–civilian relations from the start of the civil war until the period of stable peace.

The first period of violence begins with the onset of civil war, in which one or more rebel groups challenge the government in an attempt to take control of the center. The rebel groups arrive from the periphery in rural areas

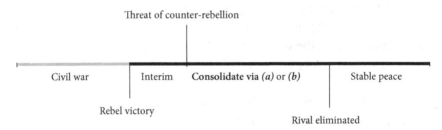

Figure 2.3 Consolidating power after civil war
(a) **Low-violence consolidation conflict:** a counter-rebellion is launched but fails to reach war levels as the rebel government quashes attempts at violence.
(b) **War-level consolidation conflict:** a counter-rebellion is launched. The rebel government faces a second civil war involving its wartime enemies but is able to consolidate its control and eliminate its rivals' military organizational capacity.

and move toward the capital using guerrilla warfare tactics. As they mount a rebellion, rebel groups rely on civilians to provide food, information, shelter, and medicine. In some cases, they begin to form connections with civilians in order to extract these basic necessities and may build basic institutions to increase the efficiency of these extractive relationships. In other cases, they are unable to form relationships with civilians, and therefore rely on coercion to extract materials and information to fight the war. While the rebel groups are attempting to gain territory and establish social control, the government tries to regain or sustain its own territorial control. In doing so, it introduces military contestation and potentially defeats the rebels in a territory through counterinsurgency and violence, which serve to break any civilian ties that rebels may have formed there. Through rebellion and contestation, the civil war may create new ethno-religious and territorial cleavages based on wartime political geography through elite manipulation, or solidify (and even exacerbate) preexisting cleavages in an attempt to galvanize support for all parties to the conflict.

Rebel victory marks the end of the first civil war and the start of the interim period, during which the country experiences an uneasy and volatile peace as a rebel group comes to power through political or military victory. The new government benefits from international humanitarian and developmental aid, which is spent on reconstruction. However, the government is constrained by a fragile political climate and limited economic resources. It is also under pressure to demobilize ex-combatants and maintain internal security concurrently with post-war social and economic reconstruction.

The rebel government responds by first relying on its wartime ties with civilians to help govern sub-nationally after the war, because these ties are the most likely to provide the least costly form of governance. In areas with no such ties, the rebel government focuses on building state capacity— expanding its influence across the territory—by deploying partisan bureaucrats and creating bureaucratic structures at the sub-national level. However, citizens in rival strongholds may not consider the rebel government legitimate, and are likely to reject new state institutions and government attempts to extend power, which may in turn foment unrest. In response to such threats to its power, the rebel government utilizes the state military to coerce cooperation from these areas, and allocates any remaining state resources to politically target public goods through its bureaucrats. If successfully implemented, these two strategies allow it to win citizen support where possible, and restructure politics in its favor.

While the rebel government is consolidating control during this post-war interim period, rivals prepare to renew violence as quickly as possible.

70 Governing after War

A successful counter-rebellion becomes less likely over time for two reasons. First, as time passes, the new rebel government's control over the state increases as reconstruction moves forward and pro-government institutions are built or repaired. Second, disarmament and demobilization efforts may decrease the availability of arms in the country, while an increasing number of ex-combatants may return to civilian jobs and choose not to participate in a renewed war.

Thus, during this interim period, there is a threat of counter-rebellion. To prevent civil war recurrence, the rebel government sends its army to consolidate control in rival strongholds, and may increase military spending as unrest worsens. The armed rivals recruit from among their supporters, relying not just on networks established during the first civil war, but also on refugees and angry civilians who stand to lose under the new government. If the rival rebellion cannot gather enough support to wage war and the rebel government can effectively carry out a counterinsurgency, the conflict will fizzle into localized and limited unrest. This outcome becomes more likely as the intensity of the victor's ties with civilians on the ground increases.

If the opposite is true, however, then conflict intensifies into civil war—ushering in the next stage of the state-building process. During this period, the rebel government fights a consolidation conflict that is in effect a continuation of the first war. While the consolidation war is a civil conflict, it also has interstate qualities because it entails conquering rival strongholds. If the new rebel government wins this second conflict and eliminates its rivals, it successfully consolidates power and thus wins control over the state. Yet if it wins the conflict militarily but is unable to sever its rival's ties with civilians—meaning, it is unable to exert social control—it may be forced to fight multiple consolidation conflicts. Thus the state will oscillate between periods of peace and war until one side is eliminated.

Finally, the new rebel government may be overthrown altogether: the costs of internal conquest may be too high, forcing the victor to increase security spending to the detriment of reconstruction and social spending—thereby losing civilian support (Figure 2.4). Unlike the successful process of consolidating power through one or more rounds of civil war, the victor may ultimately fail to establish dominance over the entire state territory. Instead of successfully conquering its rivals and co-opting neutral civilians, the opposite happens: rivals are able to leverage their own organizational capacity to win supporters. These rivals may eventually reach a point at which they are able to either defeat the rebel government outright or force a political victory through a peace process. In this case, the second civil war restarts the process from the beginning, as a second new government seeks to consolidate power.

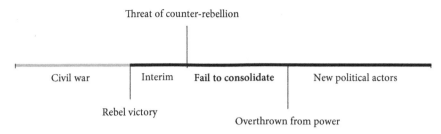

Figure 2.4 Failure to consolidate power after civil war

The logic of this theory—how war affects post-war governance and stability through organized rebel–civilian ties—applies most directly to rebel victories.[13] I test the theory's resource allocation hypotheses using the cases of the Zimbabwe Liberation War and the First Liberian Civil War in Chapters 4 and 5, respectively. In Zimbabwe, I show that a large incumbent stronghold led to a bureaucratically strong and increasingly centralized state after the war, which allowed the new government to launch a disproportionately violent military response in the rival stronghold. In Liberia, a weak and smaller rebel stronghold by the end of the war, paired with high levels of military contestation, meant that the new rebel government diverted increasing amounts of money to security rather than development.

In Chapters 6 and 7, I provide evidence to support the consolidation of power hypotheses. I argue that Zimbabwe's and Liberia's diverging trajectories can be explained by the differences in their wartime rebel–civilian ties, which affected their ability to sufficiently implement their resource allocation strategies. Specifically, overspending on security in Liberia prevented the victor from establishing control over contested terrain with bureaucratic strength and development. I complement these case comparisons with four additional cases in Angola, Côte d'Ivoire, Burundi, and Rwanda.

---

[13] The theory can be extended to make predictions about state victories where the government was created during a previous violent struggle or has extensive local party structures.

PART II

RESOURCE ALLOCATION

3
Introducing the Cases

The previous chapter laid out my theory of state-building through rebel–civilian ties. I argued that wartime experiences, through forming ties with civilians and organizing them to establish control on the ground, have subsequent implications for sub-national variation in governance and cross-national outcomes for state stability. At the *sub-national* level, ties with civilians increase post-war social control, meaning that development resources and violence are directed outside of wartime strongholds. Where possible, informal institutions—from rebel party structures to civilian militias—implemented during wartime are replicated afterwards to establish top-down control. At the *cross-national* level, the breadth and depth of rebels' ties with civilians depend on the victor's degree of social control at the start of her rule: the greater this social control, the more targeted the resource allocation, which makes the rebel group more likely to consolidate its control over the state. The state-building process I describe is characterized by internal conquest, spanning from war to post-war politics.

Part II of the book evaluates the sub-national hypotheses of my theory using two disparate cases: the Zimbabwean Liberation War (1972–1979) and the Liberian Civil War (1989–1996). These two conflicts operated under starkly different domestic, regional, and international contexts. The Zimbabwean Liberation War was an anti-colonial war for Black majority rule, fought against a White minority government that was similarly seeking independence from Britain. It took place amid a regional push for independence across southern Africa, and within the broader Cold War context during the Sino-Soviet split. The Liberian Civil War, by contrast, capitalized on inter-ethnic tensions within the country. It grew out of—and later contributed to—broader regional turmoil involving natural resources, weak states, and personalist leaders seeking a pan-African identity in the post–Cold War era.

The purpose of Part II, therefore, is to use the most-different comparative research design to examine sub-national similarities in post-war governing strategies. Qualitative and quantitative evidence combine to address two of the alternative mechanisms presented in Chapter 2—namely rebel victors' will and capacity to govern (*governing capacity*) and their will and capacity

Governing after War: Rebel Victories and Post-war Statebuilding. Shelley X. Liu, Oxford University Press.
© Oxford University Press 2024. DOI: 10.1093/oso/9780197696705.003.0003

76 Governing after War

to repress (*military capacity* and *territorial control*). While both of these mechanisms matter significantly for understanding post-war governance, they do not tell the whole story when examining sub-national outcomes. My goal is thus to illustrate how both the victor's and their rival(s)'s social control at the end of civil war matters. The victor in Zimbabwe demonstrated stronger capacity for governance and almost no territorial control, while the victor in Liberia featured the opposite. Yet, their sub-national strategies for sustaining control both still featured the same elements of local control in their strongholds, repression in rival terrain, and co-optation in areas where they had low organizational capacity but anticipated an opening to shore up state capacity.

In this introduction to Part II, I provide a historical account of these two conflicts and the broader contexts within which they occurred. Since this section of the book explores the sub-national logic of how rebel–civilian ties affect governing decisions after war can be broadly applicable to vastly different conflicts, this chapter highlights the stark differences between the wars in Zimbabwe and Liberia, and examines the sub-national variation within each case. I seek to identify parallels between these two wars: how the affected citizens viewed these wars in different parts of the country, and how their participation in and support for the rebellions shaped post-war politics despite the conflicts' differences. I then show in Chapters 4 and 5 that this sub-national heterogeneity helps explain rebel victors' post-war governing decisions in Zimbabwe and Liberia, respectively.

3.1 The Zimbabwe Liberation War: Historical Context

The fight for independence and Black majority rule in Zimbabwe—then Southern Rhodesia under a British colonial regime—began decades prior to the start of the liberation war as part of a broader regional push toward decolonization. Liberation movements in Angola, Mozambique, South Africa, and Zimbabwe moved toward a military struggle; Malawi and Zambia achieved independence through political means in the 1960s.

3.1.1 Liberation Struggles in Southern Rhodesia

Zimbabwe's liberation struggle began as a political one. Following years of engagement with southern African decolonization politics, in 1960, Joshua Nkomo founded the National Democratic Party (NDP) with a group of nationalists to demand an end to minority rule in Southern Rhodesia. The NDP was quickly banned, but reformed in 1961 as the Zimbabwe African People's Union (ZAPU). ZAPU went underground in 1963 as a resistance movement after being repeatedly banned from politics by the Rhodesian colonial government under Ian Smith. ZAPU's leadership split that year due to increasing tensions over how to pursue independence, both domestically and internationally: Nkomo sought to form a government in exile in Zambia to continue the political fight and was reluctant to engage in a completely military struggle. ZAPU leaders who advocated revolution through military means splintered to form the Zimbabwe African National Union (ZANU).

Within months, ZANU had recruited a small group of potential rebel fighters for military training. Despite Nkomo's reluctance to move toward violence, ZAPU also, at the urging of its regional allies, began recruiting for a military struggle. The two rebel groups quickly developed distinct armies: ZANU's armed wing, the Zimbabwe African National Liberation Army (ZANLA), and ZAPU's armed wing, the Zimbabwe People's Revolutionary Army (ZIPRA). ZANU/ZANLA adopted Maoist tactics for a peasant-based guerrilla warfare with a politburo (*Dare reChimurenga*) separate from the military, while ZAPU/ZIPRA based its organization on the Leninist model of a tight military vanguard that used both conventional and unconventional warfare tactics. As I discuss in greater depth in the Zimbabwe case chapter (Chapter 4), ZANU/ZANLA came to be associated with the Shona ethnic umbrella group, while ZAPU/ZIPRA recruited primarily from the Ndebele group.

From the very beginning of the conflict, ZANU's efforts were frustrated by ZAPU's widespread recognition at the domestic, regional, and international levels. Though both groups operated out of external political and military bases in Zambia at the time with President Kenneth Kaunda's approval, ZAPU was clearly preferred; ZANU was merely tolerated (Reed, 1993). ZAPU also enjoyed far greater domestic political support and access to more domestic underground networks, which it had established prior to its exile. While the extent to which ZAPU's networks permeated the country at the time—and the degree to which they were embedded in the social fabric—has been debated (Bhebe, 1995), it clearly had far greater recognition and support among civilians at the time. ZANU, as a splinter group that primarily organized in exile, was unable to establish the same sorts of political networks.

ZANU and ZAPU's fight for Zimbabwean independence and Black majority rule took place during a tumultuous political period, both domestically within Southern Rhodesia and across the broader southern Africa region. In the 1950s and 1960s, Southern Rhodesia was a British colony and was one

78 Governing after War

territory within the British Federation of Rhodesia and Nyasaland, which initially included present-day Zimbabwe, Zambia, and Malawi. When Zambia and Malawi—then Northern Rhodesia and Nyasaland—elected Black governments that became increasingly vocal about secession, the federation was no longer viable; colonial powers therefore formally dissolved the federation on December 31, 1963. In 1964, Zambia and Malawi became new independent nations under the leadership of Kenneth Kaunda and Hastings Banda, respectively. The White minority government in Southern Rhodesia had expected to be granted independence if the federation was dissolved. When it became clear that it was to remain under British rule, it unilaterally declared independence in 1965.

From 1965 until Zimbabwe's official independence in 1980, domestic politics in Southern Rhodesia was characterized by several players seeking political power and independence. The White minority government led by Ian Smith battled politically against the British on the international stage and fought against economic sanctions imposed by the British and the United Nations. Domestically, the White minority government fought against ZANU and ZAPU, which both sought independence through military means. Another African nationalist party, the United African National Council led by Bishop Abel Muzorewa, eschewed violence, fighting politically for Black majority rule and independence as a formally recognized party.[1]

3.1.2 Regional and international context

Despite their rivalry from the very beginning, ZANU and ZAPU ultimately fought for the same goal and therefore continued to loosely work together on seeking independence from the colonial government. Given the regional push for liberation, leader connections across states—with each other and with major African leaders such as Julius Nyerere of Tanzania or Tom Mboya of Kenya—were an important source of legitimacy. ZAPU leader Joshua Nkomo was popular and well known as a leader in Zimbabwe's liberation movement throughout the 1960s. He maintained strong ties to Kenneth Kaunda and Hastings Banda, the presidents of Zambia and Malawi at the time. Nkomo had also been an active and leading member of the African National Congress prior to ZAPU's inception, and maintained a strong relationship

---

[1] A fourth nationalist movement, the Front for the Liberation of Zimbabwe, sought a peaceful political struggle and operated out of Zambia. It was only a minor player as it failed to gain a foothold in Southern Rhodesia.

with the Pan-African Movement of East, Central, and Southern Africa. His ties to this movement meant that when the Organisation of African Unity was founded to support independence across the continent, ZAPU—not ZANU—received the bulk of the recognition and support from African allies. While ZANU's leaders were also active in the region, Nkomo and ZAPU were already widely recognized as the country's main organization before it was formed. Thus when ZANU's leadership split from ZAPU, they were treated as a deviant splinter group operating outside Zimbabwe's main movement. The Afro-Asian People's Solidarity Organization not only extended full support to ZAPU; it also rejected ZANU's representative to the organization (Reed, 1993).

Although ZAPU garnered greater political support in these earlier years, both rebel armies received military assistance from regional and international allies as it became increasingly clear that Zimbabwe's liberation would come through armed rebellion. Within the region, rebel troops in Angola and Mozambique had been engaging in military operations for some time, and were therefore crucial to supporting the nascent rebellion in Zimbabwe. Fighters from Angola and Mozambique trained with—and after they gained independence, provided training for—ZIPRA and ZANLA soldiers, respectively. Independent Zambia helped by providing space for ZANLA's and ZIPRA's base of operations. Its president, Kenneth Kaunda, had allowed both rebellions to establish their offices in Zambia since the 1960s; he later allowed them to set up large training camps as well. The Zimbabwean Liberation War also attracted military and economic support from several countries beyond southern Africa, including Algeria, China, Ghana, the Soviet Union, and Tanzania. Since the country's fight for independence took place within the broader Cold War context, international military and economic support for the rebellions played a significant role. The Sino–Soviet split was instrumental: ZAPU received significant support from the Soviet Union, while ZANU's ties were strongest with China.[2] This alliance shifted ZANU's ideology further toward socialism and encouraged it to form ties with other anti-imperial movements and organizations around the world.

In sum, the Zimbabwean Liberation War occurred during a period of decolonization that garnered significant international attention and support. As evidenced by British Prime Minister Harold MacMillan's famous "Wind of Change" speech in 1960, national consciousness and demands for Black

---

[2] Cold War tensions also influenced Zimbabwe's post-war politics: by the time Zimbabwe gained independence, South Africa's apartheid government was the last one standing. Thus Western nations waited anxiously to see if Zimbabwean President Robert Mugabe would meddle with South African politics.

80 Governing after War

majority rule and independence were sweeping across the continent: though the war did not begin until 1972, both rebel groups—and other liberation movements around them—had spent years laying the political groundwork for it. Cold War politics shaped how the subsequent war was fought and financed. This broader historical context influenced the character of the armed resistance from 1972 until the country's official independence in 1980.

3.2 The Liberia Civil War: Historical Context

The Liberian Civil War was a vastly different conflict, situated within a different historical context and characterized by different domestic issues. Unlike the Zimbabwean Liberation War, Liberia's Civil War was an ethnic conflict that took place in the post–Cold War period. The conflict also heavily featured opportunistic leaders who sought to profit from natural resource extraction across the Mano Basin region, including timber, diamonds, rubber, and iron.

3.2.1 Ethnic Tensions

Ethnicity—specifically the inequalities, alliances, and rivalries between the country's many ethnic groups—was at the heart of the civil war. Liberia is an ethnically heterogeneous country comprising fifteen indigenous ethnic groups, none of which constitutes a majority. These groups can be aggregated into three umbrella ethnic groups based on linguistic similarities: the Mande, the Kwa, and the Mel. The Mande make up the majority of the country, followed by the Kwa and then the Mel. The country's history as an unofficial American colony also played a significant role in stoking tensions before the war. Americo-Liberians became the sixteenth ethnic group in Liberia when settlers arrived in 1822.

Americo-Liberians have dominated politics and economics in the country since their arrival. For over a century, the Americo-Liberian True Whig Party ruled and built the country in the image of the US South. Beginning in the mid-1900s, Liberia enjoyed prosperity and economic development when the party's Willian Tubman was elected president in 1944. Tubman, considered the "father of modern Liberia," was credited with building up the state both economically and diplomatically. He was hailed in the region as a political visionary who cofounded the African Union; internationally, he was well respected as a moderate and dependable leader. Despite these strengths, Tubman's politics paved the way for Liberia's future troubles: he pushed the

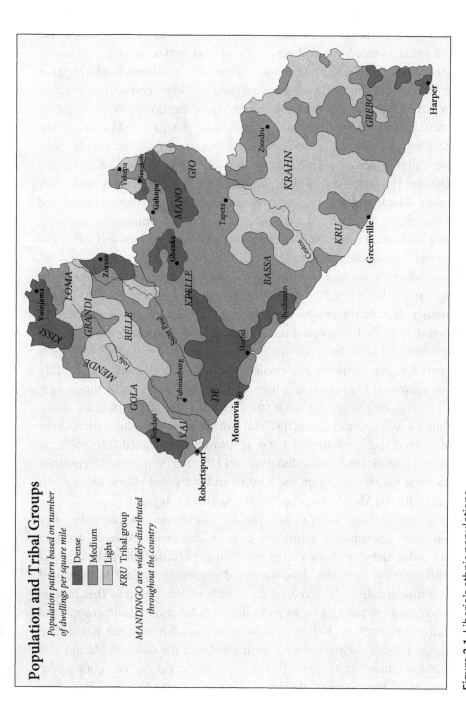

Figure 3.1 Liberia's ethnic populations
Source: UT Austin Perry-Castañeda Library Map Collection

82 Governing after War

country further toward authoritarian politics, as he chose not to leave office and remained president for almost twenty-six years until his death in 1971.[3]

Although Liberia was enjoying rapid growth, indigenous Liberians had limited political freedoms and economic opportunities in what had essentially been an apartheid state since independence. Throughout the True Whig Party's dominance, indigenous Liberians were considered second-class citizens with no political power, wealth, or freedoms. Multiple minor insurgencies and revolts from indigenous ethnic groups failed to change the political system. During his presidency, Tubman was credited with pushing for equality across ethnic groups, but his policies had not generated real change. His successor, William Tolbert (1971–1980), worked to further increase political and economic opportunities for indigenous Liberians and faced significant backlash from the Americo-Liberian community. Thus, the ongoing horizontal inequalities between indigenous Liberians and Americo-Liberians increased tensions during the mid-1900s.

These tensions erupted in violence in 1980 when Samuel Kanyon Doe, a sergeant in the Armed Forces of Liberia, seized power in a coup and infamously executed Americo-Liberian political leaders—nude and tied to wooden stakes—by firing squad on the beach. Doe was previously unknown to the Liberian public but was quickly hailed as a champion for indigenous Liberians for overthrowing the reviled political elite. However, it quickly became clear that his rule would be no better for a majority of the indigenous Liberian ethnic groups. Doe ruled as the head of the military junta, the People's Redemption Council (PRC), which banned political opposition and dissolved the legislature. To stay in power, Doe leaned into the neo-patrimonial politics that had aided previous Liberian politicians. His policies also favored his ethnic group, the Krahn, and increased efforts to establish alliances with the Mandingo people in the northwest regions.

Within the first few years of his rule, Doe developed an internal rivalry with Thomas Quiwonkpa, a military commander in the Armed Forces of Liberia and a member of the Gio ethnic group. Because Quiwonkpa threatened his position in power, Doe increased repression against the Gio and Mano ethnic groups who lived in the North of the country. This repression increased inequalities between indigenous Liberian ethnic groups and fostered resentment, in particular stoking tensions between the Krahn and Mandingo (whose allegiances were with Doe) and the Gio and Mano (who were seen as Quiwonkpa's allies). In 1985, Quiwonkpa launched a coup under the banner of the National Patriotic Front of Liberia (NPFL). This coup

---

[3] His vice president succeeded him, and stayed in power until 1980.

attempt failed; Doe increased repression against the Gio and Mano ethnic groups as punishment for their support of Quiwonkpa. The violence led to mass displacement as civilians fled to neighboring ethnic kin regions in Cote d'Ivoire and Guinea. These displaced individuals formed the eventual support base for the civil war.

3.2.2 The Charismatic Rebel Leader

In this context of ethnic rivalry and repression, another member of the Liberian government came under the spotlight during Doe's rule. Charles Taylor, a former ally of Thomas Quiwonkpa in the PRC government, fled to the United States in 1984 amid accusations of embezzlement. He was quickly imprisoned in the United States but escaped in 1985 with the help of his wife and managed to leave the country undetected. After traveling through Mexico, Ghana, and Burkina Faso, Taylor reached Libya, where he gained an audience with Libyan president Muammar Qaddafi. Qaddafi took a liking to Taylor, and trained and funded him to wage war against the Liberian government in the name of the pan-African/anti-Western movement. Between 1985 and 1989, Taylor and his Liberian allies—who had participated in Quiwonkpa's coup—recruited fighters to train in Libya and Burkina Faso under Marxist and pan-African ideology. The group planned to attack Liberia's northern border. In 1989, the rebels moved to western Cote d'Ivoire and assumed the name that Quiwonkpa had used in his 1985 coup: the NPFL.

This was how the Liberian Civil War started: not by a leader who truly represented an aggrieved sector of the civilian population, but by a charismatic man who understood how to win political support from his various audiences. While Taylor was not from either the Gio or Mano tribes—he was of Americo-Liberian and, allegedly, Gola descent[4]—he capitalized on the ethnic tensions that later came to characterize the major cleavage in the civil war. When the NPFL moved to Côte d'Ivoire, it began to recruit from among the Gio and Mano ethnic groups who lived on both sides of the Liberia–Côte d'Ivoire border. Many Gio and Mano had fled to Côte d'Ivoire to escape Doe's crackdown after Quiwonkpa's coup attempt. They enthusiastically supported the rebellion and were charmed by Taylor's leadership and vision of a democratic and equal Liberia, which he maintained could be achieved by overthrowing Doe's dictatorship.

---

[4] Taylor claimed his mother was Gola, but this has not been verified.

3.2.3 Regional and International Context

Although the Liberian Civil War was rooted in domestic ethnic inequalities, the regional and international contexts cannot be dismissed. Within this regional context, the relationships between states depended on the relationship between leaders; thus, Liberia's regional politics in western Africa were heavily influenced by the leaders in power. Clearly, the inception of Liberia's civil war owed heavily to Qaddafi's early military and financial support. Leaders of Liberia's neighbors also supported Taylor because they were against Doe's rule. In Burkina Faso, Blaise Compaore owed his position and the success of his own coup to Liberian recruits who had helped kill the former leader Thomas Sankara; in Côte d'Ivoire, Félix Houphouët-Boigny's alliance with Burkina Faso's new leader Blaise Compaore meant that Côte d'Ivoire was also now allied with the Liberian recruits. As Taylor and his men continued to travel around western Africa to form alliances, they picked up support from Togolese dissidents in Ghana and rebel forces coalescing in Sierra Leone. Taylor also formed ties with other revolutionaries at the time who fought ideological wars in Cuba, the Democratic Republic of the Congo, Uganda, and South Sudan (Ellis, 2007).

Beyond these immediate western African neighbors, Taylor's poor relationships with Guinea and Nigeria were particularly important for understanding regional politics after the civil war began. Nigeria was the clear leader of the Economic Community of West African States and its peacekeeping force, the Economic Community of West African States Monitoring Group. It had been deeply against a Taylor presidency in Liberia, and that position lengthened the civil war considerably. Guinean president Lansana Conté similarly viewed Taylor as an enemy of Guinea and a threat to West Africa. He later sponsored forces that overthrew Taylor in 2003.

Finally, the international political context was also important. Since the late 1800s, Liberia had been financially dependent on the United States, which in turn enjoyed unfettered access to the country's rubber and minerals. Throughout the mid-1900s, Cold War politics also drove US policy: the United States sought to spread democracy across Africa and thus turned a blind eye to extractive political institutions in Liberia. This was already the case in 1971, when Tolbert came to power following Tubman's death; the West lauded the peaceful transfer of power. When Doe held particularly corrupt elections in 1985, the United States again applauded the nation for its democratic processes and continued to provide economic aid. US support of Doe's regime persisted until the end of the Cold War in 1989, which coincided with the start of the Liberian Civil War.

3.3 Sub-national Heterogeneity

The Zimbabwean Liberation War and the Liberian Civil War clearly differed in many respects, including why the groups rebelled, the domestic institutional legacies, and the regional and international contexts in which they were situated. They were also received differently by the international community: while the war in Zimbabwe was heralded (and today remembered) as a programmatic rebellion that overthrew the colonial regime, Liberia's war is considered one of the most brutal, chaotic, and opportunistic rebellions on the continent. In the latter, natural resources and greed ruled, and the world lamented Taylor's rise to power; in the former, the world was cautiously optimistic about the birth of a new nation.

In the next two chapters, I show that these cross-national differences do not fully explain the two countries' diverging post-war security trajectories: subnational variation also matters. Across both cases, there are also similarities in governing strategies on the ground that complicate the lessons that should be learned. Although the international community tends to be homogeneous in its understanding of both conflicts, it is important to remember that there is persistent heterogeneity in how civilians living in various parts of both countries interpret the legacies of war and the rebel governments that emerged victorious. These differences in interpretation reflect citizens' lived experiences during wartime and peacetime.

In Liberia, for example, despite the vast number of civilian casualties and the tolls of civil war, a substantial portion of citizens supported the first civil war and believed Taylor was unfairly demonized on the international stage. These citizens—often not even from the Gio or Mano ethnic groups, which Taylor supposedly championed during the war—remember Taylor's time in government positively, when political freedoms may have been precarious but food prices were low. Others' support extended further back to the civil war. To them, it was not only the economy that made Taylor's regime popular; they also believe that he could have brought about peace, but that post-war state stability and prosperity were not achieved primarily due to a lack of support from the international community. They remember stability during the war: farmers were allowed to farm, the rebel government provided rice, and soldiers were disciplined under the watchful eyes of their commanders. Taylor's supporters blame the descent from order to chaos during the first civil war and the onset of the second civil war on outside forces. During the civil war, Taylor had proclaimed his vision a "revolution," not war; some people continue to use this term today and consider inter-ethnic peace to be one of his positive lasting legacies.

However, among people from other parts of the country, the stories and memories are very different. Many remember only brutality and chaos from the very beginning as they fled from towns to the villages to escape angry soldiers engaging in ethnic cleansing. Rebel factions had killed indiscriminately and plundered civilian households. These citizens desperately traveled through numerous counties hoping to escape the brunt of the conflict, before wearily returning home after the end of war. They had been forced to vote in 1997 under the threat of renewed warfare, and believed their ballots were forged in Taylor's favor. Despite hopes for peace and normalcy, Taylor's newly elected government provided them with no food, medicine, or reconstruction. There was only violence from the ex-rebels who were now elevated to power in the new Liberian army and other defense institutions. When the second civil war began, many of these citizens were relieved that Taylor was overthrown. For them, normalcy did not return until Ellen Johnson Sirleaf's administration in 2005.

Similar sub-national heterogeneity emerged in the Zimbabwean Liberation War: civilians were not unanimous in their enthusiasm for ZANU-PF, the victorious liberation movement at the head of the newly liberated country's government. During the war, civilian participation and support for the two liberation movements ranged from complete covert support and full participation in the war effort to chaos, confusion, and fear of all armed combatants. After the war, citizens remained divided. Some recalled major post-war reconstruction achievements under the new ZANU-PF government, and remembered the first decade of ZANU-PF's rule as a time when citizens worked with the government for the common good. On the other hand, however, others recalled state co-optation of the local government: the ruling party relied on its increasingly centralized power despite claiming to decentralize development. They remembered ZANU-PF pushing ZAPU out of politics, undermining traditional authority, and intimidating non-supporters. Some experienced the worst of all: fear for their lives as they faced indiscriminate mass violence perpetrated by the government almost immediately after the war, with no hope for an end to the conflict. This final group of citizens attributed Mugabe's first victory in the post-war election *not* to ZANU-PF's popularity in the country, but instead to the international community's desire to support him as well as the intimidating vote coercion carried out by his combatants on the ground. They believed their candidate, ZAPU's Joshua Nkomo, would have won a free and fair election to become the first leader of the free nation, setting Zimbabwean politics on the correct trajectory. To this subset of Zimbabwean civilians, Mugabe's rule had *always* been one of terror—not liberation.

Introducing the Cases **87**

In Part II, I show that despite international opinions about new rebel governments and expectations about how they will govern, the levels of domestic trust in (and mistrust of) their new ruler in different parts of the country go a long way toward constraining and explaining rebel victors' post-war governing strategies. Put another way, heterogeneity in local community experiences and civilian attitudes—including their beliefs and emotions, who they support, and collective action on behalf of their supported group—matter a great deal for political outcomes both during and after war. Part II asks: how are civilian loyalties developed and organized during war, and how does a nascent government take them into account in post-war governance? How do war and post-war conditions constrain and dictate strategies for consolidating power? Chapters 4 and 5 examine these questions in depth in Zimbabwe and Liberia, respectively.

4

The Zimbabwe Liberation War (1972–1979)

The Zimbabwean War of Liberation, also known as the Second Chimurenga, began in 1960 as a political movement under Joshua Nkomo and ended with Zimbabwe's independence and Black majority rule in 1980. During this time the two liberation parties, the Zimbabwe African People's Union (ZAPU) and the Zimbabwe African National Union (ZANU), transitioned into two opposing rebel groups with armed wings—the Zimbabwe People's Revolutionary Army (ZIPRA) and the Zimbabwe African National Liberation Army (ZANLA), respectively. A deeply politicized class of peasants actively supported both groups of rebels.

In this chapter, I show how the degree of social control exerted by the two rebel groups in different parts of the country influenced its political landscape on the eve of independence. I argue that the relationships and institutional structures underlying the groups' approaches to wartime social control shaped the governing strategies they used to consolidate postwar power. I draw on rich archival records and transcripts of interviews with a range of ex-combatants from both groups as well as civilian collaborators to illustrate how the new ruling party, the Zimbabwe African National Union-Patriotic Front (ZANU-PF), manipulated its wartime ties to its advantage. It employed a combination of local embeddedness, loyalty, and violence to project state power *not* just to sustain control over its strongholds, but also to coopt and coerce obedience from civilians across the country to create a one-party state under its control.

4.1 Conflict Overview

Zimbabwe's liberation struggle reached civil war levels in 1972, although both groups had begun military training during the 1960s (see Figure 4.1). In the beginning of the war, the two groups primarily fought out of their military bases in Zambia. However, they also operated in Zimbabwe's northernmost

Governing after War: Rebel Victories and Post-war Statebuilding. Shelley X. Liu, Oxford University Press.
© Oxford University Press 2024. DOI: 10.1093/oso/9780197696705.003.0004

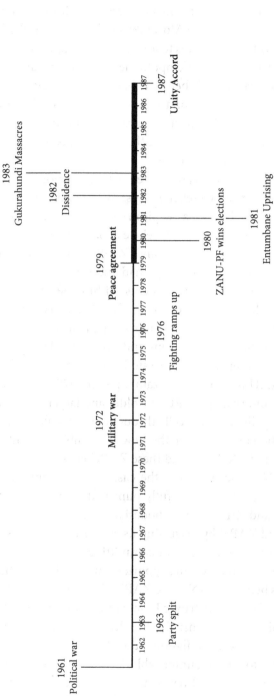

Figure 4.1 Zimbabwe conflict timeline

Notes: Figure 4.1 depicts Zimbabwe's conflict timeline. The black bar denotes the postwar period during which ZANU-PF consolidated power.

province, Mashonaland West, and in northeastern Mozambique alongside Mozambican rebels. When these Mozambican allies won independence in 1975, they invited both rebel groups to join forces and fight as one out of eastern Mozambique. After a failed attempt to merge, ZAPU returned to Zambia (where it was already well established) and opened up additional fronts along the Botswana–Zimbabwe border on the west. ZANU moved permanently to Mozambique because it had almost no infrastructure in Zambia. Its army opened up four operational zones along the entire Mozambique–Zimbabwe border on the eastern side of the country.

These new operational zones came to define their supporters and the communities controlled by the two rebel groups. By the end of the war, ZANLA was largely supported by the Shona people in eastern Zimbabwe, while ZIPRA had strong ties with members of the Ndebele tribe in the west of the country.

The relationship between ZANU and ZAPU was uneasy during the Liberation War: While the two groups had the same overarching goal of Zimbabwean independence, disagreements within the leaderships caused the two sides to fight against each other for civilian support and social control. During the initial years in Zambia, frequent disagreements led to fights for control in the training camps and on the battlefield, setting back both rebel groups in their aim to liberate Zimbabwe. These skirmishes in part motivated ZANU to move to Mozambique in 1975, cementing the two groups' separation and rivalry. ZAPU, the older and larger of the two parties, set up clandestine political party cells throughout Zimbabwe—including in the northeast of the country. After the new Mozambique front opened up on the east however, ZANU replaced these ZAPU cells with its own civilian structures. As ZANLA pushed from the east into the contested heartland of central Zimbabwe, soldiers forcefully punished civilians who were sympathetic to ZAPU and ZIPRA. The Rhodesian army exacerbated the rivalry between ZANU and ZAPU by disguising its supporters ("Selous Scouts") as guerrilla fighters from both sides and committing atrocities to sow discord and confusion among rural civilian supporters and soldiers on the ground.[1]

Despite tensions between ZANU and ZAPU, the two rebel militaries briefly teamed up again to form the Patriotic Front (PF) on the eve of independence to launch the final assault against the Rhodesian forces. Although fraught with inter-group tensions and infighting, the alliance successfully forced the colonial government to the bargaining table. Negotiations led to the Lancaster House Agreement in 1979, and national elections were held the following year. The PF split back into ZANU-PF and PF-ZAPU to contest the 1980 elections; ZANU's Robert Mugabe overwhelmingly beat ZAPU's Nkomo.

---

[1] The Selous Scouts included both Black and White Rhodesians; the latter used black makeup.

The Zimbabwe Liberation War (1972–1979) 91

Post-independence peace, however, was short-lived. Ex-ZANLA and ex-ZIPRA soldiers brought their rivalry into the newly integrated Zimbabwean military, leading to clashes in the Entumbane barracks in the Matabeleland area only a year after ZANU-PF was elected. The situation worsened further when secret ZAPU weapon caches were allegedly discovered in Gweru. ZANU used this discovery to justify its purge of ZAPU politicians from the government. Ex-ZIPRA members who were incorporated into the army deserted *en masse* in 1982 out of fear for their lives amid accusations of treasonous behavior.

While most returned home or fled to South Africa, some ex-ZIPRA deserters banded together in an attempt to fight a new war. These rebels fell into two groups: (1) ex-ZAPU "dissidents" who sought to recreate ZAPU; and (2) "Super-ZAPU," a South Africa-backed rebel group that contained both ex-ZIPRA high command members as well as Zimbabwean refugees who had fled to Botswana and South Africa. Both groups recruited from the Matabeleland provinces, which ZAPU had controlled during the war. Within Zimbabwe, the "dissidents" recruited from Matabeleland North and Matabeleland South, while Super-ZAPU recruited primarily within Matabeleland South along the border with South Africa in an effort to unseat Mugabe and wrest government control away from ZANU.

These counter-rebellion attempts were ultimately unsuccessful. Almost immediately after entering the government, ZANU-PF had filled local government positions throughout the country with partisans and maintained strict control over civilian community life through newly created rural district councils. Mugabe assembled the Fifth Brigade—a North Korean-trained army of ex-ZANLA soldiers—to brutally suppress the Matabeleland dissidents and terrorize civilians through the Gukurahundi massacres beginning in 1983.[2] Gukurahundi reached its peak in 1985 and killed an estimated twenty thousand civilians over the years through indiscriminate violence against Ndebele communities in western Zimbabwe. The network of ZANU-PF partisans, along with the brutal violence unleashed across the countryside, drastically decreased civilians' propensity to support ZAPU's revitalization. Gukurahundi and dissident activity ended with the Unity Accord in 1987, in which the ZAPU leadership agreed to disband ZAPU as a political party and join the government under the ZANU-PF coalition banner. Mugabe's brutal response to the Matabeleland dissidents, along with the successful state centralization measures, cemented the party's control over the entire country for decades to follow.

---

[2] The Shona word *Gukurahundi* translates as "the early rain which washes away the chaff before the spring rains."

4.2 Data Sources

I argue that ZANU/ZANLA's wartime experiences—particularly its relationships with civilians in the village-level party structures it created—paved the way for it to centralize power after the war. I use a mixed-methods approach to provide evidence that this was the case. Due to the historical nature of the project and the limited access to data in Zimbabwe for foreign researchers, not all hypotheses can be comprehensively tested using both qualitative and quantitative methods. I therefore combine rich historical records with quantifiable development and political outcomes to illustrate the ways in which wartime organizational structures defined the governing trajectory of postwar Zimbabwe under ZANU-PF. In this chapter, I leverage qualitative data to generate evidence of wartime rebel–civilian relations under both ZANU and ZAPU. I explore how these ties helped the rebels establish social control in parts of the country during the civil war; I also present comprehensive qualitative evidence of how the government attempted to consolidate postwar control from the top down in different areas, depending on the level of grassroots support and resistance they encountered. I then use quantitative testing to establish the observable implications of these governing strategies by examining two outcomes: (1) differential outcomes in voter registration (to demonstrate state control); and (2) strides made in education reforms across the state (to illustrate subnational variation in development efforts).

I analyzed primary documents from the Jesuit Archives (JA), the Mafela Trust (MT), and the National Archives of Zimbabwe (NAZ) with the help of two Zimbabwean research assistants.[3] Throughout this chapter, I indicate the source of the archival evidence using these acronyms. I also draw on twenty-five ZIPRA interviews (MT) and fourteen interviews with civilians who collaborated or aided the rebels during the civil war (NAZ).[4] I supplement this archival data with one ex-government employee interview, five ex-combatant interviews, two interviews with Zimbabwe experts, and secondary sources from ethnographic scholarly works conducted after the war.[5] The variety of sources consulted provides grounded insights into wartime rebel–civilian relations and the postwar political order in the 1980s. In the remainder of this section, I discuss the three primary data sources in more detail.

---

[3] Permanent access to NAZ is restricted to Zimbabwean citizens; visitors' access is limited to three days.

[4] These interviews were conducted in Shona, and were translated into English by a research assistant.

[5] Interviews were conducted in 2017, either in person in Zimbabwe or via phone or online video from the United States. See Appendix B1 for additional details.

First, the JA in Harare contains materials collected by the Catholic churches and missions in Zimbabwe. These archives are a largely impartial source of recordkeeping and independently researched materials. Documents from the Liberation War primarily detail relationships with ZANU/ZANLA, which is consistent with historical and anthropological research on ZANLA's strong relationship with the Catholic church during the civil war. I use memoirs from missionaries and church staff to determine the frequency of various missions' contact with ZANU/ZANLA, as well as the relationships between the church, local civilians, and ZANLA forces during the war. The JA also contains primary materials and independent research conducted by the Catholic church on wartime atrocities and rebel activity across Zimbabwe, as well as yearly Catholic church directories, which provide information about whether missions closed down or were downsized due to increased guerrilla activity. I use this information to identify the spread of activity for both rebel groups, depending on the locations of these mission closures. Postwar reports from the JA focus on nationwide development and security issues in Matabeleland; these were immensely helpful for understanding how ZANU-PF governed and allocated resources after the war.

Second, the NAZ in Harare contains documents primarily from the pre-independence period (up to 1979), as well as some Ministry of Education reports and oral interviews conducted in the last two decades. These materials mainly cover Rhodesian and ZANU-PF narratives. I use the oral interviews conducted with civilians and ex-combatants to assess civilian–rebel interactions, as well as the length of this contact and the strength of wartime institutions. The NAZ also houses Rhodesian military documents detailing their counter-insurgency strategy during this period. Particularly useful were the military coordinates and the number of civilians who had aided ZANU/ZANLA during the civil war who were forced into what the Rhodesian government called Protected Villages (PVs), fenced-in areas guarded by Rhodesian soldiers.

The third primary data source, the MT archives, currently housed at the South African History Archive in Johannesburg, contain wartime materials from the opposition ZAPU. These documents include correspondence, interviews, memos, and other documents collected from 1989 onward in an effort to catalog and memorialize ZAPU/ZIPRA's place in Zimbabwe's struggle for independence. They also include information about government discrimination against the Matabeleland provinces and ZAPU ex-combatants after independence. I use interviews conducted by the Trust to identify ZIPRA operational zones during the civil war, as well as relationships with civilians and local leaders and evidence of struggles against ZANU/ZANLA

94 Governing after War

soldiers in different parts of the country. The MT archives also contain information about ZAPU/ZIPRA ex-combatants who were killed during the civil war, including their location, cause of death, and place of birth for some individuals. I use these death records to determine the frequency of ZIPRA operations in different districts and as evidence of recruitment into, and local support of, ZAPU/ZIPRA.

4.3 Rebel–Civilian Relations During War

The civil war featured little *direct* military contestation between ZANU's armed wing (ZANLA) and ZAPU's armed wing (ZIPRA)—or even between ZANLA and the Rhodesian government—because both rebel armies prioritized guerrilla tactics. Thus ZANU was able to establish social control over civilian life in large parts of rural Zimbabwe's communal lands. In this section, I describe the types of ties that ZANLA established with local civilians, and then explore how these ties aided the war effort. Next, I discuss ZIPRA's wartime structures. Finally, I argue that civilian ties in the rebel groups' strongholds were cooperative under the shadow of organized coercion during war, while military contestation introduced greater *variability* in violence and coercion.

4.3.1 Organizational capacity and rebel–civilian ties

ZANLA combatants built organized civilian teams during the civil war to aid the rebels in their military activities, which increased the group's organizational capacity. Researchers and official narratives have documented ZANLA's local rebel–civilian relations during the war.[6] The group exploited existing civilian institutional structures—such as missionary staff, religious leaders, and traditional leaders who were not employed by the colonial state— to legitimate its power and build new types of civilian organizations. In the postwar period, the new incumbent used this wartime organizational structure and civilian supporters to ensure the success and stability of its governing apparatus.

In addition to partnering with existing civilian leaders, documents and interviews from NAZ and JA confirm that rebels exerted social control over civilians during the Liberation War primarily through pungwes—traditional

---

[6] See, for example, Kriger (1991), Lan (1985), and Ranger (1985).

Shona celebrations that became mandatory all-night rallies featuring ideological and political education. Revolutionary pungwes began as early as 1972 (Nhandara, 1977, 6) and continued until the end of the war; citizens were taught about freedom and imbued with nationalism. In ZANLA strongholds, pungwes were considered enjoyable experiences for civilians, as everyone gathered all night to drink beer, sing liberation songs, dance, and socialize. Rebel groups also used them to identify and punish any "sellouts" who were cooperating with the Rhodesian regime or opposition forces.

I highlight two main forms of local organization through rebel–civilian relations in areas under ZANLA control—wartime youth collaborators and village committees. ZANLA rebels created these organizations to establish relationships with civilians to serve two purposes: (1) to provide reconnaissance, some local security, and a simple liaison system between the rebels and the village; and (2) to provide logistical support and increase the efficiency of civilian assistance.

Civilian type I: Youth collaborators

A total of around fifty thousand youths are estimated to have provided secondary support to ZANU/ZANLA during the war. Male collaborators were known as mujibas and females as chimbwidos. Most were teens or young adults, although children as young as seven years old sometimes passed messages between rebel camps and the communities.

Youth collaborators primarily acted as liaisons between ZANLA and the local civilians, and their operational zones covered several villages within an area (Murambiwa, 2014). ZANLA rebel bases in Zimbabwe were hidden in the bush; their locations were often kept secret to prevent them from being discovered by government or opposition forces. When the rebels could not visit the villages themselves, the collaborators—who had intimate knowledge of the rebels' whereabouts and the location of their secret bases—would deliver messages and materials (Murambiwa, 2014; Taruvinga, 2014). A priest explained that missionaries would communicate with, and support, rebels through the youth collaborators: "The guerrillas would frequently communicate in writing, sending the letter with a mujiba [non-combatant] from the area. The letters generally were requests for medicines, though occasionally they contained political lessons..." (St. Paul's Mission, n.d.).

Youth collaborators also acted as agents of local security and defense on behalf of ZANLA. They were organized as local watch teams that could provide on-the-ground information for the rebel troops—the "eyes and ears of the struggle" (Magure, 2009) who conducted reconnaissance on Rhodesian soldiers and opposition militias sponsored by the colonial state. They also identified local residents who were providing information to the enemies. Some youth collaborators reported that they were tasked with patrolling local villages and roads to find out information about the Rhodesian soldiers' whereabouts, determine their number and traffic patterns, and learn about their operations (Murambiwa, 2014; Kwenda, 2014). ZANLA collaborators would also identify "sellouts" during the all-night pungwes, and ensure that punishments were meted out to dissuade such behavior (Mutsinze, 2014; St. Paul's Mission, n.d.).

This reconnaissance system is not unique to Zimbabwe: rebel groups around the world similarly rely on civilian spies to provide information about other civilians who do not support the group (Balcells, 2017; Kalyvas, 2006), and about other armed actors who may be advancing on particular territories. Yet these spies may be coerced into providing such information and therefore may not socially identify themselves as rebel collaborators.[7] By contrast, the Zimbabwean youth collaborators' identities during this period were intricately tied to ZANLA, and these relationships were stronger in areas with more ZANU support. Youth collaborators joined the ZANU-PF party's youth wing after the war, and many considered themselves part of the broader group of war veterans who fought for the country (Kriger, 2003, 192). While some ZANLA ex-combatants maintain that non-combatant mujibas are not "real" war veterans (Maringira, 2014), mujibas were undoubtedly considered a secondary support arm of ZANLA and sometimes operated as a militia (Magure, 2009).

Civilian type II: Village committees

Village committees served as ZANU's wartime party structures (Bhebe, 1999): these were created to organize support for ZANLA by providing combatants with food, clothing, medicines, and other materials. These committees communicated with the guerrillas through youth collaborators, while village committees also helped the youth collaborators organize and run the pungwe festivities. The youth collaborators would first let villages know that ZANLA soldiers were expecting to hold a pungwe (Jeche, 2014; Taruvinga, 2014); the village committees would then collect food and beer from the civilians and ensured that everyone in the community attended (Shumba, 1992). After the pungwes were set up, ZANU party commissars— the combatants—would come into the village to conduct the politicization (Nkiwane, 2010).

---

[7] See Chapter 5.

The Zimbabwe Liberation War (1972–1979)   97

Village committees were structured like political party cells, and were later adapted for postwar governance under ZANU-PF. These committees consisted of several members and were headed by a committee chairman. Some traditional leaders—headmen or chiefs—who supported the rebel group's goals also served as the village committee chairman.[8] Elsewhere, new leaders came to power under the rebel governing structure as chairmen (Kriger, 1991). Eight to ten village committees made up a base committee that was headed by a base chairman; base committees then organized into district and provincial committees. Lower-level committees were the most active. While there is debate over whether the village committee system represented rebel cooptation (Kriger, 1991) or a new form of peasant–guerrilla ideology that allowed citizens in rural areas to reassert control and power over those who benefited from the colonial state (Ranger, 1985), they were clearly a first step toward building local party administration for social control.

ZANLA partnered with traditional leaders such as spirit mediums to create village committees and to confer increased power and legitimacy up on them (Lan, 1985). A report from St. Albert's Mission noted that ZANLA relied on these local leaders and "would approach them to win their support" because "to ignore them or denounce them would be to risk making powerful enemies" (Nhandara, 1977, 6). In this way, ZANLA built new local administrations that were separate from the local chiefs who were associated with the British colonial government. Rather, the group relied instead on the spirits of past chiefs—who had not been tainted by association with the colonial state—and the mediums who communicated with them, to establish control. The mediums would explain the community rules and conduct rituals to initiate the ZANLA rebel commanders into the community (Marimira, 2014), thus conferring legitimacy upon the rebellion. As (Marimira, 2014) explains, "I later gave them the rules and obligations that they were supposed to follow in order to win the war... The guerrillas were then given the green light to start the war against the whites." Once these spirits—rather than the Rhodesian-appointed chiefs and headmen—were established as the new authorities of the area, the mediums "subsequently handed political authority over to the ZANU village committees" (Alexander, 2014, 132).

---

[8] Prior to the war for independence, chiefs were often viewed as appendages of the Rhodesian state since they were part of the official government structure; many lost legitimacy and credibility in local areas (Alexander, 2014, 132). However, several chiefs secretly supported the rebellion and independence movement.

4.3.2 Comparing ZANU and ZAPU's rebel–civilian ties

ZAPU maintained its own locally embedded relationships with civilians in its stronghold areas, although its own form of rebel institutions prioritized a narrow hierarchical structure rather than ZANU's method of mass engagement between guerrillas and local communities. ZAPU focused on building underground party cells during its time as a political party in the 1950s and 1960s, which it later relied on during the war to ascertain the loyalty of those who aided the ZIPRA rebels (Ex-combatants 1 and 4, 2017). ZAPU also eschewed ZANU's mass pungwes, preferring to politicize civilians and recruit new fighters through its own networks of partisan supporters. One ZAPU ex-combatant recalled that his first encounter with rebels was in 1974, when rebel soldiers approached him to ask for food. He later learned that these guerrillas were ZANLA soldiers: "ZIPRA guerrillas would not be known to the civilians, except to a few who were close to them" (Magwizi, 2014). Some ZAPU ex-combatant interviews described being recruited through their local chiefs, who had supported recruitment efforts by sending young men to the ZAPU guerrillas (Moyo, 2011). Another ex-combatant explained:

> There were a lot of political activities taking place, taking into account also that there were a number also of senior ZAPU leaders. Also even those from town they would always come home to, say, to conscientise the people about the ZAPU thing, meant to liberate the people.... Actually one of my uncles was an active member of ZAPU so he was also involved in recruiting. He was not only involved in recruiting from outside; but even from within his home . . . so as such we were also recruited accordingly (Nare, 2011).

Rebel–civilian relations cultivated for the purpose of information gathering were structured differently than those seeking food and materials. For information and reconnaissance, ZAPU used its own version of the mujiba network throughout the territory under its control (Dube, 2011). ZAPU collaborators were deeply involved with the group and were able to spread information through their networks across large distances, while ZANLA's network consisted of mass-based groups of war collaborators who were in charge of only their own zones (Ex-combatants 1 and 4, 2017). There were far fewer ZAPU collaborators, and they were less embedded in local affairs than those who operated on behalf of ZANU. They were, however, more loyal to ZAPU: while ZANU collaborators deserted or misbehaved when military contestation increased, ZAPU collaborators were better able to maintain secrecy if captured by the opposition (Ex-combatants 1 and 4, 2017). While collaborators were involved in feeding the guerrillas, ZAPU combatants collected food in a more clandestine fashion as well. ZAPU did not create civilian teams or village committees during the war; it leveraged its network of underground party cells to collect necessary items from civilians.

Because ZAPU was older and had its roots in the NDP—a party that initially operated in Zimbabwe legally—it had more time to build a robust underground civilian party structure throughout the country (MT, A4.3.2, n.d.). Yet, when ZANLA rebels took control of areas that previously supported ZAPU, ZAPU's underground party cells collapsed due to a lack of contact with the main party during the civil war (Ex-combatants 1 and 4, 2017). This allowed ZANU to easily establish social control over civilians by coopting old ZAPU structures (Sibanda, 2005, 164). In Chief Mangwende's area in Mashonaland East, for example, ZANU soldiers had gained social control by 1976 even though the area had been a ZAPU stronghold since the 1960s (St. Paul's Mission, n.d.). Thus, particularly in the eastern half of Zimbabwe, because of their war collaborators' intimate knowledge of rural areas, ZANLA enjoyed an informational advantage over ZAPU and the Rhodesian army throughout the civil war. ZANLA's pungwe rallies politicized civilians and increased the group's popularity and support over ZIPRA.[9] ZIPRA soldiers tended to view pungwes with disdain. For example, a ZIPRA ex-combatant who observed this experience from afar described:

> To be honest with every truth, do you think a fighting group of people would collect, would collect hundreds and hundreds of villagers and take them onto a mountain top ... and sing there the whole night[? And] they are fighters, they are fighting, and people hear them. "What noise is that? Oh ZANLA ZANU people" (Nkiwane, 2010).

By the end of the war, ZANU had a decentralized structure of civilians who maintained ties with the party's ex-combatants and political commissars, while ZAPU had succeeded in party building at the local level. Both approaches proved to be useful, as they allowed the rebel parties to remain locally embedded in their strongholds in different ways.

---

[9] Paradoxically, ZAPU's initial strength and ability to build a broad underground network meant that it had not needed to utilize mass mobilization to recruit and politicize its members.

4.3.3 Rhodesian counterinsurgency

I highlight two Rhodesian counterinsurgency tactics designed to sever ties between the rebels and civilians. First, in areas with frequent ZANLA operations, the Rhodesian government forced mass displacement by sending entire villages into PVs, which were designed to be new dense settlements within various chieftaincies.[10] The use of PVs as a counterinsurgency strategy began in 1974 with Operation Overload in Chiweshe Tribal Trust Land, in the northeastern Mashonaland Central province. Rebels had been operating in the region for some time, and the Rhodesian government had failed to prevent civilians from engaging with them. Communication from the Rhodesian government indicates that this strategy was explicitly implemented to prevent civilians from aiding rebels in the war:

> For a long time you have continued to feed, shelter, and assist the communist terrorists to carry out their evil deeds. You have disregarded previous Government warnings of the bitter times that will fall upon your land if you allow these communist terrorists to carry on deceiving you ... Only if you cooperate and assist the Security Forces to eliminating the communist terrorists will any consideration be given to lifting some or all of the above restrictions (Catholic Commission for Justice and Peace, 1978).

The Rhodesian government established PVs primarily along the eastern border, where ZANU/ZANLA was particularly active, starting in 1974. By 1997 there were over two hundred, housing more than half a million people— one-twelfth of the Black Zimbabwean population.

In a second tactic, the Rhodesian government used propaganda and disinformation to confuse civilians. Early in the war, it distributed propaganda pamphlets in rural ZANU/ZANLA strongholds—called, for instance, *Anatomy of Terror* (Government of Rhodesia, 1978a) and *Harvest of Fear* (Government of Rhodesia, 1978b)—in an attempt to highlight rebel violence. This tactic failed to achieve the desired results. The government also used Selous Scouts—Rhodesian agents pretending to be rebel fighters. These agents used violence to confuse and anger civilians to increase mistrust between civilian communities and the rebels. As I explain in what follows, these agents were more successful at confusing civilians in areas with low levels of rebel–civilian engagement and greater civilian mistrust.

---

[10] They were close enough to citizens' original homes that they could (and were encouraged to) walk during the day to tend to their crops.

4.3.4 Coercive and unstable rebel–civilian relations under military contestation

ZANU strongholds experienced greater organization and participation: mujibas were described as being generally well behaved and disciplined in their actions (St. Paul's Mission, n.d.), while spirit mediums and members of the village committees considered the ZANLA rebels their "children" and continued to support their activities with food and materiel despite Rhodesian counter-insurgency tactics. PVs set up to destroy rebel–civilian ties proved to be generally unsuccessful. Reflecting ZANLA's degree of local social control, civilians continued to support operations covertly despite threats to their personal security, and frequently helped rebels enter the PVs undetected. ZANLA developed strategies to help civilians escape Rhodesian soldiers' brutality:

> The comrades had taught us various tactics to survive Rhodesian attacks and intimidation . . . We [were] taught what to do when we were caught by the Rhodesian soldiers . . . In the event of intimidation by Rhodesian soldiers, the guerrilla told us that we should only show them footprints but never tell them information that would compromise their security. We did as they taught us (Magaya, 2014).

In ZANU strongholds, where rebel presence and influence were high, civilians reportedly found pungwes more enjoyable. It is important to note, however, that civilians in these areas did sometimes experience guerrilla violence and coercion; participation was not always voluntary. For civilians who chose to remain in frequent operational zones rather than flee into town, it was often in their best interest to cooperate and legitimate ZANLA control (Kriger, 1991): "We would also go to the pungwes with the guerrillas. Everyone was happy. Those who did not like it ran away to the city" (Masuku, 2014). In some cases, pungwes were even viewed as a way for lower-class citizens in rural areas to reassert control and power over those who benefited from the colonial state (Ranger, 1985). Overall, in these strongholds, ZANU/ZANLA fundamentally altered local administration during the war.

Rebel–civilian ties were less organized and structured in areas where ZANU/ZANLA found it difficult to penetrate. Low levels of penetration or military contestation for control also meant that village committees and other grassroots political structures were either sparse or not created at all (Cliffe, Mpofu, and Munslow, 1980). Citizens were suspicious of the rebels' presence: they often confused ZANU/ZANLA troops with ZAPU/ZIPRA soldiers or the Rhodesian Selous Scouts. One collaborator described how difficult it was to make initial contact with contested areas: "Villagers had thought that they were part of the [Selous Scouts] who were fighting against the guerillas and the mission of ZANU the party" (Murambiwa, 2014). This lack of trust resulted in setbacks: "villagers in Jeke area did not give full support to the guerillas and when the attack took place at our base, the guerillas had to fight off the Rhodesian soldiers in the presence of the local villagers ... we lost one Freedom Fighter that day" (Murambiwa, 2014).

In addition to the lack of local grassroots structures, in these regions mujibas were less disciplined, more coercive, and took on more militaristic duties—primarily as the war intensified in the latter half of the 1970s. When ZANLA spread from the eastern areas of the country and penetrated westward, it clashed not only with ZIPRA troops but also Rhodesian auxiliary forces. In the late 1970s, some mujibas and chimbwidos—particularly those who lived and operated in areas that experienced higher levels of conflict—acted as auxiliary fighters for ZANU. In Chikomba district, which experienced intense fighting in 1978 due to its proximity to Harare, collaborators reported being tasked with moving weapons between rebel bases and cleaning military equipment prior to rebel operations (Magaya, 2014). One collaborator recalled carrying and hiding weapons (Murambiwa, 2014), while others were given instructions on how to operate weapons and use landmines on behalf of ZANLA (Mutsinze, 2014).

In these areas with low levels of ZANU social control, rebel politicization also took on coercive and predatory functions. Pungwes were forced upon unwilling civilians in contested areas. Particularly in the last few years of the war when the conflict intensified near the battlefronts, the heightened military insecurity and the decreased likelihood of repeated interactions between rebels and the community meant the rebels were more likely to punish civilians with impunity and less likely to exercise restraint or establish rules of appropriate behavior among their own supporters. The mujibas became less disciplined and more coercive toward civilians, sometimes using their power to exact revenge against local enemies.

Thus, pungwes frequently featured violence against civilians in the community: The number of "sellout" accusations increased, as did the severity of punishments meted out by the ZANLA rebels; more individuals were shot or burned alive in front of the entire community (Mutsinze, 2014; Kwenda, 2014). Civilians in contested areas were forced not just to sing songs of resistance and nationalism, as those in strongholds were asked to do—they were also made to pledge allegiance solely to ZANU, to denounce ZAPU and its leader Nkomo, and to renounce their political and tribal identities (Cliffe, Mpofu, and Munslow, 1980). Such denouncements bred resentment among civilians in contested regions that had been early and staunch supporters of ZAPU. While civilians living in such areas often supported the overarching liberation cause, they feared rather than supported the disorderly and coercive ZANLA rebel troops.

4.4 Spatial representation of rebel social control

To understand how rebel control and contestation affected postwar politics, I code subnational variation in rebel strongholds and unsecured terrain according to the strength of their rebel–civilian ties and degree of military contestation. Since the Zimbabwean Liberation War took place several decades ago, there is no systematic dataset of conflict events. I thus rely on the qualitative data I collected during my fieldwork—colonial maps, memoirs and diary entries, death records, and Rhodesian counterterrorism strategy decisions. I also use anthropological and historical studies in different areas of the country to obtain a fuller view of events on the ground. In keeping with the typology of terrain types presented in Chapter 2, I examine each *district* in rural Zimbabwe to code their ZANLA or ZIPRA presence and the rebels' degree of influence over the district. I restrict the sample to rural districts to increase comparability, since rebel–civilian relations and postwar rebellion were a rural phenomenon in Zimbabwe: Rebel politicization largely took place in communal lands, where most rural Black Zimbabweans lived during the colonial period.

4.4.1 Coding procedure

My coding procedure entailed examining how the rebel presence in various districts corresponds to rebel groups' degree of influence and overall organizational capacity. In Chapter 2, I proposed a typology that identified four types of territories based on rebel presence and influence—strongholds, partisan areas, contested terrain, and rival strongholds; partisan and contested areas both have low organizational capacity. My theory distinguishes between partisan and contested areas: The former has greater influence but little presence, while the latter has greater presence from multiple groups and thus little overall influence from any particular group. This distinction is important because, in some cases (as I will show in Chapter 5 in Liberia), prewar identity-based support could lead to greater influence regardless of rebels' presence. In those cases, partisan and contested areas must be coded

104 Governing after War

in different ways due to underlying ethnic support (i.e., rebel group *influence*) for different armed groups regardless of whether any armed group is present in the area.

However, in Zimbabwe I only identify ZANU/ZANLA strongholds, ZAPU/ZIPRA strongholds (rival strongholds), and contested terrain because ethnic support and wartime military activity in the country overlapped almost entirely. As I argued qualitatively, ZANU's and ZAPU's roots in the liberation struggle meant that an individual's pre-war intrinsic predisposition to support one group (high *influence*) over the other *without* contact with that group (low *presence*) was unlikely without wartime politicization.[11] Areas that had an equally low *presence* of both armed groups, and thus would not have formed ties with one over the other, would have been relatively equal in their support for both independence movements. Yet areas with a high presence of one group would have been more likely to be influenced by that group. In sum, the relative neutrality of less-affected regions implies three types of territories: two high-organizational-capacity areas—*ZANU strongholds* and *ZAPU strongholds*—and one low-organizational-capacity category that is *unsecured* by either group.

I code these three territories as follows. I first code the intensity of a district's rebel operational *presence* from 0 (little or no rebel operations in the area) to 1 (frequent and intense rebel operations) in increments of 0.25. I then measure relative sociopolitical influence as the difference between the operational intensity of the two rebel groups. In Zimbabwe, the influence of either group in a territory primarily depended on whether the group was able to form party structures there. Rebel influence thus ranges from -1 (civilians were only subject to ZIPRA politicization) to 1 (complete ZANLA politicization).

Second, I code relative parity in operations between the two rebel groups, from 0 to 1 in increments of 0.25, to indicate *unsecured* civilian support. This variable is coded 0 if an area was only exposed to one rebel group (or zero groups), 0.25 if the absolute value of operational presence is 0.75 (i.e., one side had an operational presence value of 1 while the other was coded 0.25), 0.5 if the absolute value of influence is 0.5, and 0.75 if the absolute value of influence is 0.25. *Unsecured* is coded 1 if rebel operational intensities were fairly equal, leading to little or no differential influence; this gave the new government strong incentives not to "give up ground" to the opposition after the war in these areas.

---

[11] This was made clear by eastern Zimbabwe's initial support of ZAPU early in the war, before ZANU's wartime activity swept away ZAPU party cells.

The Zimbabwe Liberation War (1972–1979)   **105**

Finally, I code rebel control, which measures the intensity of rebel operations (Figure 4.2). *ZANU stronghold* (*ZAPU stronghold*) indicates that contestation is 0—meaning that ZAPU (ZANU) had no influence. In both cases, the resulting rebel stronghold coding ranges from 0 to 1 in increments of 0.25; contested areas are not considered a stronghold territory of either side.

4.4.2 Comparability between districts

Coding different districts using different district-specific data sources introduces a potential issue—that narratives and descriptions across districts are difficult to compare due to variations in data availability and reporting. To minimize this potential bias, I used four sources to code rebel operational intensity *across* districts. This data increased the comparability of rebel presence across districts.

First, the most systematic archival data available to identify rebel politicization is the location of PVs—the counterinsurgency tool used in areas where rebels were populous and rebel–civilian ties proved difficult for the colonial government to sever. I use the location of PVs to indicate a high level of rebel presence. Because these were only created in areas under ZANLA control, I geocode this data to evaluate the intensity of support for ZANU and the influence of its ideology across the country.[12]

Second, I used the official ZANU/ZANLA death records from *The Fallen Heroes of Zimbabwe*, published in 1983 by the Zimbabwean government. This book includes the names (and *noms de guerre*, where different) and general operational zones of the deceased. I use incomplete details about the location—for example, the district, chiefdom, or communal area—and method of death to code ZANLA operational intensity. While ZAPU/ZIPRA also recorded some deaths in documents at the MT archives, this data is particularly incomplete.

Third, I use chieftaincy records that are housed at the NAZ. The history of chief turnover, along with their demographic information and reasons for leaving their position, provided insights into various districts' degree of rebel presence and influence. Since chiefs were often considered colonial subjects,

---

[12] It is important to note that PVs were not *only* implemented in areas with a high level of civilian support for the rebels; they were also created for strategic reasons. However, PVs cannot be used as the only indicator of rebel–civilian ties; rebel–civilian relations were fairly strong in ZAPU-supporting western regions, but these did not feature PVs. Yet where rebel activity and civilian support were low, PVs would not have been built. In short, rebel control over civilian support is a necessary but insufficient condition for the establishment of PVs.

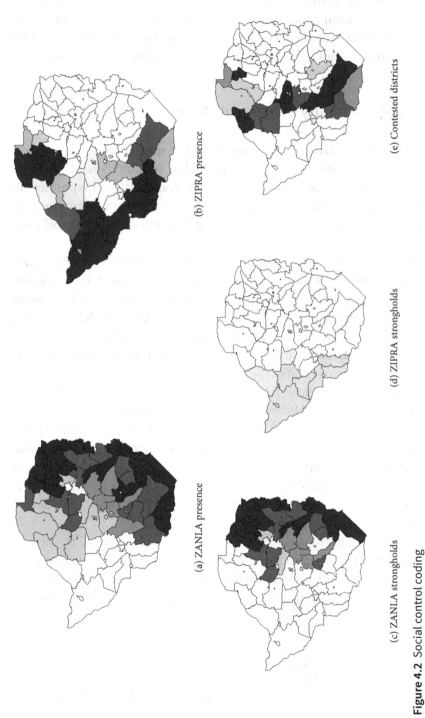

Figure 4.2 Social control coding

Note: The darker the area, the greater the degree of presence in (a) and (b); the greater the control in (c) and (d); and the greater the parity in influence in (e).

The Zimbabwe Liberation War (1972–1979)   107

the frequency with which they left their posts during the Liberation War—both voluntarily and involuntarily—provides a rough but useful measure of instability within various chieftaincies. This data, when combined with historical reports and information from memoirs about whether various chiefs covertly supported the rebellions (and thus would have been less likely to be killed) and the extent to which rebels collaborated with other traditional leaders in the chieftaincy, greatly strengthened the coding for rebel presence.

Finally, I cross-checked my coding of ZANU and ZAPU control and contestation using secondary sources from national-level reports about conflict intensity and from academics who conducted extensive fieldwork in different parts of Zimbabwe in the immediate postwar period. These sources helped confirm that the final dataset matches published accounts of rural rebel–civilian relations. Next, I present a motivating example in the Mount Darwin district, and include additional narrative examples of coding decisions in Appendix B2.

4.4.3 A motivating example: Mount Darwin district as a ZANU stronghold

Mount Darwin district, on the border of northeastern Zimbabwe and Mozambique (Figure 4.3), was one of the first ZANU strongholds. In two early Rhodesian propaganda publications (Government of Rhodesia, 1978a,b), the Rhodesian government described numerous encounters with ZANLA, suggesting a strong rebel presence from 1973 onward. There was little or no ZIPRA presence. Historical accounts suggest ZANLA exercised strong influence over civilian affairs.

Two Catholic missions served Mount Darwin district—the Marymount Mission located within the district, and the St. Albert's Mission located in the adjacent Centenary district. Both were hotbeds of ZANLA activity

Figure 4.3 Mount Darwin district

throughout the conflict. From 1973 onward, rebels maintained a base near St. Albert's Mission and routinely had contact with civilians at night while looting empty farm stores for supplies (Von Walter, n.d.). A written account from Marymount Mission illustrates the missionaries' familiarity and cooperation with rebels and their youth collaborators, the mujibas. During one interaction, mujibas questioned the missionaries about the location of Rhodesian forces, but the missionaries were not worried because "we were used to such questions" (Dakudzwa, 1979, 1). The missionaries also reported that Marymount Mission had a good relationship with ZANLA soldiers during the war (Dakudzwa, 1979, 9).

According to an independent report released by the Catholic Commission for Justice and Peace in Rhodesia (CCJP), civilians in Mount Darwin aided the ZANLA rebels (Catholic Commission for Justice and Peace, 1976); investigators who provided information for the CCJP report also noted various rebel checkpoints in or near the district (Central Africa Investigation Service Bottriell's, 1975). A clear indicator that rebels established social control over civilians was the existence of PVs, the counterinsurgency tactic designed to prevent civilians from maintaining contact with rebels. Based on data gathered from the NAZ's collection of Rhodesian files, 63 PVs were established in Mount Darwin, out of a total of 231 set up during the conflict throughout the country (Ministry of Internal Affairs, n.d.). Of these, forty were created in 1975: It was the fourth district to be subjected to the program. An additional twenty-three were set up in 1978 to counteract spreading support for the rebels.

Finally, all three chiefdoms in Mount Darwin that had consistent leadership throughout the war (two more were promoted to chieftaincy during the conflict) experienced a far higher rate of chief turnover during the war than other areas (Government of Rhodesia, 1985). One chiefdom had two turnovers (a total of three chiefs held the position due to one death and one abduction); the other two experienced one turnover each due to death. While the chiefs' causes of death were not recorded, and so natural causes cannot be ruled out, rebels were known to kill chiefs (who they considered Rhodesian administrators) and appoint new leaders. Prior to the war, chiefs in Mount Darwin had an average tenure of around eleven years; during the war they only lasted around five years. Thus, it is likely that turnovers were war related.

4.5 postwar organization and stability

Zimbabwe's postwar government under ZANU-PF prioritized stability and technocracy; its overarching goal was to develop the country while maintaining power. I first explain the new government's overall approach to sustaining power and maintaining good governance. I then investigate the subnational differences in governing decisions between strongholds, contested districts, and opposition areas to explain how wartime organizational capacity on behalf of ZANU or ZAPU affected how the new government perceived security threats and the need to consolidate state power.

4.5.1 Continuing control through wartime ties (Sub-national Hypothesis 1)

Electioneering for political victory

Between the December 1979 ceasefire and the February 1980 elections, rebels remained in contact with collaborators and village committees and continued to draw on them for assistance and political support. ZANLA exploited its relationships with the youth collaborators during this demobilization and campaigning period; under the peace agreement and ceasefire process, ex-combatants were expected to assemble in specific areas to prevent electoral violence. As a ZIPRA ex-combatant noted, while ZAPU soldiers assembled in the west, ZANU camps were filled with wartime collaborators who posed as ZANLA ex-combatants—rather than the ZANLA soldiers themselves (Ndlovu, 2010). Official estimates suggest that at least a quarter of the ZANLA soldiers did not comply with the ceasefire terms (Catholic Institute for International Relations, 1980), and allegedly remained "in their operational areas, where they worked with their war-time youth collaborators to maintain the party's military and political dominance" (Kriger, 2005, 4). Similarly, the pungwes continued to bolster rebel–civilian ties. One ZIPRA ex-combatant complained about the unfair playing field they faced during the first post-independence campaign period:

> ZANU, ZANU from word go they had seven thousand commissars, trained commissars who were being infiltrated into the country. Even toward the elections seven thousand were outside and doing the party work. There the pungwes . . . on the hills and the mountain tops throughout the nights were being done by the trained commissars (Nkiwane, 2010).

Youth collaborators who remained in the local communities continued to act as intermediaries and spokespersons for the guerrillas during this period. According to ZAPU interviews, ZANLA fighters and youths further prevented ZAPU from campaigning in ZANU strongholds (Dabengwa, 2011; Ndlovu, 2010), thereby limiting potential ZAPU influence in the eastern half

Table 4.1 Votes for main parties

	Controlled by	ZANU-PF	ZAPU-PF
Manicaland	ZANLA	84.1%	1.6%
Mashonaland Central	ZANLA	83.8%	2.3%
Mashonaland East	ZANLA	80.5%	4.6%
Mashonaland West	Contested	71.9%	13.4%
Matabeleland North	ZIPRA	10.0%	79.0%
Matabeleland South	ZIPRA	6.7%	86.4%
Midlands	Contested	59.7%	27.1%
Masvingo	ZANLA	87.3%	1.9%

of Zimbabwe. ZANU-PF set up local party offices to facilitate campaigning outside its wartime stronghold areas, but had "very little infrastructure" and "existed much more as formal party machines geared to the election, than the para-guerrilla bodies" (Cliffe, Mpofu, and Munslow, 1980, 60). In these areas, they were less successful electorally.

The 1980 election results displayed in Table 4.1 illustrate that votes broadly fell along ethnic lines: The eastern provinces are predominantly Shona, while the Matabeleland provinces are predominantly Ndebele. However, each rebel group's wartime presence also influenced the election outcome. The rows highlighted above—Mashonaland West and Midlands province—represent areas that had a strong presence from both groups during the war. Mashonaland West, along with Mashonaland Central and Mashonaland East, have high concentrations of Shona-speaking civilians, but ZAPU received a substantially higher vote share in the former than in the two latter provinces, where ZANU's organizational capacity was especially high. Similarly, Midlands province was a highly contested district where ZANU received only 59% of the vote and ZAPU 27% despite having a larger Shona majority (Rich, 1982). Finally, ZAPU's local ties to civilians played a role in the Matabeleland provinces as well. ZANU's candidate in Matabeleland South for the election was a high-level Ndebele commanding officer, Enos Nkala. Despite having ethnic ties to the region, Nkala won only 11% of the vote; his opponent was a ZAPU party leader.

Delegating local governance
After coming to power, ZANU-PF initially continued to leverage village committees to minimize the need for immediate state resources. The new government's initial successes in rebuilding the country can partially be attributed to active civilian communities that engaged in volunteerism ("self-help") to coproduce local development (Ex-combatant 4, 2017). Civilian input

The Zimbabwe Liberation War (1972–1979)   **111**

into government initiatives began soon after independence, particularly in areas that retained strong ties with ZANLA. Immediately after the war, the government identified local needs by relying on "[village committees] developed during the liberation war in the communal areas" (Lenneiye, 2000, 24). Village committees were instrumental in collecting and disbursing necessary aid to local communities (Kriger, 1991, 215). ZANU-PF ties with youth gave the younger generation a greater say over postwar development and politics, including through the government's Youth People's Service—district-level youth brigades created to implement development projects (Silveira House, 1982). The Jesuits supported the brigades by providing additional leadership training to help expedite development projects.

The new rebel government did not reward its wartime constituencies by preferentially targeting them with state resources after the war. Its backers noted—and resented—the lack of "payback" for their support. As one ex-collaborator complained: "It seems we have been forgotten if not neglected by our leaders . . . we appear as mere people, yet we played a crucial role to help the guerrillas during the liberation struggle" (Masuku, 2014). A traditional leader whose community had aided ZANLA soldiers during the war lamented the lack of postwar development assistance: "Some communities were destroyed . . . property and houses were destroyed by the Rhodesian soldiers, yet there is nothing that the government is doing to help such people" (Kwenda, 2014). Instead of engaging in community-level development, the new government rewarded ex-combatants and important supporters through a "biased" land reform program (Magaya, 2014). Such ad hoc compensation was only given to those who were "privileged to have been close to the ex-combatants" (Taruvinga, 2014).

To implement large-scale development projects in its wartime strongholds, ZANU-PF used its local party organization to provide local public goods to help offset expenses. For example, it used this approach to implement its broadly successful education reform in 1980. Immediately after the elections, ZANU-PF announced that education would be available for all children in the country (previously, only White children were eligible to attend secondary school) and began constructing schools to accommodate the increased demand for education. The new mandate largely succeeded in opening up education to Black Zimbabweans, as the number of primary schools increased from 2,401 to 4,504 and secondary schools from 177 to 1,502 within the first decade of independence (Kanyongo, 2005; Croke et al., 2016, 69). The number of school attendees increased from 890,000 to "well over 2 million" within the first 2 years (Zimbabwe Catholic Bishop's Conference, 1982). Organized community cooperation was needed to mitigate resource

112 Governing after War

constraints; a Ministry of Education Report from 1983 noted, "The increasing demand...has resulted in parents undertaking more self-help projects to provide classrooms" (Ministry of Education, 1983, 22). The government encouraged volunteer efforts, including community fundraising and help building schools using government-purchased materials (Ex-bureaucrat, 2017; Zimbabwe Catholic Bishop's Conference, 1982).

The capacity to mobilize civilians helped reduce budgetary pressures on the state in ZANU's wartime strongholds. Beyond village committee-led local reconstruction, there is evidence that ties between ex-combatants and civilians helped increase volunteerism with respect to the education reforms. In some cases, ex-combatants returned to the communities in which they had operated during the conflict to inspire local volunteerism and held friendly competitions between civilians and ex-combatants for fundraising and school construction. According to an ex-ZANLA combatant:

> When the government began to develop, began to build the schools, there was not enough budget...The news reached the war veterans who said "no problem! Let the government pay teachers with the budget. We will organize the parents to build the schools"...Remember when I told you of the organization [during the war]? (Ex-combatant 4, 2017).

The local party organizations also helped the ruling party maintain control and ensure loyalty. Where ZANLA organized wartime village committees, the government used them after the war to identify potential dissidents. The committees monitored new visitors and punished individuals who violated "party rules" (Kriger, 1991, 215). Thus, village committees continued to play an important role in the new rebel government's party hierarchy: They "conveyed information to the provincial and central party and received information from above" (Kriger, 1991, 218). The committees directed citizens to obey the ZANU-PF party authorities rather than the Rhodesian-era bureaucrats who were still in power at the time (Ranger, 1985, 292–293). In this way, they bolstered ZANU-PF's reach into rural areas by being its eyes and ears on the ground.

4.5.2 Expanding wartime institutions to establish control (Sub-national Hypothesis 2)

By 1984, ZANU-PF had more systematically implemented a hierarchical state developmental bureaucracy that mirrored its wartime village committee

The Zimbabwe Liberation War (1972–1979)   **113**

structure.[13] This bureaucracy contained multiple key actors: (a) village development committees (VIDCOs) and ward development committees (WADCOs), which oversaw several VIDCOs in the area; (b) local government promotional officers (LGPOs); and (c) district administrators.[14] VIDCOs and WADCOs comprised locally elected community members, while LGPOs and district administrators were government bureaucrats tasked with implementing ZANU-PF policy decisions. District administrators were well-educated wartime supporters who oversaw district-level development after the war.[15] LPGOs were often less educated and were therefore not eligible for higher positions such as district administrator. However, most were party political commissars during the war—in charge of conducting pungwes in villages—who would have maintained close relationships to the communities in which they operated (Ex-bureaucrat, 2017).

VIDCOs and WADCOs were created to decentralize development and to allow villages to democratically make decisions about local developmental needs. In practice, however, they enabled top-down state control over development affairs. They were modeled after the ZANU/ZANLA wartime village committees to ensure "continuity in the way war party cells were organized" (Ex-bureaucrat, 2017). LGPOs were responsible for setting up one VIDCO for every few villages; villages directly elected their representatives to the VIDCOs, which would then report village-level development needs to the ward-level WADCOs, which comprised members elected by VIDCO members. WADCOs then aggregated these reports and sent them to the district administrator. The district administrator, receiving these reports from several WADCOs, would then allocated development funds to local projects.

This developmental hierarchy was implemented throughout the country. However, because VIDCOs and WADCOs comprised local community members, state control was exercised differently in different areas. In ZANU-PF strongholds, village committees—for example (wartime party cells) were already well-established. In these areas, party cell members, particularly youth and women leaders, assumed positions in new VIDCOs and WADCOs and carried out the party's work on the ground (Lenneiye, 2000; Makumbe, 1996; Kwangwari, 2009). These leaders were critical to helping the ruling party sustain its local information channels (Kriger, 1991; Makumbe,

---

[13] Since the government had piloted several forms of grassroots-based development structures, including a variety of local committees, village community workers, and village health workers (Sadomba, 2011), a prime minister's directive formally established this hierarchical structure in 1984 to unify development.

[14] The district level was the most important politically, but provincial committees (above the district level) were also established.

[15] While both LPGOs and district administrators were technocratic and development focused, party considerations eventually overshadowed these goals.

114 Governing after War

1996). To minimize civilian demands for government services, they did not encourage peasant politicization. They instead promoted loyalty to party goals, helping the government sustain support by ensuring the continuation of successful party cells and curbing civilian voices that threatened state support.[16] Reflecting similarities to wartime social control, civilians resented empty development promises but "had learned the dangers of challenging guerrilla commands" during war and thus recognized that they "had to take orders... from ZANU-PF's top officials so that they would not invite punishments" (Kriger, 1991, 230).

Where wartime party ties were weaker or nonexistent for example outside of ZANU-PF's strongholds—community-elected VIDCO and WADCO leaders were less likely to be pro-ZANU-PF and therefore would have been less amenable to state control. For example, Alexander (1994, 327) notes that centralized development was necessary because village-level ZANU and ZAPU party committees "acted with an autonomy from the ZANU(PF) leadership... and, notably in Matabeleland and parts of Midlands and Mashonaland West, they were not loyal to ZANU(PF)." In these unsecured areas (Midlands and Mashonaland West) and rival strongholds (Matabeleland), party committees would have been far less open to state control. Similarly, civilians would not have been socialized to obey guerrillas under the threat of violence during the war, and would thus be more willing to voice discontent.

To prevent political heterogeneity at the local level, ZANU-PF's deployed bureaucrats—pro-government district administrators and LGPOs—played a significant role in establishing control by leveraging development funding from the top down. While establishing VIDCOs, GP [LGPOs] "had to carry out political re-orientation for the members of these committees; and one of the key attributes of being a member was loyalty to the state and the party" (Mabhena, 2014, 145). Further, VIDCOs and WADCOs were unable to empower citizen input because they did not control any development funding; rather, all money was funneled through the district administrator. Development schemes and funding were contingent on having a pro-government stance; thus development was distributed using a carrot-and-stick approach. Local development became "an appendage of central government, severely marginalized, under-resourced and dependent on central government for both their funding and staffing" (Murithi and Mawadza, 2011, 10).

In *unsecured areas*, the new rebel government felt that there was a political opening to cultivate loyalty by establishing bureaucratic control. There, it

---

[16] There is evidence that these development committees inspired self-help in some cases. For example, Saruchera and Matsungo (2003, 27) found that rural citizens in Wedza district—under ZANLA's social control during the war—considered these development councils a way to "channel their participation" as they believed they were "effective ways of strengthening their representation."

The Zimbabwe Liberation War (1972–1979) **115**

attempted to "firm up control for the emerging state" by advocating "development functions, drought relief, participating in vaccination campaigns, etc." (Expert, 2017). Particularly with respect to funding for programs such as drought relief, VIDCOs had little choice but to comply with LGPO politicization and party loyalty (Mabhena, 2014, 145). This strategy helped ZANU-PF establish control: Within even local government, "Loyalty ran very deep. In the rest of the country outside of [rival strongholds], loyalty to ZANU-PF was a given" (Ex-bureaucrat, 2017). Local leaders and civilians, despite having previously been sympathetic to ZAPU and ZIPRA, now declined to help ex-ZIPRA dissidents (Alexander, McGregor, and Ranger, 2000).

For example, Gokwe district—an unsecured area that was sympathetic to ZAPU during the war and was the first to establish VIDCOs and WADCOs in 1981 (Sadomba, 2011, 87)—became a "no-go zone" for ex-ZIPRA dissidents. In 1984, the local government announced that it was 100% pro-ZANU-PF and citizens began reporting dissidents to the authorities (Alexander, 1998, 170). Grant budgets indicate that pro-government sentiments were well rewarded. Gokwe's grant budget from the central government increased almost tenfold, from $Z582,397 in 1983 to $Z5,546,059 in 1984. Grant figures remained high at over 5 million for two years before being reduced to $Z1,495,49 in 1986 and $Z454,902 in 1987 (Mutizwa-Mangiza, 1992). Though these fluctuations in grant money reflect changes in government policy,[17] the sharp increase and subsequent decline in funding align with the Gokwe district council's pro-ZANU-PF position in 1984, the near elimination of the dissident threat in 1986, and the Unity Accords peace agreement signed in 1987.

The expansion of wartime institutions through this hierarchical development structure was far less successful in ZAPU strongholds than in unsecured territories because ZAPU had strong ties to civilians and maintained its own party cells in its strongholds. After the elections, citizens in the Matabeleland provinces initially "seemed to be waiting for 'permission'" from ZAPU to cooperate with the new government because they were afraid of being accused of selling out to ZANU-PF (Alexander, McGregor, and Ranger, 2000, 207). Civilians also rejected ZANU-PF bureaucrats: They only began to participate, albeit reluctantly, when veteran ZAPU leaders took control of local councils. Citizens continued to elect ZAPU leaders to local government positions throughout the first decade of independence (Ex-bureaucrat, 2017); ZANU-PF officers were sidelined. In contrast to the voluntary school-building efforts in ZANU-PF strongholds, citizens in pro-ZAPU areas

---

[17] In 1986 the government centralized teacher salaries, and in 1987 there was an overall reduction in development grants to district councils (Mutizwa-Mangiza, 1992).

refused to participate in rebuilding or raising money for government schools (Alexander, McGregor, and Ranger, 2000, 208). Development in the Matabeleland provinces suffered further after the hierarchical development structure was formalized: "VIDCO members were targets of dissidents who regarded them as sell outs, while on the other hand the state would only channel development aid through these institutions" (Mabhena, 2014, 145).

It quickly became clear that ZANU-PF was unable to control civilians through its institutions: ZAPU endorsement was necessary to legitimize local government, and "the charisma and authority of ZAPU leaders were crucial in overcoming [citizen] suspicions" (Alexander, McGregor, and Ranger, 2000, 208). Thus, while the new rebel government pursued nominal development projects in opposition areas during this period, they were underfunded and of low quality—especially because, as I show in the next section, the government used violence rather than development to coerce control. For example, Alexander, McGregor, and Ranger (2000, 248) found in Shangani district of Matabeleland North that security forces routinely harassed nurses, and rural health centers "were regularly closed or inaccessible." An ex-ZAPU combatant and politician complained that the opposition-supported Matabeleland region was not being developed as much as other parts of the country in the 1980s, and that the government was using dissidents as an excuse to refuse development and reconstruction in these provinces:

[The] government took the attitude that, if this is what you are doing in Matabeleland, then Matabeleland will not be developed, there will be no development in Matabeleland . . . and they found an excuse, because of the security situation . . . they made sure that they stopped developing Matabeleland under that excuse (Dabengwa, 2011).

Indeed, in the immediate postwar period, "the ZAPU challenge was just in [ZANU-PF's] face," and was therefore excluded from the "inclusive national project of development" that was being implemented elsewhere (Ex-bureaucrat, 2017). Development in these opposition areas only began in earnest after 1987, when ZANU-PF had centralized control.

4.5.3 Violence to coerce control (Sub-national Hypothesis 3)

As described earlier, due to relatively high levels of civilian support for ZAPU in rival strongholds, the new rebel government was not able to consolidate its control by deploying loyal bureaucrats to these areas. But ZANU-PF also faced an additional hurdle in its attempts to gain control over rival strongholds: Ex-combatants initially refused to disarm (Dabengwa, 2011). As in many postwar states, ex-rebels in Zimbabwe feared they would be marginalized if they disarmed (Walter, 1997). ZIPRA training camps outside the country were not demobilized (Nare, 2011). Armed ZIPRA ex-combatants were thus able to station themselves both inside and outside the country, and even recruited additional members in late 1980 "as a reserve against a rainy day" because "full-scale war seemed imminent" (Kriger, 2003, 116–117). Some ex-ZIPRA commanders declined to be integrated into the new national army and instead posted themselves in the capital and in ZAPU strongholds such as Bulawayo and the Gwaai River Mine in anticipation of renewed violence. The ZIPRA Revolutionary Council was "hoping for the war to continue" because it "believed that [ZIPRA] would win and ZAPU would win [militarily] because [it] had lost elections" (Ngwenya, 2010). The situation further deteriorated beginning in 1982 when ex-ZIPRA soldiers deserted the army and fled to the Matabeleland provinces, where they mounted a low-scale insurgency as ex-ZAPU dissidents. While they were in the bush, the dissidents reorganized themselves based on ZIPRA structures and attempted to recruit other ex-ZIPRA members and to recruit and incite support from local civilians (Alexander, 1998).

While the ex-ZAPU insurgency in the Matabeleland provinces was perhaps the most pressing military threat to the ruling party, ZANU-PF was also forced to contend with threats from South Africa's apartheid regime. As part of South Africa's strategy to destabilize post-independence regimes in the region, it had funded dissidents (Super-ZAPU) along the southern Zimbabwe border in Matabeleland South and insurgents in Mozambique (Resistência Nacional Moçambicana, RENAMO) to fight against the new government in Zimbabwe. The former comprised ex-ZAPU soldiers who sought to destabilize Zimbabwe, while the latter—though primarily operating to destabilize Mozambique—had ties with the Rhodesian government during the Liberation War (Young, 1990). While RENAMO operated in Mozambique after 1980, bases along the Zimbabwe–Mozambique border and refugees fleeing into Zimbabwe posed local security threats (Hall, 1990).

The ruling party handled these security issues differently in various areas based on its wartime organizational capacity (and that of its rival) in each location. Once again reflecting learned wartime experiences, one of ZANU-PF's strategies was to use its youth supporters to build new local militias to enforce security. It returned to the local self-defense security model ZANLA had perfected during the war by calling on wartime collaborators and pro-ZANU-PF youth to build the Zimbabwe People's Militia (ZPM) in 1982. As

118 Governing after War

Sadomba and Tom (2013, 3) explains, "The liberation struggle was greatly assisted by the employment of the youth as collaborators, intelligence gatherers and weapon carriers. This same segment of the population was later to play an important role in the para-military set up." The ZPM received three months of training at bases across the country before being returned to their communities "to act as the eyes and ears of the standing army" (Rupiya, 2005). In effect, the ZPM was organized as part community-level militias, and part local defense watch teams that were created to eliminate potential local unrest and weed out local opposition supporters (Sadomba and Tom, 2013, 3). The ZPM was first established in Gokwe district, the farthest western edge of ZANLA penetration during the civil war. Once established, watch teams were spread eastward to guard against cross-border operations from the RENAMO insurgency in Mozambique (Chitiyo and Rupiya, 2005, 342).

Attempts to create local ZANU-PF cells to mobilize young people into pro-government brigades, however, were unsuccessful in rival strongholds due to strong support for ZAPU. Faced with the looming threat of armed rivals and a resistant population, ZANU-PF deployed paramilitary security forces in these rival strongholds (Catholic Commission for Justice and Peace, 1997, 15). ZANU-PF exploited the isolation of the Matabeleland provinces created by the "very tightly controlled information space" (Ex-bureaucrat, 2017) to deploy massive military violence against civilians in rival strongholds.

To sever ZAPU's rebel—civilian ties—and thus destroy its organizational capacity—in the Matabeleland provinces, ZANU-PF used mass violence (Gukurahundi massacres). Mugabe created the Fifth Brigade, a North Korea-trained military force separate from the national army comprised primarily of ex-ZANLA troops who were not integrated into the national army. The Fifth Brigade began its training in August 1981 before being deployed first in Matabeleland North in January 1983, and then to Matabeleland South in February 1984 (Catholic Commission for Justice and Peace, 1997, 7–8). Figure 4.4 outlines these two provinces in black, along with the estimated population-weighted casualties of mass violence.[18] Concurrently, ZANU-PF set up three detention camps in Plumtree, Lupane, and Kezi. These areas represent ZIPRA strongholds during the war that were largely untouched by ZANLA, which were also key ZIPRA entry points from Botswana into Zimbabwe. According to Alexander (1998, 57), "anyone believed to have aided or abetted dissidents, as well as former ZIPRA combatants, members of the Rhodesian army, even serving members of the ZNA home on leave"

---

[18] Violent events include deaths, missing (presumed dead), property loss, torture, detention or kidnapping, injury, and rape (Catholic Commission for Justice and Peace, 1997, 76). I use the 2012 census to approximate the population.

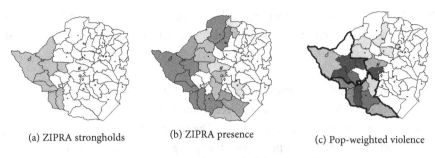

(a) ZIPRA strongholds   (b) ZIPRA presence   (c) Pop-weighted violence

Figure 4.4 Gukurahundi operations in the Matabeleland provinces
Notes: Panel (a) shows ZAPU control; Panel (b) illustrates the intensity of ZAPU operations; Panel (c) displays the population-weighted postwar violence count compiled by Catholic Commission for Justice and Peace (1997, 77–78) (the Fifth Brigade operated in provinces outlined in black). Population figures include violence carried out by dissidents as well as pro-government actors—the Fifth Brigade (Gukurahundi), various army/state security branches, police, militias, and ZANU-PF youth militias.

was brought to the detention camps to be tortured and killed. Joshua Nkomo estimated that the Gukurahundi killed twenty thousand civilians, but casualty figures vary greatly across sources (Catholic Commission for Justice and Peace, 1997, 18).

The Fifth Brigade was not created to quell dissident activity; that was the job of the official army. Rather, it was established to coerce control over civilians. It forced civilians to re-enact pungwes, sing ZANU liberation songs, and pledge support to the ruling party. The Gukurahundi created an atmosphere of civilian fear that prevented locals from supporting the ex-ZIPRA troops, and successfully blocked ex-ZIPRA efforts to recruit. Unlike in the first civil war when civilians willingly supported ZAPU, the renewed violence generated transactional relationships in which civilians aided dissidents under duress (Catholic Commission for Justice and Peace, 1997). As the CCJP wrote in its final report of the Gukurahundi massacres:

> What is apparent in retrospect... is that there were two overlapping "conflicts" going on in Matabeleland. The first conflict was between the dissidents and Government defence units... The second conflict involved Government agencies and all those who were thought to support ZAPU. This was carried out mainly against unarmed civilians in those rural areas which traditionally supported ZAPU (Catholic Commission for Justice and Peace, 1997, 15).

The Fifth Brigade was trained primarily to break down civilian resolve and prevent support for renewed violence by targeting civilians and unleashing mass atrocities across areas loyal to ZAPU (Alexander, McGregor, and Ranger,

2000, 200). Because the government had little information about the exact nature of its rivals' civilian ties, it used indiscriminate rather than targeted violence:

> Well the whole idea really was to get rid of ZAPU—not just the people, anyone who was ZAPU and as far as government was concerned everyone in Matabeleland was ZAPU and therefore people to be killed and be taught a lesson so that those that remained can never again support any other party than the ruling party ZANU PF (Dabengwa, 2011).

4.6 Quantitative evidence of postwar resource allocation

4.6.1 From wartime to postwar social control

Greater organizational capacity in ZANLA strongholds should have allowed the new incumbent government to rely on local organizational structures for postwar governance and control. In essence, these organizational efforts increased local embeddedness and state capacity through bottom-up social control. Earlier I presented evidence of this argument primarily using qualitative data related to keeping citizens in line and mobilizing self-help efforts to promote reconstruction and development. I now discuss quantitative evidence that is consistent with ensuring local support for the state (Subnational Hypothesis 1).

One way to identify the effects of local capacity to organize for political support is to examine voter registration rates—particularly during a time when the state faced very few challenges to its rule. Are residents of ZANU strongholds more likely to register to vote than elsewhere in the country, and can this be attributed to local capacity? The use of ZANU-PF youth for electioneering has been well documented, both during the initial post-independence elections—as I previously argued using qualitative evidence—and in subsequent elections (Kriger, 2005). ZANU-PF's local party cells ought to be deeply involved in mobilizing voters. I therefore argue that these local party cells are strongest where ZANU had wartime roots. Thus, I expect voter registration rates for postwar elections to be higher in controlled territories (strongholds) than in the rest of the country.

I leverage Rhodesian voter registration laws for causal identification. Prior to independence, all Zimbabweans were automatically registered to vote at birth; thus voter registration rates varied depending on the strength of the

The Zimbabwe Liberation War (1972–1979) **121**

Rhodesian bureaucracy across the country. This law ensured near-universal voter registration for those born prior to independence in 1980 (Dendere, 2015, 40). After independence, however, citizens were no longer required to register at birth; voter registration was left to the individual as well as local community-level pressures during election season. The change in voter registration levels for those born under the Rhodesian state versus those born after therefore provides a useful way to test the strength of local party cells for postwar social control while still accounting for pre-war bureaucratic strength.

Research design

I test for the effects of ZANU wartime control on postwar voter registration rates using a difference-in-differences (DiD) identification strategy, which allows me to compare the change in outcomes before and after treatment onset for those in the treated group (residents of ZANU-PF strongholds) versus the control group (those outside of ZANU-PF strongholds). To identify treatment onset using the Rhodesian voter registration law, I classify individuals as pretreatment if they were born prior to 1980, and post-treatment if they were born after 1980. I use the *voter registration* variable from Afrobarometer survey rounds 1–6 (1999–2012), coded "0" if the individual is not registered to vote and "1" if they are. Individuals who were not old enough to vote in the most recent election are coded as missing.

The DiD design can causally identify the effect of the treatment if the treated and control areas exhibit parallel trends prior to treatment onset. Thus individuals born prior to 1980, both within and outside ZANLA strongholds, should exhibit similar voter registration trends before the war. For example, if the Rhodesian bureaucracy deteriorated in one part of the country and strengthened in another, we should observe decreasing registration rates in the former and increasing rates in the latter—which would violate the parallel-trends assumption. Figure 4.5 shows that pretreatment trends were generally parallel. Thus, we can be reasonably certain that the DiD has identified the causal effect of ZANU control on postwar voter registration rates. I also use two placebo cutoffs in Appendix B4.3 to further demonstrate the parallel trends.

The Rhodesian birth registration law also helps identify electioneering through local party cells and pro-government leaders because being born after 1980 coincides with being eligible to vote in the 2000–2005 elections. In these elections, ZANU-PF was faced with a true opposition party, the Movement for Democratic Change (MDC), which was formed in 1999. ZANU-PF increased its campaign activities for the first time, focusing primarily on

122 Governing after War

its legacy as the liberators of Zimbabwe, while war veterans and ZANU-PF youths shored up support for the ruling party (Alexander and McGregor, 2001). I exclude elections from 2008 onward, as the MDC had built its own electoral organizational capacity in the west and in urban areas by that time (LeBas, 2013). Thus, the sample is attenuated to the group of individuals born prior to 1987, who would have been eligible to vote in the 2000–2005 elections.[19]

The DiD equation compares individuals who were born in 1980 or earlier— and were thus registered at birth—to those who were born between 1980 and 1986 under ZANU-PF rule. I compare the difference in pre-treatment and post-treatment registration rates between treated and control areas; the treatment variable is the intensity of ZANU/ZANLA control during the Liberation War. I estimate the following:

$$\text{registration}_{i,b,d,y} = \tau(post_b \times \text{stronghold}_d) + X_i\gamma + \kappa_b + \eta_d + \zeta_y + \epsilon_{i,b,d,y}$$

where i is the individual respondent in the Afrobarometer survey, and $X_i\gamma$ captures individual characteristics, including gender and ethnicity. I also include birth cohort fixed effects (κ_b), district-level fixed effects (η_d), and survey-year fixed effects (ζ_y). Standard errors are clustered at the district level. I limit the pre-war population to those born in 1950 or later to increase comparability between the pre- and postwar samples; however, the effect sizes do not change substantially with different bandwidths. In addition to using the full sample from 1950 to 1986, I also report the estimated effects after dropping individuals who were born during the years of political unrest— 1972 to 1980—to eliminate the potential confounding effects of the war on Rhodesian bureaucratic efficacy.

Results

Table 4.2 reports the differences in voter registration rates, comparing children born in 1980 or earlier to those born after 1980. The results demonstrate that ZANU/ZANLA's wartime strongholds were more likely to register individuals to vote after the end of the birth registration law in 1980. This effect is larger and more significant when I exclude children born during wartime, whose registration at birth may have been affected by disruptions to bureaucratic administration in rural areas. The results suggest that individuals who

---

[19] Those born prior to March 5, 1987 would have been eighteen years old and eligible to vote in 2005; however, the Afrobarometer surveys do not record birth month information. Regression estimates are stable using either 1986 or 1987 as the cutoff.

Table 4.2 Voter registration

	(1) Full sample	(2) Exclude 1972–1980 births
ZANU-PF stronghold × Post	0.057** (0.025)	0.073*** (0.026)
Observations	3606	2465
Dep mean	0.913	0.913
ZANU-PF stronghold × Post SD	0.297	0.297

Notes: $^*p < 0.1$, $^{**}p < 0.05$, $^{***}p < 0.01$. Robust standard errors in parentheses, clustered at the district level. The sample is restricted to respondents born from 1950 to 1986. The regression includes district, Afrobarometer survey round, birth year, gender, and tribe fixed effects. *Voter registration* is coded "1" if they were registered to vote in the last election and "0" otherwise. Respondents who were too young to vote in the last election are coded as missing.

lived in an area fully controlled by ZANU/ZANLA during the war were 6–7% more likely to have registered to vote compared to those living elsewhere. The parallel-trends plot in Figure 4.5 shows that while both populations experienced a decline in voter registration from the 1970s onward due to the conflict, the decline was much steeper after 1980 for areas that were not controlled by ZANLA during the war.[20]

This result accords with qualitative evidence of higher organizational capacity in areas that were ZANU/ZANLA strongholds during the war. After voters were no longer required to register at birth, voter registration depended on the existence of not just local government, but also organized partisans in rural stronghold areas who can mobilize citizens to register to vote. The results are consistent with the hypothesis that ZANU-PF structures and wartime collaborators, which were ingrained in wartime strongholds, were better able to shore up voter registration after it was no longer mandatory. Voter registration rates lagged behind in areas that were not under ZANU-PF control.

Two threats to inference must be addressed. First, the clear alternative explanation is that these results are driven purely by co-ethnicity: Residents of ZANU strongholds are primarily from the Shona ethnic group, and are therefore co-ethnics of the ruling party. Theories of ethnic collective action would thus suggest that voter registration efforts linked to co-ethnic ties could be driving these results (Habyarimana et al., 2007). As a robustness check to

---

[20] For the 2008 election, after the opposition party MDC had gained a considerable foothold in the western region, we observe a sharp change in results. Appendix B4.1 shows the parallel-trends plot extended to include everyone up to the 1994 birth cohort. Those born between 1987 and 1994 would have been eligible to vote in their first election in either 2008 or 2013.

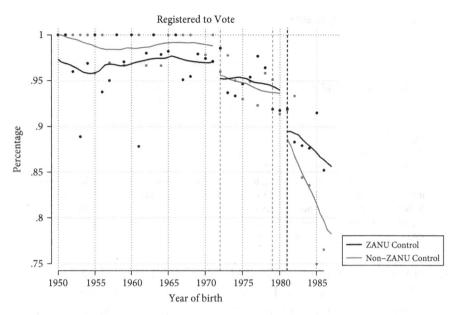

Figure 4.5 Voter registration plot

Note: Plot depicts voter registration rates for people born each year, from 1950 until 1986, in ZANU and non-ZANU-controlled areas. In the first specification, the variable post is greater than zero at the 1980 dotted line. The second specification drops those who were born between the 1972 and 1980 dotted lines.

confirm that this effect is not driven purely by co-ethnicity, I conduct the same analyses on the subsample of districts that have a population of at least 80% Shona respondents, which allows me to compare a subset of ZANU wartime strongholds to a subset of contested territories, and to drop wartime ZAPU strongholds altogether. The results, presented in Appendix B4.2, are robust to this specification.

Second, because the Afrobarometer surveys were conducted between 2000 and 2012, respondents who claim to have been registered to vote may have been registered in later years depending on the contentiousness of various elections—even if they were born during the years specified in my DiD equation. While I cannot validate what year people were registered to vote, the survey year fixed effects used for the estimation capture individual election year propensity to demand increased (decreased) registration efforts. More importantly, voters only have to register to vote once—not for each election. If people registered to vote after their first eligible election (undoubtedly common), this would bias my results toward zero: As more and more individuals outside of ZANU strongholds would be registered under the MDC's organizational structures and local party efforts, non-ZANU stronghold voter registration should continue to rise. The estimated effects are thus conservative.

4.6.2 How resource allocation strategies affect public goods provision

The three strategies for consolidating power—(a) relying on wartime supporters (Sub-national hypothesis 1), (b) deploying bureaucrats to control development (Sub-national hypothesis 2), and (c) coercion (Sub-national hypothesis 3)—should have distributional consequences. I now use a DiD identification strategy to causally identify differences in educational attainment in postwar school-building initiatives across government strongholds, unsecured terrain, and rival strongholds. My theory predicts that the greatest gains in educational attainment will be in unsecured areas, where bureaucrats use public goods to establish political control. I also expect education gains (to a lesser degree) in government strongholds, where the ruling party relies on its wartime ties to organize volunteer efforts for development while managing and limiting community demands for more resources. Increases in educational attainment should be lowest in rival strongholds, where the potential for cooptation is low.

Educational attainment is a useful test in Zimbabwe for three reasons. First, although the new ZANU-PF government undertook several public works after the civil war, the unparalleled success of its education development initiative during the first decade of independence provides a clear and measurable outcome with which to causally identify development gains across the country.[21] Before 1980, Black Zimbabweans were barred from public secondary schooling; after coming to power, the new government embarked on a large school-building initiative to accommodate the influx of new students into secondary schools. The number of secondary schools increased more than eightfold during the first decade of independence (Kanyongo, 2005, 69). This shock to the education system allows me to cleanly test development effects. Other development efforts were less pronounced, less immediately measurable, and are more likely to be confounded by pre-war factors such as preexisting public goods distribution.

---

[21] Measuring changes just after the war is crucial, because the theory pertains primarily to the immediate postwar period when the new rebel government was consolidating power. We might not expect the government to use the same strategies to stay in power after the immediate threat of counter-rebellion subsides. A good measure should therefore be able to identify change during 1980–1987.

126 Governing after War

The second reason I assess educational attainment is that school-building initiatives form part of a wider class of comparable reforms that not only (a) benefit from civilian volunteerism, as demonstrated by the qualitative evidence, but are also (b) visible goods for which the state can claim credit. The beneficiaries of distributive politics may differ based on the good (Kramon and Posner, 2013) and, where the government must win over a large sector of the population to prevent defection to its rival, broad public goods such as school-building initiatives become the more effective choice (De Mesquita et al., 2002).[22] In sum, quantitative educational attainment outcomes should clearly demonstrate the effects of the government strategies outlined in the theory and identified in the qualitative evidence.

Third, we should expect pro-government bureaucrats to be focused on education, as it is particularly important for establishing state control and cultivating pro-state constituents (Paglayan, 2020). In a 1981 speech, Prime Minister Mugabe emphasized the role of the education system in cultivating good citizens, claiming that "to change Zimbabwe we must first change our educational system...the ideological aspect must necessarily constitute an integral part of the education experiences...our schools, our entire education system, must inculcate a socialist consciousness..." (Zimbabwe Catholic Bishop's Conference, 1982). In another speech, President Canaan Banana similarly noted, "appropriate attention will be given to the role of education in imparting new values, attitudes, and motivations associated with the new society..." (Silveira House, 1982). These sentiments are echoed in various ministerial speeches, indicating the importance that the new government placed on education for modeling the ideal Zimbabwean citizen (Zimbabwe Catholic Bishop's Conference, 1982).

Research design

I use data on educational outcomes from a 5% sample of the Zimbabwe 2012 Population Census, made available through the Integrated Public Use Microdata Series. The census data records each respondent's highest level of education. I drop all individuals who identified as "White," immigrants, or non-Zimbabwean citizens. Using the remaining data, I create an aggregate variable coded from 0 to 3, where "0" indicates no formal schooling, "1" denotes some primary schooling, "2" indicates having completed primary school, and "3" some secondary schooling.

---

[22] In its strongholds, the rebel government may instead make private transfers to its local supporters who in turn organize on its behalf, rather than invest in public goods.

The Zimbabwe Liberation War (1972–1979)   **127**

I use this coding scheme for two reasons. First, because Zimbabwe's secondary schooling is split into lower (Ordinary) and upper (Advanced) levels, and as students must pass rigorous tests to continue onto the upper-secondary level, many rural Zimbabweans leave school after completing lower-level secondary schooling. I therefore do not include "completed secondary schooling" as a final category for the education attainment main regressions. Second, I collapse the coding into these categories rather than using individual grade levels in order to retain the subset of respondents in the 2012 Census that did not specify which grade level they had completed.

In Appendix B5.1, I show that the results are robust to (1) using a 0–4 coding scale that includes "completed secondary schooling" as the last category; (2) using a 0–11 scale to indicate the grade level completed, from no school to completing lower-secondary school; and (3) using a 0–13 scale to indicate the grade level completed, from no school to completing upper-secondary school.

To compare successes in education reform in *contestation* and *stronghold* areas versus *opposition* areas, treatment onset *post* captures individuals who were of secondary-school age after the war. The pretreatment group includes all who were older than 18 by 1980: these individuals should have missed the chance to benefit from the mass proliferation of education that began in 1980 under the universal education program. I further allow *post* to capture partial treatment: Individuals who were 12 by 1981 have a *post* value of 1, indicating that they were best poised to take advantage of the secondary schooling made available to Black Zimbabweans by the end of 1980. Children aged 13–17 by 1981 are coded using partial values in increments of 1/6. The equation is:

$$\text{education}_{i,b,d} = \tau_1(post_b \times \text{contestation}_d) + \tau_2(post_b \times \text{stronghold}_d)$$
$$+ \gamma_i + \kappa_b + \eta_d + \epsilon_{i,b,d}$$

where i is the individual respondent in the 2012 census, γ_i is the respondent's gender, κ_b denote birth year fixed effects, and η_d are district fixed effects.[23] Standard errors are clustered at the district level. The sample used for the education variable is individuals born between 1950 and 1971, to eliminate the potential effects of war for those born in 1972 or later. I present two regressions. First, I use the full sample of those born between 1950 and 1971. Second, as with the voter registration regressions, I drop those who were born between 1960 and 1969, as these individuals would have started secondary

---

[23] Ethnicity controls are omitted here because ethnicity information is not available in the census data.

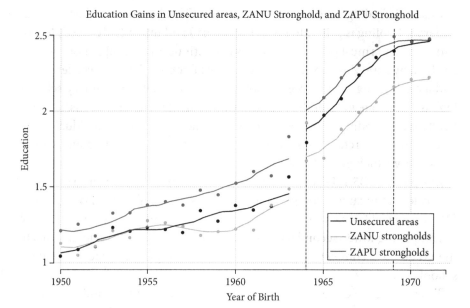

Figure 4.6 Education parallel-trends plots

Notes: Education plots show parallel trends for education gains across different territory types. Population is subsetted to rural citizens. The first specification, *post* is greater than 0 at the 1963 dotted line. In the second specification, I drop all those who were born between 1960 and 1969.

school during the war and thus may have been adversely affected by the conflict.

Results

Figure 4.6 plots educational attainment growth in unsecured areas—which featured weak or nonexistent civilian ties compared to ZANU and ZAPU strongholds—for individuals born between 1950 and 1972. Two observations should be noted. First, simply allowing Black Zimbabweans to attend secondary school had clear nationwide effects. Those who were too old to have benefited from the education reforms, individuals born before 1964— had a mean level of education lower than attending secondary school (less than a "2"), while the cohorts born in 1964 or later quickly increased their education to include some secondary school. This is the case for *all three* types of territories, indicating that simply *allowing* Black Zimbabweans to attend public secondary schools had a widespread positive effect on education.

Second, comparing across territories, there is clear evidence that is consistent with the argument: Unsecured areas grew at a faster rate than government strongholds, while rival strongholds lagged behind. The figure shows

The Zimbabwe Liberation War (1972–1979)   **129**

that the educational gap between unsecured and stronghold areas closed substantially as a result of the school construction and education reforms. As my theory suggested, unsecured areas are the primary beneficiaries of development—for example, the new rebel government did not only reward its wartime supporters. ZAPU strongholds, which started off at a similar level to unsecured areas, lag behind significantly following the post-independence education reforms. This accords with the qualitative evidence: In unsecured areas, district-level bureaucrats leveraged development funding to win supporters and dissuade communities from backing the opposition. In pro-ZANU strongholds, preexisting supporters organized communities to fundraise and build schools themselves, while local leaders discouraged residents from demanding more. Voluntary resources may have been overshadowed by state-provided resources, which is consistent with slower education gains. Both unsecured areas and government strongholds, however, performed far better than rival strongholds—unsurprising given the government's reluctance to provide resources coupled with the state-sponsored mass killings (Gukurahundi) during this period.

The coefficients reported in Table 4.3 also illustrate that educational attainment in both pro-ZANU strongholds and unsecured areas grew more quickly than in the baseline category, ZAPU strongholds (column 1). The difference between unsecured areas and ZANU stronghold territories is statistically significant at $p < 0.018$, indicating support for my argument that the government used resources for top-down control in unsecured areas that would be especially useful for consolidating power. This result is robust to excluding those who reached secondary school age during the war (column 2).

These results are robust to a variety of different specifications, including (1) alternative operationalizations of the education variable, (2) alternative operationalizations of the *post* and outcome variables, and (3) different sample populations to exclude individuals who migrated between 2002 and 2012, and districts that are 80% Shona or greater.[24] These results are presented in Appendix B5.1, and show stable and statistically significant coefficients across all specifications. Finally, I provide the results for placebo cutoffs—in which I consider false *post* birth cohorts to confirm that the estimated positive treatment effect can indeed be attributed to the postwar era—in Appendix B5.3.

Three alternative explanations may confound these findings. First, conflict may have affected residents of various parts of the country differently, given

---

[24] Because the census does not provide ethnicity information, I define these districts using respondent ethnicities from Afrobarometer surveys rounds 1–6.

130 Governing after War

their contrasting exposure to conflict and ideological or cultural differences. The DiD research design mitigates this concern: Conflict should not differentially affect only those who are of secondary school age after the start of the war compared to those who turned 18 by 1980. However, I show a variety of placebo outcomes using the same identification strategy, which provides reassurance that the estimated effects are not due to factors unrelated to development funding for education (these results are available in Appendix B5.2).

A second alternative explanation is that the treatment variables are coded such that strongholds and unsecured areas do not overlap. This may raise concerns that the coding strategy mutes the variation in rebel ties within unsecured areas by treating areas where both groups had a weak presence as similar to those in which both groups made strong efforts to form civilian ties. To explore this possibility, I ran a DiD regression interacting *unsecured* areas with the *presence* of ZANU politicization. If it is rebel *presence* (rather than social control through a monopoly over civilian ties) that is driving the variations in educational attainment I observe, this coefficient should be statistically significant. The results indicate that it is indeed parity between ZANLA's and ZIPRA's operational presence—rather than the *strength* of each group's presence—that affected education spending by deployed bureaucrats after the war. Appendix B5.1 shows that the coefficients remain stable and statistically significant for *unsecured* and *ZANU stronghold* areas. The interaction between *presence* and *unsecured* is statistically insignificant and close

Table 4.3 Educational attainment

	(1) Full sample	(2) Exclude 1960–1969 births
Unsecured × post	0.257***	0.266***
	(0.066)	(0.070)
ZANU stronghold × post	0.103**	0.127**
	(0.051)	(0.053)
Observations	48,262	27,896
Dep mean	1.853	1.853
Unsecured × post SD	0.319	0.325
Difference *p-value*	0.018	0.035

Notes: $*p < 0.1$, $**p < 0.05$, $***p < 0.01$. Robust standard errors in parentheses, clustered at the district level. The sample is restricted to respondents living in rural districts who were born between 1950 and 1971. The regressions include district fixed effects, birth year fixed effects, and gender fixed effects. *Education* is coded as follows: "0" = no formal education, "1" = incomplete primary, "2" = complete primary, "3" = incomplete secondary, and "4" = complete secondary.

to zero. This finding also partially addresses the second concern mentioned earlier—that the level of conflict does not explain the results.

Finally, ethnicity may confound the results for two reasons. First, there may be differences in preexisting intra-ethnic cooperation: Villages with stronger rebel–civilian ties may have enjoyed greater community collective action to begin with. In line with the ethnicity literature, homogeneous villages may be better able to engage in both (1) the local coproduction of reconstruction and (2) in-group policing. Thus, if strongholds are more homogeneous, this may affect local organizational capacity—regardless of the strength of rebel–civilian ties. However, this is less of a concern because in Zimbabwe, ethnic heterogeneity varies at the district level, whereas the ethnic cooperation thesis (and the collective action prescribed by rebel–civilian ties) is primarily salient at the village level. An alternative ethnic hypothesis is that district administrators engage in favoritism in the distribution of public goods. However, ethnic favoritism, both with regard to the Shona and Ndebele split as well as within-group subethnic differences, would imply greater targeting of resources toward co-ethnics. This would bias my results toward zero, since I find greater development in unsecured districts, which tend to be more heterogeneous at the district level.

To provide some evidence that ethnicity does not explain my results through either an ethnic cooperation or ethnic favoritism mechanism, I isolate my sample to districts that are 80% Shona or greater. While this does not capture subethnic differences, it does take into account the main ethnic cleavage during that period (between the Shona and Ndebele). Within this subsample, there is ethnic homogeneity at both the village and district levels. I show in Appendix B5.1 that these results are stable and statistically significant.

4.7 Conclusion

This chapter examined the Zimbabwean Liberation War, and identified the patterns of control and contestation that emerged on the eve of the country's independence. The victor (ZANU) built strong organizational capacity in its strongholds during the civil war: Citizens were folded into the war effort under village committee structures and teams of youth collaborators. These wartime governance structures allowed ZANLA soldiers to extract materiel and information while building a politicized base of supporters through *pungwes*. The resulting war machine involved locally embedded ZANU rebel party structures, which after war continued to engage in local mobilization efforts to promote control and reconstruction. While supporters and a politicized peasantry could be credited with local postwar self-help, partisans were instrumental in both sustaining control—by providing on-the-ground information and ensuring citizen support—and preventing citizens from organizing independently to make more demands of the state. In short, organic citizen political participation was minimized and participation in pro-ZANU-PF activities was encouraged.

Outside of ZANU strongholds, the new ruling party used development and violence to expand its influence. ZANU-PF spread local governing institutions—modeled on its wartime party structures—across the country under the hierarchical framework for local development. Political commissars set up these local development structures in an effort to ensure unwavering support. Wartime supporters obtained important local positions, and trusted youth and women became leaders after the war. With self-help and local organizations promoting local development projects while deployed bureaucrats exerted control from the top down through development funding, ZANU-PF's attention turned to coercive violence in the pro-ZAPU Matabeleland areas. The resulting Gukurahundi massacre caused widespread fear among opposition-supporting civilians and stamped out any potential support for the ex-ZIPRA dissidents operating in Matabeleland. The available quantitative evidence is consistent with my argument: Wartime rebel–civilian ties did lead to differences in postwar resource allocation strategies as measured through voter registration and educational attainment across the state. These results support the qualitative evidence I presented in the previous chapter and highlight how the process of postwar state-building relies heavily on wartime state-building.

In the next chapter I examine the Liberian Civil War, in which the opposite occurred. While Liberian rebels made early attempts to establish social order, they consistently lost territory in the latter half of the war as more armed groups entered the conflict—and were therefore forced into a period of heightened contestation. The result was a weak state plagued by challengers in opposition territory, leading to increased security spending and reduced support from civilians elsewhere in the country.

5
The Liberia Civil War (1989–1996)

The First Liberian Civil War captured international attention for its brutality. For seven years, rebels from different factions contested heavily for territory, power, and resource wealth while citizens suffered under rebel violence. The war ended with a rebel victory: Charles Taylor, the leader of the National Patriotic Front of Liberia (NPFL), won the 1997 election by a landslide. Although Taylor promised to reform the country and set aside the ethnic differences that had fueled the civil war, he was immediately challenged by rivals when he assumed office. Liberia quickly resumed its familiar pattern of violence: By late 1999, it had returned to a full-blown second civil war as the new government continued its power struggle against rival rebel groups from the first civil war. These rivals had lost the first war in 1996, but they successfully overwhelmed government forces in this second war. Taylor had failed to consolidate power, and was forced out in 2003.

This chapter has three goals. First, I argue that rebel–civilian ties are useful for rebels without programmatic goals: Establishing social order and organizational capacity allows rebel groups to extract resources more efficiently (Tilly, 1985; Reno, 1999; Sanchez de la Sierra, 2017). Second, I discuss how military contestation makes it very difficult to maintain rebel–civilian ties *despite* territorial control. While the NPFL had formed connections with civilians when (and where) the wartime dynamics of rebel control permitted social control, the existential military threat and territorial loss during the war reduced both the depth (quality) and breadth (spread) of rebel–civilian ties across Liberia. Although the NPFL regained territorial control in the final months of the war, it did not rebuild these ties.

Third, I demonstrate how the absence of rebel–civilian ties in Liberia affected post-war politics and the victor's ability to effectively consolidate power through the governing strategies outlined in Chapter 2. The new rebel government attempted to allocate resources to co-opt additional supporters after it won the election, but the regime's limited ties with civilians hampered efforts to ease the security concerns. I draw on interviews and focus group discussions with ex-combatants, government officials, and civilians to present

Governing after War: Rebel Victories and Post-war Statebuilding. Shelley X. Liu, Oxford University Press.
© Oxford University Press 2024. DOI: 10.1093/oso/9780197696705.003.0005

134 Governing after War

evidence that that the NPFL's limited rebel–civilian ties shaped Taylor's constraints after the war and thwarted the new rebel government's attempts to consolidate control. Since the first civil war's conclusion did little to eliminate the existential threats to regime stability, Taylor's post-war rule was preoccupied by shoring up its power through increasingly military means. The new government faced a security–development trade-off: As more resources were expended on warding off rivals from state borders, less was spent on bolstering internal state capacity and attracting potential supporters from within.

5.1 Conflict Overview

As alluded to in Chapter 3, Liberia's conflict erupted out of growing ethnic tensions between the Gio and Mano ethnic groups on one side, and the Krahn and Mandingo on the other. While not a member of any of these groups, Taylor exploited these underlying tensions to build and lead the NPFL rebel army. His struggle for power can be separated into two periods of conflict. During the first conflict (1989–1996), the NPFL fomented rebellion to take control of the state. It fought government forces as well as rival rebel groups that sought to prevent Taylor from taking control of the country. After he won the 1997 election, the new rebel government engaged in the second civil war—a failed consolidation war—from 1999 to 2003 (Figure 5.1).

5.1.1 Rebellion: The First Liberian Civil War

On Christmas Eve of 1989, Charles Taylor led the NPFL two hundred miles from Côte d'Ivoire across the border into Liberia's northernmost county, Nimba. The rebels took control of a key border crossing between Liberia and Côte d'Ivoire and bolstered their efforts to recruit disaffected young Gio and Mano men from the area. The NPFL made significant headway into the interior counties in the next few months and assumed *de facto* control over the majority of the state by mid-1990. Taylor intended to install himself as president, but the NPFL could not declare outright military victory because it was unable to take control of the capital, Monrovia, at the time. Taylor instead set up a parallel government (the National Patriotic Reconstruction Assembly Government) in Bong county, Liberia's largest and most centrally located county. Throughout most of the civil war, Taylor governed the territory under his control—known as Greater Liberia or Taylorland—from the county's capital city, Gbarnga.

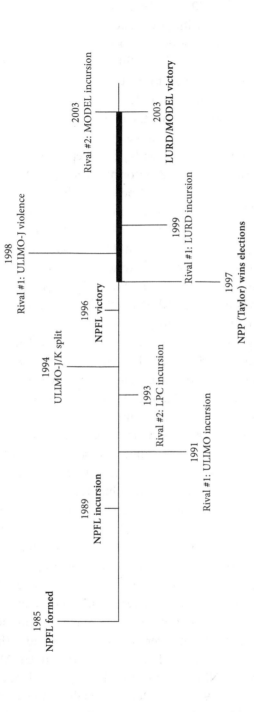

Figure 5.1 Liberia conflict timeline

Notes: The timeline depicts the entrance year of various players in the Liberia conflict. The black bar denotes the post-war period during which Charles Taylor was in power.

136 Governing after War

As the war continued, more rebel groups emerged to challenge the NPFL's territorial dominance. In 1990 the NPFL's chief military training officer, Prince Johnson, broke away with five hundred soldiers and took control of Monrovia under the banner of the Independent National Patriotic Front of Liberia (INPFL). By the time the NPFL defeated the INPFL in 1991, additional rebel groups had formed to once again prevent Taylor's outright military victory. The United Liberation Movement of Liberia for Democracy (ULIMO) formed in 1991 and became the first main rival. Its members primarily comprised people from the Krahn and Mandingo ethnic groups, and it also had ties with Guinea as well as with peacekeepers from the Economic Community of West African States Monitoring Group (ECOMOG). In 1994 ULIMO split into two factions led by Roosevelt Johnson (ULIMO-J) and Alhaji Kromah (ULIMO-K). In 1993, a second rival emerged: the warlord George Boley founded the Liberia Peace Council (LPC) and sought to take control of southeast Liberia. Homegrown militias also formed to complicate the military situation. Citizens of northwestern Lofa county, for example, founded the Lofa Defense Force to defend themselves against constant rebel military contestations between the NPFL and ULIMO. Similar militias arose in the northeast to help defend against rebel activity.

These new groups put the NPFL on the defensive. Taylorland shrank as it slowly lost control over its territories: In 1991, the NPFL maintained outright territorial control over 90% of the state (Figure 5.3). By the end of 1992, it had lost 20% of its territory (Adebajo, 2002, 55), and by April 1993 it had lost control of almost all key economic hubs that were helping it finance its military campaign (Ero, 1995). Between 1992 and 1994, ULIMO troops had swept from northwestern Lofa county to capture the entire western front, and the LPC took control of the southeast (U.S. Department of State, 1995). Although the NPFL maintained nominal territorial control over the northeast, local militias prevented its soldiers from maintaining a stable presence throughout the region. Thus, by 1994 the NPFL had lost its troop presence and social control in more than half of the country; it dominated central Liberia around Bong, Margibi, and Nimba counties.

Contestation peaked in 1994, and territorial control shifted rapidly between the various armed groups. These shifts increased uncertainty among rebel soldiers and commanders, as different battalions—even those stationed in NPFL strongholds—were sent to fight on different fronts. By the end of that year, the NPFL had even lost control of its rebel capital in Gbarnga to ULIMO-K forces and was forced to retreat to Nimba county for a brief period (U.S. Department of State, 1995). Throughout 1995, the NPFL was left defending its strongholds as ULIMO-K contested from the west, ULIMO-J from the south, and LPC

Figure 5.2 NPFL presence

Notes: This figure maps NPFL activity at the *clan* level, using polygon-level data from the Uppsala Conflict Data Program (UCDP) Georeferenced Event Dataset (GED). Darker shading indicates that the entire clan experienced a yearly NPFL presence from 1990 onward; lighter shading denotes that only parts of the clan experienced this consistent presence.

from the east (Amnesty International, 1995, 18). Harris (1999, 448) noted that during this time, "diamond mines fell to ULIMO, timber-rich areas to the LPC, and much of 'Greater Liberia' became contested, with consequent suffering among civilians."

The NPFL's final April 1996 offensive into Monrovia marked a decisive end to the First Liberian Civil War. All groups descended upon the capital, and ECOMOG and its allies attempted to prevent Taylor from taking control of the military barracks—and therefore the entire country. The war thus ended in a military stalemate that forced the rival rebel groups to the bargaining table, and post-war elections were held in 1997 as part of the peace settlement.

138   Governing after War

Charles Taylor, under the banner of the National Patriotic Party (NPP), won the presidency with 75% of the vote and an 80% turnout rate.

5.1.2 Consolidation: The Second Liberian Civil War

The new rebel government faced violent threats to its rule just months after Taylor was sworn in as president. Although the first civil war had ended, it was clear that the struggle for control had not, and multiple sovereignties existed from the start. Rebels loyal to ULIMO-J continued to control pockets of Monrovia; in September 1998 they attempted to overthrow Taylor from within the capital. While Taylor was preoccupied with unrest in Monrovia, small bands of ex-ULIMO-K soldiers began cross-border attacks from Guinea into the northwestern Lofa county.

The second civil war began in late 1999 when these ex-ULIMO soldiers united under a new name, the Liberians United for Reconciliation and Democracy (LURD). Early members were primarily from the Krahn and Mandingo tribes, and fighting was localized to western Liberia. Mirroring the ULIMO-K and ULIMO-J split during the first civil war, Krahn members split from LURD to form the Movement for Democracy in Liberia (MODEL) and opened up an eastern front from Côte d'Ivoire. MODEL entered the war through Grand Gedeh county along the Côte d'Ivoire border—a highly contested county during the first war. It moved into central Liberia through Grand Bassa county (Human Rights Watch, 2004) to reach Taylor's political stronghold, Gbarnga, from the east (Hazen, 2013, 132). MODEL also took control of the three main ports in southeast Liberia—Harper, Buchanan, and Greenville—which cut off Taylor's business dealings and weapons supply. Meanwhile, LURD attacks had spread southeast to Monrovia and reached Gbarnga from the west.[1]

The joint rebel efforts forced Taylor to flee to Nigeria in 2003. The second civil war ended in a rebel victory, but as part of the peace process all rebel group leaders agreed not to run in post-war elections. Because neither LURD nor MODEL had sufficient military or civilian support to take over the government outright, consolidating power would have been a difficult and likely fruitless endeavor. Nor did either have enough support from the international community to make any significant political demands for leadership positions in the new government. The two rebel groups thus secured their political

---

[1] The rebels launched attacks on Monrovia three times. The attacks—known colloquially in Liberia as World War I, World War II, and World War III—in June and July 2003 devastated the capital.

The Liberia Civil War (1989–1996)   **139**

futures by agreeing to occupy key positions in the ministries rather than attempt to assume full control (Gerdes, 2013, 174).

5.2 Data Sources

I argue in this chapter that the NPFL initially succeeded in establishing organizational capacity through the rebel–civilian ties it formed during the initial years of the civil war (1990–1992). However, a series of defensive battles and territorial losses during the latter years of the conflict (1992–1996) eroded the group's organized civilian ties and on-the-ground governing structures. Thus, although Taylor won the first post-war elections by a landslide, he still found it difficult to consolidate control and eliminate the threat of a counter-rebellion from discontent rivals: allocating resources to development and security was not enough to satisfy citizens *and* eliminate violent challenges. Thus, despite attempts to maintain order, the new government faced a ballooning security crisis—forcing a development–security trade-off in its resource allocation efforts. I present qualitative and quantitative evidence to support my argument, drawing on data collected from the field.

5.2.1 Qualitative Evidence

I provide qualitative evidence from interviews and focus group discussions with ex-combatants and civilians. First, I interviewed forty-six *ex-combatants* who fought in the first and second civil wars. These interviewees ranged from rank-and-file ex-combatants to elite commanders, and included fighters from all three main rebel groups—NPFL, ULIMO-K/J, and LPC. A subset of the ULIMO-K/J and LPC ex-combatants also fought in the second civil war under LURD and MODEL, while some of the NPFL ex-combatants were engaged as government forces under Taylor's regime. I contacted potential interviewees with the help of two Liberian research assistants. We first spoke to ex-commanders who were living in larger ex-combatant communities at the time—in two major slums in Monrovia, Peace Island, and West Point. We then reached rank-and-file soldiers using a snowball sampling method, primarily through introductions from these ex-commanders. Interviewing ex-combatants gave me a comprehensive understanding of how rebel–civilian ties facilitated both rebel survival and military expansion.

I then spoke with *civilians*. I interviewed three government officials who had served in an official capacity during the war—one as a clan chief and two as leaders of aid organizations. I also facilitated eighteen focus group discussions with three to ten participants per group. During the first wave, in 2016, I held eight focus groups of six to ten civilians each to build my theory. During the second wave in 2018, I conducted ten focus groups of three to six participants per group to test my theory. I reached focus group participants by speaking to local community leaders, who identified groups of civilians who were willing to speak with me.

During the second wave, I recruited focus group participants by assembling civilians who were of the *same ethnic group* and lived in the same areas during the wars to identify civilians' varied wartime experiences across the country. I conducted two focus groups for each of the following ethnic groups: (1) Gio and Mano civilians originally from Nimba county, (2) Lormah and Kissi civilians originally from Lofa county, (3) Kpelle civilians from Bong county, (4) Bassa civilians who had established roots in Monrovia prior to the war, and (5) Krahn civilians from the eastern counties. Discussions between co-ethnics from the same parts of the country helped me distinguish between the diverse experiences of different groups of people during both the first civil war and Taylor's presidency. This method allowed me to differentiate conflict intensity at different points of the war, displacement levels, and the routes that civilians from different ethnic groups tended to travel during the war. It also generated insights into how civilians viewed the first civil war, the legitimacy of Taylor's rule, and attitudes toward governance and the second civil war in different parts of rural Liberia.

5.2.2 Quantitative Evidence

I obtained quantitative data from the Government of Liberia. The Ministry of Internal Affairs gave me access to government personnel lists for 2009 to 2015, which included information about their age, gender, and the year they began their roles. I digitized these hiring records to map clan and town chief appointments that would have been made during the civil war and formalized immediately after Taylor became president. I also gathered information on clan boundaries from the United Nations Mission in Liberia (UNMIL) and geocoded locality data—denoting villages and towns in rural areas or communities and hamlets in urban areas—from the Liberia Institute of Statistics and Geo-Information Services (LISGIS) office in Monrovia. LISGIS also gave me access to the full de-identified 2008 census data, which contains individual- and household-level characteristics. I combine these data collected in the field with conflict data from the UCDP GED for quantitative analyses in the next chapter.

The Liberia Civil War (1989-1996) **141**

In the subsequent sections, I synthesize this qualitative and quantitative evidence to illustrate how rebel–civilian ties changed between the first period of rebel control and the second period of military contestation. I then explain how the shift in these ties reduced the new rebel government's ability to consolidate power after the war.

5.3 Rebel–Civilian Relations: 1990–1992

The Liberian Civil War is often characterized as motivated by greed; greed, however, can in turn motivate governance. Although Taylor was arguably not driven by programmatic objectives at any point in the conflict, his desire to win power and to profit from extracting natural resources led him to foster governance methods that would enable him to build a movement and ensure cooperation from a network of civilians under NPFL control. He was able to do this as long as he maintained clear outright control over most of the country's interior—also known as Taylorland, or Greater Liberia.

Qualitative and secondary accounts indicate that the early civil war years brought a semblance of normality to Greater Liberia even as the government collapsed under rebel activity. As the NPFL soldiers quickly captured territories, they established widespread governing structures designed to control civilian social life and movement. Between 1990 and 1992, Taylor and the NPFL exercised both territorial and social control of around 90% of the country.[2]

The NPFL established a new social order that required citizens living under the new rebel regime to learn a new set of rules, and expected rebel soldiers to follow a standard military chain of command. Taylor established a parallel government, the National Patriotic Reconstruction Assembly Government, in Gbarnga, the Bong county capital in the heart of Liberia. He paid top-level commanders well to ensure good performance—specifically, to control their rank-and-file soldiers—and these commanders in turn paid their soldiers for their obedience. This system was more successful during the initial years: Commanders held rebels to the NPFL's Standard Operating Procedures

---

[2] An exception was the northeastern county of Grand Gedeh, where NPFL troops skirmished with civilian militias and were unable to establish control; rural areas in this county had little or no NPFL presence (Focus groups #14, #15, #16). The northeastern parts of Liberia are home to the Krahn people, who were a rival ethnic group in the first civil war. One civilian living in the area recounted:

> During the 1990 war, I was in the bush with my mom . . . only LPC generals I would see coming during war, sometimes for food, because we had chickens, we were [farming] . . . we give them food, we give them meat, we give them chickens. . . so I knew a few LPC generals at that time. . . I didn't see [NPFL soldiers], I didn't hear about the attack, I didn't see them (Civilian focus group #14).

142 Governing after War

(SOP), which dictated the rebel soldiers' code of conduct, treatment of civilians, and consequences for attempted defection or bypassing the military chain of command. One ex-combatant explained:

> During the revolution time... we were instructed by our commander to take care of life and property, honor our command, and based on Standard Operation Procedure, everybody had to guard themselves, to abide by those rules (Ex-combatant #2).

Others similarly noted that rebels who did not follow these rules "would be charged" or "arrested" by their commanders (Ex-combatants #4, #8).

The degree to which these rules were followed varied: interviewees explained that this depended on whether (and how) the commander punished their men, which is corroborated by Lidow's (2016) work on spot payments and rebel conduct. There was also *temporal* variation between the 1990–1992 period of rebel control and the 1992–1996 period of military contestation: ex-combatants involved in the earlier period were more likely to mention rules and order, while ex-combatants who joined the war later were far less likely to mention it.[3]

Taylor ordered the rebels under his control to minimize their victimization of civilians so they could extract information from them. Token public goods were also provided to foster rebel–civilian cooperation (Ex-combatant #10). Civilians were Taylor's "pepper bush," a Liberian term meaning that he considered the civilian contribution to the war effort instrumental to the survival and well-being of the rebel army (Lidow, 2016). One ex-combatant who operated in Bong county—which experienced the most stability throughout the war—explained why citizen cooperation was so important: "Whenever we get around civilians, when we capture places, we make friends with the civilian population... sometimes we go around and we assist them because we need

---

[3] Rebel accounts may suffer from social desirability bias, which may encourage respondents to minimize perceptions of misconduct and emphasize order. One way to discern the differences in rebel conduct between the 1990–1992 period and the 1992–1996 period I describe below is to compare the accounts of ex-combatants who exited the war at different times. The content of my interviews with early ex-combatants was markedly different from those held with ex-combatants who fought for the entire war, and even more so from those who only participated in the second half of the war when military contestation was particularly high. The ex-combatants who exited the war early and returned to Nimba particularly emphasized the group's focus on rebel conduct (Ex-combatants #4, #8, #9); they were largely unaffected by the military contestation in subsequent years. On the other hand ex-combatants who joined the First Civil War in the later years or who were only recruited into government defense militias in the Second Civil War were far less likely to mention the SOP or any form of order. For example, one of those ex-combatants simply stated that the "SOP is death if you give the wrong information" (Ex-combatant #42).

The Liberia Civil War (1989–1996) **143**

information. They're the only people who can know the enemy location" (Ex-combatant #2). He emphasized, "so you got to make some friends." Another highlighted the same dynamic of cooperation: "It all depends on how you are taking care of them in the town. If you are not beating on them, if you are not harassing them, then they will give you good information" (Ex-combatant #21).

Civilians provided similar accounts of rebel rule. In Taylorland, civilians were allowed to farm and continue about their daily lives (Focus groups #11, #12). Ellis (2007, 129) describes how a Kissi chief reported having good relations with the NPFL soldiers because they had entered the clan territory but left them alone to their farming. When finances in Taylorland were strong, civilians enjoyed better food prices, and commanders sometimes distributed rice to citizens (Think Africa Press, 2013; Lidow, 2016).[4] In less bountiful times, the chiefs would routinely tax civilian crops (Focus groups #3, #4, #11, #12), collecting rice "either by week or by month . . . from door to door" (Focus group #11).

NPFL governance is best highlighted by citizens who lived in rebel strongholds for most of the civil war, and were therefore least affected by the violence and coercion experienced elsewhere in the country even during the later years. These civilians noted the "fine" and "cordial" relationship between rebels and civilians in rebel strongholds in general (Focus group #4), and said the rebels did not seek to overtly undermine the local community order. For example, one civilian explained: "When they get [to a locality] they wanted full control, they want full authority . . . they can't do it by initially applying violence. So sometimes they are patient, they talk to the town chief so when he opens up, they have . . . [what] they want" (Focus group #3). Another focus group participant from Bong county pointed out that appeasing citizens and civilian leaders was important for the rebel commanders. He recounted his arrest by rebel soldiers in 1990 when he was working as a clan chief's clerk; he was soon released after civilians complained to the rebel commander because the chief had been helping the rebels collect rice: "[The commander] in town said no, you don't do that. This man here is working in our interest. The clan chief is not able to come here, he sends this man to come... so they let me go" (Focus group #11).

---

[4] Other rebel groups also governed areas under their control. For example, most of Monrovia was under rival control for much of the war. In these areas, civilians also reported good relations with rebel leaders (Focus group #4); some spoke of rebels providing rice and goods to civilians under their control (Focus groups #13, #14).

5.3.1 Organizational Capacity through Rebel–Civilian Relations

During the initial war years, civilians worked with rebels in a variety of ways to strengthen the NPFL's war machine and increase its organizational capacity. I highlight two main groups of people with whom the rebels sought ties during this period of rebel control. The first group was chiefs—traditional leaders who either predated or were appointed by the rebels. The second was the "single-barrel men," who functioned as the rebels' local reconnaissance teams.

Civilian Type I: Chiefs
NPFL soldiers prioritized forming ties with traditional leaders in rural towns and villages. They were particularly successful at cultivating relationships with traditional chiefs to facilitate logistical support. In Liberia, chiefs serve not only as local traditional leaders; they also form part of the state's bureaucracy: clan chiefs at the clan level, and town and village chiefs at the locality level. When the Liberian government essentially collapsed during the first year of the war, the NPFL incorporated the chiefs into its rebel organization.[5] This practice provided helpful logistical support because the chief customarily speaks for the village and is the best source of information about where the rebels could find food and shelter in the area. As one focus group discussed, the chiefs were considered the "stranger father," a Liberian cultural institution indicating that the chief is the official host of the village. who is "obliged to provide" and is "the only person who can speak for the civilians" (Focus group #6).[6]

Chiefs also augmented the rebels' organizational capacity by acting as an informal bureaucracy within towns and villages. They were tasked with collecting food and materiel from civilians as taxation, as well as distributing food and goods to civilians when the NPFL's business ventures were going well and the rebel group maintained control over key centers of commerce (Lidow, 2016, 126–128). The chieftaincy hierarchy was leveraged to efficiently collect rice for the rebels. One Bong county resident explained how the system worked: "The quartier chief go around to collect food, and bring it to the town chief. The town chief collect and bring it to the clan chief... to

---

[5] To a lesser extent, NPFL soldiers also sought to form ties with traditional leaders of the Poro and Sande—male and female secret societies, respectively, that played a significant role in rural Liberian society. However, since Poro and Sande leaders were not locality specific, they could have only served to confer legitimacy rather than provide local logistical support.

[6] Under the "stranger–father" institution, a newcomer to a village is the "stranger" who must be adopted by a host, the "father."

feed the soldiers" (Focus group #11). Chiefs were also expected to delegate supporting tasks to civilians, such as hosting and providing shelter for the rebels, storing and hiding rebel weapons, and providing information about the comings and goings of other rebel groups that may have passed by the area (Focus group #6).

As in Zimbabwe, chiefs were replaced if they refused to cooperate with the rebels. As one civilian described, when rebels entered a town, "cooperation was demanded, not asked." Chiefs who cooperated were "treated well," and "rebels were polite" (Focus group #3), but if cooperation was not forthcoming, rebels replaced the chiefs with another village resident who was willing to support NPFL activities (Focus groups #5, #6):

> The rebels, they filled in, can I say—the government, the leadership—as they wished. They will look at us and say 'you, you are the town chief, you are the town commander for everybody... you are the head of this town, and we will entrust you.'... and that is how they ran their government (Focus group #5).

The act of replacing chiefs with more amenable individuals has been well documented. For instance, Baldwin and Mvukiyehe (2015, 698) stated that "many of the new chiefs chosen during the war were former combatants or had close connections to armed groups." Similarly, Rincon (2010) reported that the NPFL often replaced town chiefs with younger men after capturing a town—corroborating civilians' explanations of how the NPFL appointed chiefs in certain cases: "They started looking for young people ... the young men in the town and in some of the villages. They get [them] into the position" (Focus group #3). The young men that rebels installed as town chiefs were often leaders of single-barrel men groups, which I explain next.

Civilian Type II: Single-Barrel Men

Rebels organized groups of young men to gather information and provide local security. The rebels selected and armed these men with single-barrel rifles (who then became known as "single-barrel men" or "single-barrel boys") and put them in charge of security affairs within and between localities. Single-barrel men were only used when an area was under the NPFL's territorial and social control—not along battle fronts or when military contestation was high. This is because the single-barrel men, as the rebels' eyes and ears in towns and villages, could only be employed when the rebels trusted the civilians to report information truthfully. Such trust could only develop during peaceful periods when time horizons were long: "Single-barrel men started when rebels started trusting civilians a little bit ... [the rebels] will sleep and

146 Governing after War

single-barrel men will be outside watching for them. So it started when it was all peaceful" (Focus group #5). An ex-combatant similarly explained the conditions necessary to establish a single-barrel men team:

> For instance, if we capture a town and then we pass through the town two three times, then we can have single-barrel men in that town—because it's peaceful. The [other] rebels are far away from them. But if they're closer, we can't have a single-barrel men team. It's not possible. When the town is closer to the war front, it's not possible to have the single-barrel men (Ex-combatant #21).

Civilians and ex-combatants provided similar explanations of how single-barrel men teams were formed (Focus groups #3, #5; Ex-combatants #21, #22, #35, #41). After the NPFL established control of a community, it would press the community for young men who wished to serve as volunteers. They then gathered a team of six or seven young men from among the volunteers and designated one of them the team leader.[7] The NPFL rebels would collect rifles from the community and redistribute them to the team. Notably, the single-barrel men—despite being armed—were considered civilians of the local community who were distinct from the rebel troops. Both civilians and ex-combatants made this distinction: While the rebels took an oath and were considered freedom fighters under the NPFL, single-barrel men were essential civilian support teams who were holding "civilian guns" (as opposed to "real guns") to protect their village (Ex-combatants #21, #22, #41). Civilians claimed they were "not soldiers" (Focus group #3), but instead "brave boys" who volunteered to look after their community (Ex-combatant #21).

Single-barrel men were tasked with security matters, including protecting the community by establishing a presence in the towns and villages and patrolling the rural vicinity, drawing on their familiarity with the bush terrain.[8] Local civilians had superior knowledge of the areas surrounding their village and towns (Ex-combatant #41), and since the single-barrel men often maintained small farms outside town, they were far better at traveling covertly between the town and the bush, and keeping an eye out for peculiarities (Ex-combatant #21). Single-barrel teams were expected to report any evidence of rebel troops or potential military incursions to the local rebel

---

[7] When rebels replaced chiefs with younger men, these were often team leaders of the "single-barrel men."

[8] Because these tasks were primarily important in rural areas where the terrain is difficult and the population density is low, there seem to have been no single-barrel men in urban areas such as Buchanan or Monrovia. Residents of the Bassa community who remained in Monrovia throughout the war (Focus groups #13 and #14) had never heard of the single-barrel men.

commander, who would then relay the information to a higher-level town commander. Rebel commanders were able to rely on these rebel–civilian relationships to avoid engaging their troops in surveillance in unfamiliar terrain.

Single-barrel men more importantly helped man rebel checkpoints on the roads between villages. At the start of the war, when the NPFL controlled almost the entire country and Taylorland was at its height, information and security primarily centered around a large network of these checkpoints that the NPFL had set up across rural Liberia. These checkpoints were established primarily to weed out enemy supporters and rivals' spies (Ex-combatant #21, #34). Citizens going from town to town were "given passes and permission ... a piece of paper that will allow you to pass through their check point that [the rebels] have set up" (Focus group #5). While NPFL rebel soldiers initially manned these checkpoints, single-barrel men were soon put in charge. A former single-barrel man explained his general role:

> On our side, in Gbarnga—in 1990, '91, '92—we were serving as military intelligence. You know? We were not soldiers, but you know ... we used to be [assigned] to the check point. You know? We check civilians, when you come or when you're traveling, you're going. You all will get out from your car, you will come into the office, we ask you for your name, where you're going, where you're traveling, where ... you know, the rest of it ... and then we pass that to [the rebels] (Focus group #3).

These checkpoints worked well during the first two years of war; the network of single-barrel men verified everyone's comings and goings. The civilian just quoted explained that there were no exceptions even for politicians, dignitaries, or representatives of NGOs: When ECOMOG representatives sought to pass between towns within Taylorland, they were stopped at checkpoints and forced to disarm and produce evidence that they had permission to pass through (Focus group #3). The NPFL was thus able to comprehensively control movement through the single-barrel men, highlighting the organizational capacity gained by incorporating civilians into its war machine.

5.3.2 Why Taylor Sought Rebel–Civilian Ties

Charles Taylor and the NPFL prioritized rebel–civilian relationships during the initial period of relative peace because governance and extraction went

148 Governing after War

hand in hand. Taylor sought order and governance in Taylorland primarily to maintain good trade relations with international businesses that relied on Liberian materials, such as rubber, timber, and minerals. His business ventures and extractive capacity relied on establishing functioning quasi-bureaucratic structures, which explains Taylor's preference to reduce civilian victimization. During these initial years, he prioritized strong rebel–civilian relations to efficiently extract from the land. His decisions and behaviors exemplify Olson's (2000) description of nascent government as "stationary bandits": "Taylor expected his commanders to maintain order and provide security for civilians...Civilians held the key . . . to Taylor's legitimacy. Foreign firms could justify their business with Taylor only if Taylor maintained the appearance of a responsible leader" (Lidow, 2016, 120). To demonstrate its governing strength, Taylor's shadow government successfully set up other basic services that constituted a rudimentary state. It appointed bureaucratic officials to ministerial positions, and set up schools, a justice system, and a propaganda machine. Taylor also mandated a new currency to be used within NPFL territory (the "J.J. dollar"), set a minimum wage for timber workers, and worked with local chiefs (Ellis, 2007, 92).

Businesses developed strong relations with the NPFL, and were guaranteed security to continue mining and logging. They paid Taylor and locally stationed NPFL soldiers for access to these natural resources and for providing security when the companies were extracting and exporting from Liberia. In the first two years of war, under strong NPFL control, the local security system under the single-barrel men thrived (Focus group #5). During this period, the single-barrel men—who were primarily stationed in areas considered to be under NPFL control—were instrumental to maintaining security.

These business deals, made possible by civilian cooperation and the ability to provide a sense of security for the firms operating in Liberia, generated lucrative taxes for the NPFL. As further evidence that greed and governance are mutually dependent, these taxes allowed Taylor to build a fully functioning military (Reno, 1999, 93). In short, in the initial years, many of Taylor's commercial activities were conducted to finance the NPFL's military and war—facilitating Taylor's entry into Monrovia—rather than the other way around (Reno, 1999, 95). Much like state-building in Europe (Tilly, 1992), war-making and state-making were intricately linked by the relationships between the rebels who governed and the civilians on the ground who both provided for, and benefited from, the system of extraction and security set up in Taylorland.

5.4 Rebel–Civilian Relations: 1992–1996

This social order in much of Taylorland, however, did not last. New rebel groups emerged in 1992–1993, capitalizing on the ethnic dimensions of the civil war to push NPFL soldiers out of key territories. As Taylorland shrank, the NPFL relied on extreme violence to drive away these new rivals, to force ceasefire talks, and to coerce civilians to provide support and information.

Rebel–civilian ties and NPFL organizational capacity in turn shifted drastically between the first period of rebel control (1990–1992) and the second period of heightened military contestation (1992–1996). These differences exemplify the typology presented in Chapter 2: As rebels were forced into a defensive position, the time horizons decreased for both rebels and civilians. This was felt not only in contested towns and lost territory; it also affected strongholds (to a lesser degree) because more commanders and soldiers were being deployed to the battlefront to help buffer against rivals. Differences in civilian experiences during this second period highlight the key insight of this chapter: *The increase in violence after rivals gained a foothold illustrates how susceptible wartime networks are to military contestation.* By the end of the conflict, Taylor's wartime networks consisted primarily of his business ties with international rubber, timber, and mining companies—firms that sought to do business in Liberia during and after the civil war. Cooperation with these firms was a useful but insufficient tool for maintaining control and state stability after war.

5.4.1 Loss of Social Control

When inter-factional contestation increased from 1992 onward, all factions attacked areas that were originally part of Taylorland (Focus groups #11, #12). In retaliation, the NPFL launched large-scale brutality that began with the NPFL's Operation Octopus in October 1992, a devastating assault on Monrovia that sought to force ECOMOG troops to leave Liberia and withdraw their support for the rival group ULIMO. Taylor carried out a second massacre in June 1993 to drive out rival rebel groups that had begun to contest the NPFL's control of the Firestone rubber plantation—a significant business interest. When the LPC emerged in 1993, violence spiked in the southeast as it fought to take control and punished NPFL supporters in the area. In the west, the splintering of ULIMO further increased the level of violence: The two factions fought against each other, against the NPFL, and against

150 Governing after War

the homegrown Lofa Defense Force in Lofa county and community defense forces in Maryland (Amnesty International, 1995). ULIMO-K made multiple incursions into Bong county, turning large parts of the NPFL-held county into contested territory in 1994, and briefly controlled the rebel capital Gbarnga from late 1994 to early 1995.

The loss of social control over much of the country—particularly the fall of Gbarnga for a few months in 1994—"frustrated and scared" NPFL soldiers, who "turned their aggression toward civilians" (Lidow, 2016, 126). From 1992 onward, rebels were deployed to various frontlines to fight against other factions, which significantly increased the battalions' movements (Ex-combatant #9). NPFL soldiers became roving rebels (Olson, 1993) and acted accordingly. The rebels no longer attempted to maintain cordial relations with civilians: Since they were constantly on the move, it was easier for the rebels to make demands and for civilians to either flee the area or comply to save their lives. During this period, civilians living outside of NPFL strongholds reported that the rebels did not attempt to develop a relationship with them during rebel occupation, and rebels did not return or maintain any communication after they left. As one civilian put it, who lived in Bomi county during the war—which suffered military contestation from 1992 onward—"there is no communication with the rebels after. When they move, they move" (Focus group #2). The NPFL's internal cohesion broke down significantly as well, such that rebel commanders were less able to control their own fighters. This violence against civilians increased as rebel soldiers looted and used violence to steal food and goods for themselves. Roving rebels also used civilians as shields on the military frontlines (Human Rights Watch, 1993), particularly when heavy fighting occurred in enemy territories like Bomi county (Ex-combatant interview #16), Monrovia (Focus group #4), and Lofa county (Focus group #5).

A second reason for transient rebel–civilian relations is civilian flight: As military contestation increased, so did civilian displacement.[9] In focus groups, civilians complained that the war had frequently forced them to flee, which prevented them from living a normal life: "Any time we try to start something again, we experience crisis" (Focus group #3). There was also significant displacement for civilians who lived in the NPFL stronghold of Bong county; despite being under rebel control for most of the war, the rebel capital briefly fell at the end of 1994 and forced many civilians to either flee to Guinea (Focus group #12) or move with the NPFL to Nimba county (Focus

---

[9] Displacement throughout the country was high: Over 1.2 million people are estimated to have been internally displaced persons or refugees at some point during the civil war (Innes, 2005, 293).

The Liberia Civil War (1989–1996) **151**

groups #11, #12). In some cases, civilian displacement was rebel induced: Rebels abducted some civilians as secondary support (Focus groups #8, #11, #12).[10] The NPFL brought civilians along with them when ECOMOG took over Buchanan, and killed those who refused (Amnesty International, 1994).

That civilian displacement occurred throughout the state during the latter half of the war emphasizes the NPFL's loss of military and social control over Taylorland. However, sub-national variation is also informative: While civilian displacement was high during the war, there were noticeable differences in the frequency of civilian movement based on the level of local military contestation. Citizens who originated from central Liberia tended to move less than those who lived in contested zones: Two civilians from Bong county, for example, complained about having to leave Gbarnga when it fell in 1994. Other Bong county residents similarly told me about war coming in 1994 briefly, but they were able to return in 1995 "when war was over" (Focus group #11); while the war was not officially over by then, for Bong county residents the war ended when peace returned to their home county at that time. While displacement affected their lives deeply, these civilians were displaced fewer times than others elsewhere in the country.

Civilians with family in the west or southeast reported more movement spanning almost the entire period of military contestation (Focus groups #9, #10, #16). One man traveled from Monrovia eastward to Grand Bassa county in 1992, and then to Sinoe county in 1993. He found relative peace in Gbarnga in 1994 but when it fell in 1994, he escaped to Nimba (Focus group #1). Another went back and forth between the eastern and western borders, seeking shelter in four different counties and a refugee camp in Côte d'Ivoire before returning to Liberia after the end of the war (Focus group #16).[11] Finally, displacement affected the Kru and Krahn communities from the very beginning: As the NPFL swept into eastern Liberia in 1990, civilians fled to Côte d'Ivoire, where they remained until the end of the war in 1997 (Focus groups #15 and #16).[12]

---

[10] Rebels in other civil wars have engaged in this practice in areas with high levels of military contestation (see, for example, the Movimento Popular de Libertação de Angola (MPLA) in Section 7.2).

[11] My focus group participants all lived in Monrovia at the time I spoke with them. They are likely to have experienced above average levels of displacement, since they eventually ended up in the capital after leaving their home areas during the war. Displacement is likely to have been lower among people who are still in their home counties.

[12] Mass civilian displacement among the Kru and Krahn communities highlights why territorial control does not necessarily indicate *social* control: While the NPFL maintained territorial control in these districts, social control was impossible due to displacement and low influence due to ethnic enmity.

5.4.2 Displacement Eroded Stable Rebel–Civilian Ties

Civilian victimization and displacement destroyed any organized rebel–civilian infrastructure that was set up during the initial years. Among those who did not attempt to escape violence, the relationships between rebels and civilians became more temporary and coercive. Relationships with chiefs and single-barrel men broke down as military contestation increased from 1992 to 1996.

Indiscriminate violence meant that the initial ties with chiefs and single-barrel men in rebel-controlled towns and villages broke down between 1992 and 1996. While stationary rebels initially worked with traditional leadership, roving rebels were less willing to negotiate, and more likely to "take food, make demands, [and] ask for daughters" (Focus group #2). An ex-combatant who had been a child soldier since 1990 recalled harassing civilians for food primarily from 1994 onward, when he was deployed to fight against ULIMO along the iron mines (Ex-combatant #21). Increased wartime violence also meant that civilians had less food to contribute as crops were frequently destroyed by factional fighting and roving rebels (Lidow, 2010). These two factors put chiefs "in a bad position" (Focus group #3): As food became scarcer and the violence intensified, there was greater pressure on town and village chiefs to produce food and resources for the rebels who passed by their area (Focus groups #2, #3, #6). Even worse, roving rebels also meant that villages were asked to help multiple rebel groups at their own peril. If a group discovered that the chief had aided another group, he would be killed or face severe violence (Focus group #6).

Rebel brutality toward chiefs, from all armed groups involved in the conflict, destroyed rebel–civilian ties. In the contested Bomi county, for example, chiefs were "totally disrespected" and "seen as the enemy" because of their ties to the previous government (Focus group #4). In some cases, chiefs fled the area to avoid the approaching rebels: "all the people who used to be town chief during those days . . . they started running away" (Focus group #3). This was especially the case if the chief and some villagers had remained loyal to another rebel group that had since lost control. In other cases, chiefs who refused to comply were promptly killed and replaced by new elders—only for the same to happen again when a new rebel group came into town (Focus groups #3, #4, #5). Remaining in contact with chiefs after this significant period of displacement and constant chief replacement would therefore have been impossible throughout most of Liberia: Military contestation severed the NPFL's initial ties with chiefs, while citizens who were dissatisfied with their chief's ties to various armed groups were quick to replace them once the war was over.

The Liberia Civil War (1989–1996)   **153**

Similarly, relationships with the single-barrel men dissolved as civilians sought to escape violence. Single-barrel men, who were considered clear NPFL supporters, fled from their towns and became displaced when the fighting reached their surveillance areas. A civilian who lived in Lofa county explained that once the peaceful period had ended and new factions entered, single-barrel men were "the first to be killed" (Focus group #5). They therefore either fled or defected: "Why would they stay? They must stay alive, so they joined [ULIMO-K]" (Focus group #5). An ex-combatant agreed that the single-barrel men would run away if ULIMO took over a town (Ex-combatant #22). According to ex-combatants, even if their single-barrel men stayed in town during contestation, they could no longer be trusted: "Many put us in traps, many people died" (Ex-combatant #41). Teams of single-barrel men thus easily lost contact with the NPFL rebels once the NPFL was pushed out of an area by opposing rebel groups. Areas lost to rivals therefore also lost their single-barrel men very quickly.

With reduced control, a subset of the single-barrel men became more violent, and the lines between "rebels" and "civilian spies" blurred. Their violence was associated with the rebels, even though they were only armed with civilian hunting guns. As war continued and contestation increased, single-barrel men used these weapons to increase their own power and wealth. A local government official from a contested area recalled her experiences with the single-barrel men during the latter half of the war: "Anything you get they take it from you. When they get the gun, you cannot say no" (Government official interview #1). Another ex-combatant who operated in Lofa county explained that single-barrel men began exercising their power over local enemies because "they [had] the guns in the community" (Ex-combatant #19). As social order decreased and rebels left the area, the violent structures they left behind—such as the single-barrel men—continued to perpetuate and exacerbate violence.

Rebels instead relied heavily on a third group of civilians—traveling market women—for information during the latter half of the war.

Civilian Type III: Market Women

As military contestation increased, the NPFL began relying more heavily on ad hoc ties to gather information about their rivals. A common way to access such information was to ask market traders who frequently crossed the borders into neighboring countries. Unlike other civilians during the civil war, these market women were uniquely allowed to travel freely across Liberia and into different countries with little harassment or suspicion, and spoke all of the local languages (Ex-combatant #34; Focus groups #2, #5). As one ex-combatant explained, "There was those that we met, the marketeers. They are

[our] eyes... they will tell you across the Guinea border there, where they're coming from, what they saw there, how does it look like" (Ex-combatant #29). They were therefore important sources of information about ongoing events, and rebels and civilians both used them to pass messages between different areas.

NPFL ties to these market women were not organized. Because of their trade, market women were not anchored to specific areas during the civil war; rebels were also constantly on the move during the latter half of the war. This made lasting alliances unlikely: Interviewees suggested that they were unlikely to run into the same market woman consistently due to frequent movement (Ex-combatant #19). Instead, the women gave information to any rebel group that crossed their paths in exchange for food, money, or to avoid being captured. If the women entered NPFL territory, they would provide information about enemy rebel groups to the NPFL rebels (Ex-combatant #18, #34); the same applied if they found themselves in ULIMO or LPC territory. As one rebel described the soldiers' interactions with the market women, "If they go [into ULIMO territory] they will talk good. If they come they will talk good" (Ex-combatant #29).

This shift toward prioritizing civilians with greater mobility exemplifies how rebels viewed their own roving nature: Rather than prioritizing checkpoints and civilian ties within towns and villages, NPFL soldiers—and their rivals—came to prefer obtaining information from knowledgeable civilians on the road. Instead of attempting to establish some form of stability and order for the purposes of extraction, military contestation over resource-rich areas and trade hubs meant that coercive demands for information became the primary form of rebel–civilian interaction. Due to the nature of contestation and increased rebel movements, information was most valuable when it came from highly mobile citizens rather than from stable spy networks and locally based units such as the single-barrel men. Rebels recognized that the information from these mobile civilians was of low quality and may be false, but it was preferable to no information at all. The NPFL's reliance on market women for information carried forward into Taylor's presidency and the second civil war, emphasizing how few ties the NPFL had sustained from the first war.

The only reward provided to informants was not killing them; there were no attempts to renew communication on either end. Ex-rebels claimed that repeated interactions would have been impossible due to their roving nature. This short time horizon led to disposable ties that were not amenable to sub-national governance and wartime social control.

5.4.3 Rebel–Civilian Relations in Partisan Territory

As the rest of the country became a war-torn battleground between 1992 and 1996, the original starting point of the war—the northern parts of Nimba county—became peaceful (Ex-combatant interview #9; Focus groups #7, #8). One civilian reported moving to rural Nimba in 1991 to live with his grandfather, where he experienced no further conflict (Focus group #3). Another civilian corroborated this account, citing only INPFL recruitment and violence rather than NPFL presence: "There was no more violence, we were at peace... before then, we were told that Nimba experienced hectic violence because Prince Johnson's group was there recruiting people, visiting villages, destroy people's animals... but when we got there [in 1991], the violence had subsided" (Focus group #8). Consistent with the available conflict data, Galea et al. (2010, 9) notes that Nimba was primarily affected only in 1990, and that the county was generally peaceful afterwards. Similarly, Ellis (2003, 185) writes that the core NPFL troops that had been trained in Libya had retired by 1994, returning home to Nimba county where they set up small businesses.

The result of having garnered immediate support from Nimba at the start of the war meant that in rural areas of the county—particularly those that were not useful for extraction or as transport routes—there were few localized, rebel-supervised civilian institutions. Notable exceptions were areas near Bong county, where rebels retreated after Gbarnga was briefly taken over by rivals; the capital Ganta, which was a major transportation route and an important civilian hub; and the Nimba mines in Yekepa, where Taylor received taxes from the iron mining company LIMINCO in Yekepa from 1990 until production halted in 1993 (Gerdes, 2013, 122).[13]

Whereas the NPFL had set up surveillance and taxation systems in central Liberia for the purposes of feeding soldiers and obtaining information, it focused primarily on quick recruitment in Nimba before moving to the interior of the country (Galea et al., 2010, 8–9). Consequently, the rural areas of Nimba county had lower levels of organizational capacity: Although the NPFL had a high level of influence there due to ethnic ties, its brief occupation of Nimba and subsequent focus on other parts of Liberia meant a low rebel presence in much of the county for most of the war years.

---

[13] As fighting intensified, the main iron-exporting port of Buchanan—heavily contested between the NPFL, ECOMOG, and LPC by 1993—was looted and dismantled.

5.5 Spatial Representation of Rebel Social Control

Accounts of wartime Liberia provide a nuanced picture of how military contestation had eliminated many of the NPFL's rebel–civilian ties across the country and, consequently, its organizational capacity on the ground. I now turn to examine the breadth and depth of these ties across Liberia.

In Chapter 2, I typologized wartime terrain as broadly falling into one of four categories: The victor's stronghold, their rival(s)' strongholds, the victor's partisan terrain, or contested territory. Classifying a locality into one of these categories depends on armed group(s)' *presence* and the *influence* each group exercised over it. I draw on two data sources to code rebel presence and influence: (1) for rebel presence, the UCDP-GED polygon-level dataset[14] and (2) for rebel influence, ethnic homogeneity data from the 2008 Census. I then demonstrate that rebel presence and influence translated to the strength of rebel–civilian ties and the establishment of social control by analyzing patterns of the NPFL's wartime local chief replacements and appointments.

5.5.1 Coding Rebel Control and Contestation

First, I code for the NPFL's *presence* in each locality, which is defined as the number of uninterrupted years of rebel presence counting backwards from the end of the civil war in 1996. This variable is coded from 0 (no NPFL presence) to 6 (steady NPFL presence for the entire civil war).[15] I code counting backwards to better align with the theory which argues that an uninterrupted rule is important, and that a rebel group is unlikely to simply reestablish social control following mass displacement due to destabilization. Therefore, if a territory experienced constant NPFL presence from 1991 to

---

[14] The underlying conflict data draws on the UCDP-GED data that includes point-level information, such as intensity and estimated battle deaths, for local violent events between rebel groups, against civilians, and against the government. It also includes a polygon-level dataset that uses point-level information to estimate rebel group coverage in a particular year with respect to each dyad of violence, such as conflict between two rebel groups, between a rebel group and government forces, or rebel violence against civilians. The polygons are defined as "the smallest possible convex geographical area that encompasses the locations of all UCDP-GED events in each covered UCDP dyad within a specified time period" (Croicu and Sundberg, 2012). While the data is estimated and is thus imprecise, the polygon-level dataset is the best available data source from which to derive rebel presence in a given year.

[15] Although the civil war ended in 1996—for a total of seven years of conflict—the UCDP dataset notes that the violence in 1996 occurred only in Monrovia; thus there were only six years of conflict data outside the capital (1990–1995). This is empirically consistent with the military stalemate in 1995, which lasted until the April 6, 1996 invasion of Monrovia.

The Liberia Civil War (1989–1996)   **157**

1993 but was completely overtaken in 1994 and subsequently reclaimed by the NPFL in 1995, it is coded as having one year of presence at the end of the civil war—indicating that the rebel group had to start from scratch to establish civilian ties. A locality that initially had an NPFL presence but was overtaken by enemy rebel groups and never retaken by the NPFL would be coded as having no NPFL presence by the end of the war. Since the variable is defined based on yearly presence, if an area was only briefly taken over and quickly regained within the year (such as the rebel capital in Gbarnga), NPFL presence is still coded as continuous.[16]

Second, I code whether an area was predisposed to support (i.e., high *influence*) the NPFL (Gio or Mano) or rival rebel groups (Krahn and Mandingo), since ethnic identity was a key dimension of the civil war. I calculate the percentage of civilians in each locality that belonged to one of these four ethnic groups. If the *sum* of Gio and Mano (Krahn and Mandingo) residents was greater than 50%, the locality is coded as having a high level of NPFL (rival) influence. I use a 50% cutoff because the resulting spatial depictions of wartime social control best match historical accounts of the conflict. However, the quantitative results are robust to alternative percentage cutoffs (70%, 80%).

Third, using the measure of NPFL *presence*, I identify localities that experienced one to three years of NPFL presence by the end of the civil war. In practice, this subset of localities would consist of (1) areas over which the NPFL lost control for some period of time during the high-contestation years from 1992 to 1994;[17] or (2) localities that were largely unaffected by the civil war. I categorize these localities into different types of terrain based on ethnic homogeneity. I code them as pro-NPFL *partisan* territories if they had a greater than 50% population share of Gio and Mano civilians (high NPFL *influence*), and thus would have supported the NPFL from the outset of the war. Localities that had a greater than 50% share of Krahn and Mandingo

---

[16] Short-term changes in presence due to territorial switching are not possible to code accurately using this data, because it does not indicate whether a rebel group fought and lost against rivals or whether it won and sustained its presence. If a rebel group was not present for a full year after contestation, this drop in presence is likely to be long-lasting and represent a loss during military contestation. Gbarnga is an exception, as it was a particularly high-profile loss of territory switching. Since there is far less detailed information available for elsewhere in the country, presence is coded yearly for consistency.

[17] This coding makes sense, given that the NPFL had maintained *territorial* control of over 90% of the country by 1990, and had successfully exerted *social* control in most of these areas before the contestation began. If the NPFL was only present in an area for a few years counting backwards from the end of the war, that means it was likely severed from NPFL operational zones from 1992 to 1994.

158 Governing after War

civilians are coded as *rival* territories (high rival *influence*).[18] The remaining localities, which did not have at least a 50% population share of these ethnic groups, are considered *contested* territories (low NPFL *influence* with low rival *influence*).[19] I code contested territories as 1/3 if there were three years of NPFL presence, 2/3 if there were two years of NPFL presence, and full contestation if there was only one year of NPFL presence—indicating inter-rebel fighting until the very end of the civil war.

Fourth, I use the various rebel groups' *presence* in localities to code NPFL and rival strongholds during the civil war. Localities with an NPFL *presence* of four to six years were never captured by rival forces during the war; these are NPFL strongholds. For greater specificity in the depth of social control exerted over these strongholds, I code NPFL *control* as 1/3 if there were four years of NPFL presence, 2/3 if there were five years, and full control if there were six years of NPFL presence. Conversely, in localities that experienced a rival's presence and then no subsequent NPFL presence, rival rebel forces likely pushed the NPFL out during the years of contestation. I code these areas as being under rival strongholds, which are added to the localities that are rival partisans (see earlier).

This coding strategy allows us to differentiate between localities that were under NPFL control (with a degree of control between 1/3 and 1), contested terrain (with a degree of contestation between 1/3 and 1), partisan terrain, or rival terrain. The three maps in Figure 5.3 display the spatial representation of these variables, which were coded based on the rules just outlined. Because the theory considers contested and partisan terrain to both be low organizational capacity, I plot them on the same map.

The resulting coding largely follows the detailed qualitative accounts about the First Liberian Civil War: NPFL control centered primarily around Bong county (home to the rebel capital in Gbarnga) and upper Margibi county. Civilian accounts, which suggest that Margibi was at the edge of the NPFL's territory, corroborate the switch from NPFL to contested territory. However, the rival rebel groups ULIMO-K and ULIMO-J held almost the entire western border and reached Monrovia, while the rival LPC controlled the southeastern parts encompassing the important port of Buchanan. In the eastern areas of Grand Gedeh county, neither the NPFL nor rival forces exercised much

---

[18] In practice, many of these localities are better considered partisan rivals, rather than rival strongholds with local rival–civilian ties. As my theory argues, however, areas that were predisposed to support rivals should have received the same hypothesized treatment from the new rebel government after the civil war as those under rival control *even if* the rival also has low organizational capacity in these areas. This is because the government has little information about the ties between the rivals and their supporters.

[19] No territories were neutral—not military contested, yet supporting neither the NPFL nor its rivals.

The Liberia Civil War (1989–1996) 159

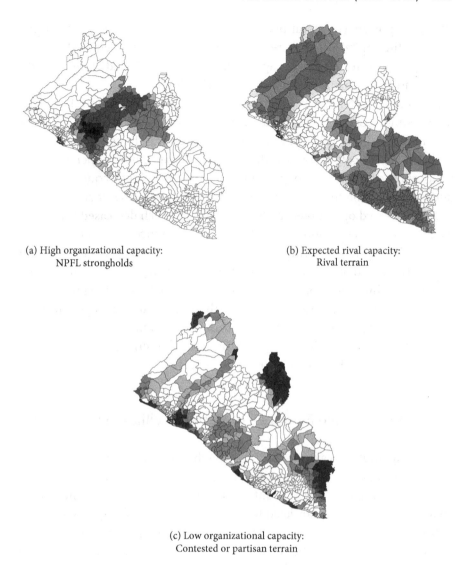

(a) High organizational capacity: NPFL strongholds

(b) Expected rival capacity: Rival terrain

(c) Low organizational capacity: Contested or partisan terrain

Figure 5.3 Territory maps

Notes: Wartime political geography is coded at the *locality* level; however, the maps display the average level of control or contestation at the *clan* level. While there are overlaps between different types of territories at the clan level, and at the locality level, each locality is coded as *one* of the categories. For example, if NPFL strongholds > 0, then rival = 0 and contested or partisan = 0.

social control over civilian lives as local militias fought against the NPFL rebels in the initial years, and the LPC and NPFL failed to consolidate control in the later years. Nevertheless, the new government would have viewed these areas as rival territories because the population was made up of the rivals'

160 Governing after War

ethnic supporters (i.e., rival partisans).[20] The areas surrounding Monrovia (but not the capital itself) were contested, as the NPFL attempted to enter the city but was never able to capture it. Monrovia is classed as being under rival control due to joint ECOMOG/ULIMO efforts.

Areas coded as NPFL *partisans* are primarily located in the central northern tip, in Nimba county. The qualitative evidence suggests that the NPFL presence in rural Nimba was strong until 1992. However, as the conflict intensified in the rest of the country, and as the NPFL shifted its military operations and political headquarters to Bong county, large parts of Nimba county were left undisturbed by the civil war.[21] This was particularly the case when iron mines in Nimba ceased operations due to the civil war, which decreased the NPFL's potential revenues. Undoubtedly, the rebels' presence in Nimba was not completely eliminated during the war. However, the NPFL's operations were primarily focused on Ganta—the county capital—and the interior areas along Nimba's southwestern border with Bong (stronghold) and along the eastern border with Grand Bassa (contested). These areas had a higher military presence during the war according to qualitative accounts, and are accurately portrayed as being NPFL strongholds or contested territories based on the variable operationalization previously detailed.

5.5.2 Quantitative Evidence of Rebel–Civilian Ties

My coding strategy captures NPFL strongholds, their rivals' strongholds, NPFL partisan terrain, and contested terrain. While I have argued that these map well onto qualitative accounts of wartime social control, I now show quantitatively that this translated to the (non)existence of rebel–civilian ties.

No area of Liberia truly escaped wartime contestation between rival groups—not even the rebel capital in Bong county. However, there was sub-national variation in the length and intensity of inter-group contestation across the country, which I examine here. I show quantitatively that (1) the NPFL formed ties during the civil war in its strongholds with individuals who

---

[20] My decision to code these as pro-rival areas highlights the difference between rebel *social* control and *territorial* control. Official accounts of the civil war indicate that the NPFL did sustain nominal territorial control over the northeast throughout most of the war. However, social control was very low: Violence between NPFL troops and homegrown militias—combined with mass displacement resulting from the NPFL's initial violent incursion into rival ethnic communities—significantly increased displacement. My interviews and focus groups indicated that the NPFL was never able to form any ties to civilians in this region.
[21] According to Ellis (2007), NPFL soldiers who retired mid-war returned home to Nimba county to start their own businesses.

The Liberia Civil War (1989–1996) **161**

could act as local leaders and (2) the depth of NPFL embeddedness—or lack thereof—contributed to Taylor's inability to fully mobilize civilian supporters on the ground. I focus on chieftaincy appointments: As I documented qualitatively, the NPFL established roots in various localities by replacing existing chiefs with new ones who were more willing to cooperate with the rebels and to supply them with food, shelter, and information. Chief replacement is similarly described in (Baldwin and Mvukiyehe, 2015), who also ascertained that war-appointed chiefs remain in power in parts of Liberia today.

Because clan chiefs in Liberia are part of the local government structure, I collected yearly government personnel lists from the Government of Liberia from 2009 (the earliest records available) to 2015. I use these hiring records to determine the dates of clan chief appointments during the civil war. Although the hiring data is only available from 2009, the payroll records identify when each chief was first officially appointed by the government as the head of his area (*chief start date*), which allows me to build a cross-sectional dataset of chief appointments for each available clan.

There are two primary concerns regarding the chiefs' data. First, because I could only obtain hiring records from 2009 onward, there is a subset of clan chiefs who were appointed in 2004 or later—after the end of the first civil war—for which I have no records of the previous chief. For those clans, I am unable to confirm the wartime chiefs' appointment dates for the relevant time periods in this study, which are those who were in power during or before Charles Taylor's rule. I therefore drop all chiefs who were appointed from 2004 onward from the analyses, and only examine the subset of clans for which the chiefs were appointed during or before Taylor's regime. The second concern with this data source is that record keeping was poor during the civil war and immediate post-war period, so each chief's exact year of appointment may not be accurate. I account for this possibility by pooling chief appointments into an indicator variable for whether the chief was appointed during the war (rather than the specific year), which reduces the level of specificity needed from the data. To further help with data missingness and data quality, I supplement this dataset with data collected by Baldwin and Mvukiyehe (2015), which contains a sample of sixty-eight self-reported chief appointment years in clans located in higher-conflict areas. My final sample contains 328 clan chiefs covering 7,727 rural localities.

I combine this chieftaincy data with the 2008 Population and Housing Census of Liberia, which provides individual-level information—including education and literacy levels—for all residents. I geocoded the census data by merging it with administrative units and locality shapefiles from LISGIS

162   Governing after War

and UNMIL. Liberia has 15 counties (administrative level 1) and 136 districts (administrative level 2). The third administrative level is the clan level, which represents either clans in rural areas or communities in urban areas; only rural areas have clan chiefs. Matching the clan boundaries and a list of rural clans obtained from the Ministry of Internal Affairs, I find 646 matchable clans in rural Liberia.

I create an indicator variable, *During war*, which is coded 1 if the chief was appointed between 1990 (when the civil war started) and 1997 (when clan chiefs were formally appointed to local governments after Taylor became president). Although the war ended in 1996, I assume that chiefs who were formally appointed in 1997—Taylor's first year in government—were acting as appointed chiefs during the war. It would not be plausible to use appointments between 1990 and 1996: Only around thirty clan chiefs were recorded as having been appointed during that time, while more than one hundred were appointed in 1997 alone, which strongly suggests that most chiefs who were appointed during the war were not formally recorded as such until 1997. Such discrepancies are unsurprising, given both the wartime insecurity and the fact that chiefs are considered government employees: They would not have been paid employees—and thus not formally recorded by the Ministry of Internal Affairs—until the new government formally appointed them in 1997. Using this method of coding chief appointments, I find that of all the clan chiefs who were appointed prior to 2004, 141 were appointed during the war (covering 4,125 localities).

Two additional challenges arise. First, since it is not possible to identify chiefs who were replaced due to conflict-related fatalities, I control for cross-locality differences in levels of fighting and civilian casualties as well as ethnic region fixed effects. I also show that the level of conflict was lowest in NPFL strongholds, which is inconsistent with the counterargument that chiefs in strongholds were more likely to be replaced during the war due to deaths. The second challenge is that the NPFL's rivals should theoretically also have appointed chiefs in their zones of control, meaning that war-appointed chiefs might be present throughout the country—not just in NPFL strongholds. I argue, however, that the NPFL was more likely than other rebel groups to replace chiefs. The qualitative evidence indeed suggests that rivals did not form ties with civilians and bypassed chiefs as local leaders (Focus group #15) since rivals never established long-term social control and thus maintained few rebel–civilian ties even in territories under their control (Lidow, 2016). Because these rival groups began and ended the war with relatively high levels of military contestation, they had very shallow (or no) ties with their alleged strongholds. I corroborate this assumption using conflict data, which

The Liberia Civil War (1989–1996)   **163**

demonstrates that opposition areas experienced the highest levels of violence during the first civil war.

Even if rivals did sometimes appoint chiefs during the war, these challenges are partially mitigated by using current-day chieftaincy data. As I argued in the qualitative section, when Taylor came to power in 1997, he installed chiefs who were amenable to his presidency. This meant formally appointing the chiefs that the NPFL had put in place during the war, and perhaps replacing some chiefs elsewhere who were reluctant to cooperate with the new government. However, in areas where the local population did not support Taylor, local civilians viewed the chiefs he put in power (along with other local government officials) with significant suspicion. As civilians from Bomi county explained, during Taylor's rule they found themselves governed by chiefs who were "young people" with "no idea of leadership" (Focus group #5). This mattered a great deal to citizens; after Taylor was overthrown, some pre-war chiefs were reinstated, while in other cases "people picked a new chief" who they believed was more suitable to govern the community (Focus group #5). Therefore, current-day data on clan chiefs would *not* indicate that these clans were governed by a war chief now: Only chiefs who enjoyed a degree of local legitimacy with civilians would still be in power.[22]

When analyzing current chieftaincy appointments, we should therefore expect that chiefs appointed in 1997 when Taylor came to power—who are still chiefs today even after Ellen Johnson Sirleaf was elected president in 2005—are primarily from areas that were NPFL strongholds. In these areas, the NPFL would have appointed new chiefs during the war, and civilians would have continued to support them even after the NPFL was overthrown. Elsewhere in the country, chiefs would more likely have been either appointed before the war but not replaced by Taylor in 1997, or replaced in 2005 by the Sirleaf regime shortly after Taylor's overthrow. While there is also attenuation in the data due to natural deaths or chief retirement beyond 2005, those factors should not differentially affect any part of the state. I estimate:

$$\text{During war}_{ljt} = \alpha + \beta \text{NPFL stronghold}_l + \zeta_l + \eta_l + \kappa_t + \epsilon_{lt}$$

where the coefficient of interest is β. ζ_l represents locality-level war controls, including the logged number of civilian deaths and whether the locality was

---

[22] I draw three descriptive conclusions from the chief appointments data: (1) NPFL strongholds now tend to be governed by chiefs who were appointed immediately after Taylor came into office, (2) ULIMO-K strongholds are now more likely to be governed by chiefs who were appointed prior to the civil war, and (3) LPC strongholds today are governed primarily by chiefs appointed by Ellen Johnson Sirleaf, who headed the new government after Taylor was ousted.

affected by the second war. η_l are locality-level demographic and distance controls: logged population, logged size of the ethnic population according to the 2008 Census, logged distance to the county capital, and logged distance to Monrovia. Finally, I include ethnic group fixed effects κ_t based on the George Murdock map of ethnographic regions for Africa (Murdock, Blier, and Nunn, 1959), which maps the boundaries of pre-war ethnic divisions. I estimate this equation using both the full universe of chiefs in Liberia and—to show that this is an outcome of war and not co-ethnicity—for the subset of chiefs excluding the co-ethnic *partisan* territories. Regressions are clustered at the clan (treatment) level.

Results

Figure 5.4a displays the spatial representation of these chief appointments. Clans shaded in light gray are either in (1) urban towns with no chiefs or rural clans missing from the government dataset (total of 13.7%), or (2) rural villages with chiefs who were replaced after 2003 (32%) and thus have no data about the chief who was affected by the war and Taylor's government. Of the clans with available data, wartime chief replacement (dark gray) clustered primarily around central Liberia within Bong and Margibi counties. This matches up well with the map of NPFL control in Figure 5.4b, where the NPFL's wartime strongholds are shown to be clearly around central Liberia as well. Besides central Liberia, most wartime chieftaincy appointments

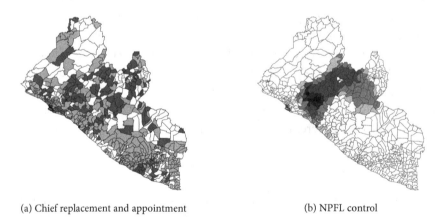

(a) Chief replacement and appointment (b) NPFL control

Figure 5.4 Chief replacement and appointment under Taylor

Notes: Figure 5.4a depicts war-appointed chiefs in dark gray. Light gray areas denote chiefdoms in which the latest chief appointments were made *after* the second civil war (i.e., after 2003). Most were, according to government records, formally appointed following the new government under Sirleaf in 2005. Areas in white denote chiefdoms in which chiefs were appointed either before the civil war (prior to 1990) or during Taylor's government (1998–2003). Figure 5.4b reproduces NPFL wartime control, for comparison.

The Liberia Civil War (1989–1996) 165

Table 5.1 Chief replacement

	(1) Full sample	(2) Excluding partisan territories
NPFL control	0.256** (0.120)	0.295** (0.124)
Observations	8,607	7,795
R^2	0.213	0.228
Conflict controls	✓	✓
Location controls	✓	✓
Fixed effects	Ethnic region	Ethnic region
Clustered SE	Clan	Clan

Notes: $^*p < 0.1$, $^{**}p < 0.05$, $^{***}p < 0.01$. Robust standard errors in parentheses, clustered at the clan level. The regression includes pretreatment ethnic region fixed effects, as measured by the Murdock map of ethnographic regions for Africa. Controls include logged civilian deaths, number of years the locality was affected by the second civil war, logged population, logged size of ethnic group, logged distance to the county capital, and logged distance to Monrovia.

(Figure 5.4a) were made in Nimba county in the central-northern tip. Nimba county—where the NPFL initially began its insurgency—is split into NPFL strongholds (nearer central Liberia) and NPFL partisan territory (toward the north, which was largely peaceful after the first one to two years of war). It is possible that these chief appointments were made during those initial years as the NPFL entered the country and established its first support base in Nimba.

Table 5.1 presents the regression estimates. In column 1, I regress the level of NPFL control on wartime chief appointment, and find that areas that were fully under the NPFL's social control throughout the war had a 25.6% higher likelihood of having a chief who was replaced during the war compared to rival-supporting or contested areas. The results remain robust and the point estimates are stable—and even slightly higher—when co-ethnic partisan territories are excluded in column 2. This evidence is consistent with my argument that the NPFL leadership made conscious efforts to increase their local control over civilian affairs by building ties with civilians through whom they could rule at the local level. These results are also robust to analyses at the clan level (Appendix C2.1),[23] which provides additional evidence in support of the qualitative data.

While the regressions in Table 5.1 include conflict and casualty controls, Table 5.2 is further evidence that wartime chief replacement cannot be entirely explained by conflict-related deaths and displacement. If chiefs were

[23] Although the outcome variable is at the clan level, NPFL control is coded at the locality level. Clan-level analyses thus operationalize NPFL control as whether the NPFL controlled *all* localities within a clan.

166 Governing after War

Table 5.2 Chief replacement

Panel A: Within 10 km	Conflict		Civilian deaths		Total deaths	
NPFL control	−1.060***	−1.060**	−0.940	−0.940	−2.354	−2.354
	(0.134)	(0.447)	(8.055)	(25.747)	(8.816)	(26.252)
Contested or partisan	0.469***	0.469	41.082***	41.082	40.263***	40.263
	(0.127)	(0.446)	(7.661)	(46.479)	(8.384)	(46.603)
Rival	0.586***	0.586*	46.580***	46.580*	54.407***	54.407*
	(0.099)	(0.347)	(5.978)	(25.059)	(6.543)	(27.997)
Observations	12,830	12,830	12,830	12,830	12,830	12,830
Clustered		✓		✓		✓
XY coord controls	✓	✓	✓	✓	✓	✓
T-test p-values						
NPFL control < cont./part.	0.000	0.000	0.000	0.231	0.000	0.227
NPFL control < rival	0.000	0.000	0.000	0.053	0.000	0.043

Panel B: Within 5 km	Conflict		Civilian deaths		Total deaths	
NPFL control	−0.259***	−0.259*	−1.846	−1.846	−1.798	−1.798
	(0.070)	(0.135)	(3.928)	(6.878)	(4.451)	(7.094)
Contested or partisan	0.054	0.054	5.569	5.569	5.166	5.166
	(0.067)	(0.139)	(3.735)	(9.935)	(4.233)	(10.054)
Rival	0.208***	0.208*	12.004***	12.004	14.248***	14.248*
	(0.052)	(0.125)	(2.915)	(7.646)	(3.304)	(8.375)
Observations	12,830	12,830	12,830	12,830	12,830	12,830
Clustered SE		✓		✓		✓
XY coord. controls	✓	✓	✓	✓	✓	✓
T-test p-values						
NPFL control < cont./part.	0.000	0.018	0.015	0.372	0.043	0.408
NPFL control < rival	0.000	0.001	0.000	0.085	0.000	0.069

Notes: $*p < 0.1$, $**p < 0.05$, $***p < 0.01$. All regressions include squared controls for X and Y coordinates. Standard errors in parentheses, clustered at the clan level where indicated. Conflict is coded as the number of violent events that took place within 10 km in Panel A, and within 5 km in Panel B. Civilian deaths is the best estimated number of civilian deaths, while Total deaths is the best estimated number of civilian and combatant deaths.

replaced due to violence, then there ought to have been greater violence in NPFL strongholds to warrant a higher incidence of chief replacement in those areas. However, my theory would predict that violence levels should be the *lowest* in strongholds, because the NPFL had sustained the most control in these areas during the civil war and therefore experienced the lowest level of military contestation. Elsewhere in the country, the NPFL enjoyed control until it lost control after high levels of military contestation. Table 5.2 shows that violence was far lower in NPFL strongholds than in contested and rival-supporting areas—in support of my theory. These results hold for conflict count, civilian deaths, and total deaths (including combatant deaths) within a ten kilometer and five kilometer radius of a locality.

5.6 Post-war Politics and the Threat of Instability

In this section I examine how these wartime rebel–civilian ties affected post-war politics. In 1997, Taylor was elected president of Liberia under the NPP by a landslide. The election was considered free and fair, which surprised and worried the international community due to the wartime conduct of Taylor and the NPFL.

5.6.1 Post-war Politics and Governance

Post-war governance in 1997 initially reflected the way that Taylor governed Taylorland between 1990 and 1992, when the NPFL sustained control. Although he undoubtedly sought to use his newfound position to extract the country's natural resource wealth and broker deals with foreign firms, such extraction is more efficient with a stable state and a supportive citizenry. Thus, for the first few months after coming to power, when the political situation was somewhat peaceful and reconciliation seemed possible, the new rebel government exhibited "a surprising financial rigor," which included paying civil servants a year's worth of back pay (French, 1998). In areas where Taylor was politically supported, chiefs—who were local government officials—were eager to comply with his government to establish a good rapport with the ruling party because this relationship dictated how government funds and public goods were distributed (Focus group #3).

While the post-war rebel government preached national reconciliation, in practice it emphasized establishing control over politics, security, and civilian lives. Taylor called for nationalism and inclusion in his inaugural speech: "we are one people, one blood, one nation, with one common destiny indivisible by God ... Let us never, ever permit ourselves to be divided again by anyone, either from within or from without" (Käihkö, 2017, 63). As in post-war Zimbabwe, however, reconciliation and unity meant support for the rebel government: dissent was not tolerated (US Department of State, 1999, 2000, 2001). Media personnel lived in fear of being harassed, abducted, and tortured for investigating government wrongdoings, and the government forcibly closed down many broadcasting institutions (French, 1998). Yet Taylor regularly participated in a phone-in radio program in which

168 Governing after War

dissenters were invited to a question—and—answer session, in effect giving him substantial control over the framing of the criticism aired on the show (Gerdes, 2013, 137).

The new government worked to promote its allies to key positions in the military. One of its first acts was to integrate ex-combatants from all factions into the national army to ease ethnic tensions (Ex-combatants #2, #19, #46). While the Armed Forces of Liberia (AFL) was previously comprised primarily of Krahn soldiers recruited during Doe's regime, the new AFL included higher-ranking rebel troops from the NPFL, ULIMO, and LPC (Ex-combatants #10, #19). Although peace processes brokered after civil wars often integrate militaries in this way (Glassmyer and Sambanis, 2008), the new government was less trusting of the AFL due to the soldiers' varied affiliations. Much like Mugabe in post-war Zimbabwe, rather than relying solely on the state army, Charles Taylor created two additional independent military units: (1) the Special Security Services (SSS) led by Taylor's right-hand man Benjamin Yeaten ("50") and (2) the Anti-Terrorist Unit (ATU) led by Taylor's son Charles Taylor Jr. ("Chucky" Taylor). The SSS was the official presidential guard, while the ATU was a new force nominally designed as an elite army. Both forces were considered Taylor's personal army and were primarily staffed by high-level NPFL commanders (Global Security, 2013).

As I argued in Chapter 2, violence is not a preferred strategy in itself. Within the national government and bureaucracy, Taylor first attempted to achieve political dominance through co-optation and patronage. He offered prior rival leaders government positions. One of his first political appointments was ULIMO-J leader Roosevelt Johnson to the post of Minister of Rural Development in order to shore up support from the Krahn ethnic group. Taylor similarly attempted to co-opt Alhaji Kromah, the Mandingo leader of ULIMO-K, along with other well-respected politicians and businessmen from multiple counties that were under rival control during the war (Gerdes, 2013, 155–160). He also appointed supporters as local government officials and bureaucrats such as ministers and chiefs. Some ex-combatants recalled Taylor trying to buy off sympathetic local leaders in rival areas with rice and tobacco (Ex-combatant interview #35) or building houses and fixing roofs for supporters in other strategic territories (Ex-combatant interview #20). Taylor also appointed allies from rival ethnic groups to local government positions (Focus group #14). Citizens from Bomi recalled that he replaced chiefs and local councilors he did not like after the war: "He can say they are dismissed, because 1997 was a special election" (Focus group #4). Taylor overhauled the governing system and installed pro-government actors to bolster the regime's ability to sustain control and gather information about local dissent.

The Liberia Civil War (1989–1996)   **169**

Taylor also attempted to win citizen support through economic means—by addressing food shortages and poverty, a tactic the NPFL also used during the war.[24] In some parts of the country, Taylor was popular for fixing the price of rice, ensuring that civilians would be able to purchase food. He curbed inflation by pegging the Liberian dollar to a fixed US dollar rate, and letting it float only when inflation was kept under control and the exchange rate remained stable (Europa, 2002, 578). These policies were popular with civilians, who were already struggling with poverty (Focus groups #2, #13; Ex-combatants #2, #7). One civilian's admiration of Taylor's presidency exemplified how he won citizen support by preventing inflation: "Though they have guns on the street... when Taylor says this, it can be normal, it can be cool" (Focus group #1). The focus group participant linked this to food prices, which had increased by late 2000 due to the second civil war: "when the second war come, prices increased again. But when Taylor says prices come down, then prices come down." Another ex-combatant similarly explained that money was "small" during this period of time, but that it was "worth something" (Ex-combatant #7). In short, Taylor sought to win support by reducing economic pressures on citizens, on whom he relied to stay in power. I demonstrate below that these policies mollified his supporters but were not sufficient to win support from neutral or rival-supporting civilians.

5.6.2 Violence Emerging from Rival Territory

I argue in Chapter 2 that co-optation does not always work—particularly in rival regions. Taylor's attempts to co-opt opposition leaders, appoint pro-government bureaucrats to establish greater control, and gather more information about ongoing dissent all failed to secure control for the new rebel government. Mirroring the post-war context in Zimbabwe, people rejected these attempts at control and considered these political appointees traitors to their own people. The threat of counter-rebellion arose just months after Taylor's inauguration from three rival-supporting regions—first within Monrovia in 1998, then from the northwestern border in 1999, and finally from a rival incursion from the east in 2003.

The Taylor regime's failure to co-opt highlights the importance of citizen support: Although the government can deploy supporters to establish control, citizens must accept them. Unlike in NPFL strongholds, where chiefs were

---

[24] Although Taylor attempted to circulate the J.J dollar used in controlled territories during the war, the British company that printed Liberian money refused to print the war currency (Gerdes, 2013, 113).

willing to work with the new government, community leaders recognized by civilians in rival areas refused to comply with government orders (Focus group #2). One civilian from Grand Gedeh county, while complaining about a co-ethnic Krahn bureaucrat in Taylor's regime, explained why they welcomed a second civil war involving the rebel group MODEL in 2003:

> During the MODEL war, the people had two main targets. Number one was Taylor, people want to get rid of Taylor. Number two was, during Taylor['s regime], we had a superintendent in Grand Gedeh . . . she was one of Taylor's eye (spy) in Grand Gedeh. At that time Taylor made her superintendent, which meant she was his eye. We wanted MODEL to catch her (Focus group #14).

To address these security concerns, the government shifted its strategy and increased security spending to break rivals' ties in rival-supporting regions. The new rebel government used violence to combat the growing insecurity in rival strongholds and citizens' rejection of government-imposed bureaucracy. From 1998 onward, as ULIMO-J combatants refused to disarm in Monrovia, security forces cracked down on Krahn civilians in the capital in an attempt to consolidate control over the city (US Department of State, 1999). Government violence expanded into two additional counties—Lofa and Bomi—by 1999 as bands of ex-ULIMO-K guerrillas, now operating under the name of LURD, crossed the border from Guinea and began to recruit in preparation for a second civil war (US Department of State, 2000). By 2000, security forces began conducting illegal surveillance of civilian homes and churches to identify rival supporters (US Department of State, 2001). There were reports of extrajudicial killings, poor prison conditions, disappearances, and torture throughout Taylor's presidency, and these occurrences increased with the outbreak of the second civil war.

Violence flared so easily because anti-NPFL sentiments from the first civil war, much of which arose from the rebel group's violence during the period of military contestation, led to early support for the new LURD rebels against Taylor. On the northwestern front, LURD enjoyed "a reasonably strong degree of support from the civilian population" Brabazon (2003, 5). In Lofa county, communal conflicts between ethnic groups were exacerbated and politicized by wartime contestation between the NPFL and ULIMO-K, fueling civilian bitterness and anger toward the new rebel government. The threat of counter-rebellion even became problematic in areas where the NPFL had initially established wartime civilian ties that were later broken due to high military contestation. The focus group discussions conducted for this study suggest that these areas faced high levels of displacement and thus increased opportunism, which led to easier recruitment into the second civil war.[25]

5.6.3 Delegating Governance within Strongholds (Sub-national hypothesis 1)

As in Zimbabwe, Taylor attempted to delegate governance within strongholds. Yet this strategy failed to produce the same results. Due to the high level of military contestation that took place from 1992 onward—and in particular the brief fall of even the NPFL stronghold Gbarnga in 1994—the NPFL failed to maintain stable and long-lasting control over much of the original Taylorland territory. The wartime structures that were put in place had significantly deteriorated, leaving only minimal capacity for security and information provision, primarily in central Liberia. Taylor tried to rely on this limited organizational capacity to help secure local stability and support in the party's wartime strongholds. This strategy enjoyed initial limited success at preventing civil war from affecting strongholds: Despite rebels attacking central Liberia from the west since 1999, civilians in strongholds described the war as minimal (Focus groups #3, #8, #9, #11) compared to those who had experience living in rival (Focus groups #15, #16) and contested areas (Focus group #13).

After the war, friendly chiefs who were appointed during the war maintained those positions and formally became government employees. Evidence from both interviews and focus groups suggest that chiefs in NPFL strongholds used their positions primarily to provide information to the government about security matters during the second war (Focus group #4; Ex-combatant #33). In a focus group with Bong county residents, everyone agreed with the assessment that chiefs in controlled territories were used as allies in the same way during the first and second wars without being paid after Taylor came to power: "During that time chiefs were not being paid by the government no ... during Charles Taylor['s] regime you couldn't see nothing of the such. You only had the respect ... chief is there to provide them with information ... chiefs could help them" (Focus group #11). Overall, the use of chiefs to ensure local support in controlled territories during the

---

[25] For example, several civilians explained that in Lofa county—a rival stronghold—civilians who were part of the NPFL war effort during the first two years of the war were later recruited into ULIMO-K during the second half of the war, and eventually became the easiest to recruit into the LURD rebellion (Focus groups #2, #5). In these areas, which exhibited little loyalty to Taylor's regime, those who had the easiest access to weapons were more likely to be targeted for recruitment and more willing to join another civil war.

172   Governing after War

second civil war accords with my theory. However, in most cases chiefs' pre-war authority did not *expand* to local community-led development in the post-war period. This reflects not only the increasingly coercive tendencies and ways in which the chiefs' power was curbed during the heightened military contestation period (1993–1996), but also the new government's preoccupation with growing security concerns resulting from the second civil war. These concerns and the quick return to war caused the new government army to rely heavily on the chiefs for security and food when their troops passed through, much in the same way as they had done during the first civil war (Ex-combatant #46).

The single-barrel men were sometimes used to provide local security and help guard NPFL strongholds against a second civil war. In Gbarnga, rebel soldiers recalled them to guard checkpoints and gates as they did during the first war (Focus group #12). Similarly, in the areas surrounding Ganta—the capital of Nimba county and an NPFL stronghold during the civil war—single-barrel men structures were positively received during the first civil war. These remained in place afterwards: Rincon (2010, 15) reported from fieldwork in Nimba that "communities and villages are still willing to organize and mobilize male youth to defend their property and their land at any time," and that during the civil war, "elders negotiated to have local militia units recognized as part of the occupying armed faction." During the second war, single-barrel groups reformed, this time to help defend the territory against the LURD incursion on behalf of both the Nimba civilians and the Taylor government. Ganta was therefore better able to stave off the LURD incursion for several years until it fell in 2003 (Focus group #12).

Beyond Ganta and Gbarnga, my fieldwork suggests that the single-barrel men were no longer community security providers. Some did become a mobile addition to the new government's security apparatus as they joined regional militias during the second civil war. Because the increasing counter-rebellion concerns grew untenable and the military and ATU became over-whelmed, Charles Taylor called on retired rank-and-file soldiers from the first war to remobilize and fight (Ex-combatant #5). Ex-single-barrel men from central Liberia added to their ranks, further blurring the line between combatants and civilian supporters. This, again, mirrored how the NPFL had dealt with growing insecurity during the first civil war. Having run out of men with whom to fight its rivals, the new rebel government deployed its supporters from relatively peaceful regions of the country elsewhere to ward against rival onslaught, paradoxically leaving these other areas less secure than before. This reliance on mobility had contributed to the destruction of rebel–civilian ties during the first civil war and to the quick fall of government

The Liberia Civil War (1989–1996) **173**

stronghold and contested regions during the second war once rivals were able to expand past their own initial strongholds.

Chiefs and single-barrel men no longer helped the NPFL engage in rebel governance due to the heightened military contestation from 1992 to 1996. The focus on information and mobility during this period of the first civil war drastically weakened the depth of its ties with civilians. By the time of Taylor's victory in 1997, much of the NPFL's war machine was based *not* on rebel–civilian relationships, but on its ties with companies that sought to do business in Liberia. These firms' regional and international networks were unaffected by the high levels of fighting, displacement, and casualties, and were able to quickly return to high-commercial areas after the conflict ended; the new government relied on them to bankroll public goods and services.

Rebel relations with local communities were only helpful through commanders' ties to ex-combatants who had returned home to civilian life. These ties were subsequently leveraged to recruit fighters for the second civil war. The new rebel government turned to its network of ex-rebels to build an army as security concerns increased. LURD activity reached war levels at the end of 1999 as it spread from the Guinean border to engulf the western counties, and Liberia returned to civil war. The SSS and ATU were no longer sufficient to conduct surveillance and maintain national security (Focus group #14). Taylor thus sought to revive the NPFL army that had theoretically been disarmed during the peace process, reassembling the ex-combatants into a wide group of what were known as the Government of Liberia militias. Interviewees reported that their commanders re-recruited them to the war either by traveling to individual communities and putting together groups of men under the command of army soldiers or travelling to their original areas of command and reconvening ex-NPFL fighters who remained in the area (Ex-combatant interviews #5, #34).[26] One ex-combatant who was a general in the post-war national army explained the latter method of re-recruiting "all the men that have been fighting before from the various divisions":

> [Taylor] called a meeting with the former commanders, to get them on board. After he had the meeting with them, he gave them instructions. The former commanders will know a previous location at a town, [they]'ll go back there where they were controlling before, and mobilize them (Ex-combatant interview #32).

---

[26] The exact number of these militias is unknown, although there were an estimated five thousand to six thousand fighters in total.

174 Governing after War

Militiamen were split into a few dozen militias organized under the name "Jungle Fire" (Käihkö, 2017, 57). Each militia loosely mimicked the wartime structures; men who had fought together during the first war were under the same commanders as before. These commanders were directly controlled by SSS Director Yeaten (Käihkö, 2017, 57).

5.7 The Security–Development Trade-Off (Hypotheses 2 and 3)

Although the new government preached order and unity, any semblance of post-war social healing and reconstruction quickly fell by the wayside when it was threatened by instability. As Taylor's focus shifted entirely toward warding off existential security threats, civilian life was once again torn apart by instability and violence.

The difficulties that Taylor faced in his attempts to maintain state stability highlight the security–development trade-off that governments must make, and how increasingly high spending on security—to the detriment of development—can thwart the consolidation of power. After a civil war, citizens expect reconstruction and development from their new government. My theory posits that if a government engages in development, it ought to prioritize forms of development that strengthen the state's capacity for control, and that such development spending should be targeted predominantly at unsecured terrain. However, development is pursued concurrently with building the security apparatus, and is *contingent* on the new government's success in addressing security threats. As insecurity increases, the focus on development must decrease. This was the case in Liberia: Although citizens demanded development, it could not be a priority when the regime's security was threatened. As one former bureaucrat explained:

> National reconciliation was primary. You had a complete breakdown of the fabric of the state, in terms of its structure, in terms of programs, in terms of policies, in terms of identifying and recruiting the professional, technical capacity that was required to run government … Gaining domestic confidence, security: these were key programs because without these, health, education, and all of the basic services, could not [be] obtained. Of course, in the process of running the government, the policies of education were developed, policies of youth were developed. But basically it must be, [first] security be restored (Ex-bureaucrat interview, 2016).

This security–development trade-off is a dangerous situation for a new rebel government. I argued in Chapter 2 that such governments face a

The Liberia Civil War (1989–1996) **175**

legitimacy crisis if security and development are imbalanced, such that development funding in one region is diverted to security funding in another. If the government is unable to invest adequately in development in areas with low organizational capacity due to an increase in security spending elsewhere, civilian dissatisfaction—combined with a lack of local capacity to impose social control—should make residents of these areas more likely to join rival rebel groups. This occurred in Liberia: The security threats that began so soon after the end of the war necessitated prioritizing security over reconstruction. Taylor's government made only nominal attempts to rebuild the country by leveraging business ties to pay for development. This angered civilians outside of NPFL wartime strongholds and served to expand the scope of the second civil war.

An increasing share of Liberia's national budget was diverted to the security apparatus. The new government increasingly relied on inconsistent expenditures to reward supporters rather than applying systematic policy decisions. For instance, it appointed pro-NPFL local bureaucrats to stabilize potential unrest rather than providing public goods for citizens (Thaler, 2018, 165). Gerdes (2013, 136) notes, for example, that government spending was based on "gifts" that were given to friendly ministers and those in their employ rather than paying salaries. These payments were for security purposes: government money "provide[d] ... for the little presents for his cronies. They represent the salaries of his police, his spies and soldiers. They pay for the weapons they carry, and for the guns he exports to arm the rebels destabilising his neighbours. Now they are paying Taylor's soldiers to fight a new civil war" (The Guardian, 2001).

Security spending was also particularly high because the new government faced international arms embargos and sanctions; Taylor was forced to source weapons through illicit means throughout his presidency. He spent more than $20 million a year to procure arms on the black market and $50 million a year to pay the Liberian security forces and paramilitaries to fight the second civil war Coalition for International Justice (2005, 22). He paid these exorbitant amounts by exploiting Liberia's natural resources (and those of Sierra Leone), which generated around $105 million a year (Coalition for International Justice, 2005, 19). To capture the resources necessary to finance his security apparatus, however, Taylor's security expenses necessarily spilled beyond Liberia's borders. He funded the Revolutionary United Front (RUF) rebels in Sierra Leone and used proxy rebels to destabilize Guinea and Côte d'Ivoire. This strategy worked in Sierra Leone: ULIMO rebels, which were reorganizing themselves as LURD along the Sierra Leone border, were pushed back with the RUF's help. These rebels found a safe haven in Guinea, however; Taylor was unable to secure the Liberia–Guinean border, and the Guinean president openly aided the LURD rebellion. Taylor therefore expended additional resources to launch border incursions into Guinea in hopes of installing a friendlier regime (Gerdes, 2013, 164). He did the same in Côte d'Ivoire along Liberia's eastern border when the Ivorian president harbored MODEL rebels, leading Taylor to support the Forces Nouvelles rebels.

5.7.1 Quantitative evidence of resource allocation and development

How did the security–development trade-off affect developmental outcomes? Since government resources were diverted to secure Liberia's borders and quash security threats, funding for reconstruction depended heavily on the international community and private firms immediately after the civil war. Taylor leveraged his wartime ties with international firms to convince them to invest in development across the country (Ex-bureaucrat interview, 2018); this dependency increased, especially as the government struggled to pay for its ballooning security apparatus and had little left over for development (Thaler, 2018, 159). However, private firms provided public goods only in areas in which they had a strong commercial interest—primarily logging and mining areas.[27] Important areas of post-war reconstruction such as health and education were not priorities for private firms. Most schools and hospitals that closed down during the war did not reopen (Focus groups #8, #10), and wartime displacement meant that the population of doctors fell by more than half compared to just before the war (Europa, 2002, 573).

Some evidence suggests that Taylor's government may have directed aid dollars—which could not be used for security—to areas where he needed to bolster civilian support. When asked about government-led development, one civilian replied, "It was not directly with the government. There were NGOs that would come into the community...those NGOs wouldn't come by themselves they would pass through the government and government would give them the go-ahead...one way you know indirectly, the government was passing it" (Focus group #2). Managing NGO activity came from both above and below: "Local chiefs work on the instruction of the executive...they are local facilitators of public policy. So peacekeepers come to your town, [the chiefs say] 'oh the government sent you, then you

---

[27] For example, the Oriental Timber Company built and repaired major roads to transport its timber in exchange for ex-combatants providing security for its logging activities (Europa, 2002, 544). Businesses sometimes financed highly visible development projects (such as rebuilding universities) in exchange for tax grants and other benefits (Europa, 2002; Nelson, 2000).

are welcome' " (Ex-bureaucrat interview, July 8, 2016). Based on reports from Liberia's independent media during that time, contested areas just outside Monrovia seem to have been targeted for school construction, although development was directed at the partisan Nimba county as well (Star Radio, 2000*a*, 1999, 2000*a*,*b*). The government also announced concrete plans to repair roads and schools in communities on the outskirts of Monrovia (Nelson, 2000). NGOs led most other health and aid projects. In 2003, the World Health Organization donated medicines and medical supplies to ten hospitals in Monrovia and Bong, Margibi, and Grand Bassa counties—all strongholds and contested areas (AllAfrica, 2003).

Quantitatively Testing Differential Development Outcomes

After the war, Taylor's government increasingly directed government funds to Liberia's security apparatus to eliminate its rivals, and spent trivial amounts on development. Although little government-led development occurred under Taylor's regime, the government used international aid- and business-led development to push reconstruction projects forward. Externally funded efforts still required government approval, which allowed the government to target some development spending. According to my theory, such development funding should have primarily been targeted at contested or partisan regions in an attempt to extend government embeddedness and increase civilian support on the ground. Compared to post-war Zimbabwe, however, the effect size should be smaller, and limited to unsecured terrain rather than strongholds.

I follow the same strategy as in Chapter 4, where I analyzed development gains in Zimbabwe through educational attainment. Here, I again test my argument of differential development efforts using individual educational attainment data from the 2008 Housing and Population Census. I use a difference-in-differences (DiD) estimation strategy to test how strongholds, contested or partisan, and rival areas differentially experienced increases or decreases in primary educational attainment and literacy rates. This estimation strategy allows me to compare pre- and post-war educational outcomes.

In Liberia, children attend primary school from the ages of six to eleven, and the mean level of education across the country is at the primary school level. To estimate post-war education changes in different parts of the country, I compare individuals who were at least eleven years old at the start of the war—and should thus have completed primary school—with those who were eleven or younger by 1997, and thus would have been affected by any new education developments after Taylor came to power. To account for the fact that an eleven year old's primary education would have been less affected by

178 Governing after War

post-war development levels than that of a six year old, I operationalize the post-war variable (*post*) to allow for partial treatment: eleven year olds are treated 1/6, ten year olds are treated 2/6, and so on. I assign six year olds a treatment value of 1. I limit birth cohorts to those born between 1970 to 1992 because those who were born after 1993 would have been eleven years old by 2003, and thus would have attended primary school after Taylor was ousted. Finally, I drop all individuals who moved to the locality when they were six years or older—after they became primary school aged.

I use two outcome variables. First, my preferred operationalization of *school* is 0 if the individual attended no primary school and 1 if they attended at least some primary school. This is because the new rebel government was in power for only five treatment years (between 1998 and 2003); thus children who started primary school after the war would not have completed their schooling by the end of Taylor's regime.[28] Second, *literacy* indicates whether the individual is listed as literate or not in the 2008 Census.

My theory predicts that educational attainment and literacy should be the highest in contested or partisan areas, followed by NPFL strongholds, if there is locally led development from the bottom up (as was the case in Zimbabwe); it should be lowest in rival terrain. As I argued in the qualitative section, there should have been no locally led development in stronghold areas. Therefore we should only expect to observe results in contested and partisan areas—if any development was targeted at all. To demonstrate these effects, I utilize two treatment variables, *contested or partisan* and *NPFL stronghold*. The baseline comparison for these treatment variables is therefore rival terrain—areas that were either controlled by rivals or were predisposed to support rivals based on their ethnic affiliation. Education outcomes—where the dependent variable is either *school* or *literacy*—are estimated using the following equation:

$$\text{education}_{ilj} = \beta_1(\text{contested or partisan}_l) + \beta_2(\text{contested or partisan}_l \times post_j)$$
$$+ \beta_3(\text{NPFL stronghold}_l) + \beta_4(\text{NPFL stronghold}_l \times post_j)$$
$$+ X_{ilj} + \zeta_l + \eta_j + \epsilon_{ilj}$$

for individual i in locality l, of birth cohort j. I include individual characteristics X_{ilj}—gender, ethnicity, and religion indicators—as controls and locality (ζ_l) and birth year (η_j) fixed effects.

---

[28] In the Appendix, I show that my results are robust to including additional levels of higher-level schooling, which may indicate lasting effects of this period.

The Liberia Civil War (1989–1996) **179**

Table 5.3 Education and literacy

	Full sample		Excluding partisan		Excluding Monrovia	
	(1) School	(2) Literacy	(3) School	(4) Literacy	(5) School	(6) Literacy
Contested or	0.098***	0.108***	0.081**	0.080**	0.035***	0.049***
partisan × post	(0.031)	(0.029)	(0.036)	(0.034)	(0.010)	(0.010)
NPFL control × post	0.015	0.036	0.026	0.043	−0.077***	−0.051***
	(0.047)	(0.045)	(0.045)	(0.043)	(0.019)	(0.019)
Observations	690,470	690,470	597,135	597,135	471,853	471,853
Adj. R^2	0.270	0.282	0.286	0.297	0.268	0.273
Dep mean	0.602	0.611	0.597	0.606	0.597	0.606
T-test p-values						
Test statistic	0.000	0.001	0.006	0.062	0.000	0.000

Notes: $^*p < 0.1$, $^{**}p < 0.05$, $^{***}p < 0.01$. Robust standard errors in parentheses, clustered at the locality level. The sample is restricted to respondents born between 1970 and 1992 who have lived in that locality since they were five years old or younger. The regressions include locality fixed effects, birth year fixed effects, ethnicity and religion fixed effects, and gender fixed effects. *Education* is coded as: 0 = no formal education, 1 = incomplete primary. *Literacy* is coded as: 0 = illiterate, 1 = literate.

For the DiD estimation to be valid, the parallel-trends assumption must be met, meaning that the three types of regions—(1) low-capacity areas (contested or partisan) during the war, (2) areas under NPFL control (strongholds) during the war, and (3) areas that were under rival control— were not substantially different in pre-war education trends. I provide parallel-trends plots for schooling and literacy in Appendix C3.1. I also use two placebo cutoffs, and find no evidence that contested or partisan areas exhibited increased educational attainment prior to the start of the civil war (Appendix C3.4).

Results

Table 5.3 presents the results for primary school attainment and literacy for the full sample and the subsample that excludes partisan areas. The results illustrate that contested territories exhibited a differential increase in primary school attainment compared to rival terrain. The point estimates show that children who turned six after the end of the war were 9.8% more likely to attend primary school, and that this point estimate is statistically significantly higher than schooling increases in NPFL strongholds. Column 2 shows that this group of children also experienced a 10.8% differential increase in literacy compared to children of the same age in stronghold areas. Columns 3 and 4, which display the same regressions dropping *partisan* areas from the analysis, suggest that the results are fairly robust and not entirely driven by redistribution back to co-ethnics. Primary schooling continues to be statistically significant at 8.1%, while literacy decreases slightly to 8.0% but remains statistically significant. Finally, it may be the case that the results are affected by the capital Monrovia, which was under rival control throughout the war but began with a higher baseline educational attainment. Excluding Monrovia, I find that primary schooling and literacy are still statistically significantly higher in contested and partisan areas compared to NPFL strongholds.

Taken together, the evidence is consistent with my argument that post-war education reconstruction was most likely to benefit areas that were contested during the civil war. However, strongholds required more robust ties with civilians—who could undertake most of the work—in order to engage in post-war reconstruction. As I showed qualitatively, the NPFL's rebel–civilian ties were *not* robust: They were shallow ties, primarily used for security and reconnaissance during the military contestation period (1992–1996) rather than for establishing organized goods provision as had occurred during the stable period (1990–1992). This meant that after the war, without top-down reconstruction efforts—which the government preferred to target at contested or partisan areas—there should be no development gains in these areas. Indeed, the DiD estimates reported in Table 5.3 indicate that NPFL strongholds were no more likely to experience education growth than rival terrain. After excluding Monrovia, the coefficients on strongholds are *negative*, indicating *lower* educational attainment than in rival areas. This finding suggests two potential possibilities: (1) that the Taylor regime also targeted some goods at rival terrain in an attempt to win support or, more likely, (2) that post-2005 reconstruction disproportionately benefited rival terrain and thus some of these effects may be due to remedial education gains. I plot education trends for *school* and *literacy* in Appendix C3.1 to show that this differentially positive effect in rival terrain is driven by children who were aged six and seven in 1998, which lends credence to the second explanation. I show that these results are robust to alternative operationalizations of *schooling* in Appendix C3.4.

I confirm that these effects on education are not confounded by other changes in demographics due to conflict. Although demographic change is unlikely to have been affected *only* for the primary school–attending population, I use the same specification to test for effects on placebo outcomes that may be plausibly distinct from development, including the individuals' marital status, whether they have children, and an indicator for disability, disability cause, and disability type (Appendix C3.3). I find a substantively large imbalance on whether the individual is *never married*; I therefore add marital status as a control variable in the educational attainment DiD specification as a robustness check (Appendix C3.2). The results, and those of other robustness checks using alternative codings of the education variable, remain robust.

5.8 Conclusion

In this chapter, I have argued that the dynamics of control and contestation in the First Liberian Civil War created a wartime landscape of high insecurity and shallow rebel–civilian relations. The initial years of the war, which featured strong rebel–civilian ties under Charles Taylor, provided a glimpse into how the new rebel government *could have* operated had Taylor enjoyed greater security during his post-war rule. From 1990–1992, the NPFL built local organizational capacity by engaging civilians to bolster its security and bureaucratic apparatuses. This in turn allowed Taylor to seek business deals with multinational corporations, wage war, and gain political power in the country. By mid-1992, however, the emergence of rivals led to greater military contestation and by 1994, the NPFL had either lost control, or was battling for control, in most of Taylorland. I use a variety of qualitative sources to show that coercion and brutality increased dramatically due to heightened tensions, mistrust, and reduced time horizons.

This deterioration of social control had implications for post-war reconstruction, which generated a sharp imbalance between security and development spending. After Taylor became president in 1997, an increasing portion of the state's budget—which was substantial due to the country's abundant natural resources—was dedicated to tamping down security threats. The threats first emerged in Monrovia, where ULIMO-J refused to demobilize. Security problems then developed along the Liberia–Guinea border as ex-ULIMO-K rebels rebranded themselves under the new rebel group LURD. Finally, MODEL formed along the Côte d'Ivoire border, opening up an eastern front in the second civil war.

In Part III, I turn from the question of *how* rebel–civilian ties affect post-war resource allocation to investigate how these ties affect the *success* of the strategy—whether power is consolidated and security is established. I return to the case of Liberia to show that this security–development trade-off bodes poorly for consolidating power because the government's incentives misalign with citizen preferences (Sub-national hypothesis 4). Unlike in

182 Governing after War

Zimbabwe, Liberia's security concerns could not be contained, and there was not enough development to appease discontented citizens. By 2003, Taylor was overspending on security while relying primarily on companies, international donors, and allied countries to help prop up development and reconstruction in Liberia. Citizens in contested areas particularly in the east, therefore willingly picked up arms to join the rebels.

PART III

CONSOLIDATING POWER

6

Divergent Trajectories across Rebel Victories

If victors strategically allocate resources across the state to consolidate their power, why does this work in some cases but not others?

In Part II, I examined war and post-war politics in Zimbabwe and Liberia to illustrate how rebel–civilian ties affect post-war resource allocation. The new rebel governments' ability to consolidate power varied greatly: While the Zimbabwean dissidents struggled to recruit new members and were unable to expand their military operations before being violently quashed by President Mugabe's Fifth Brigade militia, the Liberian rebels successfully fought against Charles Taylor's Anti-Terrorist Unit and were able to recruit and attack along multiple borders. The Zimbabwean government remained relatively stable for over forty years, while the Liberian government was overthrown after seven years. In Chapter 5, I alluded to why this was the case: Taylor faced a security–development trade-off in Liberia brought on by a lack of organizational capacity on the ground. Although he had the military strength to win *territorial* control by the end of the first civil war, and overwhelmingly won the first post-war election, Taylor was unable to sustain *social* control over much of the state. In seeking to expand control and consolidate power when faced with an existential threat, the new rebel government focused more and more on security spending—coercion—at the expense of co-optation.

Part III examines successes and failures in consolidating power during the process of internal conquest after rebel victory. I provide evidence to support my cross-national hypothesis—that rebel–civilian ties affect the victor's ability to establish control and eliminate violent rivals. I begin this chapter by returning to Liberia to explain how the security–development trade-off pushed the country toward a second civil war—and ultimately Taylor's overthrow. I then evaluate the external validity of my argument by broadening my analysis to the rest of sub-Saharan Africa. I show that rebel–civilian ties, which determine the degree of social control that rebels are able

Governing after War: Rebel Victories and Post-war Statebuilding. Shelley X. Liu, Oxford University Press.
© Oxford University Press 2024. DOI: 10.1093/oso/9780197696705.003.0006

186 Governing after War

to exert during the war, are correlated with post-war state stability. Post-war stability in this context has two elements: (1) whether the victor faces a second (consolidation) war, and (2), if so, its likelihood of consolidating power after fighting this war. In Chapter 7, I qualitatively examine four additional rebel victories to illustrate how my argument applies in different contexts.

6.1 Losing Control in Liberia

Even if victors follow the theorized sub-national logic of resource allocation, I also argued in Chapter 2 that cross-national differences in regime stability can be at least partly attributed to the strength of the victors' rebel–civilian ties when they came to power. In Zimbabwe (Chapter 4), the victor had deeper ties that were both more embedded in communities in stronghold areas and better organized to spread across the state. Within strongholds, existing ties to civilians helped sustain social control from the bottom up. Pro-ZANU-PF comrades and wartime commissars could then be safely deployed across the state after the war to exert control through development funding and institution-building from the top down. These deeper ties, coupled with their broad reach across the state, meant that the victor only had to worry about internal conquest within a limited geographical region. This facilitated the consolidation of power soon after the end of the Liberation War.

In Liberia (Chapter 5), however, by the end of the war, the new rebel government had no capacity to complete the internal conquest process. Taylor captured power with no wartime state-building and few ties to civilians, and few civilian leaders who supported his National Patriotic Front of Liberia (NPFL) were put in place during the war. Since there were no organized civilian networks when he came to power, the state's military was used to defend against dissent along the borders of his stronghold and outside this area; he also paid individuals to gather intelligence during his time in government. Because it had not created wartime institutions, the new rebel government had neither the blueprint nor the footprint to establish top-down control after coming to power. Reconstruction was instead delegated to private firms and aid organizations, which increased the civilian discontent that ultimately played a major role in Taylor's overthrow in 2003. In short, the NPFL failed to embed itself into local communities during the war, and continued to struggle to do so after winning.

6.1.1 How the Security–Development Trade-Off Affected Civilian Attitudes

At least some civilians will inevitably be unhappy with the outcome of a civil war: supporters of the victor's rival are unlikely to back the new rebel government. However, *where these citizens are* matters for post-war state stability: Taylor's fall from power in Liberia may broadly be attributable to civilian anger, but the citizens in unsecured terrain—whose minds were not yet made up about the new rebel government when the first war ended but soon chose to join a second rebellion—tipped the scales in favor of conflict recurrence. This stemmed from the NPFL's low organizational capacity during the war and its shallow rebel–civilian ties resulting from heightened military contestation. With (1) few embedded ties on the ground and (2) inadequate efforts to co-opt civilians in unsecured terrain through development and building state capacity, Taylor failed to prevent the second civil war from spreading.

Taylor's government failed to deliver on its promises to prioritize post-war reconstruction. Many schools that were destroyed during the war were not rebuilt, and by 2000, teachers' salary payments had fallen far behind (Star Radio, 2000c). In addition, Taylor promised to increase access to electricity, clean water, and technology in his campaign, but there was little improvement during his first two years in office. Civilians outside NPFL strongholds were cognizant of government failures and credited the international community and international firms rather than the government for development efforts they observed in their localities. In focus group discussions convened for this study, civilians—even Mano or Gio citizens from the highly partisan (pro-Taylor) Nimba county—indicated that Taylor's government could not be credited with development, and that it was international aid that bolstered health services in the interior (Focus groups #7, #8, #16; Government official #3).

Many citizens also criticized the government for solely relying on international support: In contested and rival strongholds, people were dissatisfied with the speed of reconstruction and the concessions that had to be made to various international companies in exchange for military-related funding. Business-provided development did little to appease citizens because, although logging firms like the Oriental Timber Corporation built roads, local residents asserted that these roads were of poor quality and not fit for the purpose. Civilians also felt that the logging firms operated above the law, especially as logging activities had a disastrous effect on community life and destroyed civilian property and homes (Global Witness, 2003).

188   Governing after War

The government's focus on security rather than development angered civilians in unsecured terrain and fueled their enthusiasm to join the new war for two reasons. First, allocating more resources to security meant that the government was fighting a losing battle with regard to civilian support, particularly among civilians who experienced significant NPFL violence during the first civil war. In the northeast, citizens readily accepted the Movement for Democracy in Liberia's (MODEL's) incursion from Côte d'Ivoire. Unsurprisingly, civilians considered MODEL to be less violent and more legitimate than the NPFL, which had failed to establish rebel governance or impose social control during the first war (Focus group #15). As one civilian who had lived in Grand Gedeh county explained, "Let me tell you, the MODEL War ... it was the best war in Liberia" because it was "not like in the 1990 war, that was [a] tribalism war. [That] was not the MODEL war ... [MODEL] had a target, the target was Taylor" (Focus group #14). Civilians also witnessed MODEL contributing to public goods in areas under its control: Gerdes (2013, 172) notes that in the eastern front, when MODEL fixed dilapidated street lights for citizens in Grand Gedeh, "youths joined the rebels *en masse*, enabling the group to occupy large territories and cut off Taylor from important revenue-generating resources as well as a major weapons consignment."

Second, where civilians faced poverty and did not benefit from reconstruction, the second civil war presented an opportunity for enrichment—*even for those who did not politically support the counter-rebellion.* This was particularly the case for areas in the west that supported LURD, where the second civil war featured high levels of military contestation, leading to the same predation and coercion that plagued the second half of the first war. Although the initial group of civilian recruits in the second civil war under LURD could be considered genuine supporters of ULIMO-K from the first war, by the end of the second war more LURD members were motivated by money than those who were affiliated with other rebel groups (Bøås and Hatløy, 2008, 45). As one ex-combatant who had defected from government forces to join LURD in 2002 recounted, "[LURD] paid me every month; everyone was paid according to rank and position" (Ex-combatant #35). He explained that this attracted many civilians to LURD: "There were civilians who joined, and we trained them ... Some of them joined because of the amount paid. Most of them were contractors."[1]

---

[1] Bøås and Hatløy (2008)'s survey also found that civilians who joined toward the end of the second civil war had opportunistic motivations that were markedly different from those of the rival supporters who were recruited during the initial cross-border incursions from Lofa county.

The attitudes of civilians who lived in NPFL wartime strongholds deviated sharply. Despite the lack of true post-war reconstruction, people in these strongholds reported generally favorable living conditions after Taylor came to power. Their leniency toward the new government reflects the importance of influence through rebel politicization and governance, which deter citizens from rebelling even when, in this case, the organizational capacity for local social control has broken down.[2]

Citizens from Bong county, for example, point to stable food prices as a benefit that carried over from wartime into Taylor's new regime. As one civilian noted, "During Taylor time, we used to call that 'normal time.' Things were fine! Very good. Yeah, things were good from 1997 [when] they voted to maybe around 2000 [when LURD attacks escalated]" (Focus group #11). When asked why Taylor was a popular president and continued to be admired by certain groups more than a decade after he was forced into exile, both ex-combatants and civilians in stronghold areas consistently mentioned food prices as a reason in the focus groups. Outside of these strongholds, civilians were more likely to express discontent with the lack of health, education, and road reconstruction after the war despite the stable food prices. Yet, among civilians in Bong and Nimba counties, the conversation primarily centered on peace, political freedom, and economic security (Focus groups #1, #2, #10; Ex-combatants #7, #9, #10, #13).

When probed further about the reconstruction efforts in their home regions, people who had lived in pro-NPFL areas during the war clearly expected public goods from the government, but were also more likely to accept security concerns as a legitimate reason for the lack of post-war development. One civilian complained about the rival rebel groups: "Yes when Taylor took over, he did not enjoy total peace because there were some people who were not satisfied" (Focus group #8). Another explained that things were "very difficult" for Taylor: "There were no good road [in Bong county] because [Taylor] only had 1998, 1999" (Focus group #11). This individual rationalized that nothing long-lasting could be put in place because the government had more pressing concerns. Civilians were grateful that central Liberia was secure, where they described life as "fine" or "good," even if they expressed some disappointment that there was no development from either the bottom up or top down (Focus groups #7, #8, #11, #12). Overall, the provision of security and allowing civilians to live normal lives was enough to garner support for the new president. This "normal life" was primarily

---

[2] It is important to note that this influence was built through rebel–civilian ties during the war in Bong county, which was not predisposed to support either Taylor or the Mano and Gio ethnic groups.

190 Governing after War

achieved in two ways. First, some ex-combatants maintained ties with chiefs, who provided intelligence when asked (Ex-combatant #29). Second, because these ties were not strong enough to allow preventative action, Taylor had to rely heavily on the military to prevent external incursions into stronghold territory. For example, as a civilian explained during a focus group about life in Bong county after the war, "sometimes the rebels come from Lofa and things [got difficult], but after two three days Charles Taylor's people will send them [back to Lofa] again" (Focus group #11).

In sum, while the new rebel government failed to engage in reconstruction or foster social unity, the degree to which citizens accepted the state of affairs mapped closely with the wartime political geography. Where the rebels enjoyed greater influence and civilian support—in the co-ethnic partisan areas of Nimba county and the cross-ethnic wartime strongholds of Bong county—attitudes toward Taylor's government were largely positive. Civilians from this area called attention to the security–development trade-off that governments must make: While they readily admitted to the lack of development, they argued that Taylor was forced to overspend on security and was never given a chance to govern due to the violence from rivals. Civilians living outside these areas were far less lenient in their assessments of the government's performance—*even if they did not support rivals either*. At best, they were indifferent to the new regime but saw an opportunity to make money from joining the second war to fight against a government that was not bettering their lives. At worst, they blamed government forces for the renewal of violence, were angered by the lack of development and reconstruction, and soon came to support the rebels' goals in the second civil war. Taylor's hasty attempts to shore up the civilian support structures in these areas by appointing new local government bureaucrats only angered civilians further. Without building influence or establishing wartime social control, Taylor was unable to maintain post-war control over these regions—which undermined his efforts to consolidate power.

6.1.2 How Violence Spread across the State (Sub-national Hypothesis 4)

Civilians' discontent and willingness to join a second rebellion increased the security threats to the new regime. In Chapter 2, I hypothesized that as a government spends more on security and less on development, conflict ought to spread beyond rival terrain to unsecured areas before finally breaking into strongholds. Within strongholds, wartime rebel–civilian ties should help the new government avoid a return to conflict. I show support for this hypothesis during Liberia's second civil war: Although counter-rebellion recruitment began in rival terrain, it easily escalated into civil war when wartime rivals— LURD and MODEL—expanded into unsecured terrain.

Data and Research Design

I use Uppsala Conflict Data Program (UCDP) data to track the spread of the fighting during the second civil war from the start of recruitment in 1999 until the end of the war in 2003. I code proxy measures of rebel *recruitment* from LURD and MODEL separately, and then code the total number of years that localities were affected by the second civil war.

The UCDP dataset records skirmishes for the second war as beginning in 1999.[3] I operationalize a proxy measure for *recruitment* for each rebel group. First, I assess LURD activity by taking the first three years of the conflict (1999–2001)—before the war engulfed the entire country—and coding each locality as a center of recruitment if it was affected by LURD (rather than government) forces. Using this coding, recruitment took place in only two counties, Lofa (1999–2001) and Gbarpolu (only in 2001), making up 3% of the country's localities. Second, I identify areas affected by MODEL recruitment by examining the group's activity in 2003 and coding each locality as being a center of recruitment if it was affected by the MODEL rebels. Measured in this way, likely MODEL recruitment zones covered roughly 8.3% of the country and spanned Grand Bassa, Rivercess, and Sinoe counties.

To code the *second war*, which accounts for all areas affected by the second civil war, I aggregate the number of years in which each locality is militarily affected by LURD, MODEL, or government troops presence, from 1999 to 2003. Based on this coding, 81.65% of the localities were affected by at least one year of conflict; the mean number of conflict years is 1.44. Figure 6.1 depicts the recruitment areas and second war coverage.

Data on the second civil war is sparse and deviates more from qualitative accounts of the war than data from the first war. Although the UCDP dataset records very few data points between 1999 and 2001, it is clear from newspaper reports that the war had spread far past Lofa and Gbarpolu counties by

---

[3] Based on qualitative accounts of the war, bands of insurgents almost certainly appeared in 1998 before they coalesced into the LURD rebel group in 1999. However, as illustrated in Figure 6.1, even by 1999 violence was still localized in the northeastern regions. Thus the civilians who were initially motivated to fight on behalf of the rivals—rather than those who later joined in Monrovia for looting purposes—should have primarily been recruited from areas where the rebels were operating.

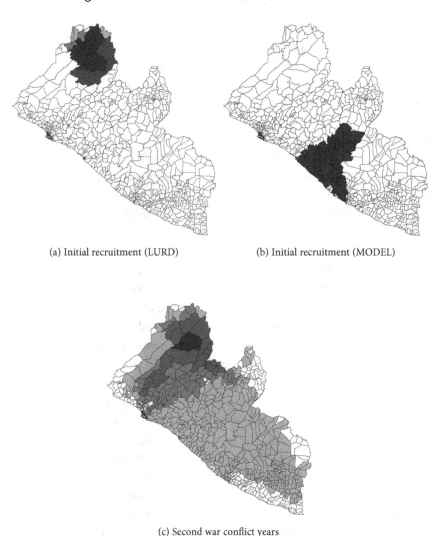

Figure 6.1 LURD and MODEL coverage

Notes: Figure 6.1 depicts chieftaincies where LURD (a) and MODEL (b) recruitment occurred; it also shows the number of years each chieftaincy experienced violence from the Second Liberian Civil War (c). In LURD recruitment (a) and conflict years (c), areas shaded in darker gray indicate a greater number of years between one to four years. MODEL recruitment (b) occurred only during one year because the rebellion entered the war late; thus, recruitment is represented as a binary.

2001 (The Perspective, 2001). Similarly, MODEL controlled important areas in other counties during this time, chiefly the rival-supporting Maryland county, which is not recorded in the UCDP data. The lack of fine-grained wartime data affects the inferences that can be made: The Second Liberian Civil War was short, and thus the coarse approximations introduce greater uncertainty when analyzing the spread of the conflict.[4] However, as it is the best approximation of wartime rebel movement and actions, I use this data to demonstrate how the second civil war spread from different parts of the country into NPFL strongholds.

I estimate three regressions. First, I compare the likelihood of being recruited by the two rebel groups during the second civil war. LURD took over the eastern front, while MODEL entered from the western front; I therefore subset the data for recruitment into the east or west of the country.[5] I then examine the likelihood of rival recruitment in NPFL wartime strongholds and in contested or partisan areas using the following equation:

$$\text{recruitment}_l = \alpha + \beta_1 \text{NPFL stronghold}_l + \beta_2 \text{Contested or partisan} + \zeta_l + \eta_l + \epsilon_l$$

where the coefficients of interest are β_1 and β_2. ζ_l controls for the logged number of civilian deaths from the first civil war, and η_l includes locality-level demographic and distance controls: logged population, logged size of ethnic group, logged distance to the county capital, and logged distance to the capital Monrovia. Robust standard errors are clustered at the clan level.

Second, I enter *contested* and *partisan* areas into the regression separately to test whether *partisan* areas, which have low organizational capacity despite supporting the NPFL, are still more likely than stronghold areas to return to conflict even if both types of territories support the new rebel government. If rebel–civilian ties affect post-war control, then *partisan* areas should theoretically still be more susceptible to conflict than strongholds; if co-ethnicity is more important, then *partisan* areas should fall last. I estimate:

$$\text{recruitment}_l = \alpha + \beta_1 \text{NPFL stronghold} + \beta_2 \text{Contested} + \beta_3 \text{Partisan} + \zeta_l + \eta_l + \epsilon_l$$

Finally, I test whether chiefs appointed during the first conflict were less likely to participate in the second war. This is an alternative test of rebel–civilian ties: Although the second war engulfed almost the entire country,

---

[4] This is less problematic for the first civil war: Though the data was also undoubtedly incomplete, by compounding multiple years of conflict between numerous actors, the resulting wartime landscape more accurately matches expert accounts of rebel presence and control during the first war.

[5] I code the eastern front to include the following counties: Grand Gedeh, River Gee, Maryland, Sinoe, Rivercess, Nimba, and Grand Bassa. I code the western front to include the following counties: Lofa, Gbarpolu, Bomi, Grand Cape Mount, Bong, Margibi, and Montserrado.

194 Governing after War

we should expect localities ruled by war-appointed chiefs to be the least susceptible to post-war violence. I thus estimate the equation:

$$\text{second war (in years)}_{ljt} = \alpha + \beta \text{During war}_{ljt} + \zeta_l + \eta_l + \kappa_t + \epsilon_{lt}$$

where ζ_l controls for the logged number of civilian deaths from the first civil war, and η_l includes locality-level demographic and distance controls: logged population, logged size of ethnic group, logged distance to the county capital, and logged distance to the capital Monrovia. I use fixed effects κ_t at the pre-war ethnic divisions level (Murdock, Blier, and Nunn, 1959), and regressions are clustered at the clan (treatment) level.

6.1.3 Results

Table 6.1 presents evidence consistent with my argument that security concerns arise from rival terrain before spreading to contested and partisan areas, and finally to strongholds. According to column 1 of Panel A, NPFL strongholds along the western front were 10.3% less likely to have been part of the brewing civil war in Lofa county and Gbarpolu than rival terrain between 1999 and 2001, while contested and partisan areas were 7.3% less likely to have been subject to LURD advances on civilians. This difference is not statistically significant ($p < 0.154$). Because the UCDP data identifies rebellion in only 3% of the western front, I estimate the same regression but subset the sample to only the affected counties, Lofa and Gbarpolu. The results, presented in column 2, demonstrate that strongholds were 28.3% less likely to be targeted for recruitment by LURD than contested areas; these findings are highly statistically significant. In column 3 of Panel A, I estimate the regression for MODEL recruitment at its inception in 2003, limiting the sample to the eastern front. Stronghold areas are 49.7% less likely to be targeted for recruitment, and the coefficient on low capacity is almost halved. The difference between these coefficients is statistically significant.

Finally, in column 4 of Panel A, I pool the recruitment between the eastern and western halves. The sample for this regression is the entire country: The western (eastern) counties are coded according to potential LURD (MODEL) recruitment areas. The recruitment areas for the two rebel groups do not overlap. The pooled results indicate that strongholds are 26.3% less likely to be in counter-rebellion recruitment zones, while low-capacity areas are 16.2% less likely to be recruited. The difference between these coefficients is also statistically significant—suggesting that low-capacity areas were more likely

Divergent Trajectories across Rebel Victories   195

Table 6.1 Recruitment areas

Panel A	(1) LURD (West)	(2) LURD (Lofa & Gbarpolu)	(3) MODEL (East)	(4) LURD & MODEL
NPFL control	−0.103*** (0.028)	−1.132*** (0.183)	−0.497*** (0.085)	−0.263*** (0.037)
Contested or partisan	−0.073** (0.034)	−0.377** (0.139)	−0.270*** (0.062)	−0.162*** (0.034)
Observations	7,102	1,067	4,730	11,978
R^2	0.506	0.515	0.362	0.360
T-test p-values				
NPFL control > cont./part.	0.153	0.000	0.003	0.004
Panel B	LURD (West)	LURD (Lofa & Gbarpolu)	MODEL (East)	LURD & MODEL
NPFL control	−0.104*** (0.029)	−1.145*** (0.185)	−0.487*** (0.088)	−0.260*** (0.037)
Contested	−0.074** (0.035)	−0.390*** (0.141)	−0.234** (0.108)	−0.138*** (0.041)
Partisan	−0.032 (0.025)	−0.089 (0.088)	−0.301*** (0.046)	−0.223*** (0.031)
Observations	7,102	1,067	4,730	11,978
R^2	0.506	0.516	0.363	0.361
T-test p-values				
Contest > partisan	0.172	0.052	0.524	0.053
Partisan > NPFL control	0.009	0.000	0.015	0.266
Contest > NPFL control	0.178	0.000	0.013	0.003
Specifications				
Conflict controls	✓	✓	✓	✓
Location controls	✓	✓	✓	✓
Ethnicity/religion controls	✓	✓	✓	✓
Clustered SE	Clan	Clan	Clan	Clan

Notes: $^*p < 0.1$, $^{**}p < 0.05$, $^{***}p < 0.01$. Robust standard errors in parentheses, clustered at the clan level. Controls include logged civilian deaths, logged size of ethnic group, logged distance to the county capital, and logged distance to the capital Monrovia. LURD recruitment is coded 1 if there was LURD activity between 1999 and 2001. MODEL recruitment is coded 1 if there was MODEL activity in 2003. Western counties are coded as the NPFL stronghold, Bong county, and those to the west that were affected by LURD activity between 1999 and 2001 (Lofa, Gbarpolu, Bomi, Grand Cape Mount, Margibi, and Montserrado). The eastern counties are to the east of Bong county and were affected by MODEL activity (Grand Gedeh, River Gee, Maryland, Sinoe, Rivercess, Nimba, and Grand Bassa).

196 Governing after War

to be recruited than strongholds but both were still less likely to be recruited than civilians living in rival terrain.

Organizational capacity from rebel–civilian ties, my theory's core mechanism, would suggest that although partisan areas support the new NPFL government due to co-ethnicity, they should still be more likely to fall to the counter-rebellion because (1) the new government has a low capacity to identify potential rival supporters or dissenters early on in these areas and (2) there are no on-the-ground structures to help defend against rebel incursion, such as the single-barrel men in Liberia. In Panel B, I disaggregate these unsecured areas into *contested* and *partisan* areas to test the differences between strongholds, contested, and partisan territories. In columns 1 and 2, partisan areas are statistically significantly more likely than strongholds to be recruited into LURD; subsetting the data to include only the affected counties similarly shows that strongholds are the least likely to fall to the counter-rebellion, followed by contested areas. The results presented in Table 6.1 strongly support my theory that organizational capacity has important effects on post-war state stability. I find that there were substantive differences between stronghold and contested areas with respect to MODEL recruitment in column 3, as well as between stronghold and partisan areas. Lastly, column 4 provides the pooled results. The coefficients are ordered in accordance with the theory: Stronghold areas are the least likely to be recruited, followed by partisan and then contested areas.

Finally, to further examine the impact of wartime organizational capacity on the second civil war, I test the effect of war-appointed chiefs on the conflict's duration in various areas. Although the second war affected almost the entire country at some point, Table 6.2 illustrates that areas

Table 6.2 War-appointed chiefs and second war conflict years

	Second war conflict years
War-appointed chief	−0.143**
	(0.068)
Observations	8,607
R^2	0.568
Controls	Conflict, location
Fixed effects	Ethnic region
Clustered SE	Clan

Notes: *$p < 0.1$, **$p < 0.05$, ***$p < 0.01$. Robust standard errors in parentheses, clustered at the clan level. Regressions include ethnic region fixed effects. Controls include logged civilian deaths, logged size of ethnic group, logged distance to the county capital, and logged distance to the capital Monrovia.

with war-appointed chiefs experienced fewer years of conflict exposure. The coefficient represents a 0.21-standard-deviation decrease in conflict years. This result, along with those presented in Table 6.1, provide evidence that (1) rival terrain was the most likely to experience conflict, but this easily spread to contested areas; and (2) strongholds were the last to be affected by war because local organizational capacity allowed these territories to stave off civil war for as long as possible.

6.2 Rebel–Civilian Ties and Consolidating Power

The preceding analyses, combined with evidence from Part II, point to the importance of thinking about the victors' and rivals' social control on the ground. This argument builds upon two complementary alternative arguments about rebel will and capacity to govern (*governing capacity*) and to repress (*military capacity*). In short, despite strong will and capacity to govern in Zimbabwe, the victor still engaged in mass violence; despite low military capacity and lack of territorial control during war, violence successfully repressed rivals. The opposite story emerged in Liberia, where the resource-hungry victor still demonstrated the will to govern during war (although wartime governance ultimately failed); despite its greater military capacity and territorial control, it did not escape conflict recurrence.

I now explore external validity—whether Liberia's post-war experience generalizes across cases, and whether the divergence in outcomes between Zimbabwe and Liberia are replicable across other rebel victories. As I argue in Chapter 2, a new rebel government is more likely to be able to consolidate its power if it has embedded rebel–civilian ties (*depth*), and if they are already spread across the state (*breadth*). Geographic distribution across the state helps territorially concentrate the regions where the new rebel government must allocate resources after the war. The existence of strong rebel–civilian ties helps the victor deepen its control in strongholds and provides the blueprint and cohort of partisans needed to spread control across the state from the top down. Social control increases with the geographic spread of these ties. In Liberia, because rebel–civilian ties were weak, post-war politics featured low social control; in Zimbabwe, the victor established strong rebel–civilian ties that were also spread across significant portions of the state, and thus enjoyed high social control.

I categorize rebel victories in sub-Saharan Africa according to the strength and geographic spread of their wartime rebel–civilian ties to demonstrate how these links correlate with wartime social control, post-war state stability, and conflict resumption overall. With respect to considerations about consolidating post-war power, I include only rebel victors that had rivals after the war. This excludes the current ruling parties in Guinea-Bissau and Namibia. Since World War II, eighteen rebel regimes—ruling parties emerging out of rebel victories—have governed fifteen countries in the region. These regimes captured state power either by winning an outright military victory (the rebel group took control of the state capital by force and unseated the government) or through a political victory (the war ended with a negotiated settlement but one armed group subsequently won complete control of the state through elections).

Table 6.3 clearly illustrates the correlation between rebel civilian ties and civil war recurrence. I categorize rebel victories into three types. First, in rebel victories with *widespread control*, the war reached most of the country and the eventual rebel victor dominated by establishing social control through strong rebel–civilian ties. These rebel victories featured both breadth and depth in their rebel–civilian ties. In the second type, wars that had *regional control*, rebels were able to build regional strength in a small part of the country where they operated and sustained strong rebel–civilian ties, but did not conduct operations or spread influence in a significant portion of the state during the civil war. In these cases, rival forces also often failed to expand beyond their own limited region of control. The result is that sizable parts of the country have low organizational capacity on behalf of any armed group in the civil war. The rebel victor thus enjoyed deep ties with restricted breadth. The third type of rebel victory features wars in which the victorious group experienced *contested control*—meaning that it failed to establish rebel–civilian ties and thus won the war with low social control. These rebellions fought for control against other rebel groups, but were unable to sustain prolonged support in a significant portion of the country; they instead relied on (1) transnational bases and/or (2) military contestation without meaningful citizen engagement. They took control of the capital and won the civil war but had only limited contact with citizens on the ground. These rebel victories thus came to power with both low breadth and depth in their rebel–civilian ties.

Four of the five cases that exhibited widespread control were able to retain power and avoid a return to civil war, although all faced threats to the regime after a rebel victory. The exception is South Sudan, which arguably exhibited strong social control during the war and had built quasi-bureaucratic structures, but many of its ties were muddled by a breakaway faction. Riek Machar and his troops capitalized on ethnic tensions within South Sudan and introduced an internal ethnic split within the Sudan People's Liberation

Table 6.3 Rebel social control and post-war state stability

Case	Reb.-civ. ties	Conflict spread	Social control	War recurred	Retained power	Recurrences
Widespread control						
Burundi	Strong	Wide	High			
Côte d'Ivoire	Strong	Wide	High			
Ethiopia (Eritrea)	Strong	Wide	High			
South Sudan	Strong	Wide	High	✓	[ongoing war]	
Zimbabwe	Strong	Wide	High			
Regional control						
Congo-Brazzaville	Strong	Limited	Low	✓	✓	1
DRC	Strong	Limited	Low	✓	✓	3
Ethiopia (Tigray)	Strong	Limited	Low	✓	✓	1
Mozambique	Strong	Limited	Low	✓	✓	1
Rwanda	Strong	Limited	Low	✓	✓	1
South Africa	Strong	Limited	Low		✓	
Uganda	Strong	Limited	Low	✓	✓	1
Contested control						
Angola	Weak	–	Low	✓	✓	3
CAR (Bozizé)	Weak	–	Low	✓		
Chad (FROLINAT)	Weak	–	Low	✓		
Chad (Habré)	Weak	–	Low	✓		
Chad (Déby)	Weak	–	Low	✓	[Assassinated]	5
Liberia (NPFL)	Weak	–	Low	✓		
Liberia (LURD/MODEL)	Weak	–	Low	[Exit]		

Movement/Army (SPLM/A) during the war. Thus, while I code the SPLM/A as a rebel victory with relatively high levels of rebel–civilian ties, its rival enjoyed similarly high levels of such ties. Indeed, the victorious rebel party faced contestation from a significant portion of its own supporting civilian structures; this internal split led to the second civil war in South Sudan.

There are fourteen rebel regimes that began their post-war governance with fairly low levels of social control and a larger territory to conquer either because they formed no rebel–civilian ties (contested control), or because their ties were geographically limited (regional control). These conflicts were far more likely to recur after the rebel government came to power. However, there are clear differences between the seven regionally strong rebellions with in-depth rebel–civilian ties and the seven contested rebellions with shallow ties. As Table 6.3 shows, regional rebels tend to only experience one consolidation war, which they are more likely to win. My theory suggests that this is because their wartime social control—although limited in its spread across the state—still provided the necessary foundation to expand their wartime structures throughout the state. However, the more regionally limited the rebellion, the longer it takes the rebel government to expand its influence across a large territory over which it has little control—which works against its ability to consolidate power quickly. On the other hand, because the conflict spread was relatively limited, its rivals must also work harder to recruit. Ultimately, rivals may enjoy some initial success in fomenting rebellion (even if the rebellion is not particularly strong)—which increases the victor's resource and time constraints—making civil war recurrence more likely.

Uganda is an illustrative case. It approaches the ideal type of a regional rebellion with strong internal institutions centering around the Luwero Triangle. During the civil war, the Ugandan rebels—the National Resistance Movement (NRM)—established Resistance Councils that were similar to Zimbabwe's wartime village committees and rebel party structure. However, while the Resistance Councils were deeply embedded in areas in which the rebels had operated, they were concentrated in a geographically small area given the rebels' lack of territorial expansion at the time. The NRM thus faced rebellions in areas where it had a weak presence and thus "there did not seem to be a large chance of being discovered and arrested for planning a rebellion" (Lewis, 2020, 77). However, the Resistance Councils proved helpful in the long run: After the war, the NRM began to expand its wartime institutions for development, bureaucratic capacity, and intelligence. According to Lewis (2020, 180–184), "Almost entirely unappreciated in existing scholarship on Uganda is the *intelligence* function of these councils ... After gaining control of the country in 1986, the NRM extended it throughout the entire country, much of which the NRM had not reached during the Bush War." Over time, nascent rebellions fizzled as the NRM government expanded its reach, which "allow[ed] it to monitor threats emerging throughout its territory" (Lewis, 2020, 92).

Unlike regionally strong rebellions, conflicts with low levels of social control may feature *contested* control. These conflicts tend to return to war, and their ability to ultimately consolidate power exhibits much more variation depending on the strength of their rivals. Sub-Saharan Africa has experienced seven such rebellions (in Angola, Central African Republic [CAR], Chad, and Liberia); the new rebel governments had to expend more effort to consolidate post-war control. Four of these rebel victors (CAR, twice in Chad, and Liberia) *lost* their consolidation wars because they had no wartime rebel–civilian ties to rely upon and no institutions to use as a blueprint. They faced one or more rivals with equal or stronger ties to civilians, and succumbed to high military expenditures when faced with an immediate return to civil war at the expense of development.

The remaining three rebel governments were not overthrown, but experienced similar difficulties in consolidating power. First, the LURD rebels in Liberia agreed not to even contest for political power in large part due to their lack of support within the country, and thus never controlled the government after victory. Second, the People's Movement for the Liberation of Angola (MPLA) eventually won dominance, but at a high cost: Unlike the regional rebellions that consolidated power after fighting one consolidation war, the MPLA faced serious challenges and nearly lost power as it fought three consecutive civil wars that spanned a total of twenty-seven years. During this time, it transitioned from a highly ideological and organized vanguard party focused on development to one that relied on oil wealth, predation, and patronage to remain in power. I explore Angola's difficult path to consolidating power in the next chapter.

Third, Idriss Déby and his party, the Mouvement Patriotique du Salut (MPS) in Chad, survived four civil wars. Déby was killed on the frontlines in 2021 while the conflict was escalating into a fifth war; however, the MPS remains in control at the time of writing. Déby's ability to maintain control for thirty-one years was in large part due to the fragmented nature of the rebellions, which lacked organizational capacity and relied heavily on cross-border havens in Sudan to overthrow Déby. During the process of putting down four rebellions, Déby incrementally completed the process of internal conquest: The ruling party spread its influence across the patrimonial state and established state control—much like the rebel victories in the second category, regional rebellions. The MPS was "the only political party with enough resources to be present in every region of the country... Because of its resources, which it uses in a patronage system to co-opt cadres across the country, the MPS appears the only truly national party" (Tubiana and Debos, 2017, 8).

Across sub-Saharan Africa, the patterns presented here are consistent with my argument that the existence of strong rebel–civilian ties decreases the likelihood of conflict recurrence and increases the likelihood of consolidating of power. Where wartime social control was widespread, the new rebel government was better able to consolidate power quickly. However, as wartime social control decreases, post-war struggles to consolidate power increase. In some cases where wartime social control was almost entirely absent and yet rebels emerged victorious, the new rebel government soon lost its grip on power.

6.3 Conclusion

This chapter presented evidence related to new rebel governments' failure to consolidate power. I examined the Liberian case once again to explain how the rebel victor not only failed to prevent a consolidation war, but lost power altogether—at least partially due to Taylor's lack of organizational capacity on the ground. Although citizens in NPFL strongholds accepted the government's inability to provide public goods, civilians outside those areas did not. Dissent from rival strongholds was expected, but discontent from unsecured terrain proved to be the tipping point: as civilians grew angrier over the rebel government's inability to provide, they joined the second civil war for political change as well as financial gain. Without rebel–civilian ties, there were no institutions or organized supporters to help manage and quash dissent. This forced the new rebel government to increasingly concentrate on security concerns, which increased civilians' discontent.

Since Zimbabwe and Liberia vary along many dimensions, I approach the issue of external validity by examining correlations between rebel–civilian ties and post-war consolidation of power across sub-Saharan Africa. I showed that there are three types of rebel victors: (1) those that enjoyed widespread control during the war, (2) those that fought regionally strong but territorially limited rebellions, and (3) those that were unable to form ties with civilians on the ground. These categories correlate with the rebel victor's need to return to war to consolidate power, the number of consolidation wars required to obtain complete control, and whether the victor fails to win control and is overthrown.

In the next chapter, I further explore this cross-national hypothesis by undertaking a qualitative comparative examination of four other rebel victories in sub-Saharan Africa. I choose rebel victories emerging out of conflicts in Angola (1961–1974) and Côte d'Ivoire (2002–2011) as close comparisons to the Zimbabwe and Liberia cases. I also examine rebel victories in Burundi (1991–2005) and Rwanda (1990–1994) as close comparisons to each other. These four cases allow me to hold constant factors such as ethnic or religious cleavages, pre-war institutions, and ideology. I show that wartime control and local ties with civilians remains a strong predictor of post-war power consolidation following a rebel victory.

7
External Comparisons

This chapter presents four secondary case studies—the Angolan War for Independence, the Ivorian Civil War, the Burundian Civil War, and the Rwandan Civil War—to further illustrate how social control and wartime rebel–civilian ties have helped rebel victors consolidate power after civil war. Section 7.1 discusses the methodology I employ in this analysis, including why I choose these cases and how they help evaluate the alternative explanations I introduced in Chapter 2. Sections 7.2–7.5 explore the four secondary cases in turn, highlighting important points of comparison with my two main cases and generating qualitative evidence to support my theory and argument. Section 7.6 briefly concludes.

7.1 Methodology and Case Selection

I cannot simply compare Zimbabwe's and Liberia's post-war trajectories as a test of my cross-national hypothesis because the cases were so different at their outset—meaning that subsequent divergent pathways may be attributed to pre-war conditions. Thus to complement the evidence presented in Chapters 4, 5, and 6 of their post-war experiences, in this chapter I conduct cross-national comparisons using a most-similar research design. The intuition behind this research design is to examine cases that are similar at their outset but have different outcomes. This comparative method allows us to "control" for pretreatment variables—in this case pre-war factors that may affect post-war outcomes. These pretreatment variables, as I discussed in Chapter 2, may be alternative explanations for the observed outcomes.

Using this comparative method, I select four secondary cases—the Angolan Civil War, the Ivorian Civil War, the Burundian Civil War, and the Rwandan Civil War—and examine them in contrast to the civil wars in Liberia and Zimbabwe to highlight divergences in outcomes. Because the research design holds pre-war factors constant, the comparisons primarily address two of the alternative hypotheses in Chapter 2: Case comparisons had similar levels of

Governing after War: Rebel Victories and Post-war Statebuilding. Shelley X. Liu, Oxford University Press.
© Oxford University Press 2024. DOI: 10.1093/oso/9780197696705.003.0007

predisposed *political support* (ideology and ethnicity) and similar *pre-war political factors*, both domestically (institutions) and internationally (time period). In addition, the comparisons also examine *civil–military relations* as an alternative explanation even though it is not a pre-war factor: All four cases feature long periods of civil–military power sharing in the post-war period.[1] Finally, within all possible comparison cases, I also prioritize selecting cases that span a broad time period: I include one of the oldest rebel victories in sub-Saharan Africa (Angola) as well as one of the youngest (Côte d'Ivoire). Table 7.1 summarizes the key aspects of all six primary and secondary cases examined in this book.

7.1.1 Comparing Angola to Zimbabwe

I begin by examining two secondary cases that are similar to the two primary cases. The first is the Movimento Popular de Libertação de Angola (MPLA) victory emerging out of the Angolan War for Independence (Section 7.2). During the revolutionary conflict, the MPLA fought alongside—and against—two other rebel groups that also aimed to overthrow the Portuguese colonial government and take control of the state. Throughout the conflict, MPLA forces contested for control across significant portions of the country but faced significant military contestation against other rebel groups in the war. By the end of the war, the MPLA's influence was restricted to the capital city; it had no organizational capacity on the ground in rural areas. Its chief rival, however—the União Nacional para a Independência Total de Angola (UNITA)—had started to build a significant governing apparatus in rural parts of the country. The MPLA subsequently faced a series of major counter-rebellions from UNITA spanning twenty-seven years before the former was eventually able to consolidate control over the state.

The genesis of the conflict in Angola resembled that of Zimbabwe. The MPLA in Angola and the Zimbabwe African National Union–Patriotic Front (ZANU-PF) in Zimbabwe both arose under similar circumstances during the same time period: Both were Marxist rebellions that emerged during a liberation movement, fighting against other liberation rebel groups for ultimate control over the newly liberated country. Both groups began as revolutionary regimes and soon produced a ruling party that featured cohesive cores, strong civil–military relations, and loyal armies. The wars fought in Zimbabwe and Angola were also similar with respect to pre-war institutions

---

[1] In Meng and Paine's (2022) dataset, defense minister appointments were stable from 60% of the regime's duration (Zimbabwe) to 100% (Liberia, Côte d'Ivoire), indicating minimal shuffling.

Table 7.1 Comparisons: Primary and secondary cases

Case	Chapter or section	Conflict cause	Pre-war institutions	Cross-ethnic rival	Civil military power-sharing	Time period	Returned to war
Zimbabwe	Ch. 4	Independence	Strong	Yes	Yes	Cold War	No
Angola	Sec. 7.2	Independence	Strong	Yes	Yes	Cold War	Yes
Liberia	Ch. 5, 6	Ethnic	Weak	Yes	Yes	Post–Cold War	Yes
Côte d'Ivoire	Sec. 7.3	Ethnic	Weak	Yes	Yes	Post–Cold War	No
Burundi	Sec. 7.4	Ethnic	Strong	No	Yes	Post–Cold War	No
Rwanda	Sec. 7.5	Ethnic	Strong	Yes	Yes	Post–Cold War	Yes

and broader regional politics: Both were rebellions operating within settler colonial regimes—and Angola and Zimbabwe had similarly high percentage of settlers by Acemoglu, Johnson, and Robinson's (2001) account—that had imposed their own institutions and language. Finally, the two liberation wars were preceded by a lengthy period of underground political organization that often brought the political and military leaders of various African liberation movements into contact.

Yet, the victors of the two conflicts had very different wartime experiences, and Angola's post-war politics paralleled Liberia's post-war experience more than Zimbabwe's. While ZANU-PF was able to establish social control during the Liberation War, the MPLA was unable to do so; it experienced high levels of military contestation and thus fought several additional conflicts after winning the war to consolidate power. The MPLA's experience demonstrates that ideology or a commitment to development policies is not enough to maintain stability during the post-war period: When faced with an existential security threat, the movement's initial commitment to development was quickly replaced by a strategy of natural resource extraction to finance its military forces. By the 1990s, the international community compared Angola to Liberia or Somalia, conflicts characterized by state breakdown and an overdependence on resources, despite its revolutionary roots (Munslow, 1999).

7.1.2 Comparing Côte d'Ivoire to Liberia

The second case I examine in this chapter (Section 7.3) is the ten-year Ivorian Civil War, which was triggered by ethnic grievances and frustration over definitions of Ivorian citizenship. This war pitted the Forces Nouvelles (FN) rebels (led by Alassane Ouattara) against the pro-government forces, the Forces Armées Nationales de Côte d'Ivoire (who supported then-President Laurent Gbagbo). The rebels engaged in conventional warfare and exerted territorial and social control in the northern half of the country, while the government controlled the southern half. For almost a decade, the two halves were at a stalemate, divided by a buffer zone extending across the middle of the country. FN commanders established strong rebel governance in communities under their control, providing security as well as goods and services. They also formed alliances with local institutions such as the traditional Dozo hunters, who helped maintain security during the war. These ties became important in the post-war period, when the Ivorian government warded off a counter-rebellion attempt and cross-border violence from Liberia.

Like the Angolan War for Independence, the Côte d'Ivoire case more closely mirrors the First Liberian Civil War at its outset, but its post-war trajectory better parallels Zimbabwe's experiences after the hostilities ended. As a civil war fueled by ethnic grievances in the post–Cold War period, the Ivorian Civil War began as far more similar to the First Liberian Civil War than the revolutionary independence movements in Angola or Zimbabwe in three ways. First, with respect to pre-war institutions and grievances, both Liberia and Côte d'Ivoire enjoyed a period of economic growth under strong leaders (William Tubman and Félix Houphouët-Boigny, respectively), but their underlying political institutions were weak. Both countries featured patrimonial pre-war politics and a predatory state, which concentrated power in a single leader. As in Liberia, these factors triggered a civil war fueled by ethnic grievances in the post–Cold War period. The second similarity relates to wartime dynamics that are independent of their rebel–civilian ties: Côte d'Ivoire and Liberia share a porous border with cross-border ethnic and cultural ties. Their civil wars thus featured significant spillover across both sides of the border, and rebels from both wars recruited from the other country's rebellion. The final shared characteristic is associated with military cohesion: Neither civil war was a revolutionary rebellion, and both rebel armies were fractionalized rather than centralized. Although their civil–military relations were qualitatively weak in comparison to revolutionary regimes such as Zimbabwe and Angola, both regimes featured stable defense minister appointments throughout their tenure.

Although Liberia and Côte d'Ivoire were similar across these dimensions, their post-war trajectories diverged. In Section 7.3, I present evidence that Côte d'Ivoire's post-war politics aligned much more closely with those of Zimbabwe with regard to both patterns of resource allocation after the war and the types of tensions in civil–military relations after power was consolidated. I argue that much of these similaries can be attributed to Côte d'Ivoire's wartime experiences with rebel governance and the formation of deep rebel–civilian ties across the north. The rebel victors had established social as well as territorial control throughout much of the war, so they targeted post-war resource allocation toward areas that may once again rebel, which helped them consolidate power relatively quickly after the conflict ended.

7.1.3 Comparing Burundi and Rwanda

In Sections 7.4 and 7.5, I explore two additional secondary cases, Burundi and Rwanda, as a most-similar comparison with divergent outcomes. These two adjacent countries are natural comparisons beyond their geographic proximity because they share similar pre-war institutions and contexts. The two countries comprised a single administrative unit under Belgian colonial rule, and thus they were subject to the same pre-war institutions and laws. Post-independence, both countries were governed by strong authoritarian regimes and their per capita GDP shared a similar trajectory. Most importantly, violent ethnic conflict was central to the politics of both countries even before the civil wars. Therefore, the two countries were comparable when their civil wars began; their post-war trajectories diverged, however, and highlight how wartime legacies influence post-war governing strategies.

In Section 7.4 I trace the wartime to post-war trajectory of the Conseil National Pour la Défense de la Démocratie–Forces pour la Défense de la Démocratie (CNDD-FDD), the victor in Burundi's civil war in 2005. I show that the CNDD-FDD initially had a low presence and little influence over civilians as it competed with other rebel groups for control over the western provinces of Burundi. However, it increased its control over the majority of the country during the second half of the civil war. Much like the ZANU-PF in Zimbabwe, rebel control under the CNDD-FDD led to the creation of quasi-bureaucratic structures, including the use of youth for reconnaissance and setting up a parallel administration for taxation and logistical support. This local organizational capacity later helped the CNDD-FDD political party maintain control and consolidate power.

In addition to serving as a strong comparison to Rwanda, the Burundi case allows me to eliminate two potential alternative arguments. First, the CNDD-FDD was not revolutionary, and indeed held very few ideological convictions during or after the civil war. However, it used development and violence by proliferating its wartime institutions to expand its control after the war. Its wartime experiences with rebel governance and post-war consolidation of power help demonstrate that ideology is not necessary for post-war governance. Second, the Burundian Civil War and its post-war politics holds pre-war ethnic cleavages constant. Although the war began as a Hutu conflict against the Tutsi ruling elite, the CNDD-FDD's rivals during and after the war were all Hutu rebel groups: All rebel groups in Burundi were Hutu throughout the war and post-war periods, and the CNDD-FDD was neither the most hardline pro-Hutu party nor the most inclusive. Thus, the CNDD-FDD's victory over other rebellions, and its subsequent ability to dominate its rival after the war, cannot be attributed to ethnic allegiance alone.

In Section 7.5, I describe how the Rwanda Patriotic Front (RPF) maintained a low presence and influence throughout the Rwandan Civil War

210   Governing after War

but moved quickly in the final months to take over the entire country. The RPF established a blueprint for state-building in a very limited territory, where it engaged in rebel governance using lessons from Uganda's Bush War but failed to expand these institutions during the war and struggled to do so after the war. Instead, the RPF transitioned after the conflict into a non-ideological, ethnic-minority (Tutsi) government that faced a brewing counter-rebellion from the ethnic majority (Hutu) along its western border. Ultimately, counter-rebellion attempts from the ex-government forces led to a second civil war because the new RPF government could only rely on top-down control: It could not leverage civilian support from the very beginning, which limited its "eyes and ears" on the ground. However, the RPF succeeded by acting quickly: It ultimately won its consolidation war with speedy bureaucratic control and a military offensive that drove its rivals out of the country.

7.2 Angolan War for Independence (1961–1974)

The Angolan War for Independence featured weak wartime social control with limited rebel–civilian ties. This short case study illustrates how a rebellion with similar beginnings and motivations as the Zimbabwean Liberation War led to post-war outcomes resembling those of Liberia. During the Angolan War, three rebel groups simultaneously fought for the country's independence but competed against each other for control of the state. The ultimate victor, the MPLA, was an ideological revolutionary rebel group that sought to establish a strong bureaucratic state after winning a military victory. However, as in Liberia, it faced civilian resistance and was forced to engage in a consolidation conflict against its rivals. To address this existential threat, the MPLA increasingly diverted resources from development to security—which increased civilian discontent.

I argue that this outcome resulted from a lack of wartime rebel–civilian ties—and thus organizational capacity on the ground. The MPLA's wartime experience followed a similar path to that of the National Patriotic Front of Liberia: Although the MPLA initially formed party structures in rural areas under its control, it was forced to retreat from these territories when its rivals took control. Its chief rival was also particularly successful at forming its own ties with civilians and increasing its grassroots social control. After the war, civilians in these rival strongholds resisted the victor's attempts to impose control, while those in unsecured terrain were motivated by high levels of underdevelopment to join the rival's counter-rebellion. The MPLA faced far greater challenges than the ZANU-PF in Zimbabwe after the former took control of the new government; the MPLA ultimately faced nearly three more decades of civil war before it was able to consolidate power. Like in Liberia, the MPLA in Angola increasingly relied on the sale of natural resources to fund its security apparatus.

7.2.1 Conflict Background

The war began in March 1961 with rural revolts against Portuguese colonialism. Three rebel groups quickly emerged to fight against the Portuguese government. First, Agostinho Neto led the MPLA, a Marxist rebel group with links to the Soviet Union and other Marxist movements in Mozambique, Zimbabwe, and South Africa. Second, the Frente Nacional de Libertação de Angola (FNLA), led by Holden Roberto, was founded in 1961 as an ethnic rebellion on behalf of the Bakongo people living in northern Angola. The FNLA built significant military strength during much of the War for Independence, and enjoyed support from Zaire and China. In 1966, a group of FNLA soldiers splintered to form the third rebel group, UNITA, under Jonah Savimbi. UNITA also began as a Marxist organization but drew its support from both China and South Africa's apartheid government. Partly due to its late entry into the war, UNITA was the smallest and militarily weakest group, but it sustained the strongest ties with civilians on the ground.

The war intensified throughout the 1960s, as the rebel groups fought against the Portuguese forces as well as each other. The war's trajectory changed in 1974: Portugal's dictatorship was overthrown in a coup during the Carnation Revolution, when Portuguese citizens revolted against both the dictatorship and colonialism. Under the new leftist government, Portugal withdrew its troops from Angola (and its other colonies); the Alvor Agreement signed in January 1975 stipulated that Angola would become an independent nation with power sharing between the three rebel parties. Yet, in the months leading up to independence, military contestation resumed between the three rebel groups. By July 1975, the MPLA had won control of the state in a military victory and assumed power in the first post-war government.

7.2.2 Rebel Control and Contestation

The Angolan War for Independence unfolded in much the same way as the Zimbabwean Liberation War less than a decade later. Because they all

212 Governing after War

sought independence, all the rebel groups were able to achieve a high level of influence over civilians in their own theaters of operation.[2] Yet they maintained varying levels of wartime social control due to differing levels of rebel presence. The three groups clashed with each other on the ground as they fought for control over civilians, recruits, and resources with different degrees of success: The FNLA was primarily situated in Zaire and thus exerted very little social control inside Angola, while UNITA and the MPLA were primarily based in Angola and thus vied heavily for control over civilians. At different points during the war, the rebel groups allied with each other to open up new fronts of attack, while the Portuguese government used chemical warfare against them to sow discord.

Given the relatively high levels of military contestation, the MPLA exerted little social control over the civilian population by the end of the War for Independence. Yet as in Liberia, it was the largest and militarily strongest group at the beginning, when it sustained a troop presence across large portions of Angola. At the time, MPLA activity in rural areas was concentrated in the southeast and the north, in provinces dominated by the Mbundu ethnic group. It also sustained strong engagement in urban areas, particularly in the northwest around the capital, Luanda. However, military contestation escalated as UNITA grew stronger and strengthened its presence in the country; Portuguese attacks also increased. The MPLA was forced to retreat from its Angolan bases altogether and could only launch hit-and-run attacks in the eastern part of the country. Although the MPLA won the war militarily, it "controlled the city of Luanda but little else" (Vines, 1999). UNITA, on the other hand had sustained its ability to exert social control over the rural highlands of Angola.

Governance and Violence during War (Implications 1 and 2)

The MPLA's initially widespread social control, followed by a sharp decline due to military contestation, helps explain patterns of rebel governance and violence during the civil war. In keeping with its ideological commitments, the MPLA had originally sought to establish complete social control during the war by creating local party structures and engaging in mass politicization. As the largest and most stable rebel group in the country at the start of the war, it was initially successful: According to Pearce (2012, 9), "The MPLA . . . tried to implement a rudimentary social contract with peasants in their respective zones of control . . . [T]his represented a first exercise in state-like engagement

---

[2] The MPLA rebels enjoyed a particularly high degree of influence over the Mbundu ethnic group—the second-largest ethnic group that makes up about 25% of the country's population.

with civilians." During this time, the group was able to build "rudimentary health care, schools, people's stores, and committee-based local government to replace the eroded or eliminated traditional authority" (Henriksen, 1976, 388). However, military losses from 1966 onward reduced the MPLA's presence in rural Angola—and thus ended its influence over civilians and destroyed its local organizational capacity. As Portuguese government forces and UNITA grew stronger, MPLA civilian structures in rural areas collapsed completely (Pearce, 2012, 9); it was only able to continue civilian organization and mobilization in the capital, Luanda, which it managed to maintain control of for the duration of the conflict (Stevens, 1976, 138).

When the MPLA lost control in rural areas due to military contestation, it resorted to violence to coerce civilians into playing supporting roles (Brinkman, 2003). It kidnapped civilians and forced them to move into the bush to serve as porters and cooks. The MPLA also "killed those who disobeyed them and abused accusations of treason to get rid of anybody whom they perceived to be a political opponent" (Brinkman, 2003, 310). Unlike using targeted violence to punish sellouts under scenarios of rebel control (Kalyvas, 2006), the MPLA engaged in indiscriminate and "less patterned" (Brinkman, 2003, 320) killings—indicative of the low-information environment resulting from a lack of local rebel–civilian ties. Through violence and forced displacement, the MPLA hoped to prevent civilians from providing information to, and supporting, rival armed groups. There is little evidence of any cooperation with local leaders during this period.

Rebel Governance and Social Control under UNITA Forces

Unlike the MPLA, which lost more and more control of rural Angola as the war progressed, UNITA was able to maintain its organizational capacity on the ground as a coherent but regionally limited guerrilla force—despite being far weaker militarily than the MPLA or FNLA, both of which received significant military aid from international sources and had more recruits. As Pearce (2012, 9) noted, "later, only UNITA was to build on [local governance] while the MPLA shifted the focus of its political engagement to the towns."

UNITA exerted social control over civilians from its own ethnic group (Ovimbundu) in its ethnic stronghold in the eastern highlands, where it leveraged the organized support of members' families and their ties to the Protestant church. Together, they "formed their own clandestine organisations, and mobilised the population in support of UNITA" (Heywood, 1989, 54). It also tasked its non-Ovimbundu members with engaging and winning over their own tribes (Dash, 1977, 72), which facilitated partnerships with leaders along the Zambian and Namibian borders. UNITA thus maintained

214 Governing after War

a strong presence in areas outside its stronghold, which allowed it to win over the local population and set up a "proto-state" (Heywood, 1989, 54) with quasi-bureaucratic structures.

Thus UNITA sustained broader local support than the MPLA during the War for Independence. UNITA maintained this social control and organizational capacity after the war: When the MPLA's consolidation war—the second Angolan civil war—began in 1975, UNITA leader Jonas Savimbi commanded control over a significant portion of the population (Dash, 1977, 13). UNITA's ability to organize more local support than the MPLA became a significant factor in the development of post-war politics under the MPLA government.

7.2.3 Post-war Patterns of Development and Violence

Although the MPLA won a military victory in 1975, its lack of social control meant that subsequent years were "devoted to coming to terms with their enemies and winning the peace" (Birmingham, 1988, 1). Patterns of development and violence under the MPLA government thus emerged within the context of multiple protracted civil wars fought to consolidate control over the country's borders. During the nearly three decades of war, the new rebel government faced substantial difficulties winning influence over the population due to strong local ties to UNITA bases. The MPLA therefore relied on military dominance, the civilian population's growing war-weariness, and UNITA's tactical mistakes (Malaquias, 2001) to eventually win complete control following the death of UNITA's leader in 2002. By then, the MPLA had morphed from an ideological political party with programmatic goals and technocratic bureaucrats into a patrimonial state relying on oil wealth and violence to sustain power and pay for protracted wars (Munslow, 1999, 565).

The Three Consolidation Wars after the War for Independence

The first consolidation war began immediately after the War for Independence ended in 1975. The MPLA was initially successful due to its military strength: It quickly defeated the FNLA, which retreated to the Democratic Republic of the Congo (DRC) by early 1976 due to a lack of civilian structures in place within Angola. The FNLA launched guerrilla attacks from its bases in the DRC until 1979 before surrendering to the MPLA. UNITA similarly faced military setbacks during the first two years as it attempted to switch from guerrilla to conventional warfare too soon (Malaquias, 2001, 318). UNITA quickly realized it was militarily weaker than the MPLA and returned to its original rural bases to resume guerrilla warfare against it. Relying on its existing organizational structures, UNITA focused on strengthening its ties with civilians in the south and expanding its parallel quasi-bureaucratic structures. This strategy allowed it to continue fighting the MPLA until the two sides brokered a peace agreement in 1991. The agreement was a political loss for the MPLA, as both sides agreed to hold another election in 1992. Because the MPLA was unable to sever UNITA's ties with civilians in vast parts of the country, it was still unable to consolidate control.

The second consolidation war, which began in 1992, once again ended with the MPLA unable to consolidate control. After losing the highly contested 1992 elections, UNITA's leader Savimbi returned to the group's stronghold in Huambo and launched attacks in four southern provinces in October of that year. Unlike the first consolidation war, which was fought exclusively in rural areas, the second featured fighting in urban centers, which were commonly considered MPLA strongholds. UNITA quickly gained the upper hand, taking complete control over the four southern provinces as ex-rebels left demobilization camps to fight. It partially took over other provinces as MPLA bureaucrats fled: "some days as many as a dozen municipalities changed hands" (Brittain, 1998, 61). The MPLA regained some territory in December 1992, but lost it again the following month. By that point, UNITA had spread its operations to 105 of the country's 164 municipalities as the MPLA failed to project state strength beyond its urban strongholds. Following significant military exchanges, both sides agreed to sign the Lusaka Protocol in October 1994 and lay down arms.

The third and final consolidation war for the MPLA began in 1998, which marked the breakdown of the Lusaka Protocol. Despite the brokered ceasefire in 1994, there were small episodes of ongoing violence and UNITA had built a parallel governing structure within the country. The MPLA government realized that "gaining control of [UNITA] strongholds was now a top political and military priority" because "its claims of legitimacy rested heavily on the ability to fully implement the Lusaka Protocol" (Malaquias, 2001, 321). As it was unable to force UNITA soldiers to demobilize, the MPLA launched a large-scale military offensive into UNITA territory in March 1999. The operation was unsuccessful in weeding out the rebel administration, leading to years of stalemate.

The MPLA finally consolidated its control over the country in 2002 after UNITA's leader Savimbi was killed in action. By then, the civilian population had become disillusioned with war and the rebel soldiers deserted.

The Rise and Decline of State-Led Development (Sub-national Hypothesis 2)

At the outset of independence, the MPLA's internal party structure featured a strong organization with ideological goals. In keeping with its Marxist ideology, the educated elite at the group's core controlled its political structure, which featured mass party organizations of youth, women, and workers (Young, 1988, 172). MPLA supporters "monopolised" the state to impose control (Birmingham, 1988, 3). As in Zimbabwe, control was not established through patronage but still featured partisans: The MPLA's bureaucracy was staffed with educated technocrats (Péclard, 2012, 172); it sought to "control the countryside" and "construct a political order in which the party monopolizes power but creates popular structures for agitational and mobilizational purposes... under tight party control" (Young, 1988, 172).

Because the MPLA was unable to exert *wartime* social control over civilians in rural areas or build embedded party structures at the local level, *post-war* governance relied almost entirely on top-down control. The new post-independence MPLA government vigorously pursued economic development after 1975 and focused heavily on spreading state control to rural areas. It attempted to create economic institutions that would help it centralize power and ensure state ownership over the productive sectors (Young, 1988, 170). It emphasized the rural agricultural sector: three years after independence (in 1978), the government implemented a villagization policy that forced Angolans living in Luanda to move to rural areas to engage in "productive labor" (Young, 1988, 181). This policy highlighted the government's desire to exert top-down control and expand its bureaucratic capacity in rural regions, where it had limited political influence and weak social control.

Despite these attempts to implement a centrally planned economy and bureaucracy that would allow the MPLA to expand its influence, the Angolan government failed to develop or build a strong bureaucratic apparatus. It was difficult to consolidate social control using a top-down approach because much of the country's territory was not only unsecured, it was controlled by rivals: UNITA commanded social control in the Angolan highlands despite the MPLA's military victory at independence. In these areas—much the same as in Zimbabwe's rival territories—the government's attempts to extend its structures across the country were poorly received. The new administration's bureaucrats, who were MPLA cadres, "were not integrated into the local administrative structures" (Péclard, 2012, 172). In UNITA territory, for example, rather than co-opting citizens through development and deployed bureaucrats, MPLA supporters only served to increase support for UNITA as civilians living in these opposition (rival-supporting) areas viewed the MPLA as the "new colonisers" (Péclard, 2012, 174).

In addition to this rejection of government bureaucrats in UNITA territory, state-led development also withered due to the resumption of conflict. Once the MPLA became embroiled in an expensive civil war against UNITA, it started to rely on oil wealth—which was entirely under state control—to fund its military apparatus. The focus on oil came at the expense of developing rural Angola, which had been the new rebel government's original goal. Rather than implementing social programs and building the agricultural sector, Birmingham (1988, 13) explains that "After independence . . . peasant incomes dropped, opportunities for marketing farm produce declined, the city fed itself on imported produce paid from oil revenue."

Increasing Commitment to Security (Hypotheses 3 and 4)

While the FNLA was quickly defeated by 1979, UNITA's influence over the local population expanded after independence was declared. Although the MPLA attempted to sever civilian ties with UNITA through deployed bureaucrats, it was difficult for the new government to control resentful civilians from the top down rather than from the bottom up (as UNITA was doing). The MPLA's treatment of civilians in opposition areas indicated it was fighting a losing battle for civilian loyalty. While the initial years featured fewer indiscriminate attacks against civilians as the MPLA attempted to implement its bureaucratic structures, its failure to build state strength in opposition areas—along with its increasing reliance on oil and patronage— soon led to a sharp increase in attacks on civilians.[3] Dash (1977, 25) notes that by 1977, civilians bore the brunt of government violence. During long periods of government attacks, those who were "even suspected of aiding the guerrillas with food or information about troop movements were slaughtered when their villages were attacked" (Dash, 1977, 25).

As in Liberia, the MPLA faced a development–security trade-off due to the costs of violence: Since it faced a growing UNITA army, the MPLA began to spend more on security than development. According to Birmingham (1988, 8), within the first decade of independence, "Army power has risen steadily . . . and is the main rival to bureaucratic power in the central councils of the ruling party. It is said that the army is the most powerful unifying factor in the country." Oil profits funded the army's rise, while the civil aspects of the MPLA were "gradually squeezed out" (Birmingham, 1988, 9).

---

[3] The MPLA was not alone in this: UNITA quickly began to rely on diamond wealth to pay for its own expensive military operations.

218 Governing after War

These priorities were also reflected in the government budget. Although the MPLA had initially allocated funding to social services and development, the national budget increasingly financed the security sector. By 1993—after two consolidation wars in which the MPLA was unable to dismantle UNITA strongholds—around 48% of the national budget was spent on defense and security according to official Ministry of Finance figures (Munslow, 1999, 554). An additional 33%–50% of government expenditures were estimated to take place "outside the normal budgetary process" to "mask the extent of defence spending" (Munslow, 1999, 554).

Neglecting development to pay for security made it easier for rival groups to recruit support for their counter-rebellion in contested areas. In the years following the War for Independence, the MPLA's declining development spending further allowed UNITA to "recruit sympathisers in the west and north with whom they had no ethnic affinity but who were distressed at the rapid decline of rural opportunity" (Birmingham, 1988, 13). UNITA's growth—from the militarily weakest rebel group at the end of the War for Independence in 1975 to a large force that militarily controlled more than half of the country's territory during the late 1980s—reflects civilian discontent with the MPLA's neglect of development and growing support for UNITA's parallel governance.

By the early 2000s, the MPLA won the third consolidation war largely because UNITA's social control and rural administration had collapsed after years of protracted warfare and near-constant military contestation. Bakonyi and Stuvøy (2005, 369) note that UNITA's rebel structures lasted until 1992, but that "From the mid-1990s, the insurgent authority disintegrated, and in 1998, their administrative structure was nearly dissolved." UNITA had lost much of the initial support of the Ovimbundu population by that time, as civilians grew war weary and "people no longer believe that their daily struggle...is only the result of the machinations of the other party" (Munslow, 1999, 554). The length of the consolidation period and the ongoing decades of civil war thus eventually helped sever UNITA's ties with civilians. When its charismatic leader Savimbi was killed in 2002, this enabled the MPLA to finally consolidate power over Angola through military dominance.

7.2.4 Summary

The lines between war and peace were blurred in Angola, highlighting the book's central argument—that the process of consolidating power extends far beyond the initial rebel victory. Thus rebel groups that fail to establish wartime social control can win a civil war but fail to govern afterwards. The MPLA was unable to maintain its ties with civilians during the war, and was too affected by military contestation to establish grassroots institutions that could be used to institute control in rural areas. The MPLA thus became a political party that was strong only in urban areas, while UNITA maintained ties with civilians and a parallel system of administration in southern Angola. After the War for Independence, the MPLA's limited reach in rural areas crippled its ability to govern. Despite its attempts to build a technocratic developmental state with a centralized structure to consolidate power, the MPLA faced a security–development trade-off due to significant support for its rival. When its post-war priorities shifted heavily toward building its army and quashing the UNITA insurgency, it neglected its political and developmental objectives. Agriculture and other productive sectors grew increasingly underdeveloped, while the MPLA funded its military with oil exports. As rural opportunities withered, undecided civilians aligned with UNITA, which exacerbated the new government's security problems.

The MPLA's experience in Angola shows how, once in power, it is difficult for an incumbent party to build embedded local structures in the same way that guerrillas can do. After occupying the capital city, the MPLA was unable to galvanize rural support without any party structures on the ground. Its attempts to do so were implemented from the top down by deploying bureaucrats. While this strategy may help the government cement control in undecided regions with low rival organizational capacity as in the case of Zimbabwe, it failed to win over the local population in Angola that resented and rejected the ruling party's legitimacy in favor of its rivals. As the MPLA sought to fund expensive conflicts, Angola quickly became a patrimonial oil state that resembled Liberia under Charles Taylor. The MPLA eventually consolidated control *not* because it won additional support or succeeded in building rural capacity, but because UNITA lost its own civilian ties through protracted warfare. The Angola case highlights the important constraints that governments face when confronted with a rival that has greater rural reach: When security concerns threaten its ability to stay in power, the government must shift its focus to state security to the detriment of development—despite its initial intentions.

7.3 Ivorian Civil War (2002–2011)

The Ivorian Civil War is an example of strong wartime social control. In this short case study, I explore how rebel control and military contestation shaped the patterns of governance and violence during the two periods of conflict in Côte d'Ivoire. As rebels took control of the north, they formed relationships with local civilians, built partnerships with local leaders, and instituted informal governing structures that allowed them to tax and recruit from the local population. After the rebel victory in 2011, these rebel–civilian ties factored heavily into the new rebel government's post-war governing strategy. This new government relied on wartime ties in its strongholds in the north to diminish demands for development and reform and to prevent instability. The decentralized wartime rebel governance structure—through zone commanders across the north—provided an additional link between citizens and the state after the war. Outside of the north, where rebels maintained their stronghold, it used development in politically important urban regions and violence in the rival-supporting south to consolidate control.

The Ivorian Civil War began with the same conflict motivations and institutional background as Liberia, but its post-war politics resemble those of Zimbabwe. As in Liberia, the rebels were motivated by ethnic grievances arising from pre-war politics rather than ideology. The two states share co-ethnics as well as a border, which was particularly porous with respect to refugees and rebel combatant flows during the civil wars in both states. Although the Ivorian Civil War is commonly described as being fought using conventional rather than guerrilla tactics, both conflicts' rebel–civilian encounters featured the same fractionalized rebel structure that was more indicative of warlordism than a cohesive rebel political party.

Despite these similarities, however, Côte d'Ivoire and Liberia diverged in the post-war period: Unlike the Taylor regime in Liberia, the Ouattara government in Côte d'Ivoire successfully consolidated power and has enjoyed relative stability since winning the civil war. I argue that wartime rebel–civilian ties contributed to these divergent outcomes, pushing Côte d'Ivoire toward Zimbabwe's political experiences after consolidating power. As in post-consolidation Zimbabwe, the main political challenge in Côte d'Ivoire arose from within the ruler's ex-combatant ranks rather than from external rivals.

7.3.1 Conflict Background

The civil war in Côte d'Ivoire was waged over the notion of birthright and the struggle for equal citizenship. In the mid-1990s, President Henri Konan Bédié instituted the *Ivoirité* doctrine as a strategy to win the 1995 and 2000 elections. Although ethnic tensions had simmered for decades, the doctrine defined true Ivorians as those who were originally indigenous (primarily those living in the southern half of the country), in contrast to those who were historically immigrants to Côte d'Ivoire (primarily citizens from the northern half). This move prevented his main opponent Alassane Ouattara from entering the presidential race, denied those in the north of the country their Ivorian identity, and assured himself victory at the polls. *Ivoirité* laws would later strip northern Ivorians of their citizenship rights by institutionalizing stringent definitions of Ivorian nationality (Bah, 2010, 602). These birthright policies made those in the north second-class citizens and ignited the grievances that led to civil war.

Tensions between the north and south escalated into civil war in 2002. The war pitted rebels representing the north, the FN fighting on behalf of opposition candidate Alassane Ouattara, against the southerner-supported government under President Laurent Gbagbo. Officially, the war took place in two distinct periods, first between 2002 and the end of 2004, and second between 2010 and 2011, with nominal peace between 2005 and 2010 as the two groups agreed to a ceasefire. Throughout the first period of civil war (2002–2004), the FN was able to capture and control the entire northern half of the country while it briefly contested for power against government forces in the southern half. During the five-year ceasefire, the country remained divided; the rebels retained social and territorial control in the north while the government maintained control in the south. The ceasefire broke down in 2010 when Ouattara was elected president. The FN resumed violence after Gbagbo refused to abide by the election results and cede power. The FN emerged victorious at the end of 2011 as it militarily took control of the country while Ouattara was sworn in as the new president.

7.3.2 Rebel Control and Contestation

Full territorial control over northern Côte d'Ivoire, as well as social control over civilian life, was quickly and easily established during the civil war. When FN rebels first initiated the conflict, their initial aim was to overthrow President Gbagbo in a coup. Failure to capture the country's largest city, Abidjan, outright forced the FN rebels to restrategize and retreat northward, where they faced little difficulty establishing control over the central, northern, and western regions of the country (Förster, 2013, 13). Government forces were unable to defeat the FN and regain control of the north despite numerous attempts to conclude a ceasefire agreement.

To prevent the FN from returning to Abidjan, the government "created a number of paramilitary movements in the west and south of the country" where FN soldiers initially contested for power, and hired mercenaries from Liberia to bolster the army's ranks (Banegas, 2011, 4–5). UN peacekeepers and French troops similarly sought to contain the violence by instituting a buffer zone between the north and south in 2003 that formally partitioned the country into rebel-held and government-held territory (Dabalen et al., 2012, 14). This partition solidified the parallel administration in the north throughout the ceasefire period (2005–2010). Reunification attempts during this peaceful interim period as a part of the disarmament, demobilization, and reintegration program were unsuccessful. Thus rebel control and governance persisted until the end of the civil war in 2011.

Fighting between the rebels and pro-government forces occurred primarily in Abidjan and along the border of the Dix-Huit Montagnes and Moyen Cavally districts in the west.[4] This contestation took place during the first and last years of the civil war as the FN attempted to expand into the south, but not during the years in between: The buffer zone prevented both sides from making military incursions beyond their controlled territory. During periods of war, the fight for control between the government and rebels led to heightened insecurity and disorder for civilians living in these areas.

Governance under Rebel Control (Implication 1)

The north, under rebel control, was in effect ruled by the FN's parallel government. Some areas enjoyed greater bureaucratic order under the rebels than under the state during the civil war (Förster, 2015). The FN divided its territory into ten zones, each with its own commander, and each zone was further divided into sectors headed by sector commanders (Martin, 2020, 13). The FN was more decentralized than ideological rebellions such as the ZANU-PF in Zimbabwe, and there was greater variation in the degree of rebel governance under zone commanders within controlled territories. Yet rebel governance was almost universal in these areas: Zone and sector commanders maintained wartime order through rebel–civilian ties.

At a minimum, FN rebel governance involved security provision throughout almost the entire territory, and commanders regulated land and property disputes in most areas (Martin, 2020, 16). Some commanders provided education, health care, infrastructure, and loans (Martin, 2020, 16). In the

---

[4] These districts were combined into a single district in 2011.

city of Korhogo, for example, rebels established governance by providing security and collecting taxes (Förster, 2015). Similarly, in the province of Man, a rebel-controlled territory in the western Dix-Huit Montagnes district bordering government-controlled territory, "everything concerning security or taxation, customs and justice was... firmly in the hands of the [FN]" (Heitz, 2009, 124). During the peaceful interim period between 2005 and 2010 within Man, even government agents cooperated with the rebels because "it is the [FN] who will offer them protection—and not the state—in the case of factional insurgency" (Heitz, 2009, 124).

As in Zimbabwe, the rebels in Côte d'Ivoire bargained and consulted with local leaders and traditional authorities and adopted local norms and customs to gain legitimacy and maintain control (Martin, 2020, 17). Rebels also partnered with local institutions to provide security: Dozo hunters played a significant role as security providers during the civil war in northern Côte d'Ivoire. The Dozo, who are part of a larger class of Mande hunters—a secret society stretching across multiple states in West Africa—held cultural significance and commanded respect in the north. The Ivorian rebels' alliance with the Dozo hunters bestowed legitimacy as well as security with little manpower (Förster, 2015, 216).

Treatment of Civilians under Contestation (Implication 2)
Contestation was brief but especially intense after the 2010 elections. After Gbagbo refused to cede power to Ouattara, who had won the popular vote, violence once again flared up. This time, the FN managed to push past the buffer zone from the north to attack government-held territories from the west and center. As it fought for control and began to occupy territories in pro-Gbagbo areas, "this offensive led to human rights abuses...and led to an exodus of people" (Amnesty International, 2011, 11). Contestation (and thus civilian victimization) was primarily high in two areas. First, the economic capital, Abidjan, experienced the highest levels of military contestation as the FN and pro-Gbagbo forces fought for control over the government. Where there was a mix of pro-Ouattara and pro-Gbagbo neighborhoods, each side committed atrocities against the opponent's supporters. Government forces also "signaled to potential defectors within his party or the state military that disloyalty would be punished violently" (Straus, 2011, 485).

The second area that suffered high levels of civilian abuse was the Dix-Huit Montagnes and Moyen Cavally districts, where tensions between the far west and southwest pro-Gbagbo communities and the northwest pro-Ouattara communities had remained heightened throughout the conflict (Amnesty International, 2011, 32). Civilians living in these areas bore the brunt of FN and government brutality when violence erupted again at the end of 2010. On the southern side of the ceasefire buffer line, the FN launched "perhaps the worst massacre during the electoral crisis" (Straus, 2011, 486) as it used indiscriminate ethnic violence against pro-Gbagbo communities. Because this area had been historically contested, Gbagbo concentrated on building militias there immediately after 2002 while the FN enlisted the Dozo hunters as auxiliary security forces. After the 2010 elections, the FN began its assault on the south by entering through the Dix-Huit Montagnes district, battling the government army and pro-Gbagbo militias. In doing so, "the two parties to the conflict committed serious violations of international humanitarian law, including war crimes, as well as crimes against humanity" (Amnesty International, 2011, 34).

7.3.3 Post-war Patterns of Development and Violence

After Ouattara won power, the new government focused its efforts on winning support through development and eliminating potential challengers using violence. To pursue both of these strategies, the national government relied on its ties with local communities—particularly those that rebel zone commanders (the *comzones*) maintained with the communities they governed during the civil war.

Development after War (Hypotheses 1 and 2)
The new government used development and post-war recovery to "increase legitimacy" and "make people forget the legacy of ethnic polarization and violence" (BTI Project, 2018). Indeed, the international community has praised the country's post-war development, and Ouattara's government has been credited with accelerating economic growth and reconstruction. Immediately after the end of the civil war, Côte d'Ivoire began implementing its 2012–2015 National Development Program, which aimed to reduce poverty, achieve 8%–10% economic growth per year, and embark upon post-war reconstruction (Republic of Côte d'Ivoire, 2012). The government broadly met these goals: The country's economy grew by an average of 9% each year, and GDP per capita increased by 21% during this period (Republic of Côte d'Ivoire, 2015). The government's focus on infrastructure development was broadly successful in roads, education, health, and electricity (Republic of Côte d'Ivoire, 2015). By 2018, the country was considered "one of the best performing economies on the continent" (World Bank, 2019).

Despite this commitment to development however, the government strategically targeted development funding to visible projects in important localities. Improvements were concentrated in Abidjan—where the new government was most able (and most needed) to win the support of the civilian population—to the detriment of the rest of the country. Neither the north nor the south, controlled by the FN and by rival ex-Gbagbo forces during the civil war, respectively, has benefitted from major reconstruction or development efforts; economic inequality and poverty remain high (Sturm, 2013). Development inequalities persisted: Despite the fast pace of growth, the number of people living in poverty remained roughly the same even five years after the end of the civil war; according to the World Bank, between 2015 and 2020, urban poverty continued to decline quickly while rural poverty increased (World Bank, 2019).

In wartime rebel strongholds, post-war aid and development came not from the central government, but from the *comzones* who controlled these areas. Because the government focused most of its aid dollars in Abidjan, reconstruction and small-scale development relied significantly on the wartime ties established by the *comzones*. During the civil war, many rebel commanders governed on behalf of the FN, for example by providing material support or helping to pay for building schools, hospitals, and mosques. More than half of the *comzones* continued to play this important role in the local community after the war, providing reconstruction aid and development out of their own pockets where the government was reluctant to spend aid dollars (Martin, 2020).

Internal Security Concerns (Sub-national Hypotheses 1 and 3)
After winning the civil war, Ouattara's government faced security threats but was able to prevent the conflict from escalating into a counter-rebellion in part by leveraging its wartime ties in rural areas alongside its security and police forces. State security and police forces were primarily used to sever civilian ties with pro-Gbagbo forces in rival areas (Sub-national Hypothesis 3), while the new rebel government leveraged its wartime ties to maintain security and order in stronghold areas and along the contested border regions (Sub-national Hypothesis 1). This mirrors the post-war strategies that the governments in Zimbabwe and (as I later show) Burundi pursued, highlighting the importance of ties to local intermediaries who can act as security providers.

Threats to security emerged primarily in the west in the pro-Gbagbo side of the Dix-Huit Montagnes district along the Liberian border and along the

226 Governing after War

Ghanaian border in the east.[5] After the civil war, pro-Gbagbo militias fled to Liberia and Ghana, where they intended to regroup and foment a counter-rebellion against the Ouattara government (Human Rights Watch, 2012*b*). Cross-border incursions began immediately after the end of the civil war in 2011, to which the new rebel government responded harshly in 2012. Ouattara's forces "undertook neighborhood sweeps, arrests, interrogations, and detentions" that were arbitrary and indiscriminate (Human Rights Watch, 2012*a*, 4). Although the violence did not reach the scale of the Zimbabwean Fifth Brigade's actions during the Gukurahundi massacres (see Chapter 4), the purpose of these drastic security measures was the same—to prevent pro-Gbagbo forces from recruiting from among the civilian population during the cross-border attacks. An anonymous diplomat quoted in a Human Rights Watch report noted the government's fear of rival ties to the local population: " 'The language they use is very concerning: 'eradication,' 'terrorism,' 'clean the country up.' They're so convinced they're right [about the nature of the threat and the extent of grassroots involvement] ... that they've decided to put reconciliation aside" (Human Rights Watch, 2012*a*, 37).[6]

The FN's wartime ties with existing local institutions also helped enhance post-war security. The traditional Dozo hunters, who allied with the FN during the civil war in the pro-Ouattara side of the Dix-Huit Montagnes district, became a pro-government militia that aided the new rebel government after the war. In the immediate post-war period, the Dozo hunters were instrumental in leveraging their organizational capacity in western Côte d'Ivoire to help keep the peace in the face of pro-Gbagbo cross-border incursions along the Liberia border. According to Amnesty International (2013, 17), "the Dozos have gained considerable importance over the whole territory and their presence has increased notably in the west of the country," where they assumed "a self-appointed policing role" to help curb cross-border activity and prevent the spread of conflict. The Dozo hunters continued to work with the government until 2014, and were even armed by the government to bolster the state security and gendarmerie forces.

Long-Run Consolidation of Power?

The Ivorian Civil War is the most recent case examined in this book; its future trajectory may be anticipated based on how politics has developed in the other cases. By 2014, the threat of a pro-Gbagbo counter-rebellion had

---

[5] As noted in Section 7.3.2, the Dix-Huit Montagnes district faced brief periods of intense contestation at the start and end of the conflict, but was separated into pro-Gbagbo and pro-Ouattara strongholds by the buffer zone.

[6] Bracketed text in the original.

been eliminated and the Ouattara government had succeeded in preventing a return to civil war. Since then, it has followed Zimbabwe's path in consolidating post-war power: As the government grows comfortable in its position, its wartime ties have begun demanding patronage and resources in return for their continued support—shifting the ruling party's attention away from development toward placating its supporters.

Like in Zimbabwe at the turn of the century, since eliminating the security threat from the pro-Gbagbo ex-soldiers, new security concerns have instead emerged from *within* the victorious rebel group. Ex-combatants in the national army mutinied against the Ouattara government first in 2014, and again in 2017, primarily over issues related to compensation. The mutinies were accompanied by protests as ex-combatants who were demobilized after the civil war—and who had returned to civilian life—demanded "paid bonuses promised upon demobilization, in addition to demanding jobs in the army and other state institutions" (Schiel, Faulkner, and Powell, 2017, 108). The protesters' calls for payment and government jobs mirror the Zimbabwean government's contention with its own ex-combatants in the 1990s and 2000s after it had eliminated the ZAPU threat in the 1980s. As in Zimbabwe, Côte d'Ivoire's next threat to security came from its own disgruntled ex-combatants who seek compensation for their wartime support. These protests and mutinies illustrate two important points in the post-war landscape.

First, as I have argued throughout the book, wartime control decreases the cost of post-war governance. In Côte d'Ivoire, wartime control may also allow the government to escape a full-blown security problem in the future from within its own ranks and from its demobilized ex-combatants. To de-escalate the threats from protests, the government relied heavily on the wartime linkages that current top commanders developed in stronghold areas. These links have proven to be instrumental to keeping the peace: When protests flared, former *comzones* who had retained ties with local communities were key to maintaining social order and calming down the protesters while brokering the negotiations between ex-combatants and the government. Important *comzones* retain key military and government positions to ensure they continue to broker peace on behalf of the government.

Second, the government de-escalated threats from the national army by diverting resources to pay their promised bonuses, which resulted in "the cancellation of a variety of public projects, including the construction of schools and healthcare and cultural centres, and the delay of Ouattara's plan to vastly expand access to electricity" (Schiel, Faulkner, and Powell, 2017, 117). This was only possible because the Ouattara government had quickly

228 Governing after War

eliminated the security threat from pro-Gbagbo forces, thus rendering development a less pressing concern. If the security threat had continued or flared into a civil war, the protests from ex-FN combatants and mutiny from the national army would have forced the new government to make hard choices about how to allocate resources. This shift in priorities mimics Zimbabwe's step back from rigorous development after it quashed the dissidents in 1987. Between the 1990s and early 2000s, the Zimbabwean government was focused on bringing ex-combatants back in line, which resulted in a combination of patronage and policy disasters.[7] Zimbabwe's past problems may therefore provide some indication of the Ivorian ruling party's future political trajectory as ex-combatants become more autonomous from the new government. The Ivorian government has already been forced to pay off its supporters to maintain its control over the state.

7.3.4 Summary

Côte d'Ivoire's pre-war institutional context resembled Liberia's, but its post-war trajectory mimics that of Zimbabwe. It was embroiled in the same regional conflict as neighboring Liberia, and some of the same combatants fought in both wars along the countries' border. Neither civil war was ideological in nature, and Côte d'Ivoire's military command structure—which featured decentralized rebel governance and autonomous *comzones*—was perhaps even more fragmented than Liberia's. Unlike in Liberia, however, the rebels in Côte d'Ivoire established significant social control over the northern half of the country, which allowed the *comzones* to govern. Civilians in this area were provided with a variety of benefits including security, goods and services, and a justice system.

Rebel ties with local communities and community institutions were sustained after the war ended in 2011, which allowed the government to focus on winning support where it mattered—in the highly contested city of Abidjan—by swiftly investing in development and reconstruction. The rest of the country, which was split into either pro-Ouattara or pro-Gbagbo areas, benefitted from relatively few government development projects. Instead, *comzones* continued their wartime governing activities and funded development in former rebel–controlled areas, highlighting the new government's need to

---

[7] The Fast Track Land Reform, for example, is one such policy: the Zimbabwean government allowed the expropriation of farmland held by White farmers, to appease ex-combatants as elections became more competitive and coup threats became more likely.

sustain their support in order to maintain control. In previously government-controlled zones, there has been no development at all: "many people, including community leaders and traditional chiefs, find themselves sleeping on the ground and unable to eat more than once a day" (Sturm, 2013). Rather than developing these areas, the Ouattara government focused on military repression when a security threat arose: As ex-Gbagbo militiamen threatened to restart the civil war from the Liberian border, the government quelled the spread of violence by relying on (1) ties with the Dozo hunters to police communities and (2) formal state forces to eliminate the potential military threat. The rebel government's path to consolidate power therefore closely tracks post-war Zimbabwe's experience, emphasizing how wartime rebel–civilian ties shape post-war governing strategies.

7.4 Burundian Civil War (1991–2005)

I now turn to compare the Burundian Civil War and the Rwandan Civil War—fought in contiguous countries with similar pre-war institutions and a history of violent inter-ethnic rivalry between the Hutus and Tutsis.

The Burundian Civil War is a case of strong wartime social control with widespread and institutionalized rebel–civilian ties. The victor emerged as the strongest of the three Hutu rebellions that were contesting the minority Tutsi government for power. In this case study, I describe how the victorious rebel group's wartime dominance allowed it to form rebel–civilian ties on the ground, establish social control across much of the state, and engage in rebel governance. I argue that these wartime activities helped the victor cement its post-war dominance and consolidate power against wartime rivals.

7.4.1 Conflict Background

The Burundian Civil War erupted after decades of ethnic tensions between the Hutus and Tutsis that featured several episodes of one-sided violence and attempted genocide. The civil war primarily pitted two rival Hutu rebel groups—the Conseil National Pour la Défense de la Démocratie–Forces pour la Défense de la Démocratie (CNDD-FDD) led by Pierre Nkurunziza and the Parti pour la libération du peuple Hutu–Forces Nationales de Libération (Palipehutu-FNL) led by Agathon Rwasa—against the minority Tutsi government. A third Hutu rebel group, the Front de Libération Nationale (Frolina), sustained only limited influence during the civil war.

These rebel groups aimed to take over the government on behalf of the Hutu ethnic group.

The war formally ended when the CNDD-FDD agreed to lay down arms in 2005 and participate in democratic elections. Because the CNDD-FDD enjoyed strong support from civilians, it won an electoral victory and has remained in power ever since. Palipehutu-FNL continued fighting—this time against the CNDD-FDD government—until the end of 2008 (Falch, 2008). Palipehutu-FNL soldiers were formally integrated into the army in 2010, but groups of ex-Palipehutu-FNL rebels maintained bases in the DRC and attempted to rekindle civil war in 2015 (MONUSCO, 2015; Nkurunziza, Jean-Baptiste, and Obi Anyadike, 2016).

7.4.2 Rebel Control and Contestation

Although the civil war began in 1991 with the Palipehutu-FNL uprising, it was not until 1994 that the CNDD-FDD coalesced to rebel against the Tutsi minority government. In the beginning, the CNDD-FDD's influence was limited; it maintained bases in the DRC amid Palipehutu-FNL bases and fought against both the Burundian government and Palipehutu-FNL. Due to the intermingling between the two rebel groups and the proximity of Burundi's capital, Bujumbura, to the DRC border, it was difficult for either group to expand beyond the western border. These initial years featured high civilian casualties as both rebel groups sought to gain a foothold in the country.

From 1996 onward, the CNDD-FDD established cross-border bases in Tanzania, substantially increasing its degree of control across the country. Much like the ZANU-PF in Zimbabwe, establishing these new rebel bases along the Burundi–Tanzania border allowed the rebels to infiltrate the country and open up a new front of attack, this time farther away from the capital. From the eastern border, the CNDD-FDD's authority was largely unchallenged: The rebels were able to build significant support among civilians moving from east to west. By the 2000s, the CNDD-FDD had spread throughout the country and was able to sustain intensive operations in almost all parts of the country at the same time (International Crisis Group, 2002, 4). The exception was the northwestern provinces, where it maintained a somewhat smaller presence; it had particularly limited influence over the provinces surrounding the capital (Bujumbura Rurale, Bubanza, and Muramvya), where its main rival (Palipehutu-FNL) enjoyed greater influence and civilian support throughout the war.

As the CNDD-FDD grew in size and expanded its control during the second half of the war, Palipehutu-FNL's control declined. It lost significant territory, as well as civilian support, during military contestation against the CNDD-FDD. Although Palipehutu-FNL was the only rebel group between 1991 and 1994, the inception of the CNDD-FDD substantially increased contestation along the western border. By 1997, after the CNDD-FDD opened up its bases in Tanzania, Palipehutu-FNL had already lost considerable support to the newer group (Wittig, 2016, 148). By the early 2000s, Palipehutu-FNL's presence was limited primarily to the northwest and near the capital (Sculier, 2003). After the CNDD-FDD was elected to government in 2005, Palipehutu-FNL continued to fight within Bujumbura Rurale and Bubanza provinces until the late 2000s.

In Burundi's case, the rebels were not unique in their ability to build local organizational capacity: From 1994 onward the Burundian government used tactics similar to the CNDD-FDD to establish local security. The government maintained a local presence in some rural areas through its state-sponsored militia, the Guardians of Peace. The militia initially focused on arming Tutsis and training them to create self-defense groups in their communities, but later began to train Hutu civilians who were living under government control. The Guardians of Peace program increased the government's social control in the north in the Kibira forest and Kayanza province, as well as in the south in Bururi, Makamba, and Rutana provinces by 1997. In 2001, as the rebels grew stronger, the government attempted to expand the program throughout the country but failed to replicate the process of local control. The Guardians of Peace began to resemble government soldiers rather than community self-defense militias (Human Rights Watch, 2001). As the CNDD-FDD increased its presence, there was evidence of deteriorating paramilitary morale and government control in areas it captured. A small number of ex-Guardians of Peace members reportedly joined the rebels; some gave their weapons to the rebels in exchange for protection, and others fled to avoid persecution (Human Rights Watch, 2001, 12–13).

Governance under Rebel Control (Implication 1)

In areas under CNDD-FDD control during the war, the rebel group established a parallel government that typified governance when rebels are "stationary bandits" (Olson, 2000). Rebel governance in CNDD-FDD areas included security, bureaucracy, and taxation in rural Burundi, and involved both youth groups as well as the older population.

The CNDD-FDD's rebel governance structures mirrored those in Liberia and Zimbabwe in two ways. First, much like other guerrilla rebel groups that successfully established control over civilians, the CNDD-FDD engaged rural youths—some as young as eight years old, but most in their teens—to take part in the rebellion (Dilworth, 2006, 7). Youths were primarily used to sustain local security. They formed watch teams for reconnaissance, local security provision, and passing messages between rebel soldiers (Dilworth, 2006, 8). The CNDD-FDD youth militia, called the Imbonerakure ("those who see far" in Kirundi), played a significant role in the group's success during the civil war and helped establish the foundation for its expansive and deep-rooted control over much of rural Burundi (Wittig, 2016, 149). Second, the CNDD-FDD also established a strong system of quasi-governing structures that bypassed the government in areas under its control. By 1996, "the CNDD had established a parallel administration in their area" and "FDD combatants received material support from residents" (Longman, 1998, 17). This administration included police, provincial governors, and policy administrators (Nindorera, 2012, 18). A key group of civilians—teachers—were particularly useful to the CNDD-FDD because of their social standing in rural areas. According to Chemouni (2016, 145), "teachers were regularly courted by the CNDD-FDD during the civil war" because they were identified as "local opinion leaders, who were able to foster support for the rebellion."

Together, the Imbonerakure youth and the CNDD-FDD parallel administration established a system of wartime taxation in which they "systematically collected contributions from the population in the area under their control" (Sabates-Wheeler and Verwimp, 2014, 1482). Individuals were compelled to provide monetary support or livestock for the rebels, and were given a receipt in exchange for their contribution. Such receipts would protect civilians from rebel violence in controlled communities or at rebel checkpoints (Sabates-Wheeler and Verwimp, 2014, 1483). Beyond taxing the civilian population for food and material support, there is some evidence that the CNDD-FDD also "founded revenue-generating associations" and "taught the local population how to grow its own food, and helped small businessmen develop market gardening" (Nindorera, 2012, 18–19). The CNDD-FDD also established tribunals in some areas, where civilians as well as captured government soldiers were tried under CNDD-FDD laws (Dilworth, 2006, 4).

Violence under Contestation (Implication 2)

Although the CNDD-FDD collaborated more with civilians in the latter half of the war when it was able to establish widespread social control, contested areas where it fought the Palipehutu-FNL for control were subject to far greater violence. Where the two rebel groups contested for influence over civilians, they were less able to build their parallel administration. Since they could not engage in taxation in these areas, the CNDD-FDD rebels looted and pillaged to gather supplies (Longman, 1998, 141), as they often did by the end of the war in areas with heavy fighting such as Bujumbura Rurale, Bubanza, and Muramvya provinces (Sculier, 2003).

In addition to looting and coercion, all parties to the conflict killed civilians. Where fighting between the CNDD-FDD and Palipehutu-FNL was especially intense and the government implemented its Guardians of Peace militia program, all civilians were treated as "proxy targets" (Longman, 1998). In the beginning of the civil war when the CNDD-FDD was first gaining a foothold in the country, civilian targeting was high throughout areas with a rebel presence; by the late 1990s, civilians were indiscriminately targeted primarily around the Palipehutu-FNL stronghold surrounding Bujumbura and in the southeastern provinces where the government's Guardians of Peace program was successfully implemented (Human Rights Watch, 2000). In these areas, although the CNDD-FDD primarily targeted Tutsis to retain Hutu support, civilians of both ethnicities who were considered government collaborators or supporters of rival rebel groups were often targeted and killed (Longman, 1998, 131,138). Rebels also frequently attacked government-run civilian displacement camps (known as regroupment camps) to force civilians to return to rural communities under rebel control (Human Rights Watch, 1999).

By the early 2000s, toward the end of the war, military contestation between the CNDD-FDD and Palipehutu-FNL further increased civilian abuse in the northwestern provinces. Rape, for example, was common from all sides involved in the war, and "increased as a result of the conflict between the FNL and the FDD" (Sculier, 2003, 42). Similarly, the FNL and FDD both engaged in civilian abuses along the western border between the DRC and Burundi (Sculier, 2003). This violence continued until the end of the war.

7.4.3 Post-war Patterns of Development and Violence

Organizational Capacity as a Legacy of War (Sub-national Hypothesis 1)
Like in Zimbabwe, the CNDD-FDD's penetration into rural Burundi was key to its success in the 2005 elections (Wittig, 2016, 149). Because the rebel party was able to set up parallel administrative organizations with an entrenched system of political mobilization among the youths as well as local elites, the CNDD-FDD easily won over 60% of the popular vote in the legislative elections, and was especially successful in rural regions.[8] Unlike Zimbabwe, however, this success could not be attributed to ethnicity: The CNDD-FDD's

---

[8] Only legislative and communal elections were held in 2005. The legislative branch then chose the president.

electoral rivals were also Hutu. The Front pour la Démocratie au Burundi, the main civilian Hutu political party up until the end of the civil war, received far fewer votes—less than 20% in the legislative elections—while the third Hutu rebel group, Frolina, failed to win any seats in parliament.[9]

Once elected, the CNDD-FDD's control over local politics relied significantly on its wartime networks. Van Acker (2015, 7) described the CNDD-FDD government as "determined by institutions, networks and individuals rooted in its former existence as a rebel movement. [They]...stretch from the level of high ranking elites...to the former combatants of the FDD rebellion at the grassroots level." In areas that fell under CNDD-FDD control during the war, post-war administration and local power were delegated to individuals who were loyal to the party rather than to qualified or elected leaders. This informal party-based hierarchy bypassed the formal state hierarchy, empowering wartime party commissars and local administrators due to their ties to the new ruling party. This strategy helped sustain wartime institutions and ensured party control at the local level.

In addition to using an informal bureaucratic hierarchy to exert local political control after the war, the Imbonerakure youth militias were carried over from wartime to post-war politics. They were used to mobilize electoral support in rural areas. In the 2010 and 2015 elections, the Imbonerakure were instrumental in ensuring local support for the CNDD-FDD and blocking opposition parties from participating in the political arena (Van Acker, 2016; Arieff, 2015). Beginning in 2017, the Imbonerakure were used in rural areas to collect election taxes for the ruling party ahead of the 2020 elections. This echoed the CNDD-FDD's wartime administration, in which CNDD-FDD administrators and the Imbonerakure would collect money, livestock, and manual labor as taxes. According to a 2019 Human Rights Watch report, although "members of the Imbonerakure do not have any legal authority to conduct administrative duties, including tax collection, or law enforcement activities," they have actively "intimidated, threatened, and beaten people to force them to donate food, livestock, and money to the ruling CNDD-FDD and take part in the construction of local ruling party offices" (Human Rights Watch, 2019, 3). Following the system used during the civil war, individuals who were taxed would be issued receipts for their contributions. These practices highlight how wartime organizational capacity and rebel institutions carry over to state politics after rebels win the civil war.

---

[9] Palipehutu-FNL did not participate in the elections. While it threatened to police, disrupt, and intimidate civilians at the polls, there is little evidence of intimidation and the elections proceeded smoothly (Stenberg, 2005).

Maintaining and Expanding Control through Local Development (Sub-national Hypotheses 1 and 2)

CNDD-FDD bureaucrats led development in post-war Burundi, which helped sustain the party's influence in controlled territories and extended its control into contested areas. Development planning and funding in Burundi is primarily disbursed at the commune administrative level, thus the CNDD-FDD bureaucrats who were in charge of development were the communal administrators. The CNDD-FDD ensured that these administrators were not elected directly, but were CNDD-FDD partisans who had ties to the rebel party during the war. Although nominally democratic, citizens within a community could only vote a political party into the commune council, which then elected a communal administrator who was considered a loyal party worker (Chemouni, 2016, 144).

Beginning in 2006, CNDD-FDD leader Nkurunziza implemented a system of "communal works" to encourage local community development efforts by mobilizing civilians to participate in building schools, health centers, and other projects on Saturdays (Theunynck and Rabakoson, 2017, 12). This mirrored the development strategies in Zimbabwe, in which villages were encouraged to engage in self-help after the war under the top-down-funded VIDCO and WADCO developmental committee system (see Chapter 4). In addition to being in charge of communal works, CNDD-FDD communal administrators "were active politically. They regularly organised political meetings for the CNDD-FDD" and attended communal works "often in the party uniform and singing party songs" Chemouni (2016, 145). Local party officials exploited the Saturday communal works for political mobilization where necessary (Chemouni, 2016, 145). In effect, much like ZANU-PF had done in Zimbabwe, the CNDD-FDD exported its wartime parallel administration to the rest of the country and "worked on extending its grass-roots penetration in the hillsides to build a mass party presence" (Wittig, 2016, 149).

This strategy proved successful for consolidating control. Besides engaging in development (the communal works system increased the rate of post-war reconstruction),[10] the CNDD-FDD's deliberate spread of party bureaucrats increased its expansion into rural Burundi and cemented its control in areas where it had a weaker hold, as evidenced by its increasing vote shares across elections. The CNDD-FDD won 55% of the vote in the 2005 communal (local) elections immediately after the war,[11] and 65% in the

---

[10] For example, between 2005 and 2012, a majority of the schools constructed in the country were built under the communal works program. These were, however, of poor quality as they were not constructed by qualified builders (Theunynck and Rabakoson, 2017, 12–13).

[11] Palipehutu-FNL did not run in this election because it had not yet laid down arms.

2010 communal elections (Abdellaoui, 2010). Even after Palipehutu-FNL contested the 2010 communal elections, the CNDD-FDD won a majority in its wartime strongholds as well as in provinces that were disputed during the war. The CNDD-FDD only failed to win a majority in three opposition (rival-supporting) areas—the capital city (Bujumbura), Bujumbura Rurale province (a rival stronghold where Palipehutu-FNL enjoyed significant support throughout the war), and the Tutsi-dominated Bururi province.[12] The international community assessed the 2010 election as free and fair with slight irregularities (Abdellaoui, 2010, 4).

Organizational Capacity and Security Concerns (Sub-national Hypotheses 1 and 3)

The CNDD-FDD's primary concern after coming to power was ensuring state stability and consolidating its control (Burihabwa and Curtis, 2019, 560). While the government implemented a number of development reforms and communal works for public goods provision and reconstruction, it also relied on violent and authoritarian tactics to eliminate potential threats to the regime. To do so, it leveraged both formal state institutions—the police and military—and its ties with the Imbonerakure.

Between 2005 and 2009, Palipehutu-FNL continued to fight against the CNDD-FDD regime. As such, security concerns arose first in Bujumbura Rurale, where Palipehutu-FNL enjoyed the greatest relative control, and then in the contested Bubanza and Muramvya provinces, where Palipehutu-FNL also maintained influence over civilians and continued to sustain some clandestine wartime party structures (Wittig, 2016, 150). In these provinces, the CNDD-FDD attempted to demonstrate its strength through brutal and repressive crackdowns (Wittig, 2016, 149). From 2008 onward, as support for the Palipehutu-FNL remained strong in northwest Burundi, the CNDD-FDD remilitarized its youth supporters, the Imbonerakure, who had been active in these areas during the civil war. Up until 2008, the Imbonerakure had primarily been used to mobilize for the ruling party in its strongholds, although it was accused of electoral intimidation during the 2005 elections. By 2008, it began operating once again as a paramilitary organization on behalf of the government.

Security concerns worsened between 2015 and 2018 as the CNDD-FDD faced a constitutional crisis, an attempted coup from within the ruling party's ranks, and the threat of civil war resumption under (1) Palipehutu-FNL

---

[12] The opposition party boycotted the presidential and legislative elections in 2010, leading to a landslide CNDD-FDD victory across all levels of government.

ex-combatants and (2) breakaway members of the CNDD-FDD party. In 2015, Nkurunziza was reelected to a third term as president (in violation of the constitution's two-term limit) amid protests. Ex-Palipehutu-FNL soldiers formed a new rebel group, Résistance pour un État de Droit au Burundi, while an ex-CNDD-FDD general formed another rebel group with breakaway CNDD-FDD members who wished to oust Nkurunziza (International Crisis Group, 2017, 5). From 2015 onward, to combat these security threats, Nkurunziza increased crackdowns against protesters and curbed civilian freedoms. Government violence continued into 2018, when a successful constitutional referendum was held to increase the presidential term from five to seven years. The referendum also allowed Nkurunziza to run for president in two more elections.

During this constitutional crisis, wartime institutions and ties to grassroots organizations through the Imbonerakure played a significant role in bolstering state forces and preventing low-level violence from reigniting the civil war. They did so by sustaining control in wartime strongholds, which freed up the official state forces—the Burundi military and police forces—to subdue protesters and prevent the resumption of war. The Imbonerakure was used to subdue the civilian population to ensure that (1) rural civilians continued to vote for Nkurunziza as president, (2) supporters voted "yes" on the constitutional referendum, and (3) election taxes were collected on behalf of the CNDD-FDD to finance its campaign.

Who engaged in violence—and where—illustrate how the CNDD-FDD delegated violence to formal (police and military) and informal (Imbonerakure) institutions. Based on data collected by the Armed Conflict Location and Event Dataset (ACLED), Imbonerakure violence increased beginning in 2010 after the Palipehutu-FNL laid down arms and formed a political party (Raleigh et al., 2010). In contested areas where there was substantial support for Palipehutu-FNL, the Imbonerakure primarily targeted ex-Palipehutu-FNL combatants as well as supporters of the FNL party (Human Rights Watch, 2009). During the 2015–2018 constitutional crisis, the ACLED database recorded a total of 2,524 violent acts committed by formal and informal CNDD-FDD institutions. Of these, violence from the Imbonerakure made up 45% of the events. Population-weighted violence from *formal* state institutions (military and police) was highest in the capital, Bubanza, Makamba, and Bujumbura Rurale—where the CNDD-FDD's wartime rival, Palipehutu-FNL, had maintained civilian ties and set up some governing structures of its own. The ratio of Imbonerakure to formal violent events was highest in rural provinces in north, east, and central Burundi, which were CNDD-FDD strongholds during the civil war (Raleigh et al.,

2010). In those areas the Imbonerakure were best able to broker support for the ruling party, thus formal military and police forces were not needed to sustain security.

7.4.4 Summary

The case of Burundi illustrates the importance of wartime control through a large rebel presence and influence over the civilian population. The CNDD-FDD contested the government and other rebel groups for control during the first few years of the civil war, but gained a foothold throughout much of the country by the late 1990s. The CNDD-FDD cemented its control sub-nationally and established rebel governing institutions by enlisting youth organizations (Imbonerakure) for reconnaissance and scouting as well as local leaders and teachers in the bureaucracy. The CNDD-FDD therefore set up a parallel administration that facilitated local control, which strengthened its local organizational capacity for warfare. This sub-national variation in control persisted after the war: The CNDD-FDD's primary rival, Palipehutu-FNL, maintained a strong influence over the northwestern part of Burundi, while the CNDD-FDD's organizational capacity was lower in the south due to the ex-government's local militia program, Guardians of Peace. Everywhere else, the CNDD-FDD's hold over the local population helped the new rebel party comfortably win the election.

Post-war politics under the CNDD-FDD relied significantly on the organizational capacity it had built during the civil war. To maintain and expand its reach in rural Burundi, the CNDD-FDD ensured that rural communes were controlled by administrators who were loyal to the party. These administrators were local leaders who maintained ties to the rebels during the war, and would continue to remain loyal to the political party after civil war. Because development was primarily administered at the commune level, this system promoted adherence to the ruling party. Similarly, the CNDD-FDD utilized its local network of Imbonerakure to broker votes, collect taxes, and weed out opposition supporters. These tactics were particularly useful during the constitutional crisis of 2015–2018, when President Nkurunziza amended the constitution to win a third term. As the threat of civil war recurrence loomed, the Imbonerakure youth became instrumental informal violent actors; formal government forces—the state military and police—focused on quashing potential counter-rebellion in provinces where the CNDD-FDD had little support. Burundi's post-war experience highlights how the relationships and institutions cultivated during war can bolster the rebel party's post-war security and governing apparatuses, increasing its chances of surviving rival challenges.

7.5 Rwandan Civil War (1990–1994)

The Rwandan Civil War is the book's final case study. Unlike the CNDD-FDD in Burundi, the victor in Rwanda established very little social control during the civil war due to its lack of military presence across the state. However, it also faced relatively low levels of military contestation throughout much of the conflict. Rwanda's new rebel government thus did not have the option of leveraging ties with civilians or wartime structures for delegated governance. It also faced threats of violence from its rivals—ex-government troops and militias that had fled to the DRC.

To maintain state stability and stay in power after the war, the new RPF government therefore had to win over the uncertain population by engaging in top-down technocratic development throughout the country—*despite* having maintained no ideological or developmental stance during the civil war. It also violently suppressed counter-rebellion threats both in-country and across the border in the DRC. The rebel government in Rwanda did face a consolidation conflict; however, given its quick efforts to consolidate control—and its rivals' low capacity to recruit—it was able to win the second civil war and stay in power.

7.5.1 Conflict Background

Much like the Burundian Civil War, Rwanda's civil war was the result of ethnic tensions between the Hutus (85%) and Tutsis (14%) that had been brewing in the region since the late 1950s during decolonization. The refugee opposition Tutsi party—the Rwandaise Alliance Nationale de Unite (RANU)—was established in 1979. RANU became the militant RPF in 1988 while the party leaders were exiled in Kampala, Uganda.

On October 1, 1990, rebel leader Paul Kagame led the Tutsi-dominant RPF from Uganda into Rwanda to fight for state control. His troops fought the Hutu-majority ruling party, the Mouvement Républicain National Pour La Démocratie et le Développement (MRND), which commanded the Forces Armées Rwandaises (FAR) and the MRND youth wing, the Interahamwe. The RPF rebels enjoyed some early success as they targeted key areas in northeastern Rwanda and gained control of some of the country's northern-most towns. Despite its military strength, however, the RPF did not make significant headway into Rwanda. By 1993, the rebels were only able to hold 2% of the country's territory. It was not until President Juvenal Habyarimana's assassination on April 6, 1994—which triggered the Rwandan genocide—that the RPF soldiers swept across the nation in a widespread military attack; they advanced into the capital, Kigali, soon thereafter. The war ended with a military victory for the RPF on July 16, 1994.

7.5.2 Rebel Control and Military Contestation

Unlike the CNDD-FDD in Burundi, rebel governance and social control under the RPF in Rwanda was exceedingly limited throughout the war. When the war began in 1990, the RPF had bases in Uganda along Rwanda's northern border. Rebel troops sought to make military gains into the country through cross-border incursions, but were rebuffed by the government military. The RPF thus eventually settled in and controlled only a thin band of territory in northern Rwanda. It established its headquarters in the Virunga mountains in the northwest, which allowed the rebels to travel between Uganda and Rwanda (Reed, 1996, 491). The RPF also sustained bases and a presence in northernmost towns such as Mulindi and Byumba (Des Forges, 1999).

The ruling party, the MRND, retained its greatest support and strength from Hutus living in Gisenyi and Ruhengeri—northwestern prefectures bordering the DRC where President Habyarimana and his wife were from. These regions enjoyed a disproportionate amount of state resources, jobs, education, and other favors (Des Forges, 1999, 36). As early as 1990, local government leaders in Gisenyi began organizing on behalf of the MRND. They called killing Tutsis a "communal work obligation," and "other community leaders, such as teachers, health workers, the staff of developments projects, and party heads also helped turn out killers" (Des Forges, 1999, 65). Later in the war, when Hutu hardliners created their own radio station in 1993, "of the fifty original founders, forty were from the three prefectures of northern Rwanda, all but seven of those from Gisenyi and Ruhengeri, the region identified with Habyarimana" (Des Forges, 1999, 51).

Unlike the other cases presented in this book, the RPF rebels prioritized attacking government strongholds rather than expanding to other parts of the country. The rebel group aimed to win the war through military victory, so it sought to increase its military presence in government strongholds. The proximity of these strongholds to rebel-controlled areas motivated the rebels to amass in the northwestern prefectures during the first three years of the war in an attempt to take over these areas and quickly end the war. The RPF rebels maintained very little presence, if any, elsewhere in the country until the last few months of the conflict.[13]

The RPF rebels started to escalate their military attacks after the genocide began—partially to save Tutsi lives, but primarily to win a military victory by capturing Kigali (Des Forges, 1999). They swept through the country at remarkable speed: while some rebel soldiers stayed back and continued to fight pro-government Hutu forces in government strongholds in northwestern Rwanda, the RPF focused most of its attention on capturing the rest of the country. It first captured the east, south, and then west, where it faced limited resistance from government troops. In these areas, the RPF did not stop to form relationships with civilians, but neither did government forces; these areas therefore experienced little contestation over civilian support. When RPF forces captured the government stronghold in the northwest, it won control of the state through a military victory.

Governance under Rebel Control (Implication 1)

Although the RPF failed to expand its presence and influence throughout the country, it engaged in local governance in its strongholds in northern Rwanda. The group, founded by refugees in Uganda, was loyal to—and learned from—the rebel-turned-incumbent Yoweri Museveni and the National Resistance Movement (NRM) during the Ugandan Civil War. The RPF leadership adopted many of the NRM's wartime governing institutions to successfully govern its own territories in northwestern Rwanda. Civilians displaced into RPF territories were told that "they would be expected to elect their own leaders, to form work committees to build houses and gather food, to settle conflicts peacefully and to 'forget who is Hutu and who is Tutsi'" (Des Forges, 1999). The RPF rebels focused on politicizing civilians to ensure they were "mobilized, resettled, and empowered with political education" (Lyons, 2016, 1033).

The RPF rebels set up local quasi-bureaucratic institutions by cooperating with local leaders who were not explicitly allied with the genocidaires (Des Forges, 1999, 474). The minority (Tutsi) RPF preached unity between the Hutus and Tutsis and rejected the Habyarimana government's ethnic rhetoric

---

[13] The MRND also had little local organizational capacity outside the northwest. Efforts to establish a civilian self-defense militia throughout the country were considered several times but quickly abandoned (Des Forges, 1999); the government's capacity to organize was primarily channeled through the Interahamwe and government institutional structures. There was little civilian-led organizational capacity left on the ground after the MRND and the Interahamwe were driven from the country in 1994.

242 Governing after War

to politicize and mobilize civilian support. This allowed the RPF to recruit moderate Hutus into the rebellion and build organizational capacity on the ground. Hutus living in RPF territories were "heavily pressured" to join the RPF's ranks as soldiers (Des Forges, 1999, 474). Those who refused would instead work in the RPF civilian administration or as RPF political liaisons. In exchange for their cooperation, the RPF offered security in their strongholds. These institutional structures were exceptionally small in scale, given the RPF's territorially limited scope of operations.

Violence during Brief Military Contestation (Implication 2)

Areas outside the rebel and government strongholds—both located in the northernmost part of Rwanda—experienced very little violence until the final days of the civil war when the genocide targeted civilians indiscriminately. Yet the entire country was exposed to violent rhetoric: The MRND had begun preparing to fight the RPF through politicization across the country and creating the *Interahamwe* youth wing, "whose sole purpose was terrorizing the perceived enemies of the Habyarimana regime" (Orth, 2001). These perceived enemies included the RPF as well as moderate Hutu politicians and other opposition parties that "controlled key government posts," while "segments of the military were openly siding with the opposition" (Straus, 2013, 43). The genocide was primarily perpetrated by the *Interahamwe* and Hutu citizens, many of whom were pressured by the ruling party to kill (Straus, 2013).

The RPF perpetrated indiscriminate violence as well. As it advanced throughout the country in 1994, it viewed any uncontrolled territory as favoring its Hutu rivals due to the ongoing genocide, the significant Hutu majority, and the pervasiveness of the *Interahamwe*. Its lack of presence throughout the country meant that it had no information to distinguish between moderate and hardline Hutus, and was unable to identify the perpetrators of the genocide. This uncertainty meant that the RPF "took no care to distinguish militias who were armed and potentially dangerous from civilians" (Des Forges, 1999, 480). In eastern, central, and southern Rwanda, the RPF massacred civilians even after government forces had fled to punish them for potentially having taken part in the genocide.

7.5.3 Post-war Patterns of Development and Violence

The post-war arena was largely unsecured. After its military victory, the RPF had to consolidate power as the minority ethnic group while preventing the ex-FAR from resuming the civil war from its bases in the DRC. Unlike post-war Burundi, which relied on patronage and grassroots coercion using the party's name to sustain control in much of the country, the RPF had no grassroots capacity: it failed to establish any control in the majority of Rwandan territory, and thus "maintained virtually no civilian administrative structures" (Reed, 1996, 498). Yet the ex-FAR also lacked the capacity to organize a new rebellion deep within Rwanda. As the ex-genocidal forces fled to the DRC, their organized supporters escaped with them, including "the bulk of the FAR and Hutu militias, along with hundreds of thousands of Hutu civilians" (Orth, 2001, 234). The ex-FAR's only capacity within Rwanda consisted of family ties in the northwest, along the border with the DRC, where they could count on support for a new rebellion (Orth, 2001, 254).

Exerting Top-Down Control as a Bureaucratic State (Sub-national Hypothesis 2)

Faced with the need to conquer largely unsecured terrain, the new Rwandan government emphasized a strong development policy through good governance and "efficiency in bureaucracy" (Takeuchi, 2019, 125). The government had to build organizational capacity by exerting top-down control as a bureaucratic state, and thus post-war development occurred almost entirely through loyal bureaucrats as a "pragmatic approach" (Reed, 1996, 500). The RPF was able to do this quickly: It may have benefited from knowledge gathered during its exile in Uganda, from the rudimentary rebel governance during the war, and from preexisting state institutions. Bureaucrats who had served under the previous government were quickly replaced with RPF partisans—many of whom were Tutsis—at every level of the state (Reyntjens, 2004, 188–189). Staffing the government with pro-RPF bureaucrats continued even after local governments began democratizing in 2001. Although candidates were not allowed to be officially affiliated with any political party, "the RPF recruited candidates anyway" and "the local authorities appointed by the RPF . . . gave the electors to understand which candidates they were expected to elect" (Reyntjens, 2004, 183).

The RPF's post-war bureaucratic system ensured centralized control over local development and helped the new ruling party gain legitimacy across much of the country. Unlike Burundi, which had already established social control over civilians by the end of the war, the RPF faced the task of establishing such social control after war. Thus, "the necessity to build legitimacy as a condition of collective political and physical survival provides a . . . powerful explanation for the endurance of the RPF's organisational culture" (Chemouni, 2016, 235). The government went to great lengths to ensure civilians recognized its ongoing efforts with local development. After the war, when the international community contributed significant amounts of aid to post-genocide reconstruction, development successes bolstered the RPF's strength and legitimacy in rural areas.

The ruling party cultivated this image of developmental strength by ensuring that international aid was perceived as working in conjunction with the RPF. It engaged heavily in credit-claiming: For example, on leaflets explaining development projects to residents, the government ensured that its logos featured more prominently than those of donors (Chemouni, 2016, 199). Rwanda proceeded with post-war development quite similarly to Zimbabwe in this sense. In 2001, the government created Community Development Committees (CDCs) at the cell, sector, and district levels (Ministry of Local Government, 2001). These committees comprised elected local leaders—almost always RPF partisans—who initiated, coordinated, and managed funding for local development based on community needs. CDCs were tasked with overseeing *all* development projects, including those funded and implemented by international donor agencies (Cheema and Rondinelli, 2007, 89–90).

From the outset, the new rebel government emphasized strong rural development to ensure that rural areas did not lag behind and to expand state social control beyond urban centers (Takeuchi, 2019, 131). Many rural areas had been completely destroyed in the final months of the genocide, and rural economic sectors suffered substantially immediately after the war (Kumar et al., 1996, 25). While the government adopted a *laissez-faire* development policy in urban centers, it was involved in seed and aid distribution, land policies, and gender equality in rural agricultural sectors. The government also created the Community Health Workers program to improve health in rural areas (Chemouni, 2016, 247).

The government sought to eliminate pre-war ethnic quotas for school enrollment, opening up primary and secondary school education for all to maintain post-war peace and stability. The government used the school curriculum to achieve this goal: In the first decade after the conflict, history was banned from Rwandan schools. After it was reintroduced in 2005, history texts emphasized nationalism through a common Rwandan identity and "contrast[ed] the bad governance of the past to 'the RPF [who] wanted to bring national unity to Rwanda and establish real democracy again'" (King, 2013, 133). The government sought to discourage deviations from the "government-approved narrative" and has responded harshly to "divergent versions of history" (King, 2013, 137).

Security Concerns and Government Violence during the Second Civil War (Sub-national Hypothesis 3)

The Rwandan government initially believed it faced significant security concerns throughout most of the country after the civil war. This was largely because Hutus comprised the majority of the population, and because the RPF had no information about most of the country, including which Hutus were moderate or hard liners, and who would support the ex-government. Thus, when the RPF committed violence against Hutu civilians, it was brutal and indiscriminate, particularly in the south and the eastern prefectures (Straus, 2019). Violence in these areas was quickly replaced with development and pro-RPF local leaders when it became clear that civilians had no systematic local ties to the previous government. As the security situation became clearer, the new Rwandan government focused its military efforts in the northwest, Despite stabilization efforts through development and security, Rwanda still returned to civil war—the RPF's consolidation war.

In their bases in eastern DRC, the ex-FAR, along with refugees and the *Interahamwe*, had reorganized themselves as the Armée pour la Libération du Rwanda (ALiR) (Human Rights Watch, 2011, 6). Due to difficult terrain for the DRC forces and a particularly porous border between the DRC and Rwanda, ALiR was able to easily organize among the Hutu population living in eastern DRC and northwestern Rwanda. The insurgency began in 1996 and escalated into a second civil war by 1998. In 2001, ALiR merged with the DRC-based rebel group Forces Démocratiques de Libération du Rwanda, also made up of ex-FAR members. The conflict continued into the late 2000s, but had dropped below war levels in the early 2000s.

During this second civil war, the violence was carried out primarily by small cross-border units that entered the two ex-government strongholds of Gisenyi and Ruhengeri prefectures. These units sought to "conduct acts of banditry to gain resources (money and cattle) to purchase weapons and other military supplies, and to murder and intimidate local Hutus into not supporting the new government" (Orth, 2001, 235). The ALiR had significant organized support in the northwest, where it was able to continue mobilizing citizens against the RPF. Citizens aided ALiR rebels in numerous ways; they "provided food and shelter, served as messengers, and alerted the rebels when the army was near" (Orth, 2001, 240).

The RPF eliminated the security threat using violence in two ways. First, in large parts of the country that had low organizational capacity—where neither the RPF nor the ex-government had exercised substantial control over the civilian population during the civil war—the RPF began to build a local security force that would help extend state control over rural Rwanda on top of the developmental measures it was implementing. This entailed incorporating local Hutu and Tutsi civilians into Local Defense Forces, which were created in 1997 as an auxiliary police force "to address chronic shortages in policing" (Jones and Murray, 2018, 18).

Second, and more significantly, the RPF won its consolidation war by using considerable military force against civilians who supported rival forces. According to my theory, new rebel governments must prevent rebellions that might emerge in rival strongholds from spreading into unsecured terrain, as was the case in Rwanda: "Not only did the government have to reestablish control of the situation in the northwest, but it had to prevent the insurgents from expanding their operations east, to prevent the insurgency from growing and gaining increased support amongst Hutu" (Orth, 2001, 239). The RPF engaged in multiple cross-border incursions into the DRC, a preventative measure that violated international norms against inter-state invasions. Frustrated with the DRC's refusal to expel the ALiR, the Rwandan army entered the DRC to attack ALiR recruitment grounds from 1996 onward (International Crisis Group, 2000, 12), and in 2001 launched a "massive search- and-destroy operation in eastern Congo with the intention of 'cleaning up the Kivus'"(Human Rights Watch, 2011, 7). Within Rwanda, the RPF conducted "heavy-handed counter insurgency operations" against the ALiR (Orth, 2001, 236). The RPF assessed that it could not win over civilians in northwestern rival strongholds or in the DRC refugee camps who were being recruited into the ALiR insurgency. The RPF instead sought to contain the conflict and prevent the ALiR from expanding the rebellion and venturing farther into the country to reach Kigali. Its strategy was therefore to sever the ALiR's ties with citizens both within Rwanda and those living in the DRC who could pose significant problems if the ALiR insurgency spread to other parts of Rwanda.

7.5.4 Summary

The Rwandan Civil War and post-war politics under the RPF government illustrate how a government with little wartime social control—and thus limited post-war local administrative capacity—relies on top-down development and violence against civilians to assert control and sustain power. During the civil war, the RPF exerted social control in only a very small portion of northern Rwanda. It was not until 1994 that it swept across the country to win the war militarily. Similarly, the previous Hutu government under Habyarimana had maintained very few ties with civilians across the state during the civil war, instead relying on the *Interahamwe* militias who eventually fled with the ex-government forces after the RPF captured Kigali. The ex-government's main ties with civilians were primarily limited to one corner of northwest Rwanda along the DRC border, which had long enjoyed patrimonial and family ties at the local government level.

In short, the RPF inherited a state that was largely unsecured. Projecting state strength and bureaucratic capacity before the onset of a consolidation war was therefore crucial to the regime's stability. It thus developed quite differently from post-war Burundi.[14] Unlike the CNDD-FDD in Burundi, the RPF could not rely on local supporters such as schoolteachers, administrators, and youth supporters to galvanize community-led development and provide information. To combat this disadvantage, the RPF deployed bureaucrats and emphasized the importance of rural development in agriculture, health, and education to penetrate rural populations and project state power. Yet much like the CNDD-FDD, the RPF faced a growing insurgency in the DRC that found support in a small area within Rwanda. The RPF combated this problem by engaging in violence against civilians, both within Rwanda and during cross-border invasions into eastern DRC. The RPF's dual strategy of development and violence was ultimately successful: It defended itself against the ALiR forces, won its consolidation war, and has sustained tight control over Rwanda since the ALiR conflict ended in the 2000s.

7.6 Conclusion

In this chapter, I have examined the external validity of my argument across four cases in sub-Saharan Africa: The MPLA in Angola, the FN in Côte d'Ivoire, the CNDD-FDD in Burundi, and the RPF in Rwanda. Taken together, the four case studies explore the role of social control independently of other factors such as state weakness, ethnicity, natural resources, or ideological stance. I have shown that wartime ties help enhance post-war state control by decreasing the cost of governance and providing information to the state about local loyalties. By leveraging the support of their wartime administrations for sub-national control in their strongholds, rebel regimes can better target resource allocation toward development or violence where

---

[14] As Chemouni (2016, 3) explains, while both Rwanda and Burundi had fairly strong state institutions, "informal norms and organisational behaviour promoted by ruling political parties undermined developmental efforts in Burundi while supporting them in Rwanda."

they need to win support and eliminate rivals, respectively. This allows rebel regimes to successfully consolidate control.

Although these cases provide evidence to support the book's theory, they also highlight the importance of additional variables to consider, including the role of rival ties and the rebel government's ability to learn on the job after the end of the war. While wartime rebel–civilian ties help alleviate post-war resource concerns, an invaluable step toward exerting control, they do not wholly determine the post-war trajectory. In the final chapter of this book, I explore the implications of my theory and the unanswered questions that future research should investigate. I conclude by discussing the policy takeaways.

PART IV
IMPLICATIONS

8
Implications and Future Research

8.1 A Summary of the Argument

This book has examined how wartime ties with civilians affect rebel victors' post-war governing strategies. Rebel-civilian ties not only affect where the victor is eventually best able to control, but also where they may seek to shore up capacity and where they most fear the threat of subsequent insurrection. These considerations come to influence how the victor allocates resources to development versus violence for co-optation and coercion, respectively, to consolidate its power.

More broadly, my overall argument examines how civil war, rebel victory, post-war politics, and potential unrest form part of a longer state-building process. This extended view of conflict is distinct from dyadic or multi-dyadic models of civil war because it emphasizes how multiple violent actors, including victors and their rivals, continuously contest for political control of the state during both wartime and peacetime. The cases presented in this book have demonstrated that the struggle for power continues in the post-war period because rivals remain a threat to the new rebel government. Rivals capable of organizing violence or politicizing civilians threaten state stability because they could quickly reignite the civil war. Thus post-war peace is uneasy: Simmering discontent can erupt into full-blown conflict, forcing the new rebel government to fight one or more consolidation wars. If the rebel government can eliminate its rivals as a violent threat during these consolidation conflicts, it will have won the struggle for power; if it is overthrown, its rivals will restart the process of consolidating power from the beginning.

A rebel victor's wartime relationships with civilians partly determine whether it will need to fight one or more consolidation wars. A new rebel government is best able to consolidate control after a civil war if it established strong wartime relationships with civilians in an organized fashion. The likelihood of *peacefully* consolidating control increases with the breadth of the rebel group's relationships with local supporters—individuals who may have preexisting local legitimacy (such as traditional or religious leaders), or

Governing after War: Rebel Victories and Post-war Statebuilding. Shelley X. Liu, Oxford University Press.
© Oxford University Press 2024. DOI: 10.1093/oso/9780197696705.003.0008

252 Governing after War

who established legitimacy during the war due to their strong associations with a powerful rebel group (such as youth militias or village committees).

Although these rebel–civilian ties take on different forms in different contexts, rebels should generally prefer to establish ties for a variety of reasons related to politicization, organization, and efficient war-making. Within the set of cases examined in this book, ideological (Angola, Zimbabwe), ethnic (Angola, Burundi, Côte d'Ivoire, Rwanda, Liberia), and extractive (Angola, Liberia) rebellions all sought to establish links with civilians where possible. In all six cases, rebels established governing institutions that resembled quasi-bureaucracies by organizing and collaborating with local civilians. These governing institutions helped rebels levy informal taxes by collecting goods and food, and provided local security against rival violence. This pattern is consistent with the book's argument that rebel–civilian ties help rebel groups exert social control over civilian life during the war and consolidate post-war power at the *sub-national* level.

When rebels win a war, their ties with civilians remain active, and wartime collaborators become an important tool in the victor's arsenal for consolidating power at the *national* level. As the new rebel government seeks to govern the state, it attempts to consolidate power through internal conquest. Put simply, the victor should allocate resources to both violence and development to expand its footprint and capacity to control the state. Where the victor has wartime ties (i.e., in wartime strongholds), it can rely on them as an extension of itself, thereby exerting control at low cost. This frees up resources to devote to the rest of the state for co-optation and coercion. To expand its influence, the victor should attempt to extend the reach of its sub-national wartime institutions throughout the country by deploying loyal partisans to oversee the bureaucracy and exert state control from the top down. This strategy is possible in unsecured terrain, where the government can leverage development funding to co-opt civilians. In rival strongholds, however, where rivals sustain their own ties to civilians, the rebel government must resort to repression and violence to suppress the highly politicized and politically organized rival supporters.

I demonstrated support for this argument through in-depth examinations of two disparate cases, Zimbabwe and Liberia. In the former, the victorious rebel group, the Zimbabwe African National Union (ZANU), established strong and deeply embedded ties across the eastern half of rural Zimbabwe during the civil war. Thus even before it had formally come to power, ZANU already exerted social control over civilian life in these areas. Through its ties with local leaders, youth supporters, and other partisans, the new rebel government sustained support on the ground with relatively little effort and was able to set up the state in the image of its wartime institutions. Within a few years, it had spread these institutions throughout the rest of the country, leveraging centralized development funding to co-opt political support. Yet alongside this state-building, it deployed massive and indiscriminate violence in regions that resisted the imposition of its institutions and bureaucrats. The rebel government consolidated power within seven years and thoroughly eliminated its rivals as a viable political opposition by absorbing them into the ruling party and establishing a one-party state.

Liberia followed a very different path. Charles Taylor and the National Patriotic Front of Liberia (NPFL) formed ties with civilians to establish order and exert control over the group's strongholds early in the war. These initial attempts at sub-national state-building highlight how such strategies are desirable to non-ideological and extractive rebellions. However, subsequent military losses to various factions left the rebel group with few of its original institutions and derailed its organizational capacity to exert control. Instead of sustaining its longer-term relationships, the uncertain nature of this ongoing contestation forced armed groups and civilians to focus on self-preservation through temporary and transactional interactions. The loss of the NPFL's wartime organizational apparatus stymied Taylor's post-war consolidation of power. Although he sought to co-opt and coerce across the state, his efforts to do so were insufficient to win enough support or establish enough control; thus, his government was unable to manage the looming consolidation war. When faced with the prospect of all-out conflict recurrence, the rebel government diverted increasing amounts of money from development to security. Undecided civilians chose to join the counter-rebellion; eventually, even the NPFL strongholds succumbed to the second civil war. Taylor was forced out of power six years after the first civil war.

To increase the study's external validity, I examined four other conflicts—in Angola, Côte d'Ivoire, Burundi, and Rwanda. The first two featured similar ideologies and rebel beginnings as Zimbabwe and Liberia, respectively. However, differences in wartime rebel–civilian relations and the degree of social control that rebels were able to exert over the civilian population led to divergent pathways. Côte d'Ivoire's rebel victory has led to relative stability and the elimination of the ex-government as a viable rival to the newly victorious government. On the other hand, Angola's rebel victory gave way to almost three decades of consolidation wars as the government continuously failed to establish dominant control. My second set of cases, Burundi and Rwanda, are neighboring states that faced the same ethnic divides and fought civil wars during the same time period. I compared them to each other and argued that the existence of wartime rebel–civilian ties played a significant role in their post-war politics. While the victorious rebel group in Burundi laid significant groundwork during the war and thus employed its wartime structures afterwards to maintain dominance, the new Rwandan government relied primarily on shrewd post-war development and violence to prevent rivals from gaining military ground during subsequent civil wars.

My argument highlights how wartime sub-national state-building bolsters post-war efforts to consolidate power throughout the state. This link between wartime rebel–civilian ties and post-war governing strategies provides one explanation of why, overall, rebel victories may be more successful at eliminating multiple sovereignties than other forms of conflict termination (Mason et al., 2011). It also reveals insights into why some rebel governments are able to consolidate power after war while others are not.

This book contributes to scholarship on rebel governance, state-building, and political development. Prior research on rebel governance and civilian victimization provides rich insights into how rebels behave during war and the logic underpinning various patterns of cooperation and control (Kalyvas, 2006; Mampilly, 2011; Arjona, 2016; Stewart, 2018). These studies have taken important steps toward explaining the efficiency and reputational gains associated with wartime governance. This book's contribution is therefore to extend this explanation into the post-war period by linking rebels' wartime interactions with civilians to post-war governing decisions and outcomes. It adds to a growing body of work that examines how the microdynamics of war and variations in armed group behavior can lead to a variety of different political outcomes (Daly, 2016; Huang, 2016; Martin, 2020; Thaler, 2018; Daly, 2022; Liu, 2023).

The book also advances the African politics literature. On a continent where a quarter of the current ruling parties were once victorious rebel groups, the book's theory offers an explanation of these countries' post-war trajectories and explores the roots of the ruling parties' successful consolidation of power. While previous research on revolutionary regimes and rebel victors has examined their successes at the party or national level (Clarke, 2022; Levitsky and Way, 2022; Meng and Paine, 2022), this book adds rival capabilities as an additional dimension and explores how rebel victors govern at the sub-national level to consolidate power. The argument therefore expands existing theories of distributive politics (Kramon and Posner, 2013; Koter, 2013; Gottlieb and Larreguy, 2020; Bowles, Larreguy, and Liu, 2020) by adding conflict as an important nuance for understanding not just how political cleavages are developed and reinforced at the local level, but also how heightened insecurity—for example in the initial years after the end of a civil war—may change the ruling party's calculus in ways that encourage development outside ruling party strongholds.

8.2 Implications for Future Research

Although I have made the case in this book that rebel–civilian ties help explain post-war divergences in development, violence, and the consolidation of power, my argument highlights at least two additional avenues of fruitful research. The first is the ·rebel victor's ability to learn and adapt as the new government. The second is how *the way the conflict ends* affects the new government's post-war governing strategies. These variables, which may interact with my proposed mechanism, promise rich insights into how war affects post-war governance, state-building, and state stability. I discuss each in turn.

8.2.1 Ability to Learn and Adapt

Wartime rebel–civilian ties cannot explain the trajectory of post-war state-building on their own. My argument assumes that the eventual victor's ability to learn and adapt to changes in conflict and politics is endogenous to conflict incidence (i.e. whether war emerged in the first place), how the war was fought, and which group eventually won. On average, rebel groups that win may be better at learning than those that lose because victory requires successfully fomenting, fighting, and then winning a war (Toft, 2010). Still, my investigation of six rebellions reveals clear variations in the victors' ability to exert control and implement policies that could conceivably win over unsecured terrain. In Rwanda, for example, the victor's post-war successes can be at least partially attributed to appropriate decisions made within an acceptable time frame. These good choices originated from at least three factors that influenced the country's post-war outcomes: The leader's foresight, his prior experience in the Uganda Bush War where institution-building was strong, and Rwanda's pre-war institutional strength.

The evidence of variation in rebel groups' ability to learn and adapt gathered from the six cases covered in the book already warrants greater theory building. For example, we need theory to investigate how the victor's post-war learning is affected by fast-evolving post-war security threats (Angola, Liberia), prior knowledge through political activities (Zimbabwe, Angola, Rwanda), and wartime governing activities (Zimbabwe, Burundi, Côte d'Ivoire). While my theory implicitly relies heavily on the final category, the other factors are also important and should be explored in future research.

256 Governing after War

Two variables affect rebel groups' capacity to learn: (1) the *speed of innovation* and (2) the *time available to innovate*. Rwanda's experience may indicate that the rebel victor's ability to adapt may interact with the (non)-existence of wartime rebel–civilian ties in a variety of ways. In cases such as Rwanda, where rivals are relatively weak and pre-war institutions are strong enough to build upon, the ability to learn on the job can be particularly useful. Indeed, rebel groups' ability to learn from their mistakes may help to explain the variation in the length and severity of the rebel government's subsequent consolidation wars. Following this logic, the wartime spread of rebel–civilian ties helps increase the speed of innovation by providing a blueprint for exerting control, but such ties also help overcome time constraints and reduce the need to learn quickly. For example, although the victor in Zimbabwe successfully extended its control by establishing bureaucratic development committees, it took four years after the end of the civil war to fully conceive and implement them across the state. Until then, the rebel government engaged in both violence and development but took a decentralized approach with a variety of wartime supporters and partisans to test what worked in different areas. The rebel victor in Angola did not have this luxury of time because the rivals' ties to civilians were so strong. The more quickly rivals mobilize, the less time there is to learn, which puts pressure on the actor to make fewer mistakes (with fewer resources).

8.2.2 How Conflict Termination Type Affects Post-war Governing Strategies

This book has investigated transitions from war to peace after a *rebel victory*. Thus its argument does not directly apply to conflicts that end with a government victory or negotiated settlement. In this section I discuss the different considerations that must be taken into account when thinking about post-war governance under these other conflict termination types.

Government Victory

More research is needed to determine whether the argument applies to *government* (rather than rebel) victories after civil war. There are reasons to believe it may, since the post-war landscape in this scenario would also feature heightened insecurity, which should force incumbents to reassess their resource allocation strategy to increase state control. Evidence from interstate war in Schenoni (2021) suggests that victorious incumbents do rebuild institutions post-war, meaning that "victory made the state."[1] However, the argument's logic may be unique to rebel victories *because* of rebels' unrivaled ability to establish ties with civilians from the ground up.

This is the key theoretical difference between rebels and governments: Rebels can more easily form ties with civilians from the bottom up during war, whereas governments generally do not do so during counterinsurgency campaigns. Government troops instead go where the violence occurs and use force to sever ties between rebels and civilians.[2] Within the bounds of my theory, the government's post-war resource allocation strategy would instead rely on its pre-war ties, such as patronage or clientelistic networks with local leaders on the ground. The government victor's success in consolidating power after the war—i.e., eliminating the rebels altogether—would then rely on the depth and breadth of these pre-war ties with local civilians.

Even if government forces do not have to rely on civilians to provide materials, they may need them for intelligence-gathering purposes. Do governments have the opportunity to build grassroots supporting structures during war? They may: Several conflicts feature local civilian militias and counterinsurgency campaigns involving clandestine intelligence. However, governments may not take advantage of such opportunities; they may treat civil war as a battle over *territory* rather than over broad *social control*. This would mean that they eschew building local organizational capacity for control in favor of simply focusing on eliminating conflict while refusing to reconsider pre-war distributions of power and support. This latter complication points to heterogeneous expectations for government victory, which vary along multiple dimensions. Conflict intensity is an important dimension because there is no need to reorganize the state if a civil war is small and contained; the state's prior reliance on neo-patrimonial ties with its strongholds is similarly important.

This theoretical difference between rebel and government victory—that the former will form rebel–civilian ties during war while the latter is unlikely to do so—highlights the importance of accounting for *how government forces came to power in the first place*. Governments that took control through a coup, for example, are far less likely to have pre-existing civilian ties than those that won elections through grassroots party-building or experienced

---

[1] Schenoni's (2021) argument, however, follows a very different trajectory that involves bringing radical elites into the ruling coalition to engage in broader state-building. Expanding the ruling coalition would increase the size of the base, but might not change the state's strategy with regard to allocating resources disproportionately to its base.

[2] However, as I have shown in the Burundian Civil War, governments may form local militias to increase security-side control during a war, which constitutes one form of "rebel"–civilian ties.

protracted warfare as rebels themselves. Mozambique is a useful example of this distinction: After gaining independence and winning the war, the victors became the ruling party. This rebel government fought (and won) its consolidation war against its rival, the Resistência Nacional Moçambicana. The current Mozambiçan government faces an insurgency in Cabo Delgado province, a conflict that is distinct from the rivalries that emerged out of the fight for independence. If government forces win in Cabo Delgado, it would be a government victory—but one predicated on bottom-up party- and state-building that emerged from rebel–civilian ties established decades ago.

Negotiated Settlements

Cases of negotiated settlement and power sharing after war ought to present an entirely different governing logic. Unlike victories, shared power may require political strategies that strengthen support from each group's respective bases rather than winning or coercing support from the rest of the state. This is likely to be particularly applicable to consociational governments such as post-war Bosnia, where the goal of all sides is *not* to consolidate power and sustain state stability, but to remain in power by relying on their own constituencies.

Particularly with respect to shared governments emerging from competitive multiparty elections, prior research highlights the role of competitive elections in hardening wartime cleavages or reigniting violence when one side expects to win little political power (Brancati and Snyder, 2013; Flores and Nooruddin, 2012; Matanock and Staniland, 2018; Daly, 2014). In such a post-war setting, how do rivals-turned-governing partners interact with each other? Does each group's goal differ, or do they all seek to prevent conflict? And if competing and complementary incentives collide, how do they decide to allocate resources? The answers to these questions will build on, and contribute to, ongoing research that examines rebel-to-party transitions, ex-rebel politicians' incentives, and the potential development outcomes of such scenarios (Manning, 2004; Daly, 2021a,b).

8.3 Implications for Long-Term Development

While the evidence presented in this book primarily applies to the immediate post-war period when challengers pose a violent threat, the logic may also provide insights into how conflict and rebel victories can affect long-term economic and political outcomes. I propose reasonable extensions to the book's argument here, but note that this question of long-run development warrants further research.

8.3.1 Economic Development

My argument predicts that greater development gains will be made in unsecured terrain with lower organizational capacity because rebel victors must build capacity in these areas to consolidate power. But what happens after power has been consolidated? The rebel government's incentives and calculations will shift after it has eliminated potential violent challengers to its rule in opposition-supporting terrain. Will unsecured terrain continue to experience greater development in the long run, as models of swing voters in electoral and redistributive politics predict (Lindbeck and Weibull, 1987)? Should we expect the government to continue prioritizing these regions in the long run, when there is no longer a threat of violent opposition?

On the one hand, there may be path dependence in development *even if* the rebel government no longer seeks to sustain its co-optation efforts in unsecured terrain. Gains made during the consolidation period engender greater growth, which ought to increase long-term development. This logic makes sense if the government does not reallocate resources elsewhere—i.e., if the victor equalizes development spending across the state.

On the other hand, we may expect increases in development to wane because rebel governments could indeed have incentives to allocate resources differently after they consolidate power. After security threats have been eliminated, the government cares primarily about winning elections—which can be achieved by relying on its stronghold ties as long as it is able to sustain these relationships. The government therefore benefits a great deal from sustaining its ties with civilians and rewarding those who continue to galvanize support—whether it is genuine or coerced. Keeping these partisans in formalized bureaucratic positions becomes the lowest-cost way to encourage election day turnout and ensure electoral support in the long run. The ruling party will rely on loyal local leaders to help implement electoral strategies that allow it to remain in power. If this is the case, we may expect rebel governments to pursue clientelistic resource allocation strategies to stay in power. Rebel–civilian ties in strongholds become patron–broker relationships; the government must allocate the bulk of its resources to pay off these supporters as a form of vote buying or turnout buying, as occurs in Zimbabwe today.

260 Governing after War

Regardless of whether development spending remains targeted at unsecured terrain or is funneled toward clientelism in the long run, it is clear that rival terrain will lose out on development for two reasons: (1) it suffers from path dependence—it would have been set back by the violent coercion during the consolidation period—and (2) it is unlikely to ever support the government in elections, and is thus unlikely to be rewarded for doing so. Rival strongholds would not only reject the victor's imposition of control during the consolidation period; their attitudes are likely to be hardened by the subsequent state-sponsored violence. Since these areas are not politically useful to the ruling party, we should expect to see the lowest levels of long-term development in rival terrain, barring major realignments in political cleavages.

8.3.2 Political Development

In theory, rebel governance ought to increase citizens' political consciousness, since the framing techniques and rhetoric used to win over civilians during a civil war increase wartime civilian politicization at the local level. My theory thus maintains that new rebel governments partially rely on politicization and locally led social control within their strongholds to delegate bottom-up governance. Yet how do increases in citizens' political consciousness as a result of war contribute to, or hinder, political development during the consolidation period and after the threat of violence has subsided? Put differently, would the average voter in post-conflict societies be more politicized, more interested in political affairs, more likely to have learned how to participate politically during the war, and overall more willing to engage with the state to demand stronger governance? This logic underpins Huang's (2016) work on rebel governance and post-war democratization.

Because coercion and state control underlie these rebel–civilian ties, my argument suggests that civilian politicization and heightened political participation end when the rebel government has successfully consolidated power. For instance, rebel–civilian ties facilitated participatory politics in post-war Zimbabwe (Chapter 4), but were quickly exploited to suppress any form of dissent in strongholds after the war. When the victor has consolidated power, the suppression of dissent is more likely than participatory politics.

Although successful post-war state-building and power consolidation may help prevent civil war recurrence and increase civilian participation in the short run, I show in other work (Liu, 2023) that strong wartime control—which increases the likelihood of post-war stability—also increases the likelihood of political control and decreases meaningful political participation in the long run. This is because politicization-induced political participation and grassroots civilian interest in politics, which the ruling party promotes as a rebel group during the war, are discouraged once the state no longer stands to benefit from it. While political participation is the bedrock of democracy, a new rebel government will encourage it *only* if it must rely on participation to sustain local volunteerism and political support during the tense period of post-war peace. After it has consolidated power, the rebel government no longer needs to encourage participation, and may even have an incentive to stifle civil society and mute dissenting voices—particularly when appealing new opposition parties emerge. If so, the local organizational structures that were set up during the war, which have fostered the ruling party's local embeddedness during and after the conflict, can easily be repurposed to engage in coercive control when democratic participation is no longer in the ruling party's interest.

Establishing coercive political control in the long run is an intuitive extension of the book's argument, the crux of which is that rebel–civilian ties that emerge out of war may invite civilian participation, but were nonetheless established under the shadow of coercion. Thus, even though we may observe significant cooperation between rebels and civilians during war, many civilians still prefer to forego association with any of the armed groups. Because of civilian reluctance more broadly, cooperation is induced through local partisans with whom rebels have forged a relationship—meaning that supporters and rebels' power and legitimacy become increasingly intertwined. Rebels relied on their relationships with loyal local supporters to increase their own legitimacy early in the war; yet as the rebel group's power within a locality grew, so too did the power of their supporters (Balcells, 2017). Where rebel–civilian ties were strong at the end of the war, rebel group supporters would draw a significant portion of their own power and legitimacy from their association with the state. The new rebel government sometimes codified this informal power—for example by encouraging young people to join its youth militias and installing other supporters in local bureaucratic positions—which gave these civilians strong incentives to continue acting as local representatives of the new government to sustain these positions.

If this logic is correct, rebel victories that feature strong ties with civilians have positive implications for *state stability* but not for *political development*. This is because democracy is unlikely to thrive in states governed by rebels in the long term, since they seek to discourage free participation in favor of pro-government activity. Despite increased political participation due to politicization in the short run after war (Huang, 2016), long-run political

Governing after War

control increases the likelihood of competitive authoritarianism after a brief period of democracy (Lyons, 2016). Through their embeddedness in local communities and access to information, individuals with whom the state has cultivated a symbiotic relationship can continue to exert control over (and demand support from) their communities. They are therefore the key individuals who help cement the ruling party's dominance when the government needs support during election time. This dominance will likely be facilitated by coercive electoral politics—which combines voter intimidation and vote buying—in lieu of widespread development initiatives as the ruling party becomes more confident of state stability.

In Chapter 1, I presented empirical evidence of shifts toward authoritarian politics in rebel victories across sub-Saharan Africa. Of the rebel regimes that had not been violently overthrown by the opposition, all but the Democratic Republic of the Congo feature dominant parties in which the victorious rebel group has ruled since winning the war. Only two—Namibia and South Africa, where the ruling parties enjoy overwhelming support without the need for outright repressive tactics—are considered democracies according to major indices such as Freedom House, Polity, and the Economist Intelligence Unit Democracy Index; others are classed as competitive authoritarian or autocratic regimes. Although the international community initially viewed some of these rebel governments favorably (for example, Eritrea, Uganda, Zimbabwe, and Rwanda), the ex-rebels in each case have resorted to coercion when faced with electoral challengers.

8.4 Policy Considerations

While peace is of paramount concern in the immediate post-war period, the likelihood of democratic backsliding presents a new dilemma. Rebel victories with deep grassroots penetration, which decreases the likelihood of conflict recurrence in the short run but may result in authoritarian and coercive strategies to consolidate power, raise questions for the international community. Can stability be maintained without establishing complete ruling party dominance? And does consolidating power mean a breakdown in democracy as the ruling party becomes stronger while the political opposition weakens or fractionalizes? If wartime social control through rebel–civilian ties simultaneously increases state stability *and* the likelihood of long-term democratic erosion, the international community must work to ensure that the grassroots collective action developed during wartime governance continues to allow democratic participation without empowering authoritarian elites. The international community must contend with the trade-off between security and democracy. The book's findings highlight trade-offs within potential policies.

Past peace-building initiatives led by the US and other major powers have involved armed interventions in conflict zones or other forms of direct interference in political processes. However, previous studies highlight how such overt interventions may not always be helpful—and can in fact further destabilize the delicate peace (Howe, 1997; Mendelson, 2005). Direct military interference, particularly operations that support one party to the conflict, may threaten the peace because it alters the conflict dynamics on the ground and potentially leads to unforeseen consequences (Hultman, 2010; Wood, Kathman, and Gent, 2012). Introducing a new military actor increases concerns about territorial and social control, which in turn exacerbates military contestation and increases civilian victimization. Indeed, the first Economic Community of West African States Monitoring Group intervention in Liberia, as described in Chapter 5, arguably worsened the civil war from 1992 onward.

However, purely political attempts to foster peace at the elite level are not necessarily effective either. After the successful termination of civil war, the international community and domestic actors hasten to make democratic arrangements such as power-sharing agreements and post-war elections. The benefits of power-sharing are mixed, however (Hartzell and Hoddie, 2003; Le Van, 2011; Roeder and Rothchild, 2005; Walter, 2002), because elites have incentives to hold out in the peace process or to resume fighting for a bigger share of the pie, and early periods of mass-based democratization are unstable (Dahl, 1973; Mansfield and Snyder, 2007). Mediation tactics (Beardsley, 2013) designed to resolve conflicts between opposing violent groups have not been more successful at ending conflict in the long run because they are unable to resolve issues on the ground, and thus do not disincentivize civilians from supporting rivals who seek to return to war. The book's findings suggest that these results are unsurprising because the networks that rebels create involve civilians rather than elites: Just because rebel leaders acquiesce to the peace process does not mean that lower-level commanders will agree to surrender. Rivals who wish to continue challenging the rebel victor will be able to draw on their own relationships with civilians to resume the conflict— even—without their leader's blessing.

One solution to the problem of strong top-down control from an illiberal rebel regime may be to implement local community programs to build a strong civil society. However, it is not enough to simply prescribe international engagement in local communities. An important aspect of my argument is that attention must be paid to *where* these efforts are targeted, depending on the policy's goals. I demonstrate in this book that the international community must contend with the double-edged sword of grassroots citizen political action. Ultimately, if politicized citizen grievances risk fanning the flames of renewed conflict after war has officially ended, then post-war efforts should focus on ensuring peaceful political participation from a vibrant civil society rather than violent participation from a resentful one. Thus international post-war reconstruction efforts should include civil society development to promote democracy and peace.

Combining insights from the literature with the book's findings, my argument implies different possibilities for different policy goals. For example, if the international community strives to quickly increase political participation, building civil society in areas with low capacity—chiefly, partisan and contested areas—soon after a war may be the easiest way to sustain calls for democracy, resist co-optation, and begin civil society building without greater fears of destabilization. Yet if the goal is to prevent state consolidation of social control over local politics, it may be best to target civil society work in strongholds from the very beginning. Finally, if the international community seeks to offer an alternative channel of political participation for rival-supporting areas to help prevent a return to violence, more energy ought to be concentrated on peaceful participation there as an alternative to supporting rival rebels.

However, such political participation involves an inherent trade-off between stability and how various armed groups (victors and their rivals) are likely to respond. Especially when examining rebel victories and their post-war contexts, I have argued that rebel governance has different effects under different armed actors: Rival strongholds are more likely to participate violently, while the victor's strongholds are more likely to participate in support of the new government. Indeed, my theory suggests that citizens in the victor's wartime strongholds are likely to be governed and controlled by those who have ties to the ruling party; thus only pro-government actions would be tolerated. On the other hand, those living in rival strongholds have similar ties to rival armed groups that seek to destabilize the state and renew conflict; anti-state violence would thus be encouraged in the event of a counter-rebellion. Overall, both the rebel government's and their rivals' strongholds have already been co-opted during a highly polarized political period, meaning that any civil society organization that developed in these areas would likely be headed by those who are already local leaders. We may therefore expect neither type of territory to permit peaceful democratic dissent to thrive even with civil society's intervention.

Post-war reconstruction policy also heavily emphasizes aid and development for rebuilding. The rise of a seemingly programmatic victor may garner optimism as the international community looks to the new government to usher in democracy and development. However, the findings presented in this book caution against expecting post-war politics to be a blank slate and for the victor to engage in technocratic development. The potential for post-conflict reconstruction loosens the donor purse strings considerably (Galtung and Tisné, 2009), but it is important to ask not only *what* the aid will pay for, but also *where* it will be targeted. Given that post-war rebel governments tend to use both development and violence to win supporters and conquer their rivals after a civil war, the international community should understand the political landscape and the considerations underlying every government decision made in the post-conflict state. Even if the new government demonstrated a wartime capacity for development and goods provision (Burundi, Côte d'Ivoire, and Eritrea, for example) or an intent to develop these capacities after the war (such as Angola, Mozambique, Uganda, and Zimbabwe), the strategic logic of consolidating power in the face of internal security threats suggests that such programmatic efforts will be unevenly distributed across the state.

If the international community seeks to equalize development, it should then pay close attention to rival-supporting regions without discouraging development efforts elsewhere. This strategy may help counteract government targeting while also dissuading the resumption of violence. As the cases examined in this book have demonstrated, development lags primarily in rival-supporting areas for a good reason: Not only is the new rebel government least likely to win support there—ensuring low returns to such resource allocation—citizens living in rival-supporting areas are more likely to maintain strong ties to rival forces, leading them to reject government-led development even when it is offered (see, for example, rival supporters in Zimbabwe). By implementing strategies that seek to equalize development, the international community may indeed raise the costs of war for civilians and decrease the likelihood that rivals will recruit them to participate in violence again. However, such strategies should take into account the fact that the rebel government's method of disproportionately targeting aid to contested areas may indeed help keep the peace (and perhaps should not be broadly discouraged), and that rivals may threaten to spoil the peace by attacking aid projects.

Ultimately, the book's logic offers insights into how the international community can identify post-war rebel government incentives and constraints, and understand the potential decisions such governments may make as they face impending threats from rivals. By working to change the political incentives for elites and citizens—or at least mediate their effects—the international community may enhance post-war state stability.

Security Challenges after War

Table A1 Rebel victories and post-war security challenges

Country (party)	First year in power	Years until rival challenge	Years until intra-party coup	Post-war insecurity summary
Consolidated power				
Guinea Bissau (PAIGC)	1974	24	6	Wartime rivals eliminated during war; coup replaced president in 1980 but party remained in power.
Angola (MPLA)	1975	0	2	Wartime rivals UNITA and FNLA resume civil war immediately upon independence in 1975; coup attempt in 1977.
Mozambique (FRELIMO)	1975	1	16	Ex-colonial militias form RENAMO rebellion in 1976, conflict reaches civil war levels in 1977.
Zimbabwe (ZANU-PF)	1980	2	19	Ex-ZAPU combatants ("dissidence") challenge in 1982.
Uganda (NRA)	1986	0	-	Northerners (including ex-government troops) wage war under UPDA, LRA, HSM from 1986.
Chad (MPS)	1990	1	1	Southerners (including ex-government forces) wage war under MDD and CSNPD from 1991; coup attemp that same year.
Namibia (SWAPO)	1990	-	-	Wartime rivals eliminated during war; no meaningful post-war challengers.
Ethiopia (EPRDF)	1992	1	18	OLF resumed civil war in 1992.
Eritrea (EPLF/PFDJ)	1993	-	-	Although EIJM continues operations, significantly weakened prior to independence; post-war insecurity primarily from Eritrea-Ethiopia border war.
Rwanda (RPA)	1994	2	-	Ex-government forces wage war under ALiR in 1996.
South Africa (ANC)	1994	-	-	Violent contestation with IFP subsides after end of Apartheid; no meaningful post-war challengers.

(*continued*)

Table A1 Continued

Country (party)	First year in power	Years until rival challenge	Years until intra-party coup	Post-war insecurity summary
DR Congo (AFDL/PPRD)	1997	1	9	AFDL-led regional alliance splits when war ends; rebels resume war under RCD and MLC from 1998.
Congo-Brazzaville (CLP)	1997	1	-	War resumes against ex-government forces (Ninjas and Cocoyes) from 1998.
Burundi (CNDD-FDD)	2005	0	10	Palipehutu-FNL continues rebellion, lays down arms in 2009.
Côte d'Ivoire (RDR)	2010	0	-	Ex-government forces violence along Liberian and Ghanaian border in 2011. Mutiny in 2017, did not develop into a coup attempt.
Overthrown or ongoing				
CAR (Bozizé)	2003	-	-	Central African Republic Bush War takes place from 2004–2007 but no affiliation to previous wartime rivals.
Chad (GUNT)	1979	0	-	Wartime rival FAN retreats to the north. Resumes war within months and overthrows government in 1982.
Chad (FAN)	1982	0	7	Ex-government forces retreat and resume war from 1982–1987; failed coup attempt in 1989 evolved into successful rebellion under MPS in 1990.
Liberia (NPFL)	1997	1	-	Wartime rivals resume war under LURD, MODEL from 1998, overthrows government in 2003.
South Sudan (SPLA)	2011	0	2	Initial security threat from SSDM/A and SSLM/A; wartime rival Riek Machar accused of coup and rebels under SPLM-IO from 2013.

APPENDIX B

Zimbabwe Liberation War

B1 Fieldwork

Due to the heightened political tensions in Zimbabwe, it was not possible to conduct extensive interviews with civilians or rank-and-file combatants. Even though the Liberation War itself is not a contentious subject in the country—in fact, the government actively works to keep discourse on the war alive for political purposes—politics itself is considered to be an uncomfortable discussion among non-elites in Zimbabwe. In this context, I took care to minimize the need for interview data and instead focused on collecting data from archives.

Archival data was collected in-country with the help of two research assistants. Foreign researchers in Zimbabwe face restrictions on the length of time (three days) that can be spent in the National Archives of Zimbabwe (NAZ). In consultation with individuals at (1) the NAZ, (2) two Zimbabwe government ministries, and (three) the University of Zimbabwe, I determined the best course forward and engaged two research assistants to help me to retrieve materials from the NAZ and to translate/transcribe the interviews housed at the NAZ as part of their oral history collection. The research assistants who worked with me were masters students in Economic History, and had concurrently been engaged in projects for their own research as well as for other foreign researchers, all at the NAZ. Archival access and research is open to all Zimbabwean nationals, and thus they faced no risk in conducting research on behalf of this project.

The National Archives of Zimbabwe and the Mafela Trust both held a large number of interviews with ex-combatants from both ZANU and ZAPU as well as civilians living in rural areas during and after the Liberation War. These, combined with memoirs and qualitative history from the Jesuit Archives, meant that the need to conduct additional interviews was minimized. However, there were outstanding questions about which I hoped to learn more. To do so, I reached out to several other scholars in the United States with expertise in Zimbabwe, to ask who I should contact in-country and what I should keep in mind as I make my inquiries. Through their contacts, I eventually reached other scholars in Zimbabwe, who helped to put me in contact with a few people I eventually interviewed. Interviewees introduced me to other potential interviewees whose stories they felt I might find useful for my research.

In total, I was able to reach eight interviewees. Among these, five were ex-combatants; two were ex-government employees; one is an expert on Zimbabwean politics. All interviewees consented to participating in my research twice: first through the initial phone call, WhatsApp message, or email, in which I explained the purpose of my research and my request for an interview; second during the interview, during which I once again explained the interview purpose as part of the informed consent process.

Importantly, I focused only on requesting interviews with key individuals who were of high political or social standing and would face no negative repercussions from speaking to a foreign researcher. They were primarily ex-combatants who later found good positions in government or who actively work with the government in the capacity of another private organization such as an NGO. To give an indication of the types of people I was contacting for an interview, many potential interviewees recommended to me turned my interview request down not because they were afraid to speak, but because they were too often contacted by journalists

270 Governing after War

or interviewers. Several people I contacted directed me to their already-published books or memoirs of their experiences during this period of Zimbabwe's history, while another sent me a copy of his working memoir manuscript to use for my research in lieu of an interview. In short, these are not ordinary citizens or ex-combatants who have exited politics to live a civilian life. For primary evidence of experiences from people outside of public scrutiny, I gratefully relied on oral history collections—interviews and memoirs made available in archives.

B2 Selection of Coding Narratives

In this section, I provide narratives for six of the rural districts in Zimbabwe to illustrate the types of evidence used and to explain typical coding decisions for rebel territorial control and contestation. I present two cases for each type—ZANU control, ZAPU control, and highly contested. In each type, I choose one district that might be considered the ideal type, and another district is chosen by randomly sample. In all cases, I use Rhodesian records to provide some context about the size of the potential affected population, which are primarily Black Zimbabweans living in the colonial Tribal Trust Lands and Purchase Areas.

B2.1 ZANU Control

Mount Darwin (Mashonaland Central) Mount Darwin district lies at the border of northeastern Zimbabwe and Mozambique. This was one of the first ZANU strongholds: evidence suggests that ZANLA entered the district from their Zambian camps and began consistent operations here around 1972, although there was earlier sporadic presence as well. In two early Rhodesian publications found in the Jesuit Archives—"Anatomy of Terror" and "Harvest of Fear" (Government of Rhodesia, 1978a,b), the Rhodesian government described numerous encounters with ZANLA, suggesting high rebel presence from 1973 onward.

Mount Darwin district was served by the Sinoia diocese of the Catholic Mission, specifically the Marymount Mission located within the district, and the St. Albert's Mission located in the adjacent Centenary district. These two missions were hotbeds of ZANLA activity throughout the conflict: From 1973 onward, rebels maintained a base near St. Albert's Mission and routinely had contact with civilians at night while looting empty farm stores for supplies (Von Walter, n.d.). There was also a written account about an incident in 1979, when missionary workers from Marymount Mission Hospital were abducted by the rebels and forced to walk to Mozambique. According to the account, civilian collaborators (mujibas) had entered the mission that morning, but the mission was surprised that "there was a larger than normal group of mujibhas" (Dakudzwa, 1979, 1). The mujibas asked their usual questions about the existence of Rhodesian forces, but the missionaries were not worried because "we were used to such questions" (Dakudzwa, 1979, 1). The missionaries also reported that Marymount Mission had a good relationship with the ZANLA soldiers during the war (Dakudzwa, 1979, 9). These accounts of missionary contact with rebels suggest high levels of presence.

According to an independent report conducted by the Catholic Commission for Justice and Peace in Rhodesia (CCJP) in 1978, there was collaboration between local civilians and the ZANLA rebels (Catholic Commission for Justice and Peace, 1976); investigators for the CCJP also noted various rebel checkpoints in or near Mount

Appendix B: Zimbabwe Liberation War   271

Darwin (Central Africa Investigation Service Bottriell's, 1975). A clear indicator for high rebel influence and activity is the existence of Protected Villages, a counterinsurgency tactic to prevent civilians from maintaining contact with rebels. Based on protected villages data collected from the NAZ's collection of Rhodesian files, in Mount Darwin, 63 protected villages were established in total, out of a total of 231 established during the conflict (Ministry of Internal Affairs, n.d.). Of these, forty were created in 1975: it was the fourth district to be subjected to the program. An additional twenty-three were created in 1978, given spreading support in the district despite counterinsurgency measures. All wards covering native areas were forced into protected villages.

Finally, of the three chiefdoms in Mount Darwin that existed throughout the war (two more were promoted to chieftaincy during the war), all three experienced wartime chief turnover (Government of Rhodesia, 1985). One saw two turnovers—three chiefs in total due to one death and one abduction—while the other two saw one turnover due to death. Prior to the war, chiefs in Mount Darwin had an average tenure length of around eleven years, while chiefs who were in power during the war had a tenure of around five years only. While chief deaths may have occurred due to natural causes or other causes not related to the war, there is good reason to suspect that chiefs were killed or harmed by ZANLA rebels, as the rebels were well known for killing chiefs who were seen as Rhodesian administrators.

Makoni (Manicaland) Makoni district is located in the eastern-most province Manicaland, close (not not adjacent) to the border of Mozambique. Prior to the start of the liberation war, civilians in Makoni district were already being politicized by early ZAPU nationalist party structures, which had held secret meetings in rural villages throughout the 1960s (Ranger, 1985). ZANU/ZANLA entered Makoni district in late 1975, when the entire eastern front was opened up to the rebel group after Mozambican independence. High ZANLA presence as a result of Makoni's proximity to Mozambique meant that the ZAPU party structures were destroyed (Ex-combatant interview, 2017). Under ZANLA command, Makoni district fell under the Manica war zone, Tangwena sector. The ZANLA deaths register ("Fallen Heroes of Zimbabwe") lists an estimated 189 ZANLA casualties in Makoni district alone, out of a total 3,304 deaths with location information across the country and in the Mozambique bases (Prime Minister's Office, 1983).

Makoni district contains five communal native areas—Chiduku, Weya, Makoni, Tandi, and Chikori—and three additional native purchase areas. While the Rhodesian government established no protected villages, there were five protected sub-offices in Makoni within these native areas, suggesting that there was high rebel presence (Ministry of Internal Affairs, n.d.). Of the five chiefdoms in Makoni, there were turnovers in power in four of them. One, Chief Chiduku, saw one turnover while Chiefs Chikore, Chipunza, and Tandi saw two turnovers in power between 1975 and 1980. Two chiefs were killed during the war and one was removed from power. The remainder were recorded as having died, but with no reason provided (Government of Rhodesia, 1985). Some headmen (one administrative level lower level than chiefs) were also killed because they did not support ZANU (Ranger, 1985, 284). Similarly, there were three Catholic missions in Makoni district, and all three closed down non-medical services and schools in 1977 and 1978 due to heightened rebel activity (*Catholic Directory of Rhodesia 1978/9*, 1978). These pieces of evidence suggest high levels of rebel presence during the conflict.

Ranger (1982); Ranger's (1985) fieldwork in Makoni district remains one of the most comprehensive studies on peasant ideology and politicization, from the early 1900s until

272 Governing after War

the end of the liberation war. In particular, the book demonstrated the strong levels of influence rebels had (at least in Makoni district) and describes various ways in which ZANLA rebels consulted and worked with spirit mediums to gain legitimacy in the area. In some cases they even brought spirit mediums from one native area to another in order to "make the land safe." On the civilians' end, by deriving legitimacy from spirit mediums, rebels were forced to comply with customs and ensured that the "actions of the fighting men observed some local rules." Finally, spirit mediums had an incentive to participate in this cooperative relationship because "an alliance with the guerrillas ensured that they would be given proper respect" after having been sidelined by the Rhodesian administration (Ranger, 1982, 367).

B2.2 ZAPU Control

Lupane (Matabeleland North) Lupane is a district close (but not adjacent to) the Zambia border and the Botswana border. The district was an early ZAPU stronghold during the liberation war, and fell under ZAPU's Northern Front 2 (NF2) operation zone. Out of the estimated 1,185 ZIPRA casualties, 125 were part of operations in Lupane (*Actual Grave Locations of ZPRA Guerillas*, 2006). These lists are noted as incomplete and should be taken as only a very rough estimate, but they provide some indication of the intensity of rebel operations in different parts of the country. Since the Rhodesian government did not establish protected villages in ZIPRA strongholds (some were planned in Hwange district but the program had ended before implementation), there were no protected villages in Lupane; however, there were two protected sub-offices in Lupane. In the 1990s, there was also an unsuccessful push toward building a war memorial at the Pupu Shrine in Lupane, in commemoration of ZAPU/ZIPRA efforts in the Liberation War.

There are four native communal lands in Lupane: Lupane, Lubimbi, Dandanda, and Mzola. There is also one native purchase area, Gwaai. These areas cover twenty-five of the thirty wards in Lupane while European lands were limited, suggesting high potential for ZPRA presence and influence. In a Mafela Trust interview, Dube (2011)—a soldier in the NF2 zone—reported that there were ZAPU mujibas in Lupane, and that Lupane was a central semi-liberated zone in which ZIPRA soldiers could walk freely. Similarly, McGregor (2017) writes, "Guerrillas had entered Lupane in serious numbers in 1977 and by late 1978, much of the district was semi-liberated and under the control of ZIPRA guerrillas operating through ZAPU party structures." Of the four Catholic missions in Lupane, two closed their hospitals and/or schools due to an increase in fighting during latter half of the liberation war (*Catholic Directory of Rhodesia 1978/9*, 1978). This evidence suggests that ZIPRA had a large and important presence in Lupane.

Bulilima-Mangwe (Matabeleland South) Bulilima-Mangwe district, which lies at the western border of Zimbabwe along the Botswana border, was one of the most important ZAPU strongholds during the liberation war and one of the guerrillas' main entryways from external bases into Zimbabwe. While there were no protected villages in Bulilima, there were five protected sub-offices established. Bulilima falls under the Southern Front 1 operation zone, and saw an estimated twenty-eight ZIPRA casualties (*Actual Grave Locations of ZPRA Guerillas*, 2006). Despite the low number of casualties as compared to Lupane however, there is strong evidence that ZAPU/ZIPRA presence was high and that the guerrillas had strong influence over local politicization and civilian support (Ngwenya, 2017).

Because civilians living on either side of the Zimbabwe-Botswana border in Bulilima-Mangwe were from the Kalanga tribe, borders were guarded only very loosely and both rebels and civilians were free to cross between the two countries frequently. Ammunition smuggling routes also went through Bulilima-Mangwe for the same reason, leading to near-constant ZIPRA presence (Ngwenya, 2017, 160). Based on various interviews conducted by the Mafela Trust, it is clear that the town of Plumtree was one of the main routes through which ZIPRA soldiers would travel between their Francistown base in Botswana and rural villages in Zimbabwe. It was also common for new ZIPRA recruits to travel from Plumtree to the Botswana border, where they were taken to Francistown before heading north to guerrilla training camps in Zambia. Ndebele (2011) describes his situation, which seems to typify recruits from the Bulilima-Mangwe area based on the Mafela Trust interviews: As a native of rural Plumtree area, he grew up as a farmer two kilometers from the Zimbabwe-Botswana border. When he decided to join the struggle with his friends, he crossed the border into Botswana—where he was mistaken as a cattle herder—and was brought to Francistown on ZAPU vehicles. Eventually, ZAPU made the decision that he could be a soldier, so he boarded a plane and was flown Nampundwe Transit Camp in Zambia.

In Bulilima-Mangwe—and in particular, the areas around Plumtree—there was significantly high ZAPU and ZIPRA presence. For example, one interviewee in the Mafela Trust reported: "There were a lot of political activities taking place there, taking into account also that there were a number also of senior ZAPU leaders . . . So as such it is common knowledge that those people have cultivated a lot of political activity in their areas" (Nare, 2011). There was high recruitment activity in Bulilima-Mangwe's villages (Ngwenya, 2017, 165). This was in part due to the easy border crossing: Ngwenya (2017, 158–159) reported that "ZIPRA guerrillas were always present" and that the lack of border controls from Bulilima-Mangwe "minimised danger for Bulilima youths" while recruitment in the North was "dangerous, risky, and therefore fatal."

B2.3 Contested Territories

Gokwe (Midlands) Gokwe district in Midlands province saw contestation not just between ZANLA and ZIPRA, but also other smaller militias, such as Bishop Muzorewa's breakaway faction of ZANU and Reverend Sithole's militia. These militias maintained a foothold in the area (New York Times, 1979; Rich, 1982) and while they had little effect outside of Gokwe, they added to the chaotic dynamic within Gokwe district as citizens were compelled to aid and support different armed groups that operated in the rural area. In fact, the Muzorewa militia was the first group to have gained supporters in Gokwe (Preston, 2004, 59).

With the exception of some forest lands, Gokwe is made up of native tribal trust lands and some native purchase lands. It is bordered on the north, south, and west by ZIPRA strongholds, and on the east are territories that saw moderate ZANLA operational presence (Alexander, McGregor, and Ranger, 2000). During the conflict, Gokwe saw more long-standing ZIPRA operational presence and lower levels (and shorter periods) of ZANLA presence. Gokwe had been the farthest west that ZANLA could penetrate from the Mozambique border (Chitiyo and Rupiya, 2005). ZIPRA maintained bases

274   Governing after War

in Gokwe from 1975 (Catholic Commission for Justice and Peace, 1976, 55), while it seems that ZANLA did not penetrate the district until late 1977 (Prime Minister's Office, 1983). Alexander (1998) writes that Gokwe district was "entirely under Zipra control in the 1970s," but also that there were hardened Shona/Ndebele divisions because of the Shona-dominated Sithole militias that were recruited in Gokwe and used "explicitly tribal attacks" (Alexander, 1998, 179). There is also some evidence of usual ZANLA activities such as pungwes (Mwale, 2018), and "especially in 1977/78, ... Gokwe was a 'grey' area as far as encounters of Zanla and Zipra forces were concerned and also those of the Rhodesian soldiers..." (Hove, 2001). Cliffe, Mpofu, and Munslow (1980, 59) noted that Gokwe district was one of the "borders" between ZANLA and ZIPRA, which saw "contestation for control."

Because of the additional militias in operation in Gokwe, I code ZIPRA as having moderate presence and influence, while ZANLA had little presence and influence. Overall, contestation in the district is fairly high owing not just to ZANLA and ZIPRA presence but also the increased presence and influence of additional militias.

Beitbridge (Matabeleland South) Beitbridge is located in Matabeleland South, and was an important area for both ZANU and ZAPU especially during the latter half of the war. On the southern half of Matabeleland South, ZIPRA maintained an early stronghold in Gwanda, which is adjacent to the western border of Beitbridge. It seems that both ZANLA and ZIPRA extended military operations into Beitbridge in 1977, although it seems plausible that ZIPRA entered earlier than ZANLA given ZIPRA early control over Gwanda. Beitbridge fell under ZANLA's Gaza war zone, Dubula sector, Detachment 2. Under ZIPRA, it was part of the Southern Front 2 operation zone.

In Beitbridge, thirteen out of the sixteen current-day wards were part of communal lands. Of the thirteen wards that fell under native areas during Rhodesian rule, six—on the eastern half of the district that were controlled by ZANU—were subject to protected villages (Ministry of Internal Affairs, n.d.). The remaining seven on the western half, which saw heavier ZPRA presence, were not affected by protected villages. All protected villages in Beitbridge were created in 1977, and the areas subject to them make up approximately 53.7% of the native lands. According to Cliffe, Mpofu, and Munslow (1980), ZANU/ZANLA likely had controlled approximately 40% of the civilian population in Beitbridge, although this number is a rough estimate.

Contested territories in Matabeleland South, primarily in Gwanda and Beitbridge, are best conceptualized at a broader operational level rather than within districts specifically. While ZIPRA's Southern Front came from the west, ZANLA's Gaza War Zone came from the east. The two rebel groups clashed in Gwanda and Beitbridge: ZIPRA had strong operations in Beitbridge but was unable to push past ZANLA-controlled territories in the eastern part of the district, while ZANLA penetrated ZIPRA's stronghold in Gwanda in 1977 (Bhebe, 1999) and pushed very briefly into Kezi in Matobo district to the west of Gwanda (Prime Minister's Office, 1983). There were reports of clashes in all three of these districts, although it was clear that contestation in the latter years was highest in Gwanda—where ZANLA managed to control a small portion of the native areas—and slightly less so in Beitbridge. While ZANLA entered the Kezi area of Matobo from the east and fought against ZPRA combatants (Alexander, 1998), it does not seem like ZANLA maintained much presence or gained semi-permanent foothold into Matobo district (Cliffe, Mpofu, and Munslow, 1980). I thus code Matobo as being under ZAPU control, Gwanda as being highly contested despite stronger and longer-term presence from ZAPU, and Beitbridge as having moderate levels of contestation with higher presence from ZANU than from ZAPU.

B3 Descriptive Statistics

Table B1 Post-war coercive capacity (Afrobarometer Rural Sample 1950–1986)

	Count	Mean	SD	Min	Max
Registered to vote	3,730	0.942	0.234	0	1
ZANU control	4,957	0.494	0.440	0	1
Post	4,957	0.215	0.411	0	1
Male	4,957	0.499	0.500	0	1
Shona	4,954	0.720	0.449	0	1
Ndebele	4,952	0.120	0.325	0	1
Other tribes	4,955	0.160	0.366	0	1

Table B2 Public goods provision (Census Rural Sample 1950–1971)

	Count	Mean	SD	Min	Max
ZANU control	48,602	0.515	0.438	0	1
Contestation	48,602	0.170	0.331	0	1
ZAPU control	48,602	0.090	0.274	0	1
Education (0-3 coding)	49,948	1.766	1.087	0	3
Education (0-4 coding)	49,948	1.820	1.169	0	4
Education (0-13 coding)	49,873	6.395	3.931	0	13
Education (0-11 coding)	49,873	6.278	3.758	0	11
Post	50,301	0.300	0.408	0	1
Post (Croke et al., 2016)	50,301	0.346	0.447	0	1
Male	50,301	0.425	0.494	0	1
Did not migrate	49,806	0.815	0.388	0	1
Children ever born	12,609	3.893	1.487	0	5
Labor force participation	50,301	0.062	0.243	0	2
Owns home	45,080	0.838	0.368	0	1
Disabled	50,270	0.161	0.367	0	1

B4 Sub-national Hypothesis 1: Voter Registration

B4.1 Extending to Include 1987–1994 Birth Cohorts

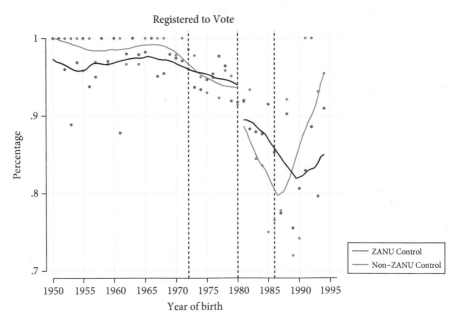

Figure App.1 Voter registration plot with additional birth cohorts

B4.2 Robustness Check for Voter Registration

Table B3 Voter registration (80% Shona)

	(1) Full sample	(2) Exclude 1972–1980 births
ZANU-PF control × post	0.043	0.054**
	(0.026)	(0.026)
Observations	2,392	1,635
Dep mean	0.913	0.913
ZANU-PF control × post SD	0.297	0.297

Notes: *p < 0.1, **p < 0.05, ***p < 0.01. Robust standard errors in parentheses, clustered at the district level. Sample is attenuated to respondents born from 1950 to 1986, from districts where there is ≥ 80% Shona population based on Afrobarometer estimates. Regression includes district, Afrobarometer survey round, birth year, gender, and tribe fixed effects. *Voter registration* is coded as "1" if they were registered to vote in the last election and "0" otherwise. Respondents who were too young to vote in the last elections are coded as missing.

B4.3 Placebo Cutoffs for Voter Registration

Table B4 Voter registration placebo checks

	(1) Post = 1965	(2) Post = 1960
ZANU control × placebo post	0.011	0.012
	(0.014)	(0.017)
Observations	1,602	1,602
Dep mean	0.913	0.913
ZANU control × placebo post SD	0.432	0.440

Notes: $^*p < 0.1$, $^{**}p < 0.05$, $^{***}p < 0.01$. Robust standard errors in parentheses, clustered at the district level. The first model codes a placebo *post* = "1" for individuals born after 1965, while the second model uses a birth cutoff of 1960. The sample is attenuated to respondents born from 1950 to 1971 for both placebo regressions. Regression includes district, Afrobarometer survey round, birth year, gender, and tribe fixed effects.

B5 Sub-national Hypothesis 2: Education Attainment

B5.1 Robustness Checks for Education Attainment

Table B5 Education attainment robustness checks

	Scale from 0–4	
	Full sample	Excluding 1960–1969 births
Contestation × educated post-war	0.259***	0.256***
	(0.070)	(0.073)
ZANU stronghold × educated post-war	0.124**	0.134**
	(0.053)	(0.054)
Observations	48,262	27,896
	Scale from 0–13	
	Full sample	Excluding 1960–1969 births
Contestation × post	0.968***	0.953***
	(0.276)	(0.275)
ZANU stronghold × post	0.497**	0.533**
	(0.216)	(0.220)
Observations	48,185	27,843

(continued)

278 Governing after War

Table B5 Continued

	Scale from 0–11	
	Full sample	**Excluding 1960–1969 births**
Contestation × post	0.960***	0.971***
	(0.266)	(0.269)
ZANU stronghold × post	0.453**	0.517**
	(0.213)	(0.218)
Observations	48,185	27,843

Notes: *$p < 0.1$, **$p < 0.05$, ***$p < 0.01$. Robust standard errors in parentheses, clustered at the district level. Sample is attenuated to respondents born from 1950 to 1971. Regressions include district, birth year, and gender fixed effects. *Education* is coded as: "0" = no formal education, "1" = incomplete primary, "2" = complete primary, "3" = incomplete secondary, and "4" = complete secondary for the 0–4 scale. The scale from 01113 is coded simply as the highest grade level from no education to completing secondary school. The scale from 0–11 is coded as the highest grade level from no education to completing lower secondary school. For these latter two codings, all individuals who responded as not knowing the exact grade level that they have completed are dropped from analysis.

Table B6 Education attainment robustness checks

	Excluding moved in last 10 years	
	Full sample	**Excluding 1960–1969 births**
Contestation × educated post-war	0.246***	0.265***
	(0.071)	(0.068)
ZANU stronghold × educated post-war	0.120**	0.141***
	(0.050)	(0.051)
Observations	39,170	22,901
	Post based on Croke et al. (2016)	
	Education (0–3 scale)	**Education (0–4 scale)**
Contestation × educated post-war	0.242***	0.248***
	(0.064)	(0.068)
ZANU stronghold × educated post-war	0.100**	0.122**
	(0.049)	(0.050)
Observations	48,262	48,262

Notes: *$p < 0.1$, **$p < 0.05$, ***$p < 0.01$. Robust standard errors in parentheses, clustered at the district level. Sample is attenuated to respondents born from 1950 to 1971. Regressions include district, birth year, and gender fixed effects. The first panel excludes individuals who reportedly migrated within the past 10 years. In the second panel, *Post* based on Croke et al. (2016) is coded as: "0" if the respondent is born before 1964, "1" if the respondent is born from 1967 onward, and increments of 1/4 for respondents born between 1964 and 1967.

Appendix B: Zimbabwe Liberation War 279

Table B7 Education attainment robustness checks (different samples)

	Including migrated population	
	Full sample	Excluding 1960–1969 births
Contestation × post	0.257***	0.253***
	(0.070)	(0.072)
ZANU control × post	0.127**	0.137***
	(0.053)	(0.054)
Observations	48,262	27,896
Dep mean	1.853	1.853
Contestation × post SD	0.319	0.325
	Only districts where Shona ≥ 80%	
	Full sample	Excluding 1960–1969 births
Contestation × post	0.320***	0.268***
	(0.056)	(0.087)
Observations	31,778	18,477
Dep mean	1.766	1.797
Contestation × post SD	0.179	0.324

Notes: $^*p < 0.1$, $^{**}p < 0.05$, $^{***}p < 0.01$. Robust standard errors in parentheses, clustered at the district level. Sample is attenuated to respondents born from 1950 to 1971. In the first panel, sample is attenuated to those who reported that they did not migrate in the past 10 years. In the second panel, sample is attenuated to individuals who reside in a district that is ≥ 80% Shona based on an estimate calculated using Afrobarometer data. Regressions include district, birth year, and gender fixed effects. *Education* is coded as: "0" = no formal education, "1" = incomplete primary, "2" = complete primary, "3" = incomplete secondary for the 0–3 scale.

B5.2 Placebo Outcomes for Education Attainment

Table B8 Placebo outcomes for educational attainment DiD

	(1) Children ever born	(2) Deaths in family (year)	(3) Owns home	(4) Disabled	(5) Did not migrate
Contestation × post	0.070	−0.008	0.011	0.013	−0.003
	(0.174)	(0.009)	(0.023)	(0.018)	(0.018)
ZANU control × post	0.077	−0.010	−0.020	0.022	0.016
	(0.156)	(0.007)	(0.018)	(0.014)	(0.013)
Observations	12,140	48,602	43,574	48,572	48,120

(coninued)

280 Governing after War

Table B8 Continued

	Age	Never married	Married	Divorced	Widowed
Contested × post	−0.000	−0.004	−0.004	−0.007	0.015
	(0.000)	(0.008)	(0.017)	(0.011)	(0.017)
ZANU control × post	−0.000	−0.012*	−0.011	0.011	0.011
	(0.000)	(0.006)	(0.014)	(0.009)	(0.010)
Observations	48,602	48,506	48,506	48,506	48,506

Notes: $*p < 0.1$, $**p < 0.05$, $***p < 0.01$. Robust standard errors in parentheses, clustered at the district level. In models 1–4, the sample is attenuated to respondents born from 1950 to 1971.

B5.3 Placebo Cutoffs for Education Attainment

Table B9 Education placebo checks

	(1) 1940–1962 sample	(2) 1934–1956 sample
ZANU control × placebo post	−0.007	−0.041
	(0.034)	(0.032)
Contestation × placebo post	−0.014	−0.097**
	(0.046)	(0.039)
Observations	38,854	29,553
Dep mean	1.853	1.853
Contestation × placebo post SD	0.327	0.327

Notes: $*p < 0.1$, $**p < 0.05$, $***p < 0.01$. Robust standard errors in parentheses, clustered at the district level. Sample is attenuated to respondents born from 1940–1961 in the first model, and from 1934–1956 in the second model. In the first model, the placebo *post* is coded as "0" if the respondent is born prior to 1951, "1" if born 1956 and after, and in increments of 1/6 in between. In the second model, the placebo *post* is coded as "0" if the respondent is born prior to 1945, "1" if born 1950 and after, and in increments of 1/6 in between. Regressions include district, birth year, and gender fixed effects.

APPENDIX C

First Liberia Civil War

C1 Descriptive Statistics

Table C1 Wartime chief appointments (rural sample)

	Count	Mean	SD	Min	Max
War chief appointment	9,327	0.442	0.497	0	1
NPFL Control	9,327	0.286	0.349	0	1
Second war	9,327	1.195	0.797	0	5
Dist. county capital (logged)	9,327	3.406	0.620	.0391001	4.656
Dist. Monrovia (logged)	9,327	4.880	0.618	2.924642	6.046
Civilian deaths (logged)	8,894	8.144	0.929	0	8.780
Population (logged)	8,607	4.044	1.433	0	10.685
Bassa	9,327	0.950	1.566	0	8.353
Belle	9,327	0.088	0.467	0	7.525
Dey	9,327	0.075	0.392	0	5.595
Gbandi	9,327	0.237	0.812	0	8.843
Gio	9,327	0.477	1.241	0	9.201
Gola	9,327	0.478	1.159	0	8.550
Grebo	9,327	0.436	1.206	0	9.842
Kpelle	9,327	1.852	1.835	0	10.343
Kissi	9,327	0.442	1.100	0	9.878
Krahn	9,327	0.219	0.907	0	9.645
Kru	9,327	0.319	0.959	0	7.871
Lorma	9,327	0.467	1.069	0	8.598
Mandingo	9,327	0.235	0.789	0	8.572
Mano	9,327	0.487	1.239	0	10.132
Mende	9,327	0.177	0.632	0	6.394
Sapo	9,327	0.097	0.584	0	7.300
Vai	9,327	0.336	0.948	0	7.229
Other Liberian	9,327	0.057	0.365	0	6.260
Other African	9,327	0.114	0.478	0	6.538
Non-African	9,327	0.015	0.153	0	4.111
Christian	9,327	3.875	1.490	0	10.617
Muslim	9,327	0.906	1.513	0	8.845
No religion	9,327	0.221	0.711	0	6.534
Other religion	9,327	0.087	0.375	0	5.011
Traditional religion	9,327	0.422	0.989	0	6.644

282 Governing after War

Table C2 Education attainment (Census sample 1970–1992)

	Count	Mean	SD	Min	Max
NPFL control	1,088,885	0.125	0.248	0	1
Contested or partisan	1,088,885	0.160	0.338	0	1
Schooling (0-2)	1,089,140	1.043	0.915	0	2
Literacy	1,089,140	0.611	0.488	0	1
Primary school by year	1,089,140	3.222	2.797	0	6
Including secondary school	1,089,140	1.535	1.504	0	4
Secondary school by year	1,089,140	4.632	4.505	0	12
Sex	1,089,140	1.521	0.500	1	2
Urban	1,089,140	0.500	0.500	0	1
Christian	1,089,140	0.884	0.320	0	1
Muslim	1,089,140	0.097	0.296	0	1
Traditional African Religion	1,089,140	0.004	0.067	0	1
Other religion	1,089,140	0.001	0.035	0	1
No religion	1,089,140	0.013	0.115	0	1
Bassa	1,089,140	0.149	0.356	0	1
Belle	1,089,140	0.009	0.094	0	1
Dey	1,089,140	0.004	0.060	0	1
Gbandi	1,089,140	0.027	0.161	0	1
Gio	1,089,140	0.080	0.271	0	1
Gola	1,089,140	0.043	0.204	0	1
Grebo	1,089,140	0.096	0.295	0	1
Kpelle	1,089,140	0.219	0.413	0	1
Kissi	1,089,140	0.038	0.190	0	1
Krahn	1,089,140	0.035	0.183	0	1
Kru	1,089,140	0.066	0.249	0	1
Lorma	1,089,140	0.049	0.216	0	1
Mandingo	1,089,140	0.026	0.158	0	1
Mano	1,089,140	0.086	0.281	0	1
Mende	1,089,140	0.008	0.091	0	1
Sapo	1,089,140	0.014	0.117	0	1
Vai	1,089,140	0.042	0.201	0	1
Other Liberian ethnic group	1,089,140	0.006	0.075	0	1
Other African tribe	1,089,140	0.003	0.059	0	1
Non African tribe	1,089,140	0.000	0.019	0	1

Table C3 Education attainment placebo outcomes (Census sample 1970–1992)

	Count	Mean	SD	Min	Max
Never married	1,089,140	0.499	0.500	0	1
Has children	566,971	0.618	0.486	0	1
Disabled	1,089,140	0.976	0.155	0	1
Congenital (from birth)	1,089,140	0.002	0.049	0	1
Polio	1,089,140	0.001	0.036	0	1
Stroke	1,089,140	0.000	0.017	0	1
Epilepsy	1,089,140	0.001	0.032	0	1
War	1,089,140	0.003	0.056	0	1
Occupational injury	1,089,140	0.001	0.029	0	1
Transport accident	1,089,140	0.001	0.026	0	1

Appendix C: First Liberia Civil War   283

Other accident	1,089,140	0.002	0.040	0	1
Aging process	1,089,140	0.000	0.000	0	0
Other causes	1,089,140	0.005	0.074	0	1
Other diseases	1,089,140	0.008	0.087	0	1
Limited use of leg(s)	1,089,140	0.004	0.063	0	1
Loss of leg(s)	1,089,140	0.001	0.032	0	1
Limited use of arm(s)	1,089,140	0.001	0.034	0	1
Loss of arm(s)	1,089,140	0.000	0.021	0	1
Hearing difficulty	1,089,140	0.002	0.047	0	1
Unable to hear (death)	1,089,140	0.001	0.024	0	1
Sight difficulty	1,089,140	0.005	0.073	0	1
Loss of sight (blindness)	1,089,140	0.001	0.023	0	1
Speech impairment	1,089,140	0.000	0.019	0	1
Unable to speak (mute)	1,089,140	0.000	0.021	0	1
Mental retardation	1,089,140	0.001	0.025	0	1
Mental illness (strange behaviour)	1,089,140	0.001	0.032	0	1
Deaf and dumb	1,089,140	0.000	0.017	0	1
Other multiple disabilities	1,089,140	0.001	0.036	0	1
Others	1,089,140	0.005	0.071	0	1

Table C4 Post-war security

	Count	Mean	SD	Min	Max
NPFL control	12,830	0.246	0.334	0	1
Contested or partisan	12,830	0.184	0.337	0	1
Contested	12,830	0.145	0.295	0	1
Partisan	12,836	0.039	0.194	0	1
LURD recruitment	12,836	0.030	0.171	0	1
MODEL recruitment	12,836	0.083	0.276	0	1
Recruitment (pooled)	12,836	0.113	0.317	0	1
Civilian deaths (logged)	12,291	8.146	0.944	0	8.780
Dist. county capital (logged)	12,830	3.376	0.616	.0391	4.656
Dist. Monrovia (logged)	12,830	4.802	0.651	0	6.046
Population (logged)	12,836	4.058	1.429	0	13.786
Bassa	12,836	1.186	1.692	0	11.984
Belle	12,836	0.094	0.474	0	8.9370
Dey	12,836	0.075	0.403	0	8.3440
Gbandi	12,836	0.245	0.819	0	10.332
Gio	12,836	0.447	1.180	0	10.699
Gola	12,836	0.499	1.165	0	10.193
Grebo	12,836	0.486	1.259	0	11.449
Kpelle	12,836	1.802	1.846	0	11.884
Kissi	12,836	0.429	1.069	0	10.809
Krahn	12,836	0.197	0.832	0	9.988
Kru	12,836	0.371	1.035	0	11.514
Lorma	12,836	0.467	1.053	0	11.186
Mandingo	12,836	0.228	0.766	0	10.906
Mano	12,836	0.466	1.182	0	10.594
Mende	12,836	0.190	0.665	0	9.485
Sapo	12,836	0.101	0.593	0	9.338
Vai	12,836	0.384	1.036	0	10.848

(continued)

284 Governing after War

Table C4 Coninued

	Count	Mean	SD	Min	Max
Other Liberian	12,836	0.071	0.430	0	9.243
Other African	12,836	0.129	0.529	0	10.339
Non-African	12,836	0.020	0.200	0	8.139
Christian	12,836	3.857	1.473	0	13.645
Muslim	12,836	0.902	1.518	0	11.719
No religion	12,836	0.184	0.645	0	6.865
Other religion	12,836	0.083	0.370	0	7.249
Tradition religion	12,836	0.384	0.936	0	7.803

C2 Implication 1: Chief Replacement

C2.1 Clan-Level Analysis

Table C5 Chief replacement (clan level)

	(1) Full sample	(2) Excluding partisan territories
NPFL control over clan	0.285**	0.292**
	(0.126)	(0.123)
Observations	297	260

Notes: *$p < 0.1$, **$p < 0.05$, ***$p < 0.01$. Robust standard errors in parentheses, clustered at the tribe level. Regression includes tribal areas fixed effects. Controls include logged civilian deaths, number of years locality was affected by the second civil war logged population, logged size of ethnic group, logged distance to the county capital, and logged distance to the capital Monrovia. NPFL control over clan is coded as "1" if the NPFL controlled at least 75% of the clan.

C3 Sub-national Hypothesis 2: Educational Attainment

C3.1 Parallel Trends Plots

The figures that follow plot the education levels for each birth cohort across the three types of areas, and shows no substantive differences prior to the first set of treated individuals who were born in 1987. In Figure App.2, the stark difference between education in rival territories versus elsewhere is in part due to the capital, Monrovia, where education is higher. I therefore drop Monrovia to show parallel trends in the rest of the country in Figure App.3.

Although areas with low wartime organizational capacity see higher schooling and literacy, it should be noted that these effect sizes are small. This small effect is visually reflected in Figure App.2: While strongholds and opposition territories see a greater drop in post-war schooling—and in particular, stronghold areas become less educated than contested and partisan regions—there is little change in educational attainment overall for all three types of

Appendix C: First Liberia Civil War 285

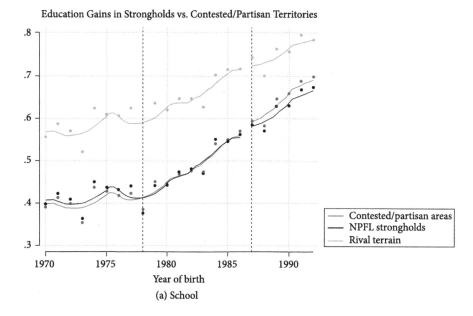

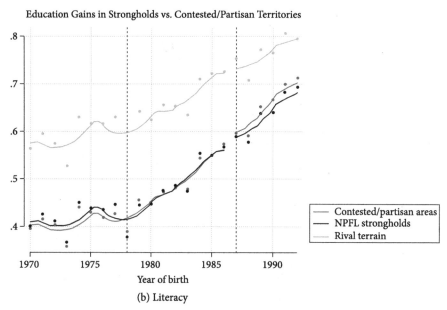

Figure App.2 Parallel Trends for Gains in Educational Attainment
Notes: School is coded as: "0" = no formal education, "1" = incomplete primary. *Literacy* is coded as: "0" = illiterate, "1" = literate.

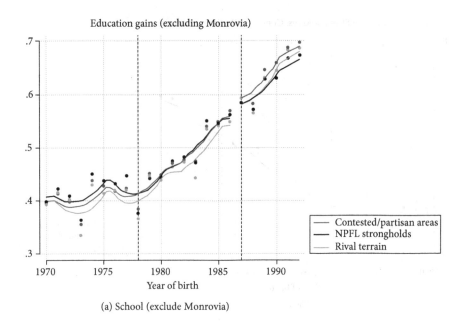

(a) School (exclude Monrovia)

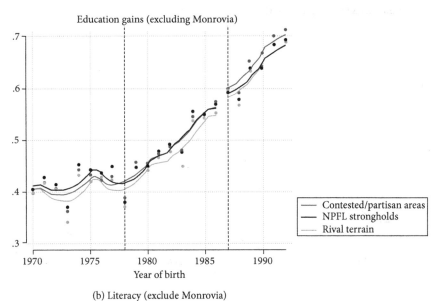

(b) Literacy (exclude Monrovia)

Figure App.3 Parallel trends for gains in educational attainment (excluding Monrovia)

Notes: *School* is coded as: "0" = no formal education, "1" = incomplete primary. *Literacy* is coded as: "0" = illiterate, "1" = literate.

Appendix C: First Liberia Civil War **287**

territories. This accords with qualitative evidence from Chapter 5, Section 5.7, in which the Charles Taylor continuously diverted development funding towards paying for the security apparatus that was fighting the second civil war. Thus, although nominal improvements were made with the help of the international firms and NGOs, the effect was slight overall.

C3.2 Robustness Checks for Educational Attainment

Table C6 Education and literacy robustness checks

	Alt. primary school coding	
	(1) Add complete primary	(2) Pri. school coded 0–6
Contested or partisan × post	0.104** (0.052)	0.219 (0.139)
NPFL control × post	−0.025 (0.080)	−0.238 (0.215)
Observations	686,336	690,470
Dep mean	1.036	3.222
Cont./part. > NPFL control	0.002	0.000
	Control for "never married"	
	(1) School	(2) Literacy
Contested or partisan × post	0.092*** (0.029)	0.102*** (0.027)
NPFL control × post	0.010 (0.044)	0.030 (0.042)
Observations	690,470	690,470
Dep mean	1.043	0.611
Cont./part. > NPFL control	0.000	0.001

Notes: $^*p < 0.1$, $^{**}p < 0.05$, $^{***}p < 0.01$. Robust standard errors in parentheses, clustered at the locality level. Sample is attenuated to respondents born from 1970 to 1992 who have lived in that locality since they were five years old or younger. Regressions include locality fixed effects, birth year fixed effects, ethnicity and religion fixed effects, and gender fixed effects. *Add complete primary* is coded as: "0" = no formal education, "1" = incomplete primary, "2" = complete primary. *Primary School by Year* is coded from "0" to "6" based on years of primary school education, and post-primary school is coded as "6." *School* is coded as: "0" = no formal education, "1" = incomplete primary. *Literacy* is coded as: "0" = illiterate, "1" = literate.

C3.3 Placebo Outcomes for Educational Attainment

Table C7 Balance across placebo outcomes for educational attainment DiD

	Contested/Partisan		NPFL control	
	Coefficient	SE	Coefficient	SE
Never married	0.078**	(0.033)	0.079*	(0.048)
Has children	0.010	(0.017)	0.009	(0.027)
Disabled	0.002	(0.002)	−0.001	(0.003)
Cause: Congenital	0.000	(0.001)	0.001	(0.001)
Cause: Polio	0.000	(0.000)	−0.000	(0.001)
Cause: Stroke	0.000	(0.000)	−0.000	(0.000)
Cause: Epilepsy	0.000	(0.000)	0.001**	(0.001)
Cause: War	0.000	(0.001)	0.001	(0.001)
Cause: Occupational injury	−0.001***	(0.000)	−0.001	(0.001)
Cause: Transport accident	−0.000	(0.000)	0.000	(0.000)
Cause: Other accident	−0.001**	(0.001)	−0.000	(0.001)
Cause: Other causes	0.000	(0.001)	0.000	(0.002)
Cause: Other diseases	−0.001	(0.001)	−0.001	(0.001)
Type: Lim. use of legs	−0.001*	(0.001)	0.000	(0.001)
Type: Loss of legs	−0.000	(0.000)	0.000	(0.000)
Type: Lim. use of arms	−0.001*	(0.000)	0.001	(0.001)
Type: Loss of arms	−0.000*	(0.000)	0.001	(0.000)
Type: Hearing difficulty	0.001**	(0.001)	−0.000	(0.001)
Type: Deaf	0.000	(0.000)	−0.000	(0.000)
Type: Sight difficulty	−0.000	(0.001)	0.002	(0.002)
Type: Blind	−0.000	(0.000)	0.000	(0.000)
Type: Speech impaired	0.000	(0.000)	−0.000	(0.000)
Type: Mute	0.000	(0.000)	0.000	(0.000)
Type: Mentally impaired	0.000	(0.000)	0.000	(0.000)
Type: Mental illness	0.000	(0.000)	0.001	(0.001)
Type: Deaf and dumb	−0.000	(0.000)	0.000	(0.000)
Type: Other multiple disabilities	−0.001**	(0.000)	−0.001*	(0.001)
Type: Others	−0.000	(0.001)	−0.002*	(0.001)

C3.4 Placebo Cutoffs for Educational Attainment

Table C8 Education and literacy

	Treatment begins 1963		Treatment begins 1955	
	(1) School	(2) Literacy	(1) School	(2) Literacy
NPFL control × placebo post	−0.059*** (0.010)	−0.062*** (0.010)	−0.035*** (0.013)	−0.034** (0.014)
Contested or partisan × placebo post	−0.019** (0.008)	−0.020** (0.008)	−0.008 (0.009)	−0.009 (0.009)
Observations	609,678	609,678	417,101	417,101
Dep mean	0.868	0.478	0.791	0.433

Notes: $^*p < 0.1$, $^{**}p < 0.05$, $^{***}p < 0.01$. Robust standard errors in parentheses, clustered at the locality level. Sample is attenuated to respondents to pretreatment years. Regressions include locality fixed effects, birth year fixed effects, ethnicity and religion fixed effects, and gender fixed effects. *Education* is coded as: "0" = no formal education, "1" = incomplete primary. *Literacy* is coded as: "0" = illiterate, "1" = literate. For treatment = 1963, sample is attenuated to those born between 1956 to 1978. For treatment = 1955, sample is attenuated to those born between 1948 to 1970.

Bibliography

Abdellaoui, Jamila El. 2010. Burundi: Overview of the 2010 Elections and Observations on the Way Forward. Institute for Security Studies. https://www.files.ethz.ch/isn/140542/14Oct2010BurundiVer2.pdf.

Acemoglu, Daron, Simon Johnson, and James A. Robinson. 2001. "The Colonial Origins of Comparative Development: An Empirical Investigation." *American Economic Review* 91(5):1369–1401.

Actual Grave Locations of ZPRA Guerillas. 2006. Mafela Trust, A2.2.14.

Adebajo, Adekeye. 2002. *Building Peace in West Africa: Liberia, Sierra Leone, and Guinea-Bissau.* Lynne Rienner Publishers.

AFP. 1980. "Western Help Urged for Zimbabwe: London, July 6." *South China Morning Post*, July 7, 1980, 8. https://www.proquest.com/historical-newspapers/western-help-urged-zimbabwe/docview/1553790382/se-2?accountid=14496.

Albertus, Michael. 2020. "Land Reform and Civil Conflict: Theory and Evidence from Peru." *American Journal of Political Science* 64(2):256–274.

Albertus, Michael, and Oliver Kaplan. 2012. "Land Reform as a Counterinsurgency Policy." *Journal of Conflict Resolution* 57(2):198–231.

Alexander, Jocelyn. 1994. "State, Peasantry, and Resettlement in Zimbabwe." *Review of African Political Economy* 21(61):325–345.

Alexander, Jocelyn. 1998. "Dissident Perspectives on Zimbabwe's Post-Independence War." *Africa* 68(2):151–182.

Alexander, Jocelyn. 2014. "Things Fall Apart, The Center Can Hold: Processes of Post-War Political Change in Zimbabwe's Rural Areas." *Occasional Paper* (8):131–162.

Alexander, Jocelyn, and JoAnn McGregor. 2001. "Elections, Land, and The Politics of Opposition in Matabeleland." *Journal of Agrarian Change* 1(4):510–533.

Alexander, Jocelyn, Joanne McGregor, and Terence O. Ranger. 2000. *Violence and Memory: One Hundred Years in the "Dark Forests" of Matabeleland, Zimbabwe.* Heinemann and James Currey.

AllAfrica. 2003. "WHO Donates US$85,000 Drugs, Medical Supplies—to MOH, Phebe, Others."

Amnesty International. 1994. "Amnesty International Report 1994—Liberia." http://www.refworld.org/docid/3ae6a9f40.html.

Amnesty International. 1995. "Liberia: An Opportunity to Introduce Human Rights Protection." AFR 34/01/95.

Amnesty International. 2011. "'They Looked at His Identity Card and Shot Him Dead:' Six Months of Post-Electoral Violence in Cote d'Ivoire." AFR 31/002/2011.

Amnesty International. 2013. The Victor's Law: The Human Rights Situation Two Years after the Post-Electoral Crisis. Technical Report, AFR 31/001/2013.

Ansell, Ben W., and Johannes Lindvall. 2020. *Inward Conquest: The Political Origins of Modern Public Services.* Cambridge University Press.

Arieff, Alexis. 2015. Burundi's Electoral Crisis: In Brief. Technical Report, Congressional Research Service.

292 Bibliography

Arjona, Ana. 2015. "Civilian Resistance to Rebel Governance." In *Rebel Governance in Civil War*, ed. Ana Arjona, Nelson Kasfir and Zachariah Mampilly. Cambridge University Press.

Arjona, Ana. 2016. *Rebelocracy*. Cambridge University Press.

Arjona, Ana, Nelson Kasfir, and Zachariah Mampilly. 2015. *Rebel Governance in Civil War*. Cambridge University Press.

Arreguin-Toft, Ivan. 2001. "How the Weak Win Wars: A Theory of Asymmetric Conflict." *International security* 26(1):93–128.

Atzili, Boaz. 2011. *Good Fences, Bad Neighbors: Border Fixity and International Conflict*. University of Chicago Press.

Auerbach, Adam Michael, and Tariq Thachil. 2018. "How Clients Select Brokers: Competition and Choice in India's Slums." *American Political Science Review* 112(4):775–791.

Axelrod, Robert. 1980. "Effective Choice in the Prisoner's Dilemma." *Journal of Conflict Resolution* 24(1):3–25.

Azam, Jean-Paul. 2001. "The Redistributive State and Conflicts In Africa." *Journal of Peace Research* 38(4):429–444.

Bah, Abu Bakarr. 2010. "Democracy and Civil War: Citizenship and Peacemaking in Côte d'Ivoire." *African Affairs* 109(437):597–615.

Bakonyi, Jutta, and Kirsti Stuvøy. 2005. "Violence & Social Order beyond the State: Somalia & Angola." *Review of African Political Economy* 32(104–105):359–382.

Balcells, Laia. 2017. *Rivalry and Revenge: The Politics of Violence during Civil War*. Cambridge University Press.

Baldwin, Kate. 2013. "Why Vote with the Chief? Political Connections and Public Goods Provision in Zambia." *American Journal of Political Science* 57(4):794–809.

Baldwin, Kate, and Eric Mvukiyehe. 2015. "Elections and Collective Action: Evidence from Changes in Traditional Institutions in Liberia." *World Politics* 67(4):690–725.

Banegas, Richard. 2011. "Post-Election Crisis in Côte d'Ivoire: The Gbonhi War." *African Affairs* 110(440):457–468.

Barter, Shane. 2016. *Civilian Strategy in Civil War: Insights from Indonesia, Thailand, and the Philippines*. Springer.

Barter, Shane Joshua. 2015a. "The Rebel State in Society: Governance and Accommodation in Aceh, Indonesia." In *Rebel Governance in Civil War*, ed. Ana Arjona, Nelson Kasfir, and Zachariah Mampilly. Cambridge University Press.

Barter, Shane Joshua. 2015b. "Zones of Control & Civilian Strategy in the Aceh Conflict." *Civil Wars* 17(3):340–356.

Bates, Robert H. 1974. "Ethnic Competition and Modernization In Contemporary Africa." *Comparative Political Studies* 6(4):457–484.

Bates, Robert H. 2015. *When Things Fell Apart*. Cambridge University Press.

Bates, Robert H., and Da-Hsiang Donald Lien. 1985. "A Note on Taxation, Development, and Representative Government." *Politics & Society* 14(1):53–70.

Beardsley, Kyle. 2013. "Using the Right Tool for the Job: Mediator Leverage and Conflict Resolution." *Penn State Journal of Law & International Affairs* 2:57.

Beath, Andrew, Fotini Christia, and Ruben Enikolópov. 2012. *Winning Hearts and Minds Through Development? Evidence from a Field Experiment in Afghanistan*. World Bank.

Bellin, Eva. 2004. "The Robustness of Authoritarianism in the Middle East: Exceptionalism in Comparative Perspective." *Comparative politics* 36(2):139–157.

Berman, Eli, Jacob N. Shapiro, and Joseph H. Felter. 2011. "Can Hearts and Minds Be Bought? The Economics of Counterinsurgency in Iraq." *Journal of Political Economy* 119(4):766–819.

Berwick, Elissa, and Fotini Christia. 2018. "State Capacity Redux: Integrating Classical and Experimental Contributions to an Enduring Debate." *Annual Review of Political Science* 21:71–91.

Besley, Timothy, and Torsten Persson. 2009. "The Origins of State Capacity: Property Rights, Taxation, and Politics." *American Economic Review* 99(4):1218–44.

Bhebe, Ngwabi. 1995. *Soldiers in Zimbabwe's Liberation War*. J. Currey Heinemann.

Bhebe, Ngwabi. 1999. *The ZAPU and ZANU Guerrilla Warfare and the Evangelical Lutheran Church in Zimbabwe*. Mambo Press.

Birmingham, David. 1988. "Angola Revisited." *Journal of Southern African Studies* 15(1):1–14.

Bøås, Morten, and Anne Hatløy. 2008. "'Getting In, Getting Out': Militia Membership and Prospects for Re-Integration in Post-War Liberia." *Journal of Modern African Studies* 46(1):33–55.

Bodea, Cristina, Masaaki Higashijima, and Raju Jan Singh. 2016. "Oil and Civil Conflict: Can Public Spending Have a Mitigation Effect?" *World Development* 78:1–12.

Bowles, Jeremy, Horacio Larreguy, and Shelley Liu. 2020. "How Weakly Institutionalized Parties Monitor Brokers in Developing Democracies: Evidence from Postconflict Liberia." *American Journal of Political Science* 64(4):952–967.

Brabazon, James. 2003. Liberia: Liberians United for Reconcilitation and Democracy (LURD). Briefing Paper No. 1. Royal Institute of International Affairs. https://www.chathamhouse.org/sites/default/files/public/Research/Africa/brabazon_bp.pdf

Brancati, Dawn and Jack L. Snyder. 2013. "Time to Kill: The Impact of Election Timing on Postconflict Stability." *Journal of Conflict Resolution* 57(5):822–853.

Brierley, Sarah. 2020. "Unprincipled Principals: Co-opted Bureaucrats and Corruption in Ghana." *American Journal of Political Science* 64(2):209–222.

Brierley, Sarah, and Noah L. Nathan. 2019. "The Connections of Party Brokers." *Journal of Politics*.

Brinkman, Inge. 2003. "War, Witches and Traitors: Cases from the MPLA's Eastern Front in Angola (1966–1975)." *Journal of African History* 44(2):303–325.

Brittain, Victoria. 1998. *Death of Dignity: Angola's Civil War*. Pluto Press.

BTI Project. 2018. "Côte d'Ivoire Country Report." https://www.bti-project.org/en/reports/country-reports/detail/itc/CIV/.

Burihabwa, Ntagahoraho Z., and Devon E. A. Curtis. 2019. "The Limits of Resistance Ideologies? The CNDD-FDD and the Legacies of Governance in Burundi." *Government and Opposition* 54(3):559–583.

Call, Charles T. 2012. *Why Peace Fails: The Causes and Prevention of Civil War Recurrence*. Georgetown University Press.

Calvo, Ernesto, and Maria Victoria Murillo. 2004. "Who Delivers? Partisan Clients in the Argentine Electoral Market." *American Journal of Political Science* 48(4):742–757.

Catholic Commission for Justice and Peace. 1976. "Civil War in Rhodesia: Abduction, Torture and Death in the Counter-Insurgency Campaign." Jesuit Archives Box 320.

Catholic Commission for Justice and Peace. 1978. "Justice and Peace Reports on Protected Villages." Appendix No. 9/10/11/12/13, Jesuit Archives Box 321.

Catholic Commission for Justice and Peace. 1997. *A Report on the Disturbances in Matabeleland and the Midlands, 1980-1988*. Catholic Commission for Justice and Peace.

Catholic Commission for Justice and Peace. 1980. "Halfway To The Elections: Some Notes on the Present Situation in Rhodesia." Jesuit Archives, 430/2.

Catholic Directory of Rhodesia 1978/9. 1978. Mambo Press.

Cederman, Lars-Erik, Andreas Wimmer, and Brian Min. 2010. "Why Do Ethnic Groups Rebel? New Data and Analysis." *World Politics* 62(1):87–119.

Cederman, Lars-Erik, Nils B Weidmann and Kristian Skrede Gleditsch. 2011. "Horizontal Inequalities and Ethnonationalist Civil War: A Global Comparison." *American Political Science Review* 105(3):478–495.

Centeno, Miguel Angel. 1997. "Blood and Debt: War and Taxation in Nineteenth-Century Latin America." *American Journal of Sociology* 102(6):1565–1605.

294 Bibliography

Central Africa Investigation Service Bottriell's. 1975. "Confidential Report Re: Destruction of Kraals at Kamanika School." Jesuit Archives Box 322.

Chandra, Kanchan. 2007. *Why Ethnic Parties Succeed: Patronage and Ethnic Head Counts in India*. Cambridge University Press.

Cheema, G. Shabbir, and Dennis A. Rondinelli. 2007. *Decentralizing Governance: Emerging Concepts and Practices*. Brookings Institution Press.

Chemouni, Benjamin. 2016. "The Politics of State Effectiveness in Burundi and Rwanda: Ruling Elite Legitimacy and the Imperative of State Performance." PhD thesis. London School of Economics and Political Science (LSE).

Chitiyo, Knox, and Martin Rupiya. 2005. "Tracking Zimbabwe's Political History: The Zimbabwe Defence Force from 1980–2005." In *Evolutions and Revolutions: A Contemporary History of Militaries in Southern Africa*. Pretoria: Institute of Security Studies, ed: Martin Rupiya.

Christia, Fotini. 2012. *Alliance Formation in Civil Wars*. Cambridge University Press.

Chung, Fay. 2006. *Re-living the Second Chimurenga: Memories From the Liberation Struggle in Zimbabwe*. African Books Collective.

Clarke, Killian. 2022. "Revolutionary Violence and Counterrevolution." *American Political Science Review*: 1–17.

Clausewitz, Carl. 1982. *On War*. Vol. 20. Penguin UK.

Cliffe, Lionel, Joshua Mpofu, and Barry Munslow. 1980. "Nationalist Politics in Zimbabwe: The 1980 Elections and Beyond." *Review of African Political Economy* (18):44–67.

Coalition for International Justice. 2005. "Following Taylor's Money: A Path of War and Destruction." http://allafrica.com/download/resource/main/main/idatcs/00010642: e0bc9e66f665f2c7b2fb8a942ff328ea.pdf.

Cobb, Charles. 2001. "Eritrean Critic Urges Government to Relent on Dissidents." https://allafrica.com/stories/200110050467.html.

Cohen, Dara Kay. 2016. *Rape During Civil War*. Cornell University Press.

Collier, Paul, and Anke Hoeffler. 2004. "Greed and Grievance In Civil War." *Oxford Economic Papers* 56(4):563–595.

Collier, Ruth Berins, and David Collier. 1991. *Shaping the Political Arena: Critical Junctures, the Labor Movement, and Regime Dynamics in Latin America*. Princeton University Press.

Croicu, Mihai, and Ralph Sundberg. 2012. "UCDP GED Conflict Polygons Dataset." http://www.ucdp.uu.se/downloads/.

Croke, Kevin, Guy Grossman, Horacio A. Larreguy, and John Marshall. 2016. "Deliberate Disengagement: How Education Can Decrease Political Participation in Electoral Authoritarian Regimes." *American Political Science Review* 110(3):579–600.

Dabalen, Andrew L., Ephraim Kebede, and Saumik Paul. 2012. Causes of Civil War: Micro Level Evidence from Côte d'Ivoire. Technical Report, Households in Conflict Network.

Dabengwa, Dumiso. Interview. 2011. "Zenzo Nkobi Photographic Archive, AL3291/B03." Mafela Trust.

Dahl, Robert Alan. 1973. *Polyarchy: Participation and Opposition*. Yale University Press.

Dakudzwa, Sr. Gregor Munyaradzi. 1979. "Abduction of LCLB Sisters and Bro Herman Toma SJ from Marymount Mission 1979." Jesuit Archives Box 535.

Daly, Sarah Zukerman. 2014. "The Dark Side of Power-Sharing: Middle Managers and Civil War Recurrence." *Comparative Politics* 46(3):333–353.

Daly, Sarah Zukerman. 2016. *Organized Violence after Civil War: The Geography of Recruitment in Latin America*. Cambridge University Press.

Daly, Sarah Zukerman. 2019. "Voting for Victors: Why Violent Actors Win Postwar Elections." *World Politics* 71(4):747–805.

Bibliography 295

Daly, Sarah Zukerman. 2021*a*. "How Do Violent Politicians Govern? The Case of Paramilitary-Tied Mayors in Colombia." *British Journal of Political Science* 52:1–24.

Daly, Sarah Zukerman. 2021*b*. "Political Life after Civil Wars: Introducing the Civil War Successor Party Dataset." *Journal of Peace Research* 58(4):839–848.

Daly, Sarah Zukerman. 2022. *Violent Victors: Why Bloodstained Parties Win Postwar Elections*. Vol. 196. Princeton University Press.

Dash, Leon De Costa, Jr. 1977. "Savimbi's 1977 Campaign Against The Cubans and MPLA-Observed For 7 1/2 Months and Covering 2,100 Miles Inside Angola."

David, Paul A. 1994. "Why Are Institutions the 'Carriers of History'?: Path Dependence and the Evolution of Conventions, Organizations, and Institutions." *Structural Change and Economic Dynamics* 5(2):205–220.

De La O, Ana L. 2013. "Do Conditional Cash Transfers Affect Electoral Behavior? Evidence from a Randomized Experiment in Mexico." *American Journal of Political Science* 57(1):1–14.

De Mesquita, Bruce Bueno, Alastair Smith, Randolph M. Siverson, and James D. Morrow. 2005. *The Logic of Political Survival*. MIT Press.

De Mesquita, Bruce Bueno, James D. Morrow, Randolph M Siverson, and Alastair Smith. 2002. "Political Institutions, Policy Choice and the Survival of Leaders." *British Journal of Political Science* 32(4):559–590.

Dendere, Chipo. 2015. "The Impact of Voter Exit on Party Survival: Evidence from Zimbabwe's ZANU-PF." PhD thesis, Georgia State University.

Des Forges, Alison. 1999. "Leave None to Tell the Story:" Genocide in Rwanda. Technical Report, Human Rights Watch.

Dietrich, Simone, and Amanda Murdie. 2017. "Human Rights Shaming through INGOs and Foreign Aid Delivery." *Review of International Organizations* 12(1):95–120.

Dilworth, Alison. 2006. Burundi: The CNDD - FDD (Nkurunziza) and the Use of Child Soldiers. In *Forum on Armed Groups and the Involvement of Children in Armed Conflict*.

Ding, Iza. 2022. *The Performative State: Public Scrutiny and Environmental Governance in China*. Cornell University Press.

Downes, Alexander B. 2007. "Draining the Sea by Filling the Graves: Investigating the Effectiveness of Indiscriminate Violence as a Counterinsurgency Strategy." *Civil Wars* 9(4):420–444.

Dube, Richard. Interview. 2011. "Zenzo Nkobi Photographic Archive, AL3291/B05." Mafela Trust.

Dube, Oeindrila, and Juan F. Vargas. 2013. "Commodity Price Shocks and Civil Conflict: Evidence from Colombia." *Review of Economic Studies* 80(4):1384–1421.

Ellis, Stephen. 2003. "Young Soldiers and the Significance of Initiation: Some Notes from Liberia." *Afrika-Studiecentrum: Leiden*.

Ellis, Stephen. 2007. *The Mask of Anarchy Updated Edition: The Destruction of Liberia and the Religious Dimension of an African Civil War*. NYU Press.

Ero, Comfort. 1995. "ECOWAS and the Subregional Peacekeeping in Liberia." https://www.africabib.org/rec.php?RID=P00017859.

Esteban, Joan, Laura Mayoral, and Debraj Ray. 2012. "Ethnicity and Conflict: Theory and Facts." *Science* 336(6083):858–865.

Europa. 2002. "Africa South of the Sahara 2003". *Psychology Press*. (Accessed June 20, 2018).

Ex-bureaucrat interview. 2017. Cambridge, Massachussetts.

Ex-combatant interviews 1 and 4. 2017. Harare, Zimbabwe.

Expert interview. 2017. Cambridge, Massachussetts.

Ex-combatant interviews 1, 4, 5, 7, 8, 9, 10, 11, 13, 16, 19, 20, 21, 22, 29, 32, 33, 35, 41, 42, 46. 2016. Monrovia, Liberia.

296 Bibliography

Falch, Åshild. 2008. "Power-Sharing to Build Peace? The Burundi Experience with Power-Sharing Agreements." *Centre for the Study of Civil War (CSCW).*

Fazal, Tanisha M. 2011. *State Death: The Politics and Geography of Conquest, Occupation, and Annexation.* Princeton University Press.

Fearon, James D., and David D Laitin. 2003. "Ethnicity, Insurgency, and Civil War." *American Political Science Review* 97(01):75–90.

Fearon, James D., and David D. Laitin. 2011. "Sons of the Soil, Migrants, and Civil War." *World Development* 39(2):199–211.

Flores, Thomas Edward, and Irfan Nooruddin. 2012. "The Effect of Elections on Postconflict Peace and Reconstruction." *Journal of Politics* 74(2):558–570.

Focus groups 1–8. 2016. Monrovia, Liberia.

Focus groups 9–18. 2018. Monrovia, Liberia.

Förster, Till. 2013. "Insurgent Nationalism: Political Imagination and Rupture in Côte d'Ivoire." *Africa Spectrum* 48(3):3–31.

Förster, Till. 2015. "Dialogue Direct: Rebel Governance and Civil Order in Northern Côte d'Ivoire." In *Rebel Governance in Civil War*, ed. Ana Arjona, Nelson Kasfir, and Zachariah Mampilly. Cambridge University Press.

French, Howard. 1998. "Liberia Waits: Which Charles Taylor Won?" New York Times, January 17, 1998. https://www.nytimes.com/1998/01/17/world/liberia-waits-which-charles-taylor-won.html.

Galea, Sandro, Peter C. Rockers, Geetor Saydee, Rose Macauley, S. Tornorlah Varpilah, and Margaret E. Kruk. 2010. "Persistent Psychopathology in the Wake of Civil War: Long-Term Posttraumatic Stress Disorder in Nimba County, Liberia." *American Journal of Public Health* 100(9):1745–1751.

Galtung, Fredrik, and Martin Tisné. 2009. "A New Approach to Postwar Reconstruction." *Journal of Democracy* 20(4):93–107.

Garfias, Francisco. 2018. "Elite Competition and State Capacity Development: Theory and Evidence from Post-revolutionary Mexico." *American Political Science Review* 112(2):339–357.

Gerdes, Felix. 2013. *Civil War and State Formation: The Political Economy of War and Peace in Liberia.* Vol. 9. Campus Verlag.

Glassmyer, Katherine, and Nicholas Sambanis. 2008. "Rebel—Military Integration and Civil War Termination." *Journal of Peace Research* 45(3):365–384.

Global Security. 2013. "Special Security Service (SSS)." GlobalSecurity.org, accessed June 11, 2018. https://www.globalsecurity.org/military/world/liberia/sss.htm.

Global Witness. 2003. "Against the People, For the Resources: The Need for Stronger Enforcement of UN Timber Sanctions and Prevention of Plunder." Technical Report. Global Witness.

Golden, Miriam, and Brian Min. 2013. "Distributive Politics around the World." *Annual Review of Political Science* 16:73–99.

Goldstone, Jack A, Robert H. Bates, Ted Robert Gurr, Michael Lustik, Monty G Marshall, Jay Ulfelder, and Mark Woodward. 2005. A Global Forecasting Model of Political Instability. In *Annual Meeting of the Population Association of America, Washington DC.*

Gottlieb, Jessica, and Horacio Larreguy. 2020. "An Informational Theory of Electoral Targeting in Young Clientelistic Democracies: Evidence from Senegal." *Quarterly Journal of Political Science* 15(1):73–104.

Government of Rhodesia. 1978a. Anatomy of Terror. In *Documents Concerning the Prosecution of Members of the Executive 1977/78*. Catholic Commission for Justice and Peace in Rhodesia.

Government of Rhodesia. 1978*b*. Harvest of Fear: A Diary of Terrorist Atrocities. In *Documents Concerning the Prosecution of Members of the Executive 1977/78*. Catholic Commission for Justice and Peace in Rhodesia.

Government of Rhodesia. 1985. "Schedule of Chiefs and Headmen: Rhodesia Zimbabwe to 31.12.85." National Archives of Zimbabwe, MS746.

Green, Amelia Hoover. 2018. *The Commander's Dilemma: Violence and Restraint in Wartime*. Cornell University Press.

Green, Elliott D. 2022. *Industrialization and Assimilation*. Cambridge University Press.

Grossman, Guy, Devorah Manekin, and Dan Miodownik. 2015. "The Political Legacies of Combat: Attitudes toward War and Peace among Israeli Ex-Combatants." *International Organization* 69(4):981–1009.

The Guardian. 2001. "How a Tyrant's 'Logs Of War' Bring Terror to West Africa." May 26, 2001. https://www.theguardian.com/world/2001/may/27/theobserver.

Habyarimana, James, Macartan Humphreys, Daniel Posner, and Jeremy Weinstein. 2007. "Why Does Ethnic Diversity Undermine Public Goods Provision?" *American Political Science Review* 101(4).

Hägerdal, Nils. 2019. "Ethnic Cleansing and the Politics of Restraint: Violence and Coexistence in the Lebanese Civil War." *Journal of Conflict Resolution* 63(1):59–84.

Hall, Margaret. 1990. "The Mozambican National Resistance Movement (Renamo): A Study in the Destruction of an African country." *Africa: Journal of the International African Institute* 60(1):39–68.

Harris, David. 1999. "From 'Warlord' to 'Democratic' President: How Charles Taylor Won the 1997 Liberian Elections." *Journal of Modern African Studies* 37(3):431–455.

Hartzell, Caroline, and Matthew Hoddie. 2003. "Institutionalizing Peace: Power Sharing and Post-Civil War Conflict Management." *American Journal of Political Science* 47(2):318–332.

Hassan, Mai. 2020. *Regime Threats and State Solutions: Bureaucratic Loyalty and Embeddedness in Kenya*. Cambridge University Press.

Hazelton, Jacqueline L. 2017. "The 'Hearts and Minds' fallacy: Violence, Coercion, and Success in Counterinsurgency Warfare." *International Security* 42(1):80–113.

Hazen, Jennifer M. 2013. *What Rebels Want: Resources and Supply Networks in Wartime*. Cornell University Press.

Heitz, Kathrin. 2009. "Power-Sharing in the Local Arena: Man—A Rebel-Held Town in Western Côte d'Ivoire." *Africa Spectrum* 44(3):109–131.

Hendrix, Cullen S. 2011. "Head for the Hills? Rough Terrain, State Capacity, and Civil War Onset." *Civil Wars* 13(4):345–370.

Henriksen, Thomas H. 1976. "People's War in Angola, Mozambique, and Guinea-Bissau." *Journal of Modern African Studies* 14(3):377–399.

Herbst, Jeffrey. 2000. *States and Power in Africa: Comparative Lessons in Authority and Control*. Princeton University Press.

Heywood, Linda M. 1989. "UNITA and Ethnic Nationalism in Angola." *Journal of Modern African Studies* 27(1):47–66.

Hicken, Allen. 2011. "Clientelism." *Annual Review of Political Science* 14:289–310.

Hoffmann, Kasper. 2015. "Myths Set in Motion: The Moral Economy of Mai Mai Governance." In *Rebel Governance in Civil War*, ed. Ana Arjona, Nelson Kasfir, and Zachariah Mampilly. Cambridge University Press.

Holland, Alisha C., and Brian Palmer-Rubin. 2015. "Beyond the Machine: Clientelist Brokers and Interest Organizations in Latin America." *Comparative Political Studies* 48(9):1186–1223.

Hove, Henjeral. 2001. "Zimbabwe: The Violence of Gokwe". Zimbabwe Standard, December 16, 2001.

298 Bibliography

Howe, Herbert. 1997. "Lessons of Liberia: ECOMOG and Regional Peacekeeping." *International Security* 21(3):145–176.

Huang, Reyko. 2016. *The Wartime Origins of Democratization: Civil War, Rebel Governance, and Political Regimes.* Cambridge University Press.

Hultman, Lisa. 2010. "Keeping Peace or Spurring Violence? Unintended Effects of Peace Operations on Violence Against Civilians." *Civil Wars* 12(1–2):29–46.

Human Rights Watch. 1993. "World Report 1993 – Liberia." Refworld, January 1, 1993. http://www.refworld.org/docid/467fca5ec.html.

Human Rights Watch. 1999. "World Report 1999 – Burundi." https://www.hrw.org/legacy/worldreport99/africa/burundi.html.

Human Rights Watch. 2000. "World Report 2000 – Burundi." https://www.hrw.org/legacy/wr2k/Africa-01.htm.

Human Rights Watch. 2001. "To Protect The People: The Government-Sponsored 'Self-Defense' Program in Burundi." 13(7A).

Human Rights Watch. 2004. How to Fight, How to Kill: "Child Soldiers in Liberia." https://www.hrw.org/report/2004/02/02/how-fight-how-kill/child-soldiers-liberia.

Human Rights Watch. 2009. "Pursuit of Power: Political Violence and Repression in Burundi." Technical Report, Human Rights Watch.

Human Rights Watch. 2011. "Rwanda: Observing the Rules of War?" 13(8).

Human Rights Watch. 2012a. "'A Long Way from Reconciliation' Abusive Military Crackdown in Response to Security Threats in Côte d'Ivoire." Technical Report, Human Rights Watch, November 18, 2012.

Human Rights Watch. 2012b. "Liberia: Ivorian Government Foes Wage, Plot Attacks." Human Rights Watch, June 6, 2012. https://www.hrw.org/news/2012/06/06/liberia-ivorian-government-foes-wage-plot-attacks.

Human Rights Watch. 2019. "We Let Our Children Go Hungry to Pay." Technical Report, Human Rights Watch.

Innes, Michael A. 2005. "Denial-of-Resource Operations and NPFL Radio Dominance in the Liberian Civil War." *Civil Wars* 7(3):288–309.

International Crisis Group. 2000. "Scramble for the Congo: Anatomy of an Ugly War." ICG Africa Report no. 26.

International Crisis Group. 2002. "The Burundi Rebellion and the Ceasefire Negotiations."

International Crisis Group. 2017. "Burundi: The Army in Crisis." Technical Report, 247, International Crisis Group.

Ishiyama, John, and Michael Widmeier. 2013. "Territorial Control, Levels of Violence, and the Electoral Performance of Former Rebel Political Parties After Civil Wars." *Civil Wars* 15(4):531–550.

Jeche, Anna. Interview. 2014. "Capturing Fading National Memory." Interview, National Archives of Zimbabwe, Oral History Department.

Jok, Jok Madut, and Sharon Elaine Hutchinson. 1999. "Sudan's Prolonged Second Civil War and the Militarization of Nuer and Dinka Ethnic Identities." *African Studies Review* 42(2):125–145.

Jones, Will, and Sally Murray. 2018. "Consolidating Peace and Legitimacy in Rwanda." Technical Report. International Growth Center.

Käihkö, Ilmari. 2017. "Liberia Incorporated: Military Contracting, Cohesion, and Inclusion in Charles Taylor's Liberia." *Conflict, Security & Development* 17(1):53–72.

Kalyvas, Stathis. 2015. "Rebel Governance during the Greek Civil War, 1942–1949." In *Rebel Governance in Civil War*, edited by Ana Arjona, Nelson Kasfir, and Zachariah Mampilly. Cambridge University Press.

Kalyvas, Stathis N. 2001. "'New' and 'Old' Civil Wars: A Valid Distinction?" *World Politics* 54(1):99–118.

Kalyvas, Stathis N. 2006. *The Logic of Violence in Civil War*. Cambridge University Press.

Kanyongo, Gibbs Y. 2005. "Zimbabwe's Public Education System Reforms: Successes and Challenges." *International Education Journal* 6(1):65–74.

Kasfir, Nelson. 2005. "Guerrillas and Civilian Participation: The National Resistance Army in Uganda, 1981–86." *Journal of Modern African Studies* 43(2):271–296.

Kasfir, Nelson. 2015. *Rebel Governance–Constructing a Field of Inquiry: Definitions, Scope, Patterns, Order, Causes*. Vol. 2. Cambridge University Press.

Kilian, Michael. 1980. "Zimbabwe's Nationhood: A Miracle of Statecraft." *Chicago Tribune*, April 17, 1980, 1–b2. https://www.proquest.com/historical-newspapers/zimbabwes-nationhood-miracle-statecraft/docview/170162988/se-2?accountid=14496.

King, Elisabeth. 2013. *From Classrooms to Conflict in Rwanda*. Cambridge University Press.

Koter, Dominika. 2013. "King Makers: Local Leaders and Ethnic Politics in Africa." *World Politics* 65(2):187–232.

Kramon, Eric, and Daniel N Posner. 2013. "Who Benefits from Distributive Politics? How the Outcome One Studies Affects the Answer One Gets." *Perspectives on Politics* 11(2):461–474.

Krebs, Ronald R., and Roy Licklider. 2016. "United They Fall: Why the International Community Should Not Promote Military Integration After Civil War." *International Security* 40(3):93–138.

Kreiman, Guillermo, and Juan Masullo. 2020. "Who Shot the Bullets? Exposure to Violence and Attitudes toward Peace: Evidence from the 2016 Colombian Referendum." *Latin American Politics and Society* 62(4):24–49.

Kriger, Norma. 2005. "ZANU (PF) Strategies in General Elections, 1980–2000: Discourse and Coercion." *African Affairs* 104(414):1–34.

Kriger, Norma J. 1991. *Zimbabwe's Guerrilla War: Peasant Voices*. Cambridge University Press.

Kriger, Norma J. 2003. *Guerrilla Veterans in Post-War Zimbabwe: Symbolic and Violent Politics, 1980–1987*. Vol. 105. Cambridge University Press.

Kumar, Krishna. 2001. *Women and Civil War: Impact, Organizations, and Action*. Lynne Rienner Publishers.

Kumar, Krishna, David G. Tardif-Douglin, Carolyn Knapp, Kim Maynard, Peter Manikas, and Annette Sheckler. 1996. *Rebuilding Postwar Rwanda: The Role of the International Community*. Center for Development and Evaluation, US Agency for International Development.

Kwangwari, Christine. 2009. "Formal Politics at the District and Sub District Levels: The Case of Goromonzi." Master's thesis, University of Zimbabwe.

Kwenda, Headman. Interview. 2014. "Capturing Fading National Memory." Interview, National Archives of Zimbabwe, Oral History Department.

Lachapelle, Jean, Steven Levitsky, Lucan A. Way, and Adam E. Casey. 2020. "Social Revolution and Authoritarian Durability." *World Politics* 72(4):557–600.

Lan, David. 1985. *Guns and Rain: Guerillas and Spirit Mediums in Zimbabwe*. Number 38, University of California Press.

Le Van, A. Carl. 2011. "Power Sharing and Inclusive Politics in Africa's Uncertain Democracies." *Governance* 24(1):31–53.

LeBas, Adrienne. 2013. *From Protest to Parties: Party-Building and Democratization in Africa*. Oxford University Press.

Lebovic, James H., and Erik Voeten. 2009. "The Cost of Shame: International Organizations and Foreign Aid in the Punishing of Human Rights Violators." *Journal of Peace Research* 46(1):79–97.

Lee, Melissa M., and Nan Zhang. 2017. "Legibility and the Informational Foundations of State Capacity." *Journal of Politics* 79(1):118–132.

300   Bibliography

Lenneiye, Mungai. 2000. "Testing Community Empowerment Strategies in Zimbabwe: Examples from Nutrition Supplementation, and Water Supply and Sanitation Programmes." *IDS Bulletin* 31(1):21–29.

Levitsky, Steven, and Lucan Way. 2022. *Revolution and Dictatorship: The Violent Origins of Durable Authoritarianism.* Princeton University Press.

Lewis, Janet I. 2020. *How Insurgency Begins: Rebel Group Formation in Uganda and Beyond.* Cambridge University Press.

Lidow, Nicholai. 2010. "Rebel Governance and Civilian Abuse: Comparing Liberia's Rebels Using Satellite Data." APSA Annual Meeting Paper.

Lidow, Nicholai Hart. 2016. *Violent Order: Understanding Rebel Governance through Liberia's Civil War.* Cambridge University Press.

Lijphart, Arend. 1969. "Consociational Democracy." *World Politics* 21(2):207–225.

Lindbeck, Assar, and Jörgen W Weibull. 1987. "Balanced-Budget Redistribution as the Outcome of Political Competition." *Public Choice* 52(3):273–297.

Liu, Shelley X. 2022. "Control, Coercion, and Cooptation: How Rebels Govern after Winning Civil War." *World Politics* 74(1):37–76.

Liu, Shelley X. 2023. "Coercive Legacies: From Rebel Governance to Authoritarian Control." Forthcoming, *Journal of Politics.*

Longman, Timothy Paul. 1998. *Proxy Targets: Civilians in the War in Burundi.* Human Rights Watch.

Lyons, Terrence. 2016. "From Victorious Rebels to Strong Authoritarian Parties: Prospects for Post-War Democratization." *Democratization* 23(6):1026–1041.

Mabhena, Clifford. 2014. "Ethnicity, Development, and the Dynamics of Political Domination in Southern Matabeleland." *Journal of Humanities and Social Science (IOSR-JHSS)* 19(4):137–149.

Magaya, Rodrick. Interview. 2014. "Capturing Fading National Memory." Interview, National Archives of Zimbabwe, Oral History Department.

Magouirk, Justin. 2008. "The Nefarious Helping Hand: Anti-Corruption Campaigns, Social Service Provision, and Terrorism." *Terrorism and Political Violence* 20(3):356–375.

Magure, Booker. 2009. "Civil Society's Quest for Democracy in Zimbabwe: Origins, Barriers, and Prospects, 1900–2008." PhD Thesis, Rhodes University, Grahamstown, Department of Political and International Studies.

Magwizi, Colonel. Interview. 2014. "Capturing Fading National Memory." Interview, National Archives of Zimbabwe.

Mahoney, James. 2000. "Path Dependence in Historical Sociology." *Theory and Society* 29(4):507–548.

Makumbe, John Mw. 1996. *Participatory Development: The Case of Zimbabwe.* University of Zimbabwe.

Malaquias, Assis. 2001. "Diamonds Are a Guerrilla's Best Friend: The Impact of Illicit Wealth on Insurgency Strategy." *Third World Quarterly* 22(3):311–325.

Mamdani, Mahmood. 1988. "Uganda in Transition: Two Years of the NRA/NRM." *Third World Quarterly* 10(3):1155–1181.

Mampilly, Zachariah. 2015. "Performing the Nation-State: Rebel Governance and Symbolic Processes." In *Rebel Governance in Civil War,* ed. Ana Arjona, Nelson Kasfir and Zachariah Mampilly. Cambridge University Press.

Mampilly, Zachariah Cherian. 2011. *Rebel Rulers: Insurgent Governance and Civilian Life During War.* Cornell University Press.

Mampilly, Zachariah, and Megan A. Stewart. 2021. "A Typology of Rebel Political Institutional Arrangements." *Journal of Conflict Resolution* 65(1):15–45.

Bibliography 301

Mann, Michael. 1984. "The Autonomous Power of the State: Its Origins, Mechanisms and Results." *European Journal of Sociology/Archives Européennes de Sociologie* 25(2):185–213.

Manning, Carrie. 2004. "Armed Opposition Groups into Political Parties: Comparing Bosnia, Kosovo, and Mozambique." *Studies in Comparative International Development* 39(1):54–76.

Mansfield, Edward D., and Jack Snyder. 2007. *Electing to Fight: Why Emerging Democracies Go to War*. MIT Press.

Mao, Zedong. 1937. *On Guerrilla Warfare*. University of Illinois Press.

Marimira, Sekuru Naison. Interview. 2014. "Capturing Fading National Memory." Interview, National Archives of Zimbabwe.

Maringira, Godfrey. 2014. "Soldiers in Exile: The Military Habitus and Identities of Former Zimbabwean Soldiers in South Africa." PhD thesis, University of the Western Cape, Department of Anthropology and Sociology.

Martin, Philip. 2020. "Commander–Community Ties after Civil War." *Journal of Peace Research*.

Martin, Philip A., Giulia Piccolino, and Jeremy S Speight. 2021. "Ex-Rebel Authority after Civil War: Theory and Evidence from Côte d'Ivoire." *Comparative Politics* 53(2):209–232.

Mason, David T., Mehmet Gurses, Patrick T. Brandt, and Jason Michael Quinn. 2011. "When Civil Wars Recur: Conditions for Durable Peace After Civil Wars." *International Studies Perspectives* 12(2):171–189.

Masuku, Bertha. Interview. 2014. "Capturing Fading National Memory." Interview, National Archives of Zimbabwe, Oral History Department.

Matanock, Aila M., and Paul Staniland. 2018. "How and Why Armed Groups Participate in Elections." *Perspectives on Politics* 16(3):710–727.

McGregor, Jo Ann. 2017. Containing Violence: Poisoning and Guerilla/Civilian Relations in Memories of Zimbabwe's Liberation War. In *Trauma*. Routledge pp. 131–159.

Mehler, Andreas. 2009. "Peace and Power Sharing in Africa: A Not So Obvious Relationship." *African Affairs* 108(432):453–473.

Mendelson, Sarah Elizabeth. 2005. *Barracks and Nrothels: Peacekeepers and Human Trafficking in the Balkans*. CSIS.

Meng, Anne and Jack Paine. 2022. "Power Sharing and Authoritarian Stability: How Rebel Regimes Solve the Guardianship Dilemma." *American Political Science Review* 116(4):1–18.

Migdal, Joel S. 1988. *Strong Societies and Weak States: State-Society Relations and State Capabilities In The Third World*. Princeton University Press.

Ministry of Education. 1983. "Ministry of Education Report, 1983." National Archives of Zimbabwe.

Ministry of Internal Affairs. n.d. "Protected Sub Offices; Protected Villages; Unprotected Sub Offices; Lists." National Archives of Zimbabwe, REG-P __ INT.

Ministry of Local Government. 2001. Community Development Policy. Technical Report. Republic of Rwanda.

MONUSCO. 2015. "The Foreign Armed Groups." United Nations Peacekeeping. https://monusco.unmissions.org/en/foreign-armed-groups.

Moyo, Christopher. Interview. 2011. "Zenzo Nkobi Photographic Archive, AL3291/B08." Mafela Trust.

MT, A4.3.2. n.d. "Typescript, Including Notes on ZAPU/ZPRA War Memories." Mafela Trust.

Munslow, Barry. 1999. "Angola: The Politics of Unsustainable Development." *Third World Quarterly* 20(3):551–568.

Murambiwa, Austin. Interview. 2014. "Capturing Fading National Memory." Interview, National Archives of Zimbabwe, Oral History Department.

Murdock, George, Suzanne Blier, and Nathan Nunn. 1959. "George Murdock Map of Ethnographic Regions for Africa." *Murdock HRAF*.

302 Bibliography

Murithi, Timothy, and Aquilina Mawadza. 2011. *Zimbabwe in Transition: A View from Within*. Jacana Media.

Mutsinze, Geshem. Interview. 2014. "Capturing Fading National Memory." Interview, National Archives of Zimbabwe.

Mutizwa-Mangiza, N.D. 1992. "Rural Local Government Finance in Zimbabwe: The Case of Gokwe District Council." *Public Administration and Development* 12(1):111–122.

Mwale, Emergency. 2018. "ZANLA Forces Liberate Nembudziya." *The Patriot*, December 6, 2018. https://www.thepatriot.co.zw/old_posts/zanla-forces-liberate-nembudziya/.

Nare, Edward. Interview. 2011. "Zenzo Nkobi Photographic Archive, AL3291/B10." Mafela Trust.

Ndebele, Longman. Interview. 2011. "Zenzo Nkobi Photographic Archive, AL3291/B12." Mafela Trust.

Ndlovu, Thadeus Parks. Interview. 2010. "Zenzo Nkobi Photographic Archive, AL3291/B15." Mafela Trust.

Nelson, Estella. 2000. "Liberia; Taylor Embarks on Reconstruction."

New York Times. 1979. "Muzorewa Says Regime's Forces Began Clashes with Rival's Units. *New York Times*, August 18, 1979." https://www.nytimes.com/1979/08/18/archives/muzorewa-says-regimes-forces-began-clashes-with-rivals-units.html.

Ngwenya, Christopher. 2017. "The Role of Youths in Zimbabwe Liberation Struggle: A Case Study of Bulilima District, 1960–1980." PhD thesis, University of Venda.

Ngwenya, Amos. Interview. 2010. "Zenzo Nkobi Photographic Archive, AL3291/B17." Mafela Trust.

Nhandara, Sr. Irene-Rufaro. 1977. "Wedza: Detention 1977." Jesuit Archives.

Nichter, Simeon. 2008. "Vote Buying or Turnout Buying? Machine Politics and the Secret Ballot." *American Political Science Review* 102(1):19–31.

Nielsen, Richard A. 2013. "Rewarding Human Rights? Selective Aid Sanctions against Repressive States." *International Studies Quarterly* 57(4):791–803.

Nindorera, Willy. 2012. "The CNDD-FDD in Burundi: The Path from Armed to Political Struggle."

Nkiwane, Abraham. Interview. 2010. "Zenzo Nkobi Photographic Archive, AL3291/B20." Mafela Trust.

Nkurunziza, Jean-Baptiste, and Obi Anyadike. 2016. "Briefing: Who's Who in Burundi's Armed Opposition." Accessed January 14, 2018. https://www.refworld.org/docid/5757bbe44.html.

O'Gorman, Eleanor. 2011. *The Front Line Runs through Every Woman: Women & Local Resistance in the Zimbabwean Liberation War*. Boydell & Brewer Ltd.

Olson, Mancur. 1993. "Dictatorship, Democracy, and Development." *American Political Science Review* 87(3):567–576.

Olson, Mancur. 2000. *Power and Prosperity: Outgrowing Communist and Capitalist Dictatorships*. Basic Books.

Orth, Richard. 2001. "Rwanda's Hutu Extremist Genocidal Insurgency: An Eyewitness Perspective." *Small Wars and Insurgencies* 12(1):76–109.

Østby, Gudrun. 2008. "Polarization, Horizontal Inequalities, and Violent Civil Conflict." *Journal of Peace Research* 45(2):143–162.

Paglayan, Agustina S. 2021. "The Non-Democratic Roots of Mass Education: Evidence from 200 Years." *American Political Science Review* 115(1):179–198.

Pearce, Justin. 2012. "Control, Politics, and Identity in the Angolan Civil War." *African Affairs* 111(444):442–465.

Péclard, Didier. 2012. "UNITA and the Moral Economy of Exclusion in Angola, 1966–1977." In *Sure Road? Nationalisms in Angola, Guinea-Bissau, and Mozambique*. Brill.

Peksen, Dursun, Timothy M. Peterson, and A. Cooper Drury. 2014. "Media-Driven Humanitarianism? News Media Coverage of Human Rights Abuses and the Use of Economic Sanctions." *International Studies Quarterly* 58(4):855–866.

The Perspective. 2001. "Taylor, LURD Spar Over Bong and Cape Mount." *The Perspective*, June 8, 2001. https://www.theperspective.org/taylor_lurd.html.

Pierson, Paul. 2000. "Increasing Returns, Path Dependence, and the Study of Politics." *American Political Science Review* 94(2):251–267.

Podder, Sukanya. 2014. "State Building and the Non-state: Debating Key Dilemmas." *Third World Quarterly* 35(9):1615–1635.

Posner, Daniel N. 2004*a*. "Measuring Ethnic Fractionalization in Africa." *American Journal of Political Science* 48(4):849–863.

Posner, Daniel N. 2004*b*. "The Political Salience of cultural Difference: Why Chewas and Tumbukas are Allies in Zambia and Adversaries in Malawi." *American Political Science Review* 98(4):529–545.

Preston, Matthew. 2004. *Ending Civil War: Rhodesia and Lebanon in Perspective*. IB Tauris.

Prime Minister's Office. 1983. *The Fallen Heroes of Zimbabwe*. Jongwe.

Raleigh, Clionadh, Andrew Linke, Håvard Hegre, and Joakim Karlsen. 2010. "Introducing ACLED: An Armed Conflict Location and Event Dataset: Special Data Feature." *Journal of Peace Research* 47(5):651–660.

Ranger, Terence. 1982. "The Death of Chaminuka: Spirit Mediums, Nationalism and the Guerilla War in Zimbabwe." *African Affairs* 81(324):349–369.

Ranger, Terence O. 1985. *Peasant Consciousness and Guerilla War in Zimbabwe: A Comparative Study*. Vol. 37. University of California Press.

Reed, William Cyrus. 1993. "International Politics and National Liberation: ZANU and the Politics of Contested Sovereignty In Zimbabwe 1." *African Studies Review* 36(2):31–59.

Reed, Wm Cyrus. 1996. "Exile, Reform, and the Rise of the Rwandan Patriotic Front." *Journal of Modern African Studies* 34(3):479–501.

Reno, William. 1999. *Warlord Politics and African States*. Lynne Rienner Publishers.

Republic of Côte d'Ivoire. 2012. "National Development Plan 2012–2015." International Monetary Fund, June 2013. https://www.imf.org/external/pubs/ft/scr/2013/cr13172.pdf.

Republic of Côte d'Ivoire. 2015. "National Development Plan 2016–2020." International Monetary Fund, December 2016. https://www.imf.org/external/pubs/ft/scr/2016/cr16388.pdf.

Revkin, Mara Redlich. 2021. "Competitive Governance and Displacement decisions under Rebel Rule: Evidence from the Islamic State in Iraq." *Journal of Conflict Resolution* 65(1):46–80.

Reyntjens, Filip. 2004. "Rwanda, Ten Years On: From Genocide ro Dictatorship." *African Affairs* 103(411):177–210.

Rich, Tony. 1982. "Legacies of the Past? The Results of the 1980 Election in Midlands Province, Zimbabwe." *Africa* 52(3):42–55.

Rincon, Jairo Munive. 2010. *Ex-Combatants, Returnees, Land, and Conflict in Liberia*. Number 2010: 05 DIIS Working Paper.

Roeder, Philip G., and Donald S. Rothchild. 2005. *Sustainable Peace: Power and Democracy after Civil Wars*. Cornell University Press.

Rohner, Dominic, Mathias Thoenig, and Fabrizio Zilibotti. 2013. "Seeds of Distrust: Conflict in Uganda." *Journal of Economic Growth* 18(3):217–252.

Ross, Jay. 1980. "Zimbabwe Gains Independence: Thousands Cheer as Rhodesia Becomes a Free Zimbabwe; War-Torn Rhodesia Reborn as Independent Zimbabwe." *Washington Post*, April 18, 1980, 3. https://www.washingtonpost.com/archive/politics/1980/04/18/zimbabwe-gains-independence/185c3573-e9e4-4d3a-9dce-5fe89bf04605/

304 Bibliography

Ross, Michael L. 1999. "The Political Economy of The Resource Curse." *World Politics* 51(2):297–322.

Rueda, Miguel R. 2017. "Popular Support, Violence, and Territorial Control in Civil War." *Journal of Conflict Resolution* 61(8):1626–1652.

Rupiya, Martin R. 2005. "An Examination of the Role of the National Youth Service/Militia in Zimbabwe and its Effect on the Electoral Process, 2001-2005." *Journal of African Elections* 4(2):107–122.

Sabates-Wheeler, Rachel, and Philip Verwimp. 2014. "Extortion with Protection: Understanding the Effect of Rebel Taxation on Civilian Welfare in Burundi." *Journal of Conflict Resolution* 58(8):1474–1499.

Sadomba, Frederick, and Tom Tom. 2013. "The Role and Functions of the Para-Military in Civil Military Relations in Zimbabwe 1980-1987." *Sacha Journal of Policy and Strategic Studies* 3(1):1–11.

Sadomba, Zvakanyorwa Wilbert. 2011. *War Veterans in Zimbabwe's Revolution: Challenging Neo-Colonialism & Settler & International Capital.* Boydell & Brewer Ltd.

Sanchez de la Sierra, Raul. 2017. "On the Origin of the State: Stationary Bandits and Taxation in Eastern Congo." *Journal of Political Economy* 128(1):32–74.

Sanín, Francisco Gutiérrez, and Elisabeth Jean Wood. 2014. "Ideology in Civil War: Instrumental Adoption and Beyond." *Journal of Peace Research* 51(2):213–226.

Saruchera, Munyaradzi, and Oscar Matsungo. 2003. "Understanding Local Perspectives: Participation of Resource Poor Farmers in Biotechnology—The Case of Wedza District of Zimbabwe." Background Paper, Brighton: Institute of Development Studies, University of Sussex.

Schenoni, Luis L. 2021. "Bringing War Back In: Victory and State Formation in Latin America." *American Journal of Political Science* 65(2):405–421.

Schiel, Rebecca, Christopher Faulkner, and Jonathan Powell. 2017. "Mutiny in Côte d'Ivoire." *Africa Spectrum* 52(2):103–115.

Scott, James C. 1999. *Seeing Like a State: How Certain Schemes to Improve the Human Condition Have Failed.* Yale University Press.

Scott, James C. 2008. *Domination and the Arts of Resistance.* Yale University Press.

Scott, James C. 2009. *The Art of Not Being Governed: An Anarchist History of Upland Southeast Asia.* Nus Press.

Sculier, Caroline. 2003. *Everyday Victims: Civilians in the Burundian War.* Vol. 15, Human Rights Watch.

Shumba, Simoni Mazarire. Interview. 1992. "OH/451." Interview, National Archives of Zimbabwe, Masvingo Records Centre.

Sibanda, Eliakim M. 2005. *The Zimbabwe African People's Union, 1961-87: A Political History of Insurgency in Southern Rhodesia.* Africa World Press.

Silveira House. 1982. "Silveira House, Center for Leadership Training and Development, Annual Report, 1982." Jesuit Archives.

Sindre, Gyda Marås. 2016. "Internal Party Democracy in Former Rebel Parties." *Party Politics* 22(4):501–511.

Soifer, Hillel. 2008. "State Infrastructural Power: Approaches to Conceptualization and Measurement." *Studies in Comparative International Development* 43(3–4):231.

Soifer, Hillel David. 2015. *State Building in Latin America.* Cambridge University Press.

Spruyt, Hendrik. 1996. *The Sovereign State and Its Competitors: An Analysis of Systems Change.* Princeton University Press.

St. Paul's Mission. n.d. "St. Paul's Mission, Musami, Mrewa, Salisbury Archdiocese, Takawira Sector." Jesuit Archives, 506/2.

Star Radio. 1999. "Liberian Daily News Bulletin."

Star Radio. 2000a. "Liberian Daily News Bulletin."

Bibliography   305

Star Radio. 2000*b*. "Liberian Daily News Bulletin."

Star Radio. 2000*c*. "Liberian Daily News Bulletin."

Stenberg, Arild. 2005. Burundi Parliamentary Election July 2005. Technical Report, Norwegian Centre for Human Rights (NORDEM), University of Oslo.

Stevens, Christopher. 1976. "The Soviet Union and Angola." *African Affairs* 75(299):137–151.

Stewart, Megan A. 2018. "Civil war As State-Making: Strategic Governance in Civil War." *International Organization* 72(1):205–226.

Stewart, Megan A. 2021. *Governing for Revolution: Social Transformation in Civil War.* Cambridge University Press.

Stokes, Susan C., Thad Dunning, Marcelo Nazareno, and Valeria Brusco. 2013. *Brokers, Voters, and Clientelism: The Puzzle of Distributive Politics.* Cambridge University Press.

Straus, Scott. 2011. ' "It's Sheer Horror Here': Patterns of Violence during the First Four Months of Côte D'Ivoire's Post-Electoral Crisis." *African Affairs* 110(440):481–489.

Straus, Scott. 2013. *The Order of Genocide.* Cornell University Press.

Straus, Scott. 2019. "The Limits of a Genocide Lens: Violence against Rwandans in the 1990s." *Journal of Genocide Research* 21: 1–21.

Sturm, Nora. 2013. "Two Years after Civil War's End, Côte d'Ivoire Is Still Unstable." The Atlantic, July 30, 2013. https://www.theatlantic.com/international/archive/2013/07/two-years-after-civil-wars-end-c-te-divoire-is-still-unstable/278210/.

Suykens, Bert. 2015. "Comparing Rebel Rule through Revolution and Naturalization: Ideologies of Governance in Naxalite and Naga India." In *Rebel Governance in Civil War*, ed. Ana Arjona, Nelson Kasfir, and Zachariah Mampilly. Cambridge University Press.

Takeuchi, Shinichi. 2019. "Development and Developmentalism in Post-Genocide Rwanda." In *Developmental State Building.* Springer.

Tapscott, Rebecca. 2021. *Arbitrary States: Social Control and Modern Authoritarianism in Museveni's Uganda.* Oxford University Press.

Taruvinga, George Winston. Interview. 2014. "Capturing Fading National Memory." Interview, National Archives of Zimbabwe, Oral History Department.

Taydas, Zeynep, and Dursun Peksen. 2012. "Can States Buy Peace? Social Welfare Spending and Civil Conflicts." *Journal of Peace Research* 49(2):273–287.

Thachil, Tariq. 2014. "Elite Parties and Poor Voters: Theory and Evidence from India." *American Political Science Review* 108(2):454–477.

Thaler, Kai M. 2012. "Ideology and Violence in Civil Wars: Theory and Evidence from Mozambique and Angola." *Civil Wars* 14(4):546–567.

Thaler, Kai M. 2018. "From Insurgent to Incumbent: State Building and Service Provision After Rebel Victory in Civil Wars." Dissertation, Harvard University.

Theunynck, Serge, and Hervé Rabakoson. 2017. "School Construction for Basic Education." World Bank, May 2017. https://documents1.worldbank.org/curated/ar/751581498759557305/pdf/P161127-06-29-2017-1498759550576.pdf

Think Africa Press. 2013. "Liberia's Stockholm Syndrome: Why Bong County Still Loves Charles Taylor."

Tilly, Charles. 1978. From Mobilization to Revolution. In *Collective Violence, Contentious Politics, and Social Change.* Routledge.

Tilly, Charles. 1985. "War Making and State Making as Organized Crime." In Bringing the State Back In, ed. Peter Evans, Dietrich Rueschemeyer, and Theda Skocpol. Cambridge University Press.

Tilly, Charles. 1992. *Coercion, Capital, and European States, AD 990-1992.* Blackwell Oxford.

Toft, Monica Duffy. 2010. "Ending Civil Wars: A Case for Rebel Victory?" *International Security* 34(4):7–36.

Tubiana, Jérôme, and Marielle Debos. 2017. "Déby's Chad: Political Manipulation at Home, Military Intervention Abroad, Challenging Times Ahead." https://www.usip.org/

306 Bibliography

sites/default/files/2017-12/pw136-debys-chad-political-manipulation-at-home-military-intervention-abroad-challenging-times-ahead.pdf.

UN Geospatial Information Section. 2008. "Angola." https://www.un.org/geospatial/sites/www.un.org.geospatial/files/files/documents/2020/May/angola_3727_r3_jan04.pdf.

UN Geospatial Information Section. 2011. "Cote d'Ivoire." https://digitallibrary.un.org/record/720531?ln=en.

UN Geospatial Information Section. 2018. "Rwanda." https://www.un.org/geospatial/content/rwanda.

UN Geospatial Information Section. 2019. "Burundi." https://digitallibrary.un.org/record/3849415?ln=en.

US Department of State. 1995. "Liberia Human Rights Report, 1994." http://dosfan.lib.uic.edu/ERC/democracy/1994_hrp_report/94hrp_report_africa/Liberia.html.

US Department of State. 1999. "Liberia Country Report on Human Rights Practices for 1998." Accessed June 19, 2018. https://www1.essex.ac.uk/armedcon/story_id/Liberia%20Country%20Report%20on%20Human%20Rights%20Practices%20for%201998%20.pdf.

US Department of State. 2000. "Liberia." Accessed June 19, 2018. https://www.state.gov/j/drl/rls/hrrpt/1999/254.htm.

US Department of State. 2001. "Liberia." Accessed June 19, 2018. https://www.state.gov/j/drl/rls/hrrpt/2000/af/845.htm.

Utas, Mats. 2003. "Sweet Battlefields: Youth and the Liberian Civil War." PhD thesis, Uppsala University.

Valentino, Benjamin, Paul Huth, and Dylan Balch-Lindsay. 2004. "'Draining the Sea': Mass Killing and Guerrilla Warfare." *International Organization* 58(2):375–407.

Van Acker, Tomas. 2015. "Understanding Burundi's Predicament." *Africa Policy Briefs*.

Van Acker, Tomas. 2016. "Exploring the Legacies of Armed Rebellion in Burundi's Maquis par Excellence." *Africa Spectrum* 51(2):15–37.

Vines, Alex. 1999. "Angola Unravels: The Rise and Fall of the Lusaka Peace Process." Human Rights Watch.

Von Walter Fr. L. SJ. n.d. "Just a Pawn in Their War Games?" Jesuit Archives, Box 535.

Walter, Barbara F. 1997. "The Critical Barrier to Civil War Settlement." *International Organization* 51(3):335–364.

Walter, Barbara F. 2002. *Committing to Peace: The Successful Settlement of Civil Wars*. Princeton University Press.

Walter, Barbara F. 2004. "Does Conflict Beget Conflict? Explaining Recurring Civil War." *Journal of Peace Research* 41(3):371–388.

Walter, Barbara F. 2022. *How Civil Wars Start: And How to Stop Them*. Crown Publishing Group.

Weber, Max. 1946. "Politics as a Vocation." In *From Max Weber: Essays in Sociology*, ed. H.H. Gerth and C. Wright Mills. Oxford University Press.

Weinstein, Jeremy M. 2006. *Inside Rebellion: The Politics of Insurgent Violence*. Cambridge University Press.

Wikham Crowley, Timothy. 2015. "Del Gobierno de Abajo al Gobierno de Arriba . . . and Back: Transitions to and from Rebel Governance in Latin America, 1956–1990." In *Rebel Governance in Civil War*, ed. Ana Arjona, Nelson Kasfir, and Zachariah Mampilly. Cambridge University Press.

Wittig, Katrin. 2016. "Politics in the Shadow of the Gun: Revisiting the Literature on 'Rebel-to-Party Transformations' through the Case of Burundi." *Civil Wars* 18(2):137–159.

Woo, Byungwon, and Amanda Murdie. 2017. "International Organizations and Naming and Shaming: Does the International Monetary Fund Care about the Human Rights Reputation of Its Client?" *Political Studies* 65(4):767–785.

Wood, Elisabeth Jean. 2003. *Insurgent Collective Action and Civil War in El Salvador*. Cambridge University Press.

Wood, Reed M., Jacob D. Kathman, and Stephen E. Gent. 2012. "Armed Intervention and Civilian Victimization in Intrastate Conflicts." *Journal of Peace Research* 49(5):647–660.

World Bank. 2019. "Côte d'Ivoire Economic Outlook: Understanding the Challenges of Urbanization in Height Charts." https://www.worldbank.org/en/country/cotedivoire/publication/cote-divoire-economic-outlook-understanding-the-challenges-of-urbanization-in-height-charts.

Young, Tom. 1988. "The Politics of Development in Angola and Mozambique." *African Affairs* 87(347):165–184.

Young, Tom. 1990. "The MNR/RENAMO: External and Internal Dynamics." *African Affairs* 89(357):491–509.

Zaks, Sheryl. 2017. "Resilience beyond Rebellion: How Wartime Organizational Structures Affect Rebel-to-Party Transformation." PhD thesis, UC Berkeley.

Zhukov, Yuri M. 2023. "Repression Works (Just Not in Moderation)." *Comparative Political Studies*.

Zimbabwe Catholic Bishop's Conference. 1982. "Memorandum: Education in Zimbabwe Government Policy." Jesuit Archives, 430/2.

Index

Note: Tables and figures are indicated by a "*t*" and "*f*", respectively, following the page number.

adaptation 255–56
Africa 11. See also *specific countries*
African National Congress 6
African Party for the Independence of
    Guinea and Cape Verde 11, 15n6
African politics literature 254
African Union 80
Alexander, Jocelyn 114, 116,
    118–19, 274
Americo-Liberians 80, 83
Anatomy of Terror (pamphlet) 100
Angola
    Côte d'Ivoire and 24, 203, 253
    Democratic Republic of Congo
        and 214–15
    Frente Nacional de Libertação de Angola
        in 211–15, 217
    independence in 21, 210–19
    Mozambique 76
    MPLA 12, 16t, 201, 205, 207, 210–19,
        247–48
    People's Movement for the Liberation of
        Angola 201
    rebel victors in 256
    UNITA 7–8, 12, 211–19
    Zimbabwe and 205, 206t, 207
Armed Forces of Liberia 168
Armée pour la Libération du
    Rwanda 245–47
armies. *See* military
authoritarianism 5, 62, 86

Banda, Hastings 78
Bédié, Henri Konan 220–21
Beitbridge district 274–75
birth registration laws 121–22, 122n19
Boley, George 136
Botswana 91, 118–19, 272–73
breadth 66–67, 197
budget constraints 42
Bulilima-Mangwe district 272–73

bureaucrats
    budget constraints to 42
    bureaucratic development
        committees 256
    chiefs and 168
    civilians and 40, 115–16, 144–45, 190
    in contested unsecured
        terrain/areas 114–15
    legitimacy to 8–9
    local government promotional officers
        and 113–15
    loyal 116–17
    monopolies to 30
    to NPFL 175
    politics of 6, 8–9
    power of 252
    rebel governance and 69, 126
    in Rwanda 6
    state-building to 243–44
    strategies and 60, 112–13
Burundi
    civil wars in 229–39, 257n2
    Front pour la Démocratie au Burundi 234
    history of 21
    Résistance pour un État de Droit au
        Burundi 237
    Rwanda and 24, 203, 208–10, 229, 253
    youth in 232
    Zimbabwe and 11n4, 16

Cambodia 5
campesinos 43
Catholic Commission for Justice and
    Peace 108, 119–20, 270–71
Catholicism 93
Chad 15n5
chiefs
    in aid organizations 139–40
    appointment of 164–65, 164f, 196–97,
        196t
    bureaucrats and 168

310 Index

chiefs *(cont.)*
  chieftaincy records 105, 107
  clan 161–62
  in contested unsecured
    terrain/areas 193–94
  cooperation of 169–70
  ex-combatants and 98
  in Liberia 144–45, 281*t*, 284*t*
  NPFL to 143
  politics of 58–59
  power of 161
  rebel brutality to 152
  in rebel governance 171–72
  rebel victors to 16n8, 58–59
  replacement of 164–66, 165*t*, 166*t*, 284*t*
  in Rhodesia 97
  rivals of 163
  single-barrel men and 144, 173
  turnover rates of 108
  in Zimbabwe 145
chimbwidos 95–96, 102
China 16, 79, 211
Chiweshe Tribal Trust Land 100
citizens. *See* civilians
civilians. *See also* rebel-civilian ties
  bureaucrats and 40, 115–16, 144–45, 190
  civil-military relations 33–35, 205
  community of 96–97, 100
  in contested unsecured
    terrain/areas 223–24
  counter-rebellions by 57, 64
  displacement of 150–51, 151n12
  elections to 4
  ethnicity of 140
  guerrilla warfare to 42–43
  in Guinea Bissau 154
  influence over 54
  interviews with 269–75
  leadership of 116
  in Local Defense Forces 246
  local politics to 94
  market women as 153–54
  mass civilian displacement 151n12
  military and 61–62, 95
  mobilization of 112
  NPFL and 141n2, 171n25, 186, 187, 189
  participation of 260–61
  peace to 32
  political incentives for 265
  politics of 260

  post-war governance for 46–47
  post-war politics to 133–34
  pungwes for 94–99, 101–2, 109, 113, 119,
    131–32
  punishment of 49
  rebel governance of 66–67, 85, 87, 181–82
  rebel group presence to 52–54
  rebel victors and 65*f*, 187–90
  resentment from 102–3
  rivals and 32–33, 63, 157
  rural 14n16, 114–16, 146n8
  scholarship on 188n1
  social control of 45, 48, 69, 252–53
  strategies and 7–8
  in strongholds 175
  support of 29
  Taylor, C., and 139–40, 169–70, 176–77
  in violence 9–10, 12–13, 118–19, 119*f*,
    163–64
  as volunteers 125–26
  ZAPU and 119–20
  in Zimbabwe 86
civil society 263–64
civil wars. *See also specific topics*
  aftermath of 29–30, 34, 41–42
  in Burundi 229–39, 257n2
  in Cambodia 5
  in Cold War 15–16
  communication in 153–54
  consolidated power after 38–39, 38*f*,
    70–71, 71*f*
  in Côte d'Ivoire, 55–56, 219–29
  counter-rebellions after 70
  data on 139
  displacement in 150n9
  external comparisons of 206*t*
  institutions after 9–10, 11n4
  intra-state war 49
  leadership and 82–83
  legacy of 22
  military in 88, 89*f*, 90–92
  post-war governance after 45–46
  rebel governance after 23–24
  rebel groups in 151n10
  rebel victors after 10–12, 69
  recruitment in 171n25
  in Rwanda 21, 239–47
  scholarship on 251–54
  social control and 43–44, 160n20
  state institutions after 37–38

stronghelds in 172–73
violence in 68–69, 68f, 156n15
in Zimbabwe 4–5
clan chiefs 161–62
CNDD-FDD. *See* Conseil National Pour la
Défense de la Démocratie–Forces pour
la Défense de la Démocratie
coercion
coercive political control 261
post-war coercive capability 275t
rebel-civilian ties and 101–3
rebel governance with 51
rival 61
strategies with 62–63
as violence 14, 50
violence and 14, 50, 64, 94, 116–20,
119f, 132
in Zimbabwe 58
co-ethnic ties 123–24
Cold War 15–16, 28, 79–80, 79n2, 84
Colombia 32, 52–53
colonialism
education after 4, 111–12
elections in 90
Great Britain in 3, 75
hierarchies in 103
power in 97
reform after 128–29
in Southern Rhodesia 77–78
violence and 11
Community Development Committees 244
comzones 224–25, 227–29
conflict intensity 257
conflict recurrence 64, 67–68
conflict scholarship 27–29, 80, 81f, 82–83
conflict termination 255–58
Congo. *See* Democratic Republic of Congo
Conseil National Pour la Défense de la
Démocratie–Forces pour la Défense de
la Démocratie (CNDD-FDD)
influence of 230–40
scholarship on 209, 229–30, 247–48
consolidated power
after civil wars 38–39, 38f, 70–71, 71f
long-run 226–28
peaceful 251–52
politics of 27
post-war 44, 174–75, 186, 202, 209,
253–55
in rebel governance 59

to rebel victors 56–57, 67, 197–98, 199t,
200–202
scholarship on 20–21, 38–40, 38f, 71,
267–68
social control and 190
state-building and 63–64, 65f, 66–68, 258
strategies for 39–40, 54–57, 55t
after violence 69–70
wars for 214–15
ZANU with 186
consolidation
conflict 68f, 70
wars 70, 134, 186, 200–202, 210, 214–15,
218, 246–47, 251–52, 256–58
Conté, Lansana 84
contested unsecured terrain/areas
bureaucrats in 114–15
chiefs in 193–94
civilians in 223–24
control of 198, 199t, 200
education in 128–29
military in 101–3, 180, 240–42
partisans and 56, 60, 103–4, 159f, 166t,
178–79, 193, 195t
policy in 98–99, 127
politics of 65f
public goods provision in 275t
rebel control in 103, 211–14, 221–24,
230–33
rebel governance in 61
to rebel victors 33, 47–48, 64, 66
rivals in 190–91
scholarship on 12, 56–59, 62–66, 103,
104, 125, 273–75, 285f, 286f
social control in 54–55
spatial representation of 156–60, 159f
typology of 156
violence in 136–37, 232–33
ZANU and 129–30, 130t
in Zimbabwe 273–75
cooperation
co-optation and 8–9, 14, 19–20, 36–37,
61, 66–67, 76, 86, 168–69, 185, 251–52,
259, 264
with institutions 49–50
military 51
Côte d'Ivoire
Angola and 24, 203, 253
civil wars in 55–56, 219–29
Guinea Bissau and 83, 181

312 Index

Côte d'Ivoire *(cont.)*
  Liberia and 138, 176, 207–8
  Rwanda and 21
  Zimbabwe and 220
counterinsurgency 100
counter-rebellions
  by civilians 57, 64
  after civil wars 70
  consolidation conflict and 68f
  psychology of 61–62
  to rebel victors 33–34
  recruitment in 239
  scholarship on 28–29
  in strongholds 63
cross national politics 75, 85–87, 203

Déby Idriss 201–2
democracy 30–31, 262–63, 265
Democratic Republic of Congo
  Angola and 214–15
  Guinea Bissau and 15
  history of 243, 245–47
  influence in 47–48, 262
  politics in 15n6, 230, 233
  reputation of 239–40
depth 66–67, 197
despotic power 46
development
  bureaucratic development
    committees 256
  Community Development
    Committees 244
  democracy and 265
  development committees 114n16
  economic 259–60
  education development
    initiatives 125–26
  grassroots-based development
    structures 113n13
  hierarchies in 113–14
  laissez-faire development policy 244
  in Liberia 176–81, 178t
  local 110–11, 235–36
  long-term 258–59
  political 260–62
  post-war 177–78, 224–25
  by rebel governance 174–75
  reconstruction and 236
  security and 26
  security-development trade-offs 20–21,
    24, 66–67, 134, 174–82, 185–90, 219

  state-led 216–17
  in strongholds 115–16
  village development committees 113–16
  violence and 214–18, 224–28, 233–38,
    242–46
differences-in-differences (DiD) 121–22,
  124–25, 177, 179–81
direct military interference 263
disabilities 180–81, 275t, 288t
displacement
  of civilians 150–51, 151n12
  mass civilian 151n12
  by NPFL 170–71
  of rebel-civilian ties 152–54
  scholarship on 150n9, 151n11
  violence and 165–67
distributive politics 5–6
district administrators 113, 113n15
districts. See *specific districts*
Doe, Samuel Kanyon 82–84
Dozo hunters 207, 223–24, 226, 229

economics
  Economic Community of West African
    States Monitoring Group 136–38, 147,
    149–51, 155n13, 160
  economic development 259–60
  Economist Intelligence Unit Democracy
    Index 262
  grant budgets 115
  oil profits 217–18
  politics and 169
  of security 42–43, 174–76, 189
  of security spending 132
education
  after colonialism 4, 111–12
  in contested unsecured
    terrain/areas 128–29
  development initiatives 125–26
  in Liberia 177–78, 282t
  literacy and 178–81, 179t
  in military 50
  parallel trends in 128f
  political 53–54
  religion and 282t
  secondary schooling 127
  in strongholds 127, 179–80
  in sub-national politics 277t, 278t, 279t,
    280t, 284, 285f, 286f, 287, 287t, 288t,
    289t
  teachers 232

from war 117–18
elections. *See also* voting
  to civilians 4
  in colonialism 90
  electioneering 120
  ethnicity in 110
  main parties in 110*t*
  Movement for Democratic Change
    in 123n20
  NPFL in 133
  special 168
  Taylor, C., in 138, 163–64, 167, 173
  territorial control with 185
  village committees in 112
elite politics 33–35
El Salvador 43
Ethiopia 11n4
ethnicity. *See also specific ethnicities*
  of civilians 140
  co-ethnic ties 123–24
  in elections 110
  ethnic tensions 80, 81*f*, 82–83
  ethnic violence 224
  intra-ethnic cooperation 131
  in Liberia 47–48, 80, 81*f*, 82
  loyalty to 40
  to NPFL 20
  partisans and 179–80
  partisan ties to 28
  in politics 77–78
  to rebel governance 45
  to rebel victors 28
  religion and 59, 281*t*, 283*t*
  research on 92–93
  in Sudan 198, 200
  violence against 21
Europe 148
ex-combatants
  chiefs and 98
  peace to 145–46
  scholarship and 41, 112, 116, 270
  single-barrel men to 153
  with social desirability bias 142n3
  threats to 236–37
exploitation 59, 118
external comparisons 204–5, 206*t*, 247–48,
  253–54
extrajudicial killings 170

The Fallen Heroes of Zimbabwe 105
Fayulu, Martin 15n6

Forces Armées Rwandaises 239–40,
  243–45
Forces Démocratiques de Libération du
  Rwanda 245
Forces Nouvelles 207, 221–28, 247
France 222
Freedom House 262
Frente Nacional de Libertação de
  Angola 211–15, 217
Front pour la Démocratie au Burundi
  234

Gaddafi, Muammar 19–20
Gbagbo, Laurent 207, 221–29
genocide 229–30, 240–42, 244
Ghana 79, 83–84, 225–26
Gio ethnic group 82–83, 85
Gokwe district 118, 273–74
governance. *See specific topics*
governing capacity 29–31, 197
government victories 256–58
grant budgets 115
grassroots-based development
  structures 113n13
grassroots penetration
  262–63
Great Britain 3, 75, 77–78
Green, Elliott D. 49
grievances 64
guerrilla warfare
  to civilians 42–43
  politics in 95
  rebel governance and 111
  strategies in 68–69, 101–2
  in strongholds 272–73
  surveillance in 170
  violence of 17–18
Guinea Bissau
  civilians in 154
  Côte d'Ivoire and 83, 181
  Democratic Republic of Congo and
    15
  Namibia and 11n3
  Sierra Leone and 175–76
Gukurahundi 89*f*, 91, 119–20, 119*f*, 129,
  132, 226
Gwaai River Mine 117

Habyarimana, Juvenal 240–42,
  246–47
Harvest of Fear (pamphlet) 100

314 Index

heterogeneity 85–87
Houphouët-Boigny, Félix 84
human rights 62–63
Hutu ethnic group. *See* Rwanda

identity-based support 103–4
ideological partisans 45
Imbonerakure 43, 232, 234, 236–39
independence
  in Africa 11
  in Angola 21, 210–19
  campaigns for 109
  policy before 120–21
  rivals and 258
  wars for 214–15
  Zimbabwe after 3–4, 78
Independent National Patriotic Front of
    Liberia 136, 155
indiscriminate violence 152
Indonesia 43
ineffectual presence 55–56
influence
  over civilians 54
  in Democratic Republic of Congo
    47–48, 262
  of grievances 64
  of military presence 47
  presence and 47, 52, 104
  rebel 51
  of rivals 158
  social control and 53
infrastructural power 46
innovation 256
Inong Balee 43
instability 16–17, 101–3, 167–69
institutions
  after civil wars 9–10, 11n4
  cooperation with 49–50
  in Liberia 21
  politics of 24–25
  pre-war 29–31
  rebel 42, 60–61, 75, 234
  state 37–38
  wartime 44–45, 59, 67–68, 112–16
insurgencies. See *specific topics*
Integrated Public Use Microdata
    Series 126–27
intelligence. *See* reconnaissance
Interahamwe youth wing 239, 241n13, 242,
    245, 247

internal conquests
  post-war 8–10, 13
  scholarship on 18–20, 36, 66, 70, 75
  war and 185–86, 201–2, 252
internal security 225–26
interstate wars 256–57
intra-ethnic cooperation 131
intra-state war 49
Ivorian Civil War. *See* Côte d'Ivoire

Jesuit Archives 92–93, 94, 107
Johnson, Roosevelt 136, 168

Kabila, Joseph 15n6
Kagame, Paul 6, 239–40
Kaunda, Kenneth 77–78
Khmer Rouge 5
Krahm ethnic group 82–83
Kromah, Alhaji 168
Kwa ethnic group 80

laissez-faire development policy 244
Lancaster House Agreement 90
land reform programs 111
Latin America 6n1, 28
legibility 9, 13, 37
legitimacy 8–9, 13–14, 37, 47–49, 251–52
Leninism. *See* Marxism
liberation songs 119
Liberia
  Armed Forces of Liberia 168
  chiefs in 144–45, 281t, 284t
  consolidation in 138–39
  Côte d'Ivoire and 138, 176, 207–8
  development in 176–81, 178t
  education in 177–78, 282t
  Ethiopia and 11n4
  ethnicity in 47–48, 80, 81f, 82
  France and 222
  history of 6, 10–11, 84, 132, 134, 135f,
    136–38, 137f (See also *specific topics*)
  Independent National Patriotic Front of
    Liberia 136, 155
  institutions in 21
  interventions in 263
  Liberians United for Reconciliation and
    Democracy 138–39, 170–73, 175–76,
    181, 188–96, 191n3, 192f, 201
  Liberia Peace Council 136–39, 141n2,
    149–50, 154, 158–60, 163n22, 168

market women in 153–54
Movement for Democracy in
    Liberia 138–39, 170, 176, 181–82, 188,
    191–96, 192*f*
post-war security in 283*t*
qualitative evidence from 139–40
quantitative evidence from 140–41
rebel-civilian ties in 141–43, 149–51,
    181–82
rebel victors in 186
security-development trade-offs
    in 174–76
single-barrel men in 145–47
social control in 33
sub-Saharan Africa and 185–86
Taylor, C., for 133
Tubman for 80, 82
United Nations Mission in Liberia
    140, 162
violence in 152–53
Zimbabwe and 19–25, 43, 71, 75–76, 85,
    87, 171, 185, 202–3, 228, 253
Liberia Civil War. See *specific topics*
literacy 178–81, 179*t*, 282*t*, 284, 287*t*, 289*t*
Local Defense Forces 246
local development 110–11, 235–36
local governance 110–12, 115
local government promotional
    officers 113–15, 113n15
local legitimacy 47, 251–52
local politics 64, 94, 254, 264
local security 95–96
local strongholds 99
long-run consolidated power 226–28
long-term development 258–59
looting 51, 108, 191n3, 233, 270
low-violence consolidation conflict 68*f*
Lupane district 272

Machel, Samora 16
MacMillan, Harold 79–80
Mafela Trust 92–94, 105
Makoni district 271–72
Malawi 76, 78
male youth 172
Mamdani, Mahmood 67–68
Mande ethnic group 80, 223
Mandingo ethnic group 82–83
Manicaland 110*t*, 271–72
Mano ethnic group 82–83, 85

Maoism 77
market women 153–54
Marxism 3, 19, 28, 57n10, 59, 216
Marymount Mission 107–8
Mashonaland 100, 110, 110*t*, 114, 270–71
mass violence 86, 132, 149–50
Masvingo 110*t*
Matabeleland
    exploitation of 118
    history of 116–17, 118–19, 119*f*
    Mashonaland and 110, 114
    Mozambique and 117
    scholarship on 91–94, 272–73, 274–75
    strategies in 119–20
    voting in 110*t*
Mel ethnic group 80
Midlands 110, 110*t*, 114, 273–74
military
    capacity 197
    civilians and 61–62, 95
    civil-military relations 33–35, 205
    in civil wars 88, 89*f*, 90–92
    collaborators 98–99
    in Colombia 52–53
    contestation 52
    in contested unsecured
        terrain/areas 101–3, 180, 240–42
    cooperation with 51
    desertion 91
    direct military interference 263
    education in 50
    juntas 82
    militias and 174, 273–74
    politics 92–94, 198
    presence 8, 47, 157n16
    psychology 40–41
    qualitative evidence of 75–76
    rebel 141–42
    rebel governance and 54, 191–92
    recruitment 98
    Rhodesia 93, 95–96, 101–2
    rival terrain to 32–33
    spending 42
    strength 31–33
    strongholds 104
    taxes for 148
    training 79
    variability 94
    victories 11–12, 11n4
    violence 35, 71, 118

316 Index

military *(cont.)*
  youth population to 18, 40, 118–19, 122,
    188, 233–34, 236, 238–39, 242, 247,
    261, 273
  in Zambia 88, 90
  ZANU and 77
military presence 47, 157n16
MLPA. *See* People's Movement for the
  Liberation of Angola
Monrovia. See *specific topics*
Mount Darwin 107–8, 107*f*, 270–71
Mouvement Républicain National Pour La
  Démocratie et le Développement
  (MRND) 239–42, 241n13
Movement for Democracy in Liberia
  138–39, 170, 176, 181–82, 188, 191–96,
  192*f*
Movement for Democratic Change 121–22,
  123n20
Movimento Popular de Libertação de
  Angola. *See* People's Movement for the
  Liberation of Angola
Mozambique 16, 19, 76, 90, 117–18, 258
MRND. *See* Mouvement Républicain
  National Pour La Démocratie et le
  Développement
Mugabe, Robert 3, 16, 79n2, 86, 126, 168
mujibas 95–96, 98–99, 102, 108, 270, 272
Murdock, George 164
Museveni, Yoweri 241

Namibia 11, 11n3, 213–14, 262
National Archives of Zimbabwe 92–93, 95,
  105, 108, 269, 271
nationalism 19, 47–48
National Patriotic Front of Liberia (NPFL).
  See also *specific topics*
  bureaucrats to 175
  to chiefs 143
  civilians and 141n2, 171n25, 186,
    187, 189
  control 146–47, 157n17, 164–66, 165*t*,
    166*t*, 178–80, 179*t*, 195*t*, 281*t*, 282*t*,
    283*t*, 284*t*
  displacement by 170–71
  in elections 133
  ethnicity to 20
  history of 12, 29, 82–83
  in Operation Octopus 149–50
  organizational capacity of 149, 187
  partisans and 179*t*

presence 155–60
rebel governance and 188
rebel groups and 136–38, 137*f*, 144–45
rivals of 158n19
scholarship on 194, 287*t*, 289*t*
soldiers 144n5, 148, 150, 160n20
strongholds 150–51, 160–63, 178–79,
  193, 285*f*, 286*f*
Taylor, C., and 134, 141–43, 173–74, 253
territory 154
ZANU and 24
National Patriotic Reconstruction Assembly
  Government 141
national politics 252
National Resistance Movement 200–201,
  241
Ndebele ethnic group 77, 110, 131, 274
negotiated settlements 258
Neto, Agostinho 211
NGOs. *See* nongovernmental organizations
Nicaragua 5
Nigeria 138
Nkomo, Joshua 76–77, 86, 88, 119
Nkurunziza, Pierre 16, 229–30, 235,
  237–38
nongovernmental organizations (NGOs) 4,
  22, 176–77, 287
Northern Rhodesia 78
North Korea 91
NPFL. *See* National Patriotic Front of Liberia
Nyasaland 78

oil profits 217–18
Operation Octopus 149–50
organizational capacity
  dynamics of 14
  legacy of 233–34
  in Midlands 110
  of NPFL 149, 187
  organizational endowments 18
  organized ties 44–46
  post-war social control and 54–57, 55*t*
  of rebel-civilian ties 46–47, 94–97,
    118–19, 133, 144–47, 196–97
  security concerns and 236–38
  in strongholds 159*f*
  of Taylor, C. 202
  of traditional leaders 94, 97
  of wartime institutions 67–68
Oriental Timber Company 176n27, 187
Ouattara, Alassane 207, 220–29

Parti pour la libération du peuple
  Hutu–Forces Nationales de Libération
  (Palipehutu-FNL) 229–38
partisans
  in contested unsecured terrain/areas 56,
    60, 103–4, 159f, 166t, 178–79,
    193, 195t
  ethnicity and 179–80
  ideological 45
  NPFL and 179t
  partisan territory 155
  politics of 6, 29
  rivals and 158n18
  scholarship on 160
  territory to 155, 157–58
  in Zimbabwe 197
party structures 131–32
Patriotic Front 90
peace
  agreements 41n5
  Catholic Commission for Justice and
    Peace in 108, 119–20, 270–71
  to civilians 32
  consolidation conflict and 70
  to ex-combatants 145–46
  Liberia Peace Council 163n22
  peaceful consolidated power 251–52
  peacekeepers 176–77
  politics and 89f, 256
  rivals and 172–73
  stability and 244
People's Movement for the Liberation of
    Angola (MLPA) 12, 16t, 201, 205, 207,
    210–19, 247–48
People's Redemption Council 82–83
politics. See also *specific topics*
  African politics literature 254
  authoritarianism 5
  of brokered votes 238–39
  in bureaucratic development
    committees 256
  of bureaucrats 6, 8–9
  of chiefs 58–59
  of civilians 260
  coercive political control 261
  Cold War 79–80, 79n2
  of consolidated power 27
  of contested unsecured terrain/areas 65f
  cross-national 75, 85–87
  of democracy 262–63

in Democratic Republic of Congo 15n6,
    230, 233
distributive 5–6
in districts 105, 107
economics and 169
elite 33–35
ethnicity in 77–78
in guerrilla warfare 95
identity-based support 103–4
in instability 16–17
of institutions 24–25
in Latin America 6n1
local 64, 94, 254, 264
of local development 110–11
of local governance 115
of Marxism 3
military 92–94, 198
of military recruitment 98
Movement for Democratic
    Change 121–22
national 252
of negotiated settlements 258
of partisans 6, 29
of party structures 131–32
peace and 89f, 256
political brokers 60
political development 260–62
political education 53–54
political geography 69
political incentives 265
political rallies 99
political support 27–29, 31–32, 205
political victories 11–12
post-war 7, 39–41, 133–34, 167–69, 260
of post-war governance 35–37, 167–69
security 109
of socialization 44
state-building and 9–10, 27–29,
    33–35
in sub-Saharan Africa 15–18, 16t
of traditional leaders 107
of UNITA 12
wartime 36
youth collaborators in 95–97, 108–10,
    131–32
of ZAPU 4, 22–23
in Zimbabwe 104n11, 269–75
Polity 2 262
population groups 81f
Portugal 205, 211–13

318 Index

post-war governance
  conflict termination and 256–58
  history of 45–47
  politics of 35–37, 167–69
  scholarship on 3, 17, 26–27, 57–58
post-war issues
  post-war coercive capability 275*t*
  post-war consolidated power 44, 174–75,
    186, 202, 209, 253–55
  post-war control 44–46
  post-war development 177–78, 224–25
  post-war internal conquests 8–10, 13
  post-war interviews 92–93
  post-war legitimacy 14
  post-war politics 7, 39–41, 133–34,
    167–69, 260
  post-war power 125n21
  post-war reconstruction 9, 17, 44, 46,
    61–64, 86, 176, 180–81, 187–89, 224,
    264–65
  post-war resource allocation 120–25,
    123*t*, 124*f*, 125–31, 128*f*, 130*t*, 185–86
  post-war resources 6
  post-war security 283*t*
  post-war social control 54–57, 55*t*,
    120–25, 123*t*, 124*f*
  post-war state-building 12–15
post-war stability
  coercive violence and 116–20, 119*f*
  control and 108–10
  local governance in 110–12
  scholarship on 24, 108–10, 110*t*, 260–61
  voting in 109–10, 110*t*
  for wartime institutions 112–16
power. *See also* consolidated power
  of bureaucrats 252
  of chiefs 161
  in colonialism 97
  despotic 46
  Gaddafi in 19–20
  infrastructural 46
  of legitimacy 13
  MPLA in 201, 205, 207, 247–48
  post-war 125n21
  of rebel-civilian ties 12, 98–99, 197–98,
    199*t*, 200–202
  rebel governance with 231–32
  rebel victors and 6–10, 15–16, 16*t*,
    185–86
  strategies with 4–5

  in strongholds 57–58, 240–41
  Taylor, C., with 174–78
  top-down control 243–44
  wartime 32–33
  ZANU in 3–4
presence
  ineffectual 55–56
  influence and 47, 52, 104
  military 8, 47, 157n16
  NPFL 155–60
  rebel 156
  rebel group 50–54
  scholarship on 130–31
  state 9
  in strongholds 106*f*
pre-war institutions 29–31
propaganda 107–8
protected villages 93, 100–101, 105,
    105n12, 108
provincial committees 113n14
public goods provision 125–31, 128*f*, 130*t*,
    275*t*
public policy 176–77
pungwes 94–99, 101–2, 109, 113, 119,
    131–32
punishment 49

qualitative evidence 75–76, 139–40
quantitative evidence
  from Liberia 140–41
  of rebel-civilian ties 160–67, 164*f*, 165*t*,
    166*t*
  rebel victors and 75–76
  of resource allocation 176–82, 178*t*, 179*t*
Quiwonkpa, Thomas 82–83

rebel brutality 152
rebel-civilian ties
  coercion and 101–3
  displacement of 152–54
  in Liberia 141–43, 149–51, 181–82
  organizational capacity of 46–47, 94–97,
    118–19, 133, 144–47, 196–97
  in partisan territory 155
  post-war governance with 57–58
  power and 12, 98–99, 197–98, 199*t*,
    200–202
  psychology of 18
  quantitative evidence of 160–67, 164*f*,
    165*t*, 166*t*

Index **319**

race and 79–80
in Rhodesia 271–72
scholarship on 15, 19–25, 251–54, 270–71
social control and 200
state-building through 26–27, 29–31, 35–39, 38f, 47–49, 68–71, 68f, 71f
strategies and 105n12
to Taylor, C. 147–48, 181–82
time horizons for 49–52
wartime 255–56
in ZANU 98–99
in Zimbabwe 94
rebel control 103, 211–14, 221–24, 230–33, 240–42
rebel governance
adaptation for 255–56
bureaucrats and 69, 126
capacity of 31
chiefs in 171–72
of civilians 66–67, 85, 87, 181–82
after civil wars 23–24
with coercion 51
consolidated power in 59
in contested unsecured terrain/areas 61
development by 174–75
ethnicity to 45
external comparisons of 204–5
goals of 41n6
guerrilla warfare and 111
human rights to 62–63
leadership in 83
legibility in 37
military and 54, 191–92
to NGOs 176–77
NPFL and 188
with power 231–32
rebel institutions and 42, 60–61
rebel victors and 39–40, 251–54, 256–60
resource allocation and 265
rivals of 70–71, 71f, 143n4
scholarship on 7, 12, 14, 17n10, 18, 23, 140, 222–23, 241–42
social control and 103–5, 106f, 107–8, 107f, 213–14
state-building and 254
in strongholds 171–73
taxes and 30
Taylor, C., and 147–48
threats to 138–39

traditional leaders and 144, 152
violence and 212–13, 245–46, 265
rebel groups
in civil wars 151n10
NPFL and 136–38, 137f, 144–45
presence 50–54
recruitment by 191–94, 195t, 196–97
rebel influence 51
rebel institutions 42, 60–61, 75, 234
rebel military 141–42
rebel presence 156
rebel victors
in Angola 256
to chiefs 16n8, 58–59
civilians and 65f, 187–90
after civil wars 10–12, 69
consolidated power to 56–57, 67, 197–98, 199t, 200–202
contested unsecured terrain/areas to 33, 47–48, 64, 66
counter-rebellions to 33–34
democracy to 30–31
ethnicity to 28
in Liberia 186
in power 6–10, 15–16, 16t, 185–86
quantitative evidence and 75–76
rebel governance and 39–40, 251–54, 256–60
scholarship on 3–6, 194, 195t, 196–97, 196t, 202–3
security challenges to 267–68
social control to 156–60, 159f
strategies of 41–44, 41n6
in sub-Saharan Africa 27, 262
violence by 190–94, 192f
ZANU and 131–32
reconnaissance 96, 118, 144–47, 209, 232
reconstruction 236
recruitment 98
reform 9, 128–29
refugees 70, 91, 117, 150n9, 220, 241, 245
regional control 198, 199t, 200
religion
in Catholicism 93
education and 282t
ethnicity and 59, 281t, 283t
leadership in 111
propaganda and 107–8
security and 283t
resentment, from civilians 102–3

320 Index

resistance groups 117–18
Résistance pour un État de Droit au
  Burundi 237
Resistência Nacional Moçambicanan 258
resource allocation
  constraints with 66
  patterns of 208
  post-war, 120–25, 123t, 124f, 125–31,
    128f, 130t, 185–86
  public goods provision and 125–31, 128f,
    130t
  quantitative evidence of 176–82, 178t,
    179t
  rebel governance and 265
  scholarship on 6–12, 19, 24, 66, 71, 75,
    132, 139 (See also *specific topics*)
  in South Africa 6
  state-building with 58–63
  strategies 125–31, 128f, 130t, 247–48,
    256–59
Rhodesia. *See also* Zimbabwe
  birth registration laws in 121–22, 122n19
  Botswana and 118–19
  Catholic Commission for Justice and
    Peace in 108, 119–20, 270–71
  chiefs in 97
  counterinsurgency in 100
  government of 100
  history of 90, 108, 270–71, 274
  military 93, 95–96, 101–2
  Northern 78
  Patriotic Front in 90
  rebel-civilian ties in 271–72
  Selous Scouts 101–2
  Soames for 3
  Southern 77–78
  voting laws in 120–21
  ZAPU and 77
rivals
  of chiefs 163
  civilians and 32–33, 63, 157
  in contested unsecured
    terrain/areas 190–91
  control and 153
  depth of 66
  governing capacity and 197
  independence and 258
  influence of 158
  of NPFL 158n19
  partisans and 158n18

peace and 172–73
  of rebel governance 70–71, 71f, 143n4
  rival coercion 61
  rival strongholds 260
  rival territory 32–33, 56–58, 169–71,
    285f, 286f
  strategies of 265
  support of 190
  ULIMO as 158–60, 168–70, 175–76,
    181, 188
  violence by 149, 252
  of ZAPU 78–80
Roberto, Holden 211
rural civilians 114–16, 114n16, 146n8
Rwanda
  Armée pour la Libération du
    Rwanda 245–47
  bureaucrats in 6
  Burundi and 24, 203, 208–10, 229, 253
  civil wars in 21, 239–47
  Côte d'Ivoire and 21
  Forces Armées Rwandaises 239–40,
    243–45
  Forces Démocratiques de Libération du
    Rwanda 245
  innovation in 256
  Interahamwe youth wing in 239, 241n13,
    242, 245, 247
  MRND in 239–42, 241n13
  Rwandaise Alliance Nationale de
    Unite 239
  Rwandan Patriotic Front 6, 209–10,
    239–48
Rwasa, Agathon 229–30

St. Albert's Mission 108
Sandinistas 5
Sankara, Thomas 84
Savimbi, Jonah 211, 214–15, 218
security
  challenges 267–68
  commitments to 217–18
  concerns 219, 236–38, 245–46
  development and 26
  economics of 42–43, 174–76, 189
  internal 225–26
  local 95–96
  politics 109
  post-war 283t
  religion and 283t

security-development trade-offs 20–21, 24, 66–67, 134, 174–82, 185–90, 219
by single-barrel men 172
spending 132
to Taylor, C. 181–82, 287
trade-offs, 262–63
to ZANU 109
in Zimbabwe 227
Selous Scouts 101–2
Shona ethnic group
  Ndebele ethnic group and 77, 131, 274
  pungwes for 94–99, 101–2, 109, 113, 119, 131–32
  scholarship on 110, 274
  strongholds 123–24
Sierra Leone 84, 175–76
single-barrel men
  chiefs and 144, 173
  to ex-combatants 153
  in Liberia 145–47
  reconnaissance by 144–47
  security by 172
  violence from 153
Sirleaf, Ellen Johnson 86, 163
Soames (lord) 3
social control
  of civilians 45, 48, 69, 252–53
  civil wars and 43–44, 160n20
  consolidated power and 190
  in contested unsecured terrain/areas 54–55
  influence and 53
  in Liberia 33
  local politics and 264
  loss of 149–51
  post-war 54–57, 55t, 120–25, 123t, 124f
  rebel-civilian ties and 200
  rebel governance and 103–5, 106f, 107–8, 107f, 213–14
  to rebel victors 156–60, 159f
  social desirability bias 142n3
  socialization 44
  in sub-Saharan Africa 197–98, 199t, 200–202
  taxes and 232–33
  to Taylor, C. 149, 185–86, 189–90
  territorial control compared to 257
  typology of 24–25
  with violence 33–34

wartime 7–8, 55t, 165
  in Zimbabwe 197
South Africa 6, 76, 79n2, 91, 93–94, 262
Southern Rhodesia 77–78
South West Africa People's Organisation 11
Soviet Union 15n7, 79
special elections 168
stability. *See* post-war stability
state-building
  to bureaucrats 243–44
  consolidated power and 62–64, 65f, 66–68, 258
  in Europe 148
  politics and 9–10, 27–29, 33–35
  post-war 12–15
  post-war control and 44–46
  by pre-war institutions 30
  through rebel-civilian ties 26–27, 29–31, 35–39, 38f, 47–49, 68–71, 68f, 71f
  rebel governance and 254
  relevant actors in 39–41
  with resource allocation 58–63
  scholarship on 5–9
  state institutions 37–38
  state-led development 216–17
  strategies 13
state legitimacy 8–9
state presence 9
state stability 261–62
stationary bandits 5, 12–13, 36, 49–51, 148, 231
Stihole (reverend) 273–74
strategies
  in authoritarianism 62
  bureaucrats and 60, 112–13
  civilians and 7–8
  with coercion 62–63
  for consolidated power 39–40, 54–57, 55t
  DiD 177
  in guerrilla warfare 68–69, 101–2
  in Matabeleland 119–20
  for post-war governance 26
  for post-war stability 24
  with power 4–5
  rebel-civilian ties and 105n12
  of rebel victors 41–44, 41n6
  resource allocation 125–31, 128f, 130t, 247–48, 256–59
  of rivals 265
  state-building 13

322 Index

strategies *(cont.)*
  of Taylor, C. 138–39, 168–69
  of ZANU 112–16, 252–53
  of ZAPU 113–16
  in Zimbabwe 235
strongholds
  civilians in 175
  in civil wars 172–73
  counter-rebellions in 63
  culture of 95
  development in 115–16
  education in 127, 179–80
  exploitation of 59
  guerrilla warfare in 272–73
  history of 100
  intensity of 105
  Liberia Peace Council 163n22
  literacy in 284
  local 99
  loyal bureaucrats in 116–17
  military 104
  in Mount Darwin 107–8, 107f
  NPFL 150–51, 160–63, 178–79, 193, 285f, 286f
  oppression in 236
  organizational capacity in 159f
  power in 57–58, 240–41
  presence in 106f
  rebel governance in 171–73
  rival 260
  scholarship on 57–58, 129–30, 130t
  Shona ethnic group 123–24
  to Taylor, C. 171
  victor 54–56, 55t, 65f
  wartime 264
  ZANU 101–3, 122–23, 123t, 276f, 276t, 277t, 278t
  ZAPU 129
  in Zimbabwe 186
sub-national politics
  control and 186
  education in 277t, 278t, 279t, 280t, 284, 285f, 286f, 287, 287t, 288t, 289t
  national politics and 252
  theory and 75, 85–87
  voter registration in 276t, 277t
  voting in 276f
sub-Saharan Africa
  cross-national politics in 203
  external comparisons in 204–5, 247–48, 253–54

Liberia and 185–86
  politics in 15–18, 16t
  rebel victors in 27, 262
  social control in 197–98, 199t, 200–202
  violence in 27–28
  Zimbabwe and 10–11
Sudan 198, 200–202
surveillance 155, 170

Tanzania 19, 78–79, 230–31
taxes 13, 30, 53, 148, 155, 232–33
Taylor, Charles. *See also* Liberia
  chief appointment by 164–65, 164f
  civilians and 139–40, 169–70, 176–77
  in elections 138, 163–64, 167, 173
  leadership of 83–86, 133, 154, 161, 253
  mass violence by 149–50
  media and 167–68
  NPFL and 134, 141–43, 173–74, 253
  organizational capacity of 202
  overthrowing of 186
  with power 174–78
  rebel-civilian ties to 147–48, 181–82
  rebel governance and 147–48
  reputation of 6, 171–72, 189, 219–20
  security to 181–82, 287
  social control to 149, 185–86, 189–90
  strategies of 138–39, 168–69
  strongholds to 171
Taylor, Charles, Jr. ("Chucky") 168
technocracy 108–9
territorial control 14–15, 31–33, 133, 185, 257
Tolbert, William 82
Tom Tom 118
top-down control 243–44, 263–64
traditional leaders. See also *chiefs*
  Marxism to 57n10
  organizational capacity of 94, 97
  politics of 107
  rebel governance and 144, 152
  scholarship on 57n10, 144n5
  in war 111
tribal groups 81f
Tshisekedi, Felix 15n6
Tubman, William 80, 82, 84
Tutsi ethnic group. *See* Rwanda
typology 24–25, 156

Uganda 45, 67–68, 200–201, 241
ULIMO. *See* United Liberation Movement
  of Liberia for Democracy
União Nacional Para a Independência Total
  de Angola (UNITA) 7–8, 12, 211–19
United Liberation Movement of Liberia for
  Democracy (ULIMO)
  history of 135*f*, 136–39
  retaliation by 149–54
  as rivals 158–60, 168–70, 175–76,
    181, 188
United Nations 222
United Nations Mission in Liberia 140, 162
United States 15n7, 16, 83, 84
unsecured terrain/areas. *See* contested
  unsecured terrain/areas
Uppsala Conflict Data Program 23, 140–41,
  156, 156nn14–15, 191–94

variability 94
victimization. See *specific topics*
victor strongholds 54–56, 55*t*, 65*f*
village committees 97, 111–12
village development committees 113–16
violence
  civilians in 9–10, 12–13, 118–19, 119*f*,
    163–64
  in civil wars 68–69, 68*f*, 156n15
  coercion and 14, 50, 64, 94, 116–20,
    119*f*, 132
  colonialism and 11
  consolidated power after 69–70
  in contested unsecured
    terrain/areas 136–37, 232–33
  development and 214–18, 224–28,
    233–38, 242–46
  displacement and 165–67
  ethnic 224
  against ethnicity 21
  extrajudicial killings 170
  genocide 229–30, 240–42, 244
  of guerrilla warfare 17–18
  in Gwaai River Mine 117
  indiscriminate 152
  to legitimacy-building 48–49
  in Liberia 152–53
  looting and 51, 108, 191n3, 233, 270
  low-violence consolidation conflict 68*f*
  mass 86, 132, 149–50
  in massacres 89*f*, 91
  military 35, 71, 118

psychology of 260–61
rebel governance and 212–13,
  245–46, 265
by rebel victors 190–94, 192*f*
by rivals 149, 252
in rival territory 169–71
from single-barrel men 153
social control with 33–34
in sub-Saharan Africa 27–28
threats of 67
violent insurrections 62
volunteers 125–26, 129, 261
voting
  brokering in 238–39
  after Lancaster House Agreement 90
  laws 120–21
  for main parties 110*t*
  by Ndebele ethnic group 110
  in post-war stability 109–10, 110*t*
  in sub-national politics 276*f*
  voter registration 121–23, 123*t*, 124*f*,
    127–28, 276*t*, 277*t*
  in Zimbabwe 259

war. See *specific topics*
ward development committees 113–15
war-level consolidation conflict 68*f*
wartime institutions 44–45, 59, 67–68,
  112–16
wartime politics 36
wartime power 32–33
wartime rebel-civilian ties 255–56
wartime social control 7–8, 55*t*, 165
wartime strongholds 264
Wedza district 114n16
widespread control 198, 199*t*, 200
"Winds of Change" speech 79–80
women 43–44, 58–60, 113, 216

youth
  in Burundi 232
  collaborators 95–96, 108–10, 131–32
  Interahamwe youth wing 239, 241n13,
    242, 245, 247
  male 172
  policy for 174–75
  population 18, 40, 118–20, 122, 188,
    233–34, 236, 238–39, 242, 247, 261, 273
  reconnaissance 118, 209, 232
  women and 43–44, 58–60, 113, 216
  Youth People's Service 111

324 Index

Zaire 211
Zambia 19, 76–79, 88, 90, 213–14, 270,
  272–73
ZANU. *See* Zimbabwe African National
  Union
ZAPU. *See* Zimbabwe African People's
  Union
Zimbabwe. *See also* Rhodesia
  Angola and 205, 206*t*, 207
  Botswana and 272–73
  Burundi and 11n4, 16
  chiefs in 145
  civilians in 86
  civil wars in 4–5
  coercion in 58
  coercive violence in 116–20, 119*f*
  contested unsecured terrain/areas
    in 273–75
  control in 216, 270–73
  Côte d'Ivoire and 220
  death records from 105
  history of 88, 89*f*, 90–92, 94–97, 100,
    103–5, 106*f*, 107–8, 107*f*
  after independence 3–4, 78
  instability in 101–3
  institutions in 112–16
  Liberia and 19–25, 43, 71, 75–76, 85, 87,
    171, 185, 202–3, 228, 253
  local governance in 110–12
  Mugabe in 168
  National Archives of Zimbabwe 92–93,
    94–95, 105, 108, 269, 271
  nationalism in 47–48
  NGOs in 4
  partisans in 197
  People's Militia 117–18
  politics in 104n11, 269–75
  post-war coercive capability in 275*t*
  post-war politics in 260
  post-war resource allocation in 120–25,
    123*t*, 124*f*, 125–31, 128*f*, 130*t*, 185–86
  rebel-civilian ties in 94
  rebel party structure in 200
  research on 276*f*, 276*t*, 277*t*, 278*t*, 279*t*,
    280*t*
  scholarship on 92–94, 108–10, 110*t*,
    131–32, 269–70
  secondary schooling in 127
  security in 227
  social control in 197
  South Africa and 76

  strategies in 235
  strongholds in 186
  sub-Saharan Africa and 10–11
  territorial control in 14–15
  Uganda and 45
  voting in 259
  Zimbabwean Liberation War 19
Zimbabwe African National Union
  (ZANU). See also *specific topics*
  CNDD-FDD and 230
  with consolidated power 186
  contested unsecured
    terrain/areas 129–30, 130*t*
  control 121–22, 270–72, 274–75, 275*t*,
    279*t*, 280*t*
  history of 88, 89*f*, 90–92, 107–8, 107*f*
  leadership of 86
  military and 77
  MPLA and 207, 211
  NGOs and 22
  NPFL and 24
  in power 3–4
  rebel-civilian ties in 98–99
  rebel victors and 131–32
  rivals of 78–80
  scholarship on 269–70, 276*t*, 277*t*, 278*t*,
    279*t*, 280*t*
  security to 109
  strategies of 112–16, 252–53
  strongholds 101–3, 122–23, 123*t*, 276*f*,
    276*t*, 277*t*, 278*t*
  volunteers to 129
Zimbabwe African People's Union (ZAPU)
  civilians and 119–20
  control 270, 272–73, 274–75, 275*t*
  history of 88, 89*f*, 90–92
  politics of 22–23
  rebel-civilian ties in 98–99
  Rhodesia and 77
  rivals of 78–80
  scholarship on 4, 269–70 (See also *specific
    topics*)
  security to 109
  strategies of 113–16
  strongholds 129
Zimbabwe Liberation War. See *specific topics*
Zimbabwe National Liberation Army.
    See Zimbabwe African National Union
Zimbabwe People's Revolutionary Army.
    See Zimbabwe African People's
    Union

Printed in the USA/Agawam, MA
January 24, 2024

859971.002